The Rise and Fall
of American Science Fiction,
from the 1920s to the 1960s

The Rise and Fall of American Science Fiction, from the 1920s to the 1960s

GARY WESTFAHL

McFarland & Company, Inc., Publishers
Jefferson, North Carolina

Also of interest and from McFarland:

Bridges to Science Fiction and Fantasy: Outstanding Essays from the J. Lloyd Eaton Conferences (edited by Gregory Benford, Gary Westfahl, Howard V. Hendrix and Joseph D. Miller, 2018)

The Spacesuit Film: A History, 1918–1969 (by Gary Westfahl, 2012)

Science Fiction and the Prediction of the Future: Essays on Foresight and Fallacy (edited by Gary Westfahl, Wong Kin Yuen and Amy Kit-sze Chen, 2011)

Science Fiction and the Two Cultures: Essays on Bridging the Gap Between the Sciences and the Humanities (edited by Gary Westfahl and George Slusser, 2009)

The Science of Fiction and the Fiction of Science: Collected Essays on SF Storytelling and the Gnostic Imagination (by Frank McConnell, edited by Gary Westfahl)

Hugo Gernsback and the Century of Science Fiction (by Gary Westfahl, 2007)

LIBRARY OF CONGRESS CATALOGUING-IN-PUBLICATION DATA

Library of Congress Cataloging-in-Publication Data
Names: Westfahl, Gary, author.
Title: The rise and fall of American science fiction, from the 1920s to the 1960s / Gary Westfahl.
Description: Jefferson, North Carolina : McFarland & Company, Inc., Publishers, 2019. | Includes bibliographical references and index.
Identifiers: LCCN 2019035920 | ISBN 9781476674940 (paperback) ∞
 ISBN 9781476638515 (ebook)
Subjects: LCSH: Science fiction, American—History and criticism. | American fiction—20th century—History and criticism.
Classification: LCC PS374.S35 W435 2019 | DDC 813/.087620905—dc23
LC record available at https://lccn.loc.gov/2019035920

BRITISH LIBRARY CATALOGUING DATA ARE AVAILABLE

ISBN (print) 978-1-4766-7494-0
ISBN (ebook) 978-1-4766-3851-5

© 2019 Gary Westfahl. All rights reserved

No part of this book may be reproduced or transmitted in any form or by any means, electronic or mechanical, including photocopying or recording, or by any information storage and retrieval system, without permission in writing from the publisher.

Front cover illustration © 2019 Wood River Gallery

Printed in the United States of America

McFarland & Company, Inc., Publishers
 Box 611, Jefferson, North Carolina 28640
 www.mcfarlandpub.com

To Mark R. Kelly—a friend, a supportive editor, and one of this business's genuine good guys

Table of Contents

Acknowledgments	ix
Introduction	1

Part I. The 1920s and Thereafter

1. The Emergence of American Science Fiction and Its Impact on the World	7
2. August 1928: Science Fiction's Second Birthday	21
3. Artists in Wonderland: Towards a True History of Science Fiction Art	39

Part II. The 1930s and Thereafter

4. Pulp Science Fiction: A Student's Guide	61
5. Beyond Logic and Literacy: The Strange Case of Space Opera	77
6. Five Ways to Conquer the Universe: The Forms of Space Opera	85

Part III. The 1940s and Thereafter

7. The Tall Dark Stranger and the Boy Next Door: A. E. van Vogt and Robert A. Heinlein	99
8. The Three Golden Ages of Science Fiction	111
9. Assemblers of Infinity: The Early History of Science Fiction Anthologies	124

Part IV. The 1950s and Thereafter

10. Invasion of the Saucer Men: How the Universe of Science Fiction Expanded in the 1950s	153

11. Hard Science Fiction: An Overview   180
12. The "Big Three" Approaches to Juvenile Science Fiction and Why One Worked and the Others Did Not   196

Epilog. The 1960s and Thereafter

13. After Things Fell Apart: The Fragmentation of Science Fiction in the 1960s and 1970s   211
14. Science Fiction Today: The Triumph of the Marketplace   233

Conclusion   247
Chapter Notes   251
Bibliography   268
Index   277

Acknowledgments

I should begin by thanking the individuals who were responsible for originally commissioning, and/or publishing, early versions of some chapters in this book, with the details listed below: Gerry Canavan, Donald M. Hassler, Edward James, Rob Latham, Eric Carl Link, Farah Mendlesohn, Andy Sawyer, Lars Schmeink, David Seed, the late George Slusser, and Peter Wright. Others who made no direct contributions to this book's contents, but have long been helpful to my research and writing, should be mentioned as well: Gregory Benford, George Butler, Marika Christofides, John Clute, Arthur B. Evans, Mark R. Kelly, David Langford, Maria Mendoza, Janet Moores, David Pringle, and Willis Regier. Finally, I thank the editors and other employees of McFarland, especially David Alff, Dylan Lightfoot, and Lisa Camp for their assistance in getting this book published, and, as always, my wife Lynne, children Allison Westfahl Kong and Jeremy Westfahl, son-in-law Steven Kong, and grandchildren Serena Kong and Derek Kong for their continuing support and encouragement.

A previous version of "The Emergence of American Science Fiction and Its Impact on the World," as "The Mightiest Machine: The Development of American Science Fiction from the 1920s to the 1960s," appeared in *The Cambridge Companion to American Science Fiction*, edited by Eric Carl Link and Gerry Canavan (Cambridge: Cambridge University Press, 2015), 17–30.

A previous version of "Artists in Wonderland: Towards a True History of Science Fiction Art" appeared in *Unearthly Visions: Approaches to Science Fiction and Fantasy Art*, edited by Gary Westfahl, George Slusser, and Kathleen Church Plummer (Westport, CT: Greenwood Press, 2002), 19–38.

A previous version of "Pulp Science Fiction: A Student's Guide," as "Teaching Pulp Science Fiction," appeared in *Teaching Science Fiction*, edited by Andy Sawyer and Peter Wright (London: Palgrave Macmillan, 2011), 86–101.

A previous version of "Beyond Logic and Literacy: The Strange Case of Space Opera" appeared in *Extrapolation* 35:3 (Fall 1994), 176–185.

Acknowledgments

A previous version of "Five Ways to Conquer the Universe: The Forms of Space Opera," as "Space Opera," appeared in *The Cambridge Companion to Science Fiction*, edited by Edward James and Farah Mendlesohn (Cambridge: Cambridge University Press, 2003), 197–208.

A previous version of "The Three Golden Ages of Science Fiction" was delivered online as a lecture for the college course "A Virtual Introduction to Science Fiction," sponsored by the University of Hamburg, April 24, 2012, with its text posted as http://virtual-sf.com/wp-content/uploads/2012/04/Westfahl.pdf.

A previous version of "Hard Science Fiction: An Overview," as "Hard Science Fiction," appeared in *A Companion to Science Fiction*, edited by David Seed (Oxford: Blackwell, 2005), 187–201.

A previous version of "Science Fiction Today: The Triumph of the Marketplace," as "The Marketplace," appeared in *The Oxford Handbook of Science Fiction*, edited by Rob Latham (London: Oxford University Press, 2014), 81–92.

Introduction

In 1947, J. O. Bailey published the first history of science fiction, *Pilgrims through Space and Time: Trends and Patterns in Scientific and Utopian Fiction*, and since that time, many others have written their own histories of science fiction. I have read and benefited from a number of them, though some are better than others, and someday I may make my own contribution to this tradition. This book, however, is not that history of science fiction, though it could be accurately described as a useful supplement to other histories, covering topics that are usually omitted in other histories, or topics only addressed in a cursory fashion.

It is also incomplete in its coverage of the genre's history, since its focus is on the development of American science fiction in the twentieth century, which I continue to regard as the most significant and influential body of works in the genre, even as the contemporary scholarly community seems more and more dedicated to the study of "global science fiction." However, while critics can choose texts from all regions and all periods of time and construct their own unified histories out of those disparate parts, the twentieth-century science fiction that emerged from the pulp magazines represents a history that actually occurred, with clear connections between innumerable authors, editors, and commentators that can be verified and studied, not merely invented. First, building on the examples of distinguished precursors like Edgar Allan Poe, Jules Verne, and H. G. Wells, Hugo Gernsback launched the world's first science fiction magazine, belatedly christened the genre "science fiction," and permanently established a new category of popular literature. In its first decade as a recognized genre, noteworthy writers like E. E. "Doc" Smith, Edmond Hamilton, Jack Williamson, and Stanley G. Weinbaum appeared, and isolated organizations of science fiction enthusiasts began to coalesce into a unified community of science fiction fans. In the 1940s, editor John W. Campbell, Jr., encouraged and oversaw a new generation of writers, prominently including A. E. van Vogt and Robert A. Heinlein, who brought more energy and depth to the genre, while others carried on producing less prestigious but still popular forms of science fiction. In the 1950s, science fiction and its writers migrated from the magazines into new venues like hardcover and paperback books, juvenile fiction, film and television, comic books, and merchandise. Finally, in the 1960s and thereafter, science fiction gradually became a dominating presence in popular culture, even as it lost the sense of unity that had long distinguished the genre and ultimately was transformed in ways that many adherents resented but could not resist.

By the time that I began my career as a science fiction scholar, I had already read several versions of this story, but I was dissatisfied with the standard narrative, and several of my endeavors can be characterized as necessary correctives to conventional views, addressing the issues and traditions that others had usually neglected or ignored. One major problem, I thought, is that literary historians tend to focus primarily or exclusively on the best writers and their best works, seizing upon perceived connections between them to invent an imagined and isolated tradition of literary excellence. Yet the twentieth-century science fiction that first appeared in the magazines was very much the product of two large communities that help to explain its qualities. First, there was what one can call the visible science fiction community, consisting of the writers, editors, publishers, artists, and fans who made their presence felt by contributing primary texts to magazines and books, attending science fiction conventions, socializing with other members of that community, and writing commentaries on science fiction in the forms of editorials, book and film reviews, letters to magazines, fanzine articles, and (eventually) nonfiction books. Second, there is the invisible science fiction community of readers who enjoy science fiction of various sorts but are generally silent, communicating their opinions and preferences solely by means of the magazines and books that they purchase or request from libraries. Because they have always been more numerous than the identifiable fans, however, they have had just as much an effect on the genre as, if not more of an effect on the genre than, its more conspicuous audience, since their decisions have dictated what sorts of science fiction works will be published, particularly in recent decades when the field has become dominated by major publishers who engage in extensive market research to determine precisely what these silent readers would be most likely to buy. Much of the work of my scholarly career can be interpreted as an effort to publicize and investigate these broader contexts from which both the masterpieces and the ephemera of science fiction have emerged.

First, beginning with my 1986 dissertation, I have strived to restore Hugo Gernsback to his properly central position in the genre's history and to relate the development of science fiction to the critical commentaries, by Gernsback and his many successors, that have always accompanied and influenced the literature. My work in this area eventually yielded two books, *The Mechanics of Wonder: The Creation of the Idea of Science Fiction* (1998) and *Hugo Gernsback and the Century of Science Fiction* (2007), and it is recapitulated and extended in the first chapter of this volume, "The Emergence of American Science Fiction and Its Impact on the World." For a volume on teaching science fiction, I analyzed and celebrated works from the early magazine era that are sometimes overlooked in histories of science fiction but nonetheless can be appreciated by many readers, an essay revised here as "Pulp Science Fiction: A Reader's Guide." I have explored the nature and history of the two most distinctive subgenres that science fiction has spawned—space opera, and hard science fiction—considering how both primary texts and critical commentaries have shaped their development, with the results presented in *Cosmic Engineers: A Study of Hard Science Fiction* (1996) and three essays revised to serve as chapters in this volume: "Beyond Logic and Literacy: The Strange Case of Space Opera," "Five Ways to Conquer the Universe: The Forms of Space Opera," and "Hard Science Fiction: An Overview." In "The Three Golden Ages of Science Fiction," first presented as a lecture to a German science fiction class, I drew special attention to another form of science fiction, proven to be very popular in the invisible science fiction community, that virtually all histories of the genre have ignored because its texts are mostly despised by the visible science fiction community: purportedly factual accounts of clearly false events and phenomena, a type of science fiction masquerading as legitimate science that has remained a vibrant and impactful literary form. Noting that the history of science fiction art had always been considered separately from the history of science fiction literature, even though stories and art had always accompanied each other and were both discussed with some frequency in readers' letters, I attempted in "Artists in Wonderland: Towards a True History of Science Fiction Art" to integrate the two stories, maintaining that each era of the genre's history is characterized by both a distinctive form of fiction and a corresponding form of art. Finally, my works regularly pondered the ways that the marketplace considerations, influenced more by anonymous buyers than vocal critics and usually overlooked by scholars, have significantly affected the genre, as described in my contributions to the volume I co-edited with George Slusser and Eric S. Rabkin, *Science Fiction and Market Realities* (1996) and an essay republished here as "Science Fiction Today: The Triumph of the Marketplace."

When I began the process of assembling these materials into a book, I then had to consider what other sorts of neglected topics might warrant the creation of additional chapters. I had long wanted to take a closer look at two key moments in the development of science fiction—the August 1928 issue of *Amazing Stories* that introduced the space operas of E. E. "Doc" Smith and the adventures of Buck Rogers, and the 1939 issues of *Astounding Science-Fiction* where the science fiction stories of A. E. van Vogt and Robert A. Heinlein first appeared. Noting that other histories had focused on science fiction magazines and books, I thought it was important to examine the role of science fiction anthologies in shaping and popularizing the genre. There was one key subgenre that conspicuously emerged in the 1950s—children's science fiction—that I wanted to examine at some length, since it represented one of the ways that I encountered the genre as a child. Finally, since these were crucial eras that I had never examined at length, I wanted to offer my own surveys of what happened to science fiction in the 1950s and 1960s, the times when I first became acquainted with the genre, focusing on the ways that both the visible and the invisible science fiction communities influenced the contrasting events in those decades and essentially engendered the literature of science fiction that we observe today.

None of these old and new analyses, of course, would truly transform this book into a history of science fiction, because I knew that there were many other aspects of that history which would be receiving little attention. Certainly, although I am comfortable in arguing that the twentieth-century American tradition is most important to an understanding of the genre, one cannot overlook the significance of earlier texts by Mary Shelley, Poe, Verne, Wells, and many others that had a lasting impact on science fiction (as Gernsback and other commentators have acknowledged), and other major twentieth-century science fiction writers who had no connections to the American genre, such as Olaf Stapledon, C. S. Lewis, Stanislaw Lem, and Arkady and Boris Strugatsky, merit extended considerations that cannot be found in this volume. Further, my chapters are hardly comprehensive in describing all of the individuals and groups who contributed to the growth and maturation of American science fiction, as there are innumerable authors, commentators, and publications worth examining that are mentioned only briefly, or not at all. As indicated, then, this book only represents a helpful supplement to the many other histories of science fiction that interested readers can readily locate and consult, perhaps by consulting this volume's concluding bibliography.

In returning to the chapters that have been previously published, I have in some cases located and revised original manuscripts that usually had to be edited to meet length requirements for their first publication, so this book's chapters now include some passages that were previously excluded; I have also endeavored to update and expand all of them as seemed necessary, so that from one perspective all of this book's chapters represent new material. But most of my energies have been devoted to researching and writing the new chapters, and fitting them into the mosaic of my general argument about the genre's development. During the final editing process, I also endeavored to minimize repetitive language, though there were certain points and observations that needed to be made more than once, to serve different purposes in different contexts. A brief conclusion will endeavor to tie everything together and offer some thoughts about the future of science fiction, and to aid other scholars, as noted, the book ends with a comprehensive bibliography of useful resources for further analyses of this remarkable era in the history of science fiction.

PART I. THE 1920S AND THEREAFTER

1

The Emergence of American Science Fiction and Its Impact on the World

In 1920, a global survey of the literature now regarded as science fiction would reveal distinctive and substantive bodies of work in several nations, including Great Britain, France, Germany, the Soviet Union, China, and Japan. The United States also had its own science fiction, yet it largely consisted of adventure stories written for pulp magazines, and its writers like Garrett P. Serviss and Edgar Rice Burroughs were not particularly impressive in comparison to, say, Britain's H. G. Wells or France's J.-H. Rosny aîné. Forty years later, the situation had entirely changed: American science fiction was widely recognized as the best in the world, and the science fiction books and magazines of other countries were largely devoted to translations of American stories and original works following American models. What caused this dramatic transformation?

Needless to say, no intelligent person can attribute the triumph of American science fiction to any peculiar virtues in the American character, though I have been incorrectly accused of making such arguments.[1] A more plausible, though equally wrongheaded, answer would be that after the end of World War II, a victorious United States unaffected by the war had the power to impose its culture on other nations ravaged by the war, and its science fiction became prominent merely as one minor consequence of its subsequent political and social domination of the world. Yet one observes no universal surrender to the superiority of American works. Foreign filmmakers, rather than slavishly imitating Hollywood products, continued to develop unique national styles that garnered American attention and respect in the 1950s; there is no evidence that the world's composers, painters, choreographers, or architects felt any pressure or desire to emulate American creators; and while baseball became popular in Japan, American sports otherwise had little impact on the world, as foreign nations remained devoted to their soccer and cricket. Only a few aspects of American culture were enthusiastically embraced throughout the world—such as rock'n'roll, blue jeans, and science fiction—and these particular successes require particular explanations.

Scholars in other fields must address why rock'n'roll and blue jeans proved to be so appealing to people in other countries, but I am prepared to explain why American science fiction dramatically improved in the decades after 1920 and came to dominate the world. As I have argued elsewhere,[2] it was largely due to the work of Hugo Gernsback, who provided an inchoate genre with a name, persuasive arguments for its special importance, and a support system of organized fans; almost against his will, he also promulgated a characteristic narrative that contributed to its remarkable growth. Then, Gernsback's most prominent successor, John W. Campbell, Jr., added a final key ingredient—intellectual respectability—to further broaden its appeal. It is these singular developments that account for the special strength, and ongoing impact, of American science fiction.

While it may seem a minor matter, one cannot promote and popularize a form of literature unless it has an appropriate and resonant name; and this is one service to science fiction that Gernsback performed. At first, when he published science fiction stories in his science magazines, he called them "scientific fiction." In 1926, when he launched the world's first science fiction magazine, *Amazing Stories*, he created and copyrighted a portmanteau version of that term, "scientifiction." Finally, in 1929, when he lost control of *Amazing Stories* and his own clunky neologism, he was fortuitously obliged to abandon "scientifiction" and come up with another name, "science fiction."[3] Soon, everyone else in America was using this term.

The name "science fiction" proved effective and popular for several reasons. It firmly linked the genre to science, which was becoming more respected and prominent in the public eye as new technologies kept improving American life and as scientists ranging from inventor Thomas Alva Edison to physicist Albert Einstein became media celebrities. Seemingly similar terms that might have become standard, like "scientific romance" (used most frequently in Great Britain) and "pseudo-scientific stories" (briefly common in American pulp magazines), suggested that the science in these stories might be fanciful; "science fiction" solidly promised accurate science, an implication that Gernsback heavily stressed in proselytizing for the genre. An additional advantage of "science fiction" was that it was easy to pronounce and easy to spell, unlike the sometimes unwieldy alternatives.[4]

Still, to attract readers to a form of literature, one needs more than a catchy name; one must explain why these stories are especially important, especially valuable, and especially worth reading. Most of the discussions of

1. The Emergence of American Science Fiction

science fiction before Gernsback that one can locate had been imperfect, hesitant, even flippant; for example, in a 1923 article advising writers on how to write what he termed "Pseudo-Scientific" stories, George Allan England essentially asserted that it was all a matter of artful lying. Such stories, he said, require "Some skill in the distortion of facts," and he went on to explain that

> science-faking requires a great deal of research.... It is the progressive marshalling of minutiae, the cumulative assembling of (often willfully falsified) data that convinces the reader that: "Well it's mighty strange, but still there might be something in it, after all." On a pinch, one can quote learned authorities which never existed, and fabricate weighty conclusions out of whole cloth. If one cannot, it proves that one has not the requisite Ananiacal and analytical twist to make one a success at this peculiarly mendacious form of story-telling.[5]

Of course, England was speaking confidentially to other writers, not to the general public, but characterizing science fiction as a type of literature based on deceiving its readers would obviously do little to attract an audience and boost the genre's respectability. Indeed, Gernsback himself would have bristled at England's description of science fiction, since he always emphasized that the stories in his magazines presented accurate scientific information and thus were especially meritorious.

In his numerous editorials, introductions, and responses to readers' letters, Gernsback crafted and tirelessly promoted two other arguments for his newly christened genre, which together corresponded to its three basic elements, announced in the definition of science fiction given in his first *Amazing Stories* editorial, "A New Sort of Magazine": "a charming romance intermingled with scientific fact and prophetic vision." The editorial proceeded to elaborate on the value of each element. Gernsback conceded that, like other forms of literature, science fiction was a form of entertainment, "a charming romance," and enjoyable for that reason. However, because stories included "scientific fact," they offered the additional benefit of scientific education: "Not only do these amazing tales make tremendously interesting reading—they are also always instructive. They supply knowledge that we might not otherwise obtain—and they supply it in a very palatable form." Third, a story's "prophetic vision," firmly based on today's science, could provide useful ideas for inventors, so "Prophecies made in many of [these writers'] amazing stories are being realized—and have been realized."[6] He explained how science fiction made its predictions come true in a later editorial, "The Lure of Scientifiction": "The serious-minded scientifiction reader absorbs the knowledge contained in such stories with avidity, with the result that such stories prove an incentive in starting some one to work on a device or invention suggested by some author."[7] In these ways, unlike other types of literature, science fiction could enormously benefit the world, creating a more educated citizenry and engendering wonderful new scientific advances inspired by its stories.

It is pointless to complain that these bold claims bore little relationship to the stories that Gernsback was actually publishing in *Amazing Stories*, which only occasionally offered truly educational material and even more rarely presented provocative ideas that were not already commonplace, because this did nothing to diminish the impact of Gernsback's arguments. In the first place, even if most of his writers were ignoring his announced requirements in their stories, many young readers wholeheartedly embraced his ideas; and when some of them later began writing their own science fiction, they were determined to produce stories that would perfectly fulfill his agenda by providing intelligent new speculations firmly based on scientific information. By the 1950s, the recognition emerged that these writers were specializing in a new subgenre of science fiction, "hard science fiction," dedicated to rigorously logical extrapolations of current scientific knowledge. So it is true that, in 1930, a person asked to provide examples of stories that matched Gernsback's description might be hard pressed to find them; but by 1960, the same person could readily turn to stories by Poul Anderson, Arthur C. Clarke, Hal Clement, and many others who were doing precisely what Gernsback had urged writers to do. In essence, by inspiring his young readers to embrace aspirations that his own writers were not embracing, Gernsback belatedly made his arguments for science fiction come true.[8]

In addition, one does not need an advanced degree in marketing to realize that advertising can be persuasive even if it is not exactly true, and Gernsback's proclamations could be regarded as unusually cunning ways to sell magazines within his marketing niche. In contrast to what he dismissed in "A New Sort of Magazine" as "the love story and the sex-appeal type of magazine," his science fiction magazine, he announced, offered readers wholesome and educational entertainment: young people could learn useful scientific information and absorb interesting ideas instead of wasting their time reading tales of scantily-clad women engaged in questionable behavior. And unlike the westerns and detective stories found in "the usual fiction magazine" and "the adventure type" of magazine, his science fiction magazine was uniquely respectable, because learned scientists were examining and endorsing its contents while other scientists and inventors were purportedly reading its stories hoping to glean helpful insights that could lead them to scientific breakthroughs.[9]

To drive this point home, Gernsback's later magazine *Science Wonder Stories* (which evolved into *Wonder Stories*) established an "editorial and advisory board" including "an imposing array of scientific authorities and educators," listed above each issue's editorial.[10] No other pulp magazine could claim that its stories were being reviewed by professors at prestigious universities such as Dartmouth College, Wellesley College, the University of California, and the University of Pennsylvania with demonstrated expertise in astronomy, botany, electricity, mathematics, medicine, physics, and zoology, reinforcing the notion that reading science fiction magazines was an unusually productive and worthwhile activity. And Paul A. Carter's research indicates that these experts actually were consulted on a regular basis, as he reports that "Donald H. Menzel of the Lick Observatory" (run by the University of California), the board's astrophysicist, "has informed me that Gernsback regularly sent him story manuscripts and took due account of his criticisms."[11] Thus, Gernsback's readers could enthusiastically recommend his magazines to friends and colleagues, unlike other pulp magazines that they might wish to hide from visitors. As he summed up the argument in a later *Wonder Stories* editorial, "the public at large should begin to know the benefits of Science Fiction and be turned from meaningless detective and love trash to the elevating and imaginary literature of Science Fiction."[12]

The effectiveness of Gernsback's marketing skills is evidenced by another phenomenon that he inspired and contributed to: the emergence of science fiction fandom. First, by publishing letters with readers' addresses in *Amazing Stories*, Gernsback provided a way for science fiction enthusiasts to get in touch with each other; then, as the next logical step, readers began to propose the formation of organizations to promote science fiction. One reader's letter, in the May 1928 issue of *Amazing Stories*, expressed surprise that the magazine itself had not taken this step: "I thought at first that you would take hold of [this idea], suggest a plan of organization, and get it started ... but it is now apparent that you are determined to leave it entirely in the hands of those of your readers who are interested enough to go ahead and organize the Science Club."[13]

A year later, such an organization actually sprang into existence; in the August 1929 issue of *Science Wonder Stories*, a reader named A. B. Maloire explained that he had been too busy to read all of the magazine's stories because "corresponding with members of the recently created Science Correspondence Club has taken up much of my time." This group of "twenty-five enthusiastic science fiction fans," he added, was presently "voting for officers"; a new Boston branch of the organization was announced in a later *Science Wonder Stories* letter.[14] This organization went on to publish what is generally regarded as the first science fiction "fanzine," an amateur magazine featuring reviews, articles, and stories that was called *The Comet*, edited by a future editor of *Amazing Stories*, Ray Palmer. Many other groups and publications soon emerged; for example, a letter in the May 1930 issue of *Science Wonder Stories* announced the creation of a New York–based group, the Scienceers, and the June 1930 issue of *Wonder Stories* published the first of several letters from members of another group, the American Interplanetary Society.[15]

From the beginning, Gernsback recognized that such societies could help to make science fiction more popular and, not incidentally, sell more copies of his magazines. Thus, the editorial response to Maloire's letter supportively commented, "We are more than interested to learn about the Science Correspondence Club. Its idea is excellent and we wish to encourage it in all means within our power"; and a later letter from another member to *Wonder Stories* expressed thanks for "the assistance and sincere cooperation of the Gernsback Publications" and "the wonderful help you have extended us."[16] Eventually, as more and more reports of independent clubs emerged, Gernsback decided to do what readers had long expected him to do: bring all of these groups together into one vast organization under his magazine's supervision.

Accordingly, in an editorial in the April 1934 issue of *Wonder Stories*, he announced the formation of the Science Fiction League, "a non-commercial membership organization ... for the betterment and promotion of scientific literature in all languages."[17] As part of a longer description of the League in the next issue, "The Science Fiction League," Gernsback unveiled its Executive Directors, a then-impressive team of published authors—Eando Binder (the pen name of brothers Earl and Otto Binder—"E and O"), Edmond Hamilton, David H. Keller, P. Schuyler Miller, Clark Ashton Smith, and R. F. Starzl—as well as two prominent fans, Forrest J Ackerman and Jack Darrow.[18] The group's announced mission was to "coördinate all who are interested in science fiction, into one comprehensive international group" that would "in due time become the parent organization of innumerable local science fiction clubs throughout the world."[19] While members of local chapters would "broadcast the gospel of Science Fiction," the League itself would offer "special LEAGUE meetings ... talks by prominent Science Fiction authorities, authors, writers, etc. ... [and] exhibits or collections of Science Fiction literature and stories, so that members can get together and meet each other."[20]

One notes that Gernsback had vowed to create a genuinely "international" alliance of science fiction fans, and in fact he had already been making American science fiction popular in other nations by means of his magazines, as evidenced by letters in *Amazing Stories* from readers in Australia, Canada, Great Britain, and India, as well as letters in *Science Wonder Stories* from readers in Belgium and Mexico.[21] So, it was not surprising that, in the months after Gernsback's announcement, the magazine heard about planned chapters in Great Britain, China, and the Philippines, though only an English chapter and an Australian chapter actually materialized.

For two years, Gernsback's *Wonder Stories* published regular reports on the League's chapters and activities, but when he temporarily abandoned the field and sold his magazine in 1936, the Science Fiction League officially ceased to exist. However, many chapters kept functioning as independent organizations, new societies emerged, and Gernsback's dream of a vast coalition of science fiction fans who regularly gathered together was soon achieved

1. The Emergence of American Science Fiction 13

less formally in 1939, when several groups collectively staged the first World Science Fiction Convention in New York City; however, I can locate no evidence that any of its attendees, or the attendees as the next World Conventions in 1940 and 1941, actually came from outside the United States.

No World Conventions were held during World War II, but when they resumed in 1946, the organizers did endeavor to raise enough money to bring British fan and editor John Carnell to their Philadelphia convention, though they failed to do so, but a significant step toward making these events truly international came in 1948, when a World Convention in Toronto became the first of twenty to be held outside the United States (and there will soon be two more, as the 2019 and 2020 World Conventions will be held in Dublin, Ireland, and Wellington, New Zealand). The alliance governing this now-annual event was eventually termed the World SF Society, and in addition to gatherings around the world, it would distinguish itself by regularly raising money to bring at least one foreign guest to each convention. In addition, by means of innumerable fanzines regularly mailed to interested subscribers, and reports on fan activities in science fiction magazines, science fiction fans could now stay in contact with each other, even if they were not members of official organizations or did not attend science fiction conventions.

Science fiction fandom was crucial to the growth and progress of American science fiction in innumerable ways. Its ranks became a breeding ground for new writers, including noteworthy talents like Gregory Benford, Ray Bradbury, Arthur C. Clarke, Harlan Ellison, and Robert Silverberg; further, driven by their enthusiasm for science fiction, fans vigorously recruited new readers and tried to draw attention to its writers. Fandom also bolstered the egos of science fiction writers; they may have been spending most of their time laboring anonymously at day jobs while earning little from their writings, but they could receive an enthusiastic fan letter or serve as an honored guest at a science fiction convention and briefly feel like a star. Most significantly, the letters that fans sent to magazines, and fanzines they wrote and published, provided a forum for an intense, ongoing discussion of science fiction that called attention to its flaws and demanded better writing, contributing to small but steady improvements in its quality; thus, some regularly published writers of the 1930s, like Jack Williamson and Clifford D. Simak, matured and developed to become more prominent in the 1940s and thereafter, while many of their compatriots from the 1930s found that their unchanging stories were no longer wanted. Similarly, the work of some writers of the 1940s, like Robert A. Heinlein and Isaac Asimov, kept getting better and better in the 1950s and thereafter, making them wealthy and famous, but lesser writers of that era who never improved gradually faded from view.

The criticisms of science fiction in letters and fanzines, interestingly, often focused on a form of science fiction that was becoming more and more popular with readers. As is the case with so many aspects of science fiction, the origins of this subgenre can be traced back to Gernsback, who in 1928 serialized a novel in *Amazing Stories*, E. E. "Doc" Smith's *The Skylark of Space*, now regarded as a pioneering work of space opera. Although Smith had completed the novel several years earlier without Gernsback in mind, his tendency to include lengthy explanations of his heroes' amazing inventions accorded perfectly with the editor's priorities; yet his story was primarily popular because of the exciting adventures in space that he provided, featuring two intrepid young heroes in a spaceship who flew beyond the solar system while battling a human villain and sinister aliens with amazing weapons. Smith went on to produce similar works, as did many other writers like John W. Campbell, Jr., Edmond Hamilton, Frank K. Kelly, Leslie F. Stone, and Williamson. Readers clearly loved these stories, so much so that space opera became the most common form of magazine science fiction in the 1930s.[22]

Arguably, Gernsback should have seen this trend coming; even before Smith's novel appeared, a 1927 interview with his magazine's "youngest reader" had yielded the information "that he preferred stories of space and of interplanetarian travel,"[23] and in the issue where Smith first appeared, a reader commented that "I like all types of scientifiction stories, but have a decided preference for those about other planets."[24] Despite their popularity, the obvious problem with the era's space operas was that most stories, unlike Smith's novels, did not really address Gernsback's agenda for science fiction, offering no substantive scientific information or provocative new ideas. In 1932, he directly criticized the dubious science of some space opera stories in a special editorial that introduced Campbell's story "Space Rays":

> When science fiction first came into being, it was taken most seriously by all authors. In practically all instances, authors laid the basis of their stories upon a solid scientific foundation. If an author made a statement as to certain future instrumentalities, he usually found it advisable to adhere closely to the possibilities of science as it was then known.
> Many modern science fiction authors have no such scruples. They do not hesitate to throw scientific plausibility overboard, and embark on a policy of what I might call scientific magic, in other words, science that is neither plausible, nor possible. Indeed, it overlaps the fairy tale, and often goes the fairy tale one better.... In the present offering, Mr. John W. Campbell, Jr., has no doubt realized this state of affairs and has proceeded in an earnest way to burlesque some of our rash authors to whom plausibility and possible science mean nothing. He pulls, magician-like, all sorts of impossible rays from his silk hat, much as a magician extracts rabbits.... I have gone to this length to preach a sermon in the hope that misguided authors will see the light, and hereafter stick to science as it is known, or as it may reasonably develop in the future.[25]

Clearly, Gernsback was imposing his own didactic message on a story with no satiric intent, but he perhaps imagined that this was the gentlest way to inform Campbell and his colleagues that their colorful adventure stories were not the sort of science fiction that he admired or wanted to publish. In contrast, he made a special effort to praise a story that did not follow the usual pattern of space opera, Stanley G. Weinbaum's "A Martian Odyssey" (1934), by personally (though anonymously) writing its introduction; Weinbaum, he said, "has written a science-fiction tale so new, so breezy, that it stands out head and shoulders over similar interplanetarian stories."[26]

Since innovative writers like Weinbaum were hard to find, Gernsback had also been striving to improve space opera by sponsoring contests in *Science Wonder Quarterly* (which became *Wonder Stories Quarterly*) to obtain new "Interplanetary Plots" that experienced authors could turn into stories. The contest instructions announced what Gernsback did not want, namely, stories like "Space Rays": "A plot submitted that simply relates a war between two planets, with a lot of rays and bloodshed, will receive little consideration." Instead, he wanted stories that offered "some original 'slant' on interplanetary travel, or of the conditions on other worlds."[27] Unfortunately, the products of this contest were consistently disappointing; for example, a plot from reader Everett C. Smith that yielded the story "The Metal Moon" (1932), actually written by R. F. Starzl, did offer an imaginative setting—an immense space station orbiting Jupiter—but it was otherwise a routine tale of a future society sharply divided into a wealthy upper class living in elevated pleasure while an oppressed lower class suffers below them, here transplanted to the station's upper and lower hemispheres.[28]

Other members of the emerging science fiction community, like Gernsback, were condemning routine space operas and calling for more imaginative approaches to science fiction. The very term "space opera" was coined by a fan, Wilson Tucker, while he was criticizing "the hacky, grinding, stinking, outworn space-ship yarn."[29] Another fan, Clyde F. Beck, whose writings were collected in 1937 as the first book of science fiction criticism, *Hammer and Tongs*, offered a similar complaint while explaining what constitutes

> the real reason for the great dearth in worthy writing in the contemporary "science fiction" magazines. There is an altogether deceptive appearance of easiness about it: seemingly one needs but to take the currently popular plot of pursuit, struggle, mystery, or intrigue, salt it with rockets or ray-guns, garnish it with a few strips of mathematics, pass it through interstellar space, the fourth dimension, the realm of the infinitely small—and behold, science fiction.[30]

None of these broadsides, however, diminished the burgeoning popularity of space opera, and this was actually helpful to science fiction—because even if the subgenre was not admired by dedicated fans, it did provide science fiction with a sense of identity and a characteristic plot, attracting numerous writers and readers who might later move on to more challenging material. Simak, for example, only wrote undistinguished space adventures in the 1930s, but he later blossomed into an author who was widely admired for gentle, pastoral stories about aliens and robots. And, as a young science fiction reader, I was first drawn to routine space operas like Jack Vance's *Vandals of the Void* (1953) and Donald A. Wollheim's *The Secret of Saturn's Rings* (1954), and the space adventures of comic book superheroes like Superman and Batman, but I later came to prefer more mature and variegated material.

More importantly, space opera expanded the audience for science fiction, inspiring dozens of new magazines in the 1940s and 1950s—including a few, like *Planet Stories* (1939–1955) and *Captain Future* (1940–1944), which were exclusively devoted to space stories. It was also the form of science fiction that could be transferred most easily into other media: thus, two stories by Philip Francis Nowlan that Gernsback published in 1928 and 1929, involving a present-day man named Anthony Rogers who awakens in the far future (collected in 1962 as *Armageddon 2419 A.D.*), became the basis for a popular comic strip, *Buck Rogers* (1929–1967), that soon transformed him into a space adventurer. This inspired two similar comic strips, *Flash Gordon* (1934–2003) and *Brick Bradford* (1933–1987), and all three comic strips became the basis of film serials (*Flash Gordon* [1936]; *Flash Gordon's Trip to Mars* [1938]; *Buck Rogers* [1939]; *Flash Gordon Conquers the Universe* [1940]; *Brick Bradford* [1947]). Comic books embraced space opera as well in popular comics like *Planet Comics* (1940–1954), *Weird Science* (1950–1953), *Strange Adventures* (1950–1973), and *Mystery in Space* (1951–1966). Finally, in the 1950s, space opera ventured into film and television, represented by films like *This Island Earth* (1954) and *Forbidden Planet* (1956) and television series like *Space Patrol* (1950–1955), *Tom Corbett, Space Cadet* (1950–1955), and *Rocky Jones, Space Ranger* (1954). Like written space operas, these comic strips, serials, comic books, films, and television programs were often derided by fans, but they reached far more people than the science fiction magazines and books and hence served to strengthen the genre by increasing its visibility and popularity.

It will be recalled, though, that one element in Gernsback's campaign to promote science fiction was to make it respectable, and a genre dominated by space opera could not achieve that goal. Thus, to balance the bad image often projected by that subgenre, someone needed to establish and support an intellectual wing of science fiction, so there would be numerous stories that would merit the attention of thoughtful adult readers. This task was undertaken by editor John W. Campbell, Jr., who officially assumed control of *Astounding Stories* in 1938, renamed the magazine *Astounding Science-Fiction*, and began writing editorials and articles conveying a new vision of science fiction and new reasons to value the genre.

As noted, Campbell began his career by writing exuberant space operas like the aforementioned "Space Rays" and *The Mightiest Machine* (1934–1935), but he was soon producing more interesting and imaginative stories using the pseudonym Don A. Stuart, including an elegiac vision of humanity's far future, "Twilight" (1934), and a scientific mystery involving a shapeshifting alien found in Antarctica, "Who Goes There?" (1938), which inspired the 1951 film *The Thing (from Another World)* and two later remakes (1982, 2011). He was thus well prepared to take the field in new directions. It is true, as I have noted elsewhere, that Campbell still felt that science fiction could fulfill Gernsback's original goals, but he also wanted the genre to transcend these priorities by offering more provocative and thought-provoking sorts of entertainment, education, and ideas.

Thus, he wanted science fiction to be well-written literature: "In older science fiction, the Machine and the Great Idea predominated. Modern readers—and hence editors!—don't want that; they want stories of people living in a world where a Great Idea, or a series of them, and a Machine, or machines, form the background. But it is the man, not the idea or machine that is the essence."[31] Second, by offering readers stimulating puzzles to solve, science fiction did not simply teach them scientific facts, but rather how to think like a scientist: science fiction is "not the summer-vacation-snooze type of fun. More like the roller-coaster or mountain-climbing type, it presents a real mental challenge."[32] Finally, science fiction could intelligently examine not only new technologies, but the ways that they might affect future societies: by employing their "understanding of how political and social set-ups react to technological changes," science fiction writers could consider both "new and still undiscovered phenomena" and "what the results look like when applied ... to human society."[33] More broadly, science fiction could function as "a way of considering the past, present, and future from a different viewpoint, and taking a look at how else we *might* do things ... a convenient analog system for thinking about new scientific, social, and economic ideas—and for re-examining old ideas."[34] Unlike Gernsback, then, Campbell offered a literary agenda that even his most erudite readers could admire and appreciate.

Campbell had one advantage over Gernsback, who was largely promoting a form of science fiction that had not yet appeared; for not only had his own stories partially anticipated his ideas, but Campbell had attracted a writer in 1939, Robert A. Heinlein, who was already doing everything that Campbell wanted science fiction writers to do. In fact, Heinlein's work directly inspired some of Campbell's talking points; for example, after examining Heinlein's Future History chart, which provided a shared background for many of his early stories, Campbell wrote a 1941 editorial, "History to Come," that presented Heinlein's painstaking development of a consistent human future as a model for other writers.[35] Campbell was also unlike the reticent Gernsback because he was willing, by means of voluminous correspondence and occasional meetings, to personally train his writers, ranging from veterans like Williamson to neophytes like Asimov, to produce the new sorts of stories that he preferred. Further, his impact extended beyond the writers who worked for *Astounding* because other writers like Philip K. Dick and Walter M. Miller, Jr., who read his editorials and the stories he published, started producing their own varieties of stimulating science fiction for adults even though they mostly published in other magazines. Thus, by the late 1940s and early 1950s, there was an established cadre of talented, imaginative science fiction writers whose works could function as exemplary examples of the deep, challenging literature that Campbell wanted; and their works could be exported along with space operas in order to appeal to demanding as well as undemanding readers in other countries.

The power of Campbell's arguments for science fiction, I think, cannot be overestimated, because it identified the genre as having a virtue that other forms of popular fiction could not claim. I vividly recall a 1970 conversation with a fellow student at Carleton College about a paperback science fiction novel that I had never heard of, cannot recall today, and was by the student's own admission absolutely terrible. And yet, he said, he was glad he had read the novel because of its conclusion, of which he said, "it made me think." And that is the essence of the point that Campbell was striving to convey: science fiction is a form of literature that can make you think. It is an argument in favor of science fiction that never occurred to Gernsback, and one that defenders of detective novels, westerns, and romance novels could not credibly present. And the argument has reverberated throughout the last sixty years in repeated assertions that science fiction is a "literature of ideas," a description of the genre that has proven to be almost universally appealing.

We can now understand precisely why American science fiction became recognized as the best science fiction in the world. It had a name that conveyed and imposed a special sense of identity, firmly associated with science; it was buttressed by arguments testifying to its unique value and significance; it was vigorously supported by armies of dedicated fans eager to both promote and critique its works in order to sustain the genre and inspire improvements; it was centered upon a characteristic narrative that was exciting and colorful enough to attract a broad range of readers; and adventures along those lines were accompanied by more distinguished stories rooted in a more challenging agenda that could appeal to intellectuals and literary connoisseurs. In contrast, the imaginative literatures of other nations lacked a recognized name, were not clearly associated with science, were not buttressed by arguments about their singular virtues, did not enjoy organized support, and were not anchored by an involving narrative pattern in alliance with more thought-provoking efforts. Hence, foreign science fiction could not resist the powerful

1. The Emergence of American Science Fiction   19

juggernaut of American science fiction, which after World War II marginalized native traditions and forced writers in other nations to enlist in its ranks and emulate its strictures.

The first triumphs of American science fiction had come in Britain, where readers in the 1930s had already started reading imported American science fiction magazines and forming their own fan organizations like those in America; one such reader and fan was the young Arthur C. Clarke, who chronicled his fondness for America's *Astounding Stories* in the 1930s in his book *Astounding Days: A Science Fictional Autobiography* (1989), which he dedicated to the magazine's three editors during that decade: Harry Bates, F. Orlon Tremaine, and Campbell. Clarke went on to become one of several British writers in the 1940s, such as Eric Frank Russell, A. Bertram Chandler (later a resident of Australia), and Sam Youd (who wrote as John Christopher), who focused much of their attention on the American market. Fandom was also emerging in another English-speaking country, Australia: a chapter of Gernsback's Science Fiction League, formed in 1935, was the first of several organized groups of Australian science fiction fans, and four Australian fanzines were launched in 1939, though only one of them, *Ultra*, lasted more than a year.

Only after the trauma of World War II ended, however, could translators in France, Germany, Russia, Eastern Europe, Japan, and other countries start providing their fellow citizens with access to American science fiction in their own languages. What happened as a result can be exemplified by two popular series of publications in postwar France: the Fleuve Noir series presented French translations of American novels, while the accompanying Anticipation series featured French writers endeavoring to produce their own versions of American science fiction.[36] The 1950s also witnessed the publication of numerous translations of books by Robert A. Heinlein into Danish, Finnish, French, German, Japanese, Norwegian, Portuguese, Spanish, and Swedish, while books by Isaac Asimov were being translated into Dutch, French, German, Italian, Japanese, Portuguese, Spanish, and Swedish. Clearly, then, numerous works of American science fiction were becoming available to foreign readers, and they undoubtedly influenced the science fiction stories and novels being written in a number of foreign countries.

Though its victory was thoroughgoing, however, the complete American domination of global science fiction was relatively brief. In America, around 1960, there arose a belief that the genre was somehow becoming exhausted, losing its strength; fan Earl Kemp's alarmist manifesto *Who Killed Science Fiction?* (1960), discussed at length below, was the clearest signal of such concerns, but many others, who noted in particular the demise of many science fiction magazines, felt that a grand era of American science fiction history was coming to an end.[37]

In the meantime, while new foreign writers were initially limited to imitating American models, some grew dissatisfied with its conventions and expectations, so they naturally looked back to their own national literatures, developed new ideas, and endeavored to write science fiction that combined American priorities with their own distinctive styles. Such authors began to have an impact, on both America and the world, in the 1960s. In Britain, figures like Brian W. Aldiss, J. G. Ballard, and Michael Moorcock became leading figures in a movement, termed the New Wave, demanding science fiction that featured daring stylistic experiments, less devotion to science, and more attention to contemporary human concerns than was apparent in American science fiction. Elsewhere, writers like France's Pierre Boulle, Japan's Kōbō Abé, Poland's Stanislaw Lem, and Russia's Boris and Arkady Strugatsky both reflected American models and moved away from American influences to create imaginative novels that, when translated, impressed readers throughout the world. Foreign science fiction filmmakers also attracted and influenced American viewers with innovative works like Chris Marker's *La Jetée* (1962), Jean-Luc Godard's *Alphaville* (1965), and Andrei Tarkovsky's *Solaris* (1971). While American voices were still strong, in other words, science fiction in the 1960s and thereafter was gradually becoming a truly global genre, and the dividing lines between an American approach and a foreign approach to the genre were no longer quite as clear.

Still, signs of American ascendancy have remained visible to this day in all forms of science fiction: writers continue to respond to the agendas that were promulgated by Gernsback and Campbell; fans all over the world are still publishing fanzines (though these are now more often online) and holding conventions in the American manner; the space operas that originated in America remain the most common form of science fiction almost everywhere; and the American writers working in Campbell's tradition continue to attract most of the critical attention. Authors and critics in other nations may resent this lingering American influence; they may even attempt to deny that it exists or condemn it as an atavistic remnant of earlier days that must be purged so the genre can progress; but it is hard to explain the success of science fiction as a whole without crediting the power of the provocative American ideas and activities in the twentieth century that have presided over its remarkable expansion and development.

2

August 1928
Science Fiction's Second Birthday

In the spring of 1928, as *Amazing Stories* entered its third year of publication, publisher and editor Hugo Gernsback had every reason to regard his magazine as a success story; not only had its circulation remained high, but it had spawned an equally profitable sister magazine, *Amazing Stories Quarterly*, and the Gernsback-christened "scientifiction" in those magazines now seemed established as a new genre of popular fiction. Content with its progress, Gernsback had largely left the business of editing the magazines to his associate T. O'Conor Sloane and was focusing his energies on other projects, most notably a pioneering initiative with the experimental technology of television. Yet there were signs that Gernsback's new genre was not advancing as he had hoped, suggesting that its long-term prospects for survival were not particularly strong. Then, there appeared the August 1928 issue of *Amazing Stories*, and suddenly everything changed.[1]

The significance of that issue has long been recognized because of two stories that appeared in that issue: the first installment of E. E. "Doc" Smith's novel *The Skylark of Space*, the inspiration and model for the vast and popular subgenre of science fiction later named "space opera"; and Philip Francis Nowlan's "Armageddon—2419 A.D.," the first of two stories that became the basis for the comic strip *Buck Rogers* (1929–1967); this influential strip, which later inspired a radio series, a 1939 film serial, a television series, and toys, brought the conventions of magazine science fiction to general audiences for the first time. But commentators have paid little if any attention to the other materials in the August 1928 issue—understandably, since with the exception of Frank R. Paul's regularly reprinted cover, they are quite unremarkable: a Hugo Gernsback editorial, "The Amazing Unknown," that makes no mention of science fiction; a number of letters primarily discussing previously published stories and the scientific issues that they raised; a reprint of an obscure and little-regarded H. G. Wells story, "The Moth" (1895); two original stories by forgotten authors—Clement Fezandié's "Hicks' Inventions with a Kick: The Perambulating Home" (as by Henry Hugh Simmons) and Joe Kleier's "The Head"; and some unremarkable interior illustrations.

Still, it is precisely because of its uneven contents that the August 1928 issue of *Amazing Stories* is such a fascinating document, as its pages illuminatingly display the past, present, and future of Gernsback's science fiction. And while they did engender significant traditions and influential adaptations, I will argue more broadly that Smith's and Nowlan's contributions to that issue effectively created the modern genre of science fiction. So, the April 1926 issue of *Amazing Stories*, that introduced the genre of science fiction to the world, unquestionably remains science fiction's first birthday; but the August 1928 issue represents its second, and perhaps its more important, birthday, as indicated by the following review of its contents.

After discussing science fiction several times in his early editorials for *Amazing Stories*, Gernsback by 1928 had fallen into the habit of devoting his editorials entirely to scientific information and speculations, usually announcing his subject in a title including the word "Amazing." Thus, one finds in 1928 editorials entitled "Amazing Thinking" (March 1928), "Our Amazing Minds" (June 1928), "Our Amazing Senses" (July 1928), "Our Amazing Universe" (September 1928), "New Amazing Facts" (October 1928), "Amazing Life" (November 1928), and "An Amazing Phenomenon" (December 1928). For the August 1928 editorial, "The Amazing Unknown," Gernsback more broadly addressed how little we know about a variety of scientific matters, as indicated by a few excerpts:

> We do not know what electricity is; we do not know what light is, in their ultimate states, and there is practically nothing in the entire world that surrounds us, that we know anything about at all.... When it comes to matter, we know nothing at all about it....We have not the slightest conception of just what life is.... We only know a small fraction of a per cent of what is going on in our own bodies[2]

In writing these editorials, Gernsback undoubtedly envisioned readers as his primary audience, since he assumed that their interest in science fiction was merely one facet of their broader interest in science; but he also must have realized that there was one particular group of readers who would examine his editorials with special attentiveness: writers and perspective writers planning to submit their works to *Amazing Stories*. Such individuals, logically, would carefully study everything that Gernsback had written, looking for clues as to what sorts of stories he might be especially inclined to publish. Thus, in addition to enlightening general readers, Gernsback may have seen these editorials as ways to stimulate potential writers with information and ideas that might become the basis of an interesting story. Considered from that perspective, "The Amazing Unknown" has a clear message for writers: there are vast areas of scientific ignorance that are open for science fiction writers to explore in new and original stories, and I will provide a number of specific examples.

Surveying the sometimes abysmal quality of the stories that he published, many commentators have assumed, like Brian W. Aldiss, that "Gernsback, as editor, showed himself to be without literary understanding."[3] Yet ample evidence indicates that Gernsback could recognize an excellent story when he saw one: as shall be discussed, he obviously knew that Smith's and Nowlan's stories were something special, and in 1934, at a time when he rarely involved himself in the day-to-day business of editing magazines, he unusually decided to personally write the introduction to another story that greatly impressed him, Stanley G. Weinbaum's "A Martian Odyssey," now acknowledged as a classic. Gernsback published weak stories because, all too often, they represented the best stories that were available, and editorials like "The Amazing Unknown" subtly convey his strong desire to receive some better ones.

Needless to say, one cannot say that the readers' letters published in the "Discussions" section of *Amazing Stories* accurately represent general reactions to the magazine. For one thing, the overwhelming majority of *Amazing*'s 100,000 or so reported readers undoubtedly never bothered to write letters, and surveying the letters that did arrive, Gernsback and Sloane had an obvious incentive to favor letters generally praising the magazine over letters that generally criticized the magazine. Furthermore, they would be inclined to choose letters that made some point about the magazine's purportedly broad appeal—like letters from women or residents of foreign countries—even if their contents were idiosyncratic. Nevertheless, although R. D. Mullen once reported in personal correspondence that he had not actually written a letter attributed to him in the first issue of Gernsback's *Scientific Detective Monthly* (1930–1931), it seems reasonable to assume that the letters published in this significantly more popular magazine were authentic, and that they did reflect the honest opinions of certain readers. To buttress that impression, I did some internet research into some of the more distinctive names in the August 1928 letter column and found evidence that there were actually individuals named Frederick Bitting, Howard Fahrer, Marcley W. Felten, F. C. Haenchen, William P. Keasbey, Stanley McMichael, and Francis Uffelman living at about the right time and place to be plausibly identified as the authors of letters to *Amazing Stories*. (As it happens, Keasbey became the author of several children's books, including *Wonder Stories from Nature* [1932], with a title perhaps borrowed from one of Gernsback's later magazines, suggesting that he had a lasting influence. In addition, Keasbey's letter begins, "While I am at the writing machine, I'd like to indulge in some comments on the tales you have published recently"—suggesting that he was hard at work on a book, possibly *The Big Trick and Puzzle Book* [1929], the first book he published.[4])

Of the fourteen letters that appeared in the August 1928 issue, the most interesting comes from an author who had already published four stories in Gernsback's magazines: Miles J. Breuer. A practicing physician who was also a regular reader of *Amazing Stories*, Breuer was manifestly dissatisfied with its contents and, more explicitly than Gernsback, set out in his letter to assist other writers in improving their work in one particular area, stories about space travel, by sharing his knowledge of the human body:

> You have had a good deal many stories of space-traveling in your pages, and all of them seemed to have neglected the effect upon the human physiology of the withdrawal of gravitation. That is a question that interests me immensely; eventually I shall try to put it into a story. However, at the present I have no material nor ideas that I could work into a story of space-travel, and am giving you my ideas, for the benefit of other writers who may care to give the matter some consideration.

After discussing three issues, Breuer concludes, "I should like very much to see some writer of space stories consider this seriously."[5] The editorial response to his observations is disappointing: surely, the proper reply would have been to thank Breuer for providing stimulating information for other writers and to encourage other readers to similarly offer their own data and perspectives to assist aspiring science fiction writers. Instead, the responding editor—perhaps Gernsback himself, or Sloane prodded by Gernsback—begins by informing Breuer, "You will find in Mr. Hugo Gernsback's book, *Ralph 124C 41+*, that he has carefully considered all of the points brought out in your letter," then proceeds to provide a lengthy quotation from that novel.[6]

This reply illuminates one persistent blind spot in Gernsback's approach to editing. On one hand, he recognized well enough that he was not a particularly talented writer, as evidenced by numerous self-deprecating comments about the quality of his own work; on the other hand, becoming a writer had been one of Gernsback's original dreams, and he could never resist hoping that, with a little self-promotion, his efforts might finally earn some attention and respect. Thus, regardless of any other consideration, he would always seize upon any opportunity to boast at length about a prediction in one of his stories that seemed to be proving accurate, as in this case, and he regularly republished his own works even when other, superior material was surely available. Gernsback probably alienated some readers by republishing his novel *Baron Munchausen's New Scientific Adventures* (1915–1917) in several issues of *Amazing Stories*, and *Ralph 124C 41+: A Romance of the Year 2660* (1911–1912, 1925) in an issue of *Amazing Stories Quarterly*—one letter in the August 1928 issue, from Charles E. Roe, dryly comments, "I do not care much for your friend, the Baron"[7]—and much later, he contributed to the demise of his comeback magazine *Science-Fiction Plus* (1953) by filling its early issues with republications of his own, generally abysmal, self-published science fiction.

Other letters in the August 1928 issue offer critiques of the science in certain stories—indicating that some of his readers were coming to share Gernsback's concern for the scientific accuracy of science fiction—with particular attention to exploring the effects of traveling faster than the speed of light. But readers seemed most inclined to comment on the qualities of various stories that had appeared in *Amazing Stories* and *Amazing Stories Quarterly*, and while three letters only praised the contents of the magazines, others included critical remarks that could be taken as ominous signs that readers were growing dissatisfied with the material that Gernsback was providing. Frederick Bitting states, "Some of the stories I have not liked."[8] While other readers had praised Gernsback's numerous reprints, Marcley W. Fenten had grown tired of them: "Reprints are very well in their place, but a live modern magazine should have little use for work that is already well read and known and that was or has been 'popular' in the past."[9] Bernard Simon lists five "stories I did not care for."[10] Perhaps the most scathing criticism—though stated indirectly and politely—came in the second part of Breuer's letter, for in the course of praising one story Gernsback had published—Clare Winger Harris's "The Miracle of the Lily"—and criticizing another—David H. Keller's "The Yeast Men" (both in *Amazing Stories*, April 1928)—he made two comments conveying a certain displeasure with the current state of science fiction. First, he reports that "I am keeping a great scrap-book of all the good things in Amazing Stories, purchasing two issues if necessary to get my clippings complete. By eliminating hopeless material, and material that I already possess in book form, I have the cream of Scientifiction, comprising less than one-fifth of all the material you have published." Second, after commenting that turning Keller's "original conception" into "a dramatic plot ... would have required real literary workmanship" (presumably beyond Keller's abilities), he muses that "some day perhaps we'll have a Lord Dunsany in this field; a fellow who can do poetic things with scientific ideas." Breuer thus asserts that up to four-fifths of Gernsback's material was substandard, and that none of it rose to the level of "real literary workmanship."

In its first two years, *Amazing Stories* had devoted a considerable amount of attention to the distinguished past of science fiction: as I discuss elsewhere,[11] Gernsback effectively crafted the first history of science fiction by means of comments in editorials and responses to readers' letters, along with republications of numerous older works of science fiction, most frequently by H. G. Wells and Jules Verne. And while detractors have charged that he did so solely to save money, Gernsback and Sloane were diligent about publishing letters in support of these republications, demonstrating that they were receiving at least some positive feedback regarding their policy.

However, the August 1928 issue provided a conspicuous indication that Gernsback's supply of older stories was running out, as it offered readers Wells's "The Moth," which was not only one of Wells's least distinguished stories but also not really a work of science fiction. After his bitter rival dies, an entomologist is tormented by sightings of a new species of moth that he cannot capture to study and enhance his reputation, and the maddened scientist is soon committed to an asylum. While the moth may have been a hallucination—a sign, rather than a cause, of his eventual insanity—the story also suggests that it may represent the ghost of his deceased enemy, who returned to bedevil him in the form of a moth. Gernsback almost certainly delegated to Sloane the task of writing the story's introduction, and necessarily defending it as science fiction, but his associate editor essentially threw up his hands and made no effort to relate the story to Gernsback's definition of the genre: "We present a most curious story by H. G. Wells. We might call this an adventure in psychology. It is a queer as well as startling penetration into the realm of the human mind."[12]

This evident dearth of suitable older stories to republish would not be a problem if Gernsback was attracting large numbers of excellent new stories; but two undistinguished new stories in the August 1928 issue suggests that he had, to date, not been entirely successful in doing so.

One of those stories, "Hicks' Inventions with a Kick: The Perambulating Home," came from a long-time Gernsback favorite, Clement Fezandié, who had (from Gernsback's perspective) the endearing quality of never wanting to receive any payments for his works. After *Amazing Stories* published in 1926 two additional installments in his series "Dr. Hackensaw's Secrets," previously a recurring feature in Gernsback's science magazine *Science and Invention*, Fezandié in 1927 adopted the pseudonym Henry Hugh Simmons and started a new series, "Hicks' Inventions with a Kick," featuring a different scientist, an eccentric inventor named Hicks. One can only speculate about the reasons for this change, but it is possible that Gernsback, pondering his readers' lack of enthusiasm for Fezandié's inferior stories, theorized that his foreign-sounding name was the cause, and therefore suggested that the author relaunch his career with a reassuringly Anglo-Saxon byline.

One thing can be said in favor of "The Perambulating Home": it perfectly fulfills one of the purposes of science fiction that Gernsback had announced, providing ideas for scientists and inventors. For most of the story consists of Hicks's extended descriptions of the inventions he has developed for his new house in Los Angeles: among other features, the house itself can move, so that its residents can enjoy sunshine whenever they wish; there is a table that ascends to the ceiling to resemble a chandelier, useful for concealing then-illegal alcoholic beverages; and the house includes an "Automatic Self-Serving Dining Table."[13] But the last device malfunctions, disrupting the house and soon plunging it into the ocean, where Hicks's inventions serendipitously allow the house to function as a boat and thus prevent any harm to its occupants. The story provides so much detail about its major inventions that any inventor reading the story could effectively follow Hicks's instructions and actually construct them, perhaps adding features to prevent the mishaps that befall the story's characters.

However, the story spectacularly fails to fulfill one of Gernsback's other purposes for science fiction: to entertain readers. A sample of Hicks's lengthy description of his "Self-Serving Dining Table" will illustrate the problem:

> The shaft which ends at the base in the male member of the clutch through which the table is driven is connected to the motor by a belt at a ratio of 5 to 1, the entire drive, including the motor, of course, being placed below the floor. The motor runs constantly while the dinner is in progress. The controls of the table are, as you will note, in the shape of levers beside each place, each lever, when slightly pressed forward throwing the clutch in and when released returning and instantly putting on a brake, thereby bringing the table to an instant stop at exactly the desired place [456].

Even if Fezandié had been a better prose stylist, this sort of material would surely bore almost all of Gernsback's actual readers, lacking any interest in constructing such devices. The story also fails to live up to the slogan found on the editorial page of every issue of *Amazing Stories*—"Extravagant Fiction Today ... Cold Fact Tomorrow"—for there is absolutely nothing "Extravagant" about Fezandié's very modest "predictions" of machines that could easily be constructed by contemporary inventors. The introduction, undoubtedly by Sloane, even acknowledges this by commenting, "it is surprising that some of these inventions are not actually in use."[14]

The author of another new story in this issue, Joe Kleier, is a mystery; the only information I have been able to locate is that, between 1924 and 1930, he also published four western stories—in *Western Adventures* and *Ace-High Magazine*—and two detective stories—in *Mystery Magazine* and *Clues*. Online genealogies indicate that a man named Joseph Kleier, who lived at about the right time, had a brother named George Kleier and a wife named Josephine Walter Kleier, both from Kentucky, and is buried in Saint Michael Cemetery in Louisville, Kentucky, but there are others with the same name who cannot be ruled out. Since the use of multiple pseudonyms by prolific authors was then not as common as it became in the 1930s and 1940s, one's best guess is that he was a real person with another career, who dabbled in writing for the pulp magazines before resolving to focus all of his energies elsewhere.

"The Head" is an interesting hybrid: for most of its length, the story follows the cautious, expository pattern long associated with Gernsback's magazines, consisting of two conversations between a scientist describing his new invention and an interested listener. The novelty is that the listener is a man dying of stomach cancer, and the scientist, Dr. James Leeson, is trying to persuade him to participate in an experiment to briefly keep the man's head alive after his death, employing artificial blood pumped and filtered by an electronic device that is explained at some length. Clearly, Kleier had read enough issues of *Amazing Stories* to figure out that this was one type of story that Gernsback favored.

Yet in its final passages the story veers in an unexpected and more expansive direction. A few days after the deceased man's head is successfully attached to the device, Leeson dies in a car accident, and the authorities investigate the situation. After the courts fail to convict Leeson's assistants of any crime, they are allowed to keep the head alive, sustained by an inheritance from Leeson, and when they die, other trained technicians carry on the work. Since the head is unable to speak, he can never communicate that he fervently longs for death. After a long period of time, "the head noticed that the progress of science had stopped,"[15] and the head becomes the god of this debased society's new religion, with "priests" (421) tending to his care and interpreting a certain facial expression as "an oracle" (449) conveying the god's instructions. Finally, foreign invaders overrun the facility, and as "a dark-skinned invader ... raised a club to strike," "a look of utter content came over the Head's features as the blow that meant oblivion descended!" (449).

Needless to say, the hurried few paragraphs summarizing these developments are vastly more interesting than the preceding technical discussions, and an assertive, involved editor surely would have advised Kleier to condense the expository passages set in the present and offer more detail about the transformed world of the future; then again, this might have been difficult to do from the perspective of a human head confined to one room. There is also nothing in Kleier's other publications to suggest that he had a flair for imaginative extrapolation, and he could have been borrowing the idea of a decadent future humanity from several stories that Gernsback had already published, ranging from Wells's *The Time Machine* (1895), which appeared in the May 1927 issue of *Amazing Stories*, to G. Peyton Wertenbaker's "The Coming of the Ice" (1926). Overall, the story suggests that the better, more creative authors Gernsback was featuring in *Amazing Stories* were having some impact on other writers, but not enough impact, as many remained wedded to the unadventurous and didactic approach of Gernsback, Fezandié, and similar writers.

The introduction to "The Head"—almost certainly written by Sloane—also provides evidence that at least one editor simply did not understand what was truly meritorious about Kleier's story, because it says nothing about its intriguing vision of humanity's distant future epitomized in its final paragraphs. Rather, the piece is characterized as a horror story: "If you are at all nervous and given to nightmares, we advise you not to read this story before you go to bed. It gives an excellent thrill, and contains good science as well."[16] It is true that the man himself regards his prolonged life as a detached head as a curse, finally and blessedly ended by his death, but others who could overlook the limitations of such an existence might eagerly embrace the opportunity to survive for several centuries after their death and learn about coming events even if they lacked an ambulatory body. Horror stories, as I argue elsewhere, tend to regard innovations as unpleasant disruptions of an acceptable status quo and seek to eliminate them, as is observed here; the science fiction stories that would eventually emerge from Gernsback's initiatives instead sought to consider both the positive and negative implications of new technologies as they are integrated into society. The modern rejoinder to "The Head," then, is the animated television series *Futurama* (1999–2013), wherein scores of present-day celebrities have freely chosen to remain alive indefinitely as detached heads, apparently enjoying their immobile immortality.

It should be noted that, prior to the August 1928 issue of *Amazing*, Gernsback had attracted contemporary authors with more talent than Fezandié or Kleier: Wertenbaker, H. P. Lovecraft, and Edgar Rice Burroughs all provided Gernsback with good stories, but were alienated by his niggardly payment policies and stopped contributing, and Gernsback had also brought into science fiction two authors, A. Hyatt Verrill and David H. Keller, who occasionally demonstrated that they could be capable and interesting writers in numerous contributions to Gernsback's magazines. But even they sometimes followed the pattern of Fezandié, Kleier, and the other forgotten writers who contributed short stories to early issues of *Amazing* by featuring present-day inventors in laboratories and depicting the salutary or disastrous effects of their modest innovations. Science fiction needed to more adventurously explore significantly different new realms—such as the distant future and outer space—and the other two, groundbreaking stories in the August 1928 issue did so in a memorable fashion.

It may or may not have been the editor's intention, but placing "Armageddon—2419 A.D." immediately after "The Head" suggested that Nowlan's story might be characterized as both an expansion of, and a sequel to, Kleier's story, providing a more extensive picture of a decadent future America that falls prey to foreign invaders and describing how the victimized Americans might someday revive their civilization and rise up to regain their independence. The fact that the text of "The Head" was "Continued" so that its final paragraphs appeared on the same page as the conclusion of "Armageddon—2419 A.D." might have further served to link the two stories in readers' imaginations. As in "The Head," Nowlan's protagonist is a man from the present who lives to see the future; but Anthony Rogers, revived after a long period of accidental hibernation, is complete, mobile, and energetic, so that he can both observe and interact with the world around him, providing the basis for a much more involving narrative.

Some aspects of Nowlan's story would already have been familiar to readers of *Amazing Stories*. Even since the late nineteenth century, numerous authors had envisioned the "Yellow Peril" of sinister Asian armies attacking America who must be opposed by beleaguered American forces. Further, Nowlan recalls Gernsback's *Ralph 124C 41+* and similar stories in the way that he regularly posits the future discovery of new elements and rays with miraculous properties, always explained at some length, that are being employed by the American rebels and the Han invaders who long ago conquered the United States. Thus, the Han oppressors can destroy foes using destructive "*disintegrator* rays" and propel their airships with "*repellor* or anti-gravity waves,"[17] while the Americans can fly through the air by means of belts with the antigravity element "*inertron*" (427) and protect themselves by using another element, "Ultron," which is "*absolutely invisible and non-reflective*" (429).

However, "Armageddon—2419 A.D." has some innovative features as well. For one thing, the scientific breakthroughs in earlier stories might be described by a scientist giving his girlfriend a guided tour of a utopian future—as in *Ralph 124C 41+*—or explained by a proud inventor greeting visitors to his laboratory—the usual approach of his other authors; in contrast, Nowlan's explanations are provided by a retrospective narrator who is also relating an exciting story about future warfare. The nature of that conflict is also different: past stories about the "Yellow Peril" typically focused on a conflict occurring in the near future, an Asian invasion that is promptly thwarted by American defenders; Nowlan sets his story about future conflict five hundred years in the future, long after the Asians had successfully conquered the United States and taken control of the country.

More significantly, Gernsback and his cohorts were usually capable enough in predicting future scientific developments, but they were unable or unwilling to posit any changes in the social order that might accompany such scientific progress; for example, in *Ralph 124C 41+*, Aldiss correctly notes that although the novel is set six centuries in the future, and describes the innumerable scientific marvels of that future era, "society is unchanged. Boy meets girl in the same prissy 1911 way" (203–204). In contrast, Nowlan envisions future development in both American science and American society. Recognizing that the militarily superior Han could not be resisted by means of conventional warfare, Nowlan has his rebels adopt a form of guerrilla warfare; indeed, the way that the American "gangs" seek to blend into their forest homes in order to avoid detection seems prescient of the strategies of later guerrillas in South Vietnam and elsewhere.

Further, Nowlan anticipates that such a lifestyle would inspire changes in the status of women. Thus, Nowlan's newly awakened Anthony Rogers first encounters a woman on military patrol, Wilma Deering, and later learns that in their gang, "all able-bodied men and women alternated in two-week periods between military and industrial service, except those who were needed for household work" (429). Rogers does find it difficult to adjust to this new world of sexual equality: after he and Deering are married, and he recruits some comrades for a daring raid into a Han stronghold, it never occurs to the naturally protective new husband to invite his wife to accompany him on this dangerous mission; but she conceals herself inside their ship and comes along anyway, explaining to Rogers that "I couldn't believe my ears last night when you spoke of going without me, until I realized that you are still five hundred years behind the times in lots of ways. Don't you know, dear heart, that you offered me the greatest insult a husband could give a wife? You didn't, of course" (440).

Finally, Gernsback and authors like Fezandié and Kleier typically displayed little if any skill in their plotting and prose style, but Nowlan's story was, as reported by E. F. Bleiler and Richard Bleiler in *Science-Fiction: The Gernsback Years*, "a well-developed, professionally handled pulp work that can still be read with some enjoyment"[18]—words of praise that few other stories in Gernsback's magazines receive in that volume. It is hardly surprising, then, that someone browsing through issues of *Amazing* looking for a story to adapt as a popular comic strip might be impressed by "Armageddon 2419 A.D." and get in touch with its author—which is exactly what happened, as the head of a newspaper syndicate, John F. Dille, liked the story and its sequel and hired Nowlan and artist Richard Caulkins to create the *Buck Rogers* comic strip. In addition, as conveyed by the unusually enthusiastic editorial introduction, Gernsback and Sloane clearly recognized from the start that Nowlan's story was something special:

> Here, once more, is a real scientifiction story plus. It is a story which will make the heart of many readers leap with joy.
> We have rarely printed a story in this magazine that for scientific interest, as well as suspense, could hold its own with this particular story. We prophecy [sic] that this story will become more valuable as the years go by.... It is one of those rare stories that will bear reading and re-reading many times.
> The story has impressed us so favorably, that we hope the author may be induced to write a sequel to it soon.[19]

The requested sequel, "The Airlords of Han," duly appeared in the March 1929 issue of *Amazing Stories*—the last issue produced under Gernsback's editorship—but it proved to be, as noted by the Bleilers, "much less interesting than the first story" (311). Perhaps fearing that descriptions of the rebels' increasing success and eventual triumph over the Han would grow repetitive, and make his hero Rogers's role seem less and less important, Nowlan has

Rogers spend most of his time in the second story as a Han captive, a bystander to summarized victories as he observes the intricacies of Han society. Also, since stories about the "Yellow Peril" were already attracting negative attention for their evident racism, Nowlan implausibly stipulates that the evil Han are not human Asians, but rather a hybrid alien race.

The broad impact of the *Buck Rogers* comic strip derived from Nowlan's stories is undeniable, but since the original stories were not republished until 1962,[20] it is difficult to assess how they directly affected subsequent science fiction. Still, it is evident that the stories greatly influenced at least one reader—a young John W. Campbell, Jr.—since during the 1930s he wrote his own story, "All" (1976), about a future America conquered by Asian invaders who are eventually expelled by means of superscience. Campbell never published "All" during his lifetime, but obviously discerning some potential in the story beyond his own ability to fulfill, he later hired Robert A. Heinlein to write a novel based on its plot, *Sixth Column* (1941, 1949). More broadly, as stories that demonized Asians grew unfashionable, Nowlan's stories may have influenced later science fiction depictions of future revolutions against other sorts of occupying powers, like the corrupt religious fanatics of Heinlein's "'If This Goes On—'" (1940) or the invisible aliens of Eric Frank Russell's *Sinister Barrier* (1939). Yet some of the homegrown or alien oppressors in later science fiction do seem to recall Nowlan's sinister aliens; even Ursula K. Le Guin, hardly a writer associated with racist tendencies, chose to name the aliens who conquered Earth in *City of Illusions* (1967) the Shing—also the name of one of China's ancient dynasties.

Even if memories of Nowlan's specific story faded during the coming decades, "Armageddon 2419 A.D." had an important message for all of the magazine's readers and future authors. Critics like Aldiss have charged that the goals Gernsback announced for science fiction were simply incompatible with the standard goals of superior literature; yet Nowlan had shown that a writer could create a story that perfectly fulfilled Gernsback's agenda while also providing a well-written, entertaining story. Science fiction would never entirely abandon the scientist's laboratory as a setting for stories, but in the 1930s, more and more writers like Nowlan would liberate their protagonists from that sterile, stifling environment to have them encounter and employ advanced science in a wider world of conflict and adventure. The most renowned story in the August 1928 issue of *Amazing Stories* would have the additional effect of inspiring many of those writers to explore one particularly stimulating environment—outer space.

Like "Armageddon—2419 A.D.," the first installment of *The Skylark of Space*—officially credited to Edward Elmer Smith and Lee Hawkins Garby—appears to have been written with Gernsback's magazine in mind, as it also follows his approach of positing the discovery of a mysterious new substance with miraculous properties. Here, after a copper solution containing a new element only called "X" abruptly soars out of his laboratory into space, chemist Richard Seaton immediately recognizes that, somehow, he has "liberated the intra-atomic energy of copper! Copper, 'X,' and electric current!" and eventually learns that this magical element "shifts the plane of vibrations of the electrons!" in copper, explaining why vast amounts of energy were released.[21] After several discussions between Seaton and his partner, millionaire Martin Crane, the men begin building an immense spherical spacecraft, to be named the *Skylark*, that will employ this new energy source to propel them far into outer space.

The odd thing is that the novel had actually been written between 1915 and 1921, several years before Gernsback launched *Amazing Stories* and began preaching the gospel of stories filled with scientific information and informed speculations. As explained by Sam Moskowitz, the young chemist Smith had been encouraged by his friend, Carl Garby, to write a novel about space travel, and when he fretted that he wouldn't be able to "handle" the "love interest" in such a story, Garby's wife volunteered to write those passages in the novel.[22] (In the end, Mrs. Garby's contributions were minimal: while she assisted with writing the first third of the novel, Smith completed the novel by himself.) Due to his own keen interest in science, then, Smith had effectively stumbled upon precisely the sort of story that Gernsback would approve, though the manuscript ultimately reached Gernsback's desk solely because it had already been rejected by several other publishers.

There is one other unusual aspect of the novel to comment on: contemporary readers, knowing that *The Skylark of Space* is regularly cited as the story that launched the subgenre of space opera, will be surprised to discover that its first installment features extremely little space travel. There is one brief space flight—an experimental journey around the Moon—but it is not described, only briefly mentioned by the spacecraft's builders, Seaton and Crane, after it occurred, and all readers learn about outer space is that the far side of the Moon "is very much like this side—the most barren and desolate place imaginable" (416). The first part of the novel is instead devoted to explaining the advanced science that is enabling Smith's heroes to venture into space, and setting up the conflict between Seaton, Crane, and Seaton's fiancée Dorothy Vaneman and the sinister Steel Corporation, working in cooperation with the duplicitous Marc "Blackie" DuQuesne. One might find it puzzling, then, that Smith's story was immediately popular with Gernsback's readers, since its first installment mostly takes place in environments that would be very familiar to them—Seaton's laboratory, where he works on his inventions and describes them at length, and the offices of the Steel Corporation and DuQuesne, where various schemes to steal Seaton's "X" solution and kill him and his partner are discussed.

However, there are clearly aspects of the first installment that would naturally appeal to Gernsback's readers. In the first place, Seaton and Crane repeatedly express their determination to employ their discovery to venture into space: minutes after his solution soars into space, Seaton exclaims, "That bath is on its way to the moon, and there's no reason why I can't follow it. Martin's such a fanatic on exploration, he'll fall all over himself to build us any kind of craft we need ... we'll explore the whole solar system!" (392). We are told that Seaton stops visiting Dorothy because "his prosaic copper steam-bath had taken flight under his hand and pointed the way to a great adventure. In a car his friend was to build, moved by this stupendous power which he must learn to control, they would traverse interstellar space—visit strange planets and survey strange solar systems" (395–396). Explaining Seaton's absence, Crane tells Dorothy that "before the summer is over, we expect to go somewhere. We do not know where, but it will be a long way from this earth" (396). When Crane mentions plans to exploit Seaton's discovery by constructing a "power-plant" to produce and provide economical energy, he explains why he is not prioritizing that initiative: "Dick and I would rather be off exploring new worlds, while the other members of the Seaton-Crane Company, Engineers, build the power-plant" (403). Seaton and Crane soon invent an "object-compass" which provided "a sure means of navigation in space" and an "X-plosive bullet" to defend the future space travelers from "any possible other-world animal, a foreign battleship, or the mythical great sea-serpent himself" (405). After mentioning their trip around the moon, Crane identifies their next goal as the planet Mars (416).

The first installment also has DuQuesne outline his plans to kidnap Dorothy and take her into outer space (since he has independently studied a sample of Seaton's solution and duplicated his results), so that Smith is further promising readers that Seaton and Crane will not only travel into faraway regions of outer space, but will also be involved with a probably violent conflict with DuQuesne over Dorothy's fate. This is also foreshadowed when, realizing that the new energy source could prove to be an effective weapon, Crane tells Seaton, "When we explore new worlds it might be a good idea to have a liberal supply of such ammunition, of various weights, for emergencies" (400). Then, as readers had every reason to expect, the second and third installments of *The Skylark of Space*, published in the September and October 1928 issues of *Amazing Stories*, fulfilled all of these exuberant promises of action and adventure, explaining why they enjoyed reading the first installment and eagerly anticipated the later installments.

Second, the first installment introduces an engaging character who paradoxically is also its chief villain—Blackie DuQuesne. Although he is clearly amoral—eager to have Seaton and Crane murdered in order to ensure that he can master and control the new source of energy they are working on—

Duquesne is also intelligent, decisive, and courageous, and even as they hope that his efforts to eliminate Seaton and Crane are thwarted, readers may also find themselves admiring the character, intrigued by his mixture of despicable and meritorious qualities. Smith thus demonstrates that Gernsback's concerns for science are no barrier to effective character development, and while DuQuesne continued to function as the chief villain in this and the first two sequels to *The Skylark of Space*, he is ultimately rehabilitated to become the hero of the series' belated fourth novel, *Skylark DuQuesne* (1966).

Third, I would argue that Smith has been undervalued as a prose stylist. To be sure, there are clumsy passages that can be taken out of context to denigrate his abilities as a writer, but he did have a knack for dramatic storytelling, and his prose is usually competent—comments that one could not make about Fezandié or Kleier. Significantly, when Smith returned to his text sixteen years later to revise the novel for book publication, he did streamline and partially restructure the initial chapters, and added some background material about Seaton and Crane and how they became friends, but many paragraphs from the 1928 version were left unchanged, and the book went on to garner many appreciative readers during the coming decades.

There was a fourth feature of the first installment of *The Skylark of Space* that the editors regarded as especially appealing, as evidenced by its introduction. After saying what any later reader would expect the introduction to say—"we must shout from the housetops that this is the greatest interplanetarian and space flying story that has appeared this year. Indeed, it probably will rank as one of the great space flying stories for many years to come"— the introduction proceeds to observe that "the story is chock full, not only of excellent science, but woven through it there is also that very rare element, love and romance. This element in an interplanetarian story is often apt to be foolish, but it does not seem so in this particular story."[23]

Certainly, there are passages in the installment that might have been taken from the romance magazines of that era, like this speech from Seaton that is presumably the work of Lee Hawkins Garby:

> I love you with everything there is in me. I love you, mind, body and spirit; love you as a man should love the one and only woman. For you are the only woman, there never was and never will be another. I love you morally, physically, intellectually, and every other way there is, for the perfect little darling that you are.... You are the nearest thing to absolute perfection that ever came into this imperfect world.... Just to think of a girl of your sheer beauty, your ability, your charm, your all-round perfection, being engaged to a thing like me, makes me dizzy—but I sure do love you, little girl of mine. I will love you as long as we live, and afterward, my soul will love your soul throughout eternity [397].

Calling attention to the novel's romantic passages was in keeping with one of Gernsback's announced goals—to attract more women to science fiction—

but one has to wonder if these effusive romantic interludes were really valued by Gernsback's readers, even though at least one reader would praise *The Skylark of Space* because it "is not only Scientifiction but a double-barrelled love story as well. And the love element, or at least one half of it, is worked naturally."[24] Still, some of the aforementioned "streamlining" that occurred when the novel was prepared for book publication involved the removal of the above passage, along with others of a similar nature, which had absolutely no impact on the novel's ongoing popularity. (True, Smith also had a specific incentive to eliminate the romantic material that Garby contributed, since it enabled him to justifiably credit later republications of *The Skylark of Space* solely to himself.)

There is no need to belabor the often-made point that Smith's novel greatly increased the number of science fiction stories about the farthest reaches of outer space and soon spawned a recognizable subgenre of science fiction, space opera. One obvious illustration of its impact is the comic strip that was based on Nowlan's story, *Buck Rogers*, which began like "Armageddon 2419 A.D." and "The Airlords of Han" by describing the efforts of the reawakened Rogers and American allies to resist Asiatic invaders; however, Rogers and Deering soon encounter sinister Martians, inspiring Rogers to construct a spaceship to confront them on their own turf, and the comic strip was then devoted almost exclusively to space adventures. Other science fiction stories took similar paths; thus, after launching his Arcot, Morey, and Wade series with a story about an aerial pirate that takes place entirely on Earth, "Piracy Preferred" (*Amazing Stories*, June, 1930), John W. Campbell, Jr., quickly took his characters into outer space, ultimately providing them with the power to traverse the entire known universe—again following in the footsteps of Smith's Seaton and Crane.

No survey of the contents of the August 1928 issue of *Amazing Stories* should omit the cover painting and interior illustrations of Frank R. Paul, which were generally praised by Gernsback's readers (though there were occasional complaints that his colorful covers made the magazine seem immature—for example, in this issue, Fenten complains that his Navy crewmates reported, "they never would be seen reading a book like that until they had first torn off the covers"). In one unimpressive interior drawing, Paul merely conveys what the introduction notes is the "comical" nature of "The Perambulating Home" by depicting its characters falling amidst the water rushing in as the house proceeds toward the ocean.

More interestingly, Paul's artwork also makes a statement about the issue's two standout stories. Gernsback, of course, saw *The Skylark of Space* as the star attraction and hence had Paul's cover painting depict the scene where Seaton tests his spaceship's propulsion system by flying into the air while Dorothy and Crane watch him from the ground; this striking image, as indicated by the Internet Speculative Fiction Database, has been republished at least eight times, including the partial reproduction seen on the cover of my own book *Hugo Gernsback and the Century of Science Fiction* (2009). Smith's story is also accompanied by a large interior illustration of Seaton showing Dorothy the spherical *Skylark* being readied for its space flight. Yet Paul devotes more attention to Nowlan's story: in addition to an introductory, full-page illustration of one of the battles against the Han, Paul provides smaller illustrations of a Han woman in a short dress, contrasted with an American woman "equipped with an inertron belt and a rocket gun"; a picture of an American "setting his rocket gun for a long distance shot"; a larger drawing of a Han airship shooting its disintegrator ray; and a small drawing of an American attacking a Han soldier.[25] One cannot know if Gernsback or Sloane assigned Paul to draw these additional illustrations, or if they were Paul's idea, but they definitely suggest that Nowlan's story includes more interesting aspects to illustrate than Smith's story—at least its Earthbound first installment—and that somebody regarded "Armageddon 2419 A.D." as the best story in the issue. Based on what it provides, not what it merely promises, one finds it hard to disagree.

During the year 1928, Gernsback employed another interior artist—R. E. Lawlor—who illustrates two of the issue's lesser stories and therefore incidentally proves that they were not highly regarded by Gernsback and Sloane, since they did not assign their best artist to depict their contents. Still, the unheralded Lawlor does provide some perhaps unintentional commentary on the stories. For "The Moth," Lawlor shows the entomologist looking at the moth from the perspective of an observer, validating the interpretation that it is not a hallucination but an actual, presumably supernatural manifestation (the interpretation that would best justify the story's republication in *Amazing Stories*). And for "The Head," Lawlor calls attention to its horrific aspects, in keeping with Sloane's introduction, by depicting the detached, wrinkled head looking distressed in a room where a shelf on the wall features a human skull and the body of a birdlike creature preserved in a jar.

The importance of the August 1928 issue of *Amazing Stories* can be demonstrated by the numerous republications of the three outstanding works that it included—Paul's cover, "Armageddon 2419 A.D.," and *The Skylark of Space*—and by the noted indications of the lasting impact of Nowlan's and Smith's stories. More broadly, the issue proves, despite arguments to the contrary, that Hugo Gernsback did not inhibit the growth and development of science fiction; rather, he stimulated and enhanced that growth and development. Nowlan and Smith show that Gernsback's precepts were not an impediment to writing effective fiction, and that he was always willing to publish—and celebrate—the best stories that reflected his concerns, even if he was often obliged to publish, and more guardedly praise, less admirable works. And, after Gernsback abandoned science fiction in 1936, other editors would follow in his footsteps to encourage the further improvement of the genre he had founded. In sum, the August 1928 issue of *Amazing Stories* may qualify as the first memorable science fiction magazine, but it would not be the last.

3

Artists in Wonderland
Towards a True History of Science Fiction Art

While there have been several books about science fiction art, none of them, from the perspective of a literary scholar, seem to be well organized in the manner of a true history, which would divide the field into different eras, explain the principles and philosophies that guided artists in each era, and describe how artists of following eras either built upon or rejected the approaches of their predecessors. Instead, books on science fiction art tend either to proceed mechanically in chronological order or to group artworks by their artists or subject matter, with chapters on art featuring aliens, women, spacecraft, and so on.[1] Surely, one might argue, we need a more systematic framework for such discussions.

There are two basis hypotheses one might employ as a premise for such an organized history of science fiction art. First, one could assume that science fiction art is an essentially autonomous tradition that has developed and evolved entirely according to its own internal dynamics, or perhaps in parallel to the general history of high art or commercial art. But that assumption is intuitively implausible; after all, the vast majority of science fiction artworks in the twentieth century were based on and published alongside specific science fiction stories, and in a few cases, science fiction artworks have inspired original stories. Science fiction literature and art were long supervised by the same editors and publishers and presented to the same readers; and both writers and artists were accepted as members of the same science fiction community. (In fact, the Guest of Honor at the first World Science Fiction Convention in 1939 was artist Frank R. Paul.) It is true that some later artworks do display a certain autonomy from the stories they accompany—Brian W. Aldiss argued in 1979 that "today their relationship to text is often generic rather than specific"[2]—and I will note that in the twenty-first century, works of science fiction art have emerged that are not based on written texts; yet if one surveys the twentieth century, it is difficult to argue that there was no relationship at all between science fiction literature and science fiction art.

If we turn to the alternative hypothesis—that the history of science fiction art is closely connected to the history of science fiction literature—we must decide how to characterize the history of science fiction. According to one argument, science fiction is one current in western literature that first emerged as a distinctive form in Mary Shelley's *Frankenstein, or The Modern Prometheus* (1818, 1831) and was later best represented by writers like Jules Verne, H. G. Wells, Olaf Stapledon, Philip K. Dick, Stanislaw Lem, Ursula K. Le Guin, and William Gibson. To produce a history of science fiction art following this model, we would seek out the texts of these great writers, observe the art that accompanied those texts, and deduce a tradition that would situate that art within a coherent pattern of development and evolution. By another argument, which I favor, science fiction is best regarded as those texts that emerged from an understanding of the *idea* of science fiction, so that the genre was born in 1926 with Hugo Gernsback's *Amazing Stories*, and its central texts are the works published in the subsequent magazines and books that were inspired by Gernsback's ideas and written for the science fiction community that he established. To produce a history of science fiction art following this model, we would begin with the art in *Amazing Stories* and continue to observe the art of other science fiction magazines and, later, the art on the covers of the science fiction paperback and hardcover books that first appeared in the 1940s and 1950s, relating that art to major developments in the literature of that tradition.

Evidence that this later approach would be superior ironically comes from a critic who vigorously promoted the first approach to science fiction literature—Brian W. Aldiss. Having maintained in *Billion Year Spree: The True History of Science Fiction* (1973—expanded as *Trillion Year Spree: The History of Science Fiction* in 1986, co-authored by David Wingrove) that science fiction is a form of Gothic literature first seen in *Frankenstein*, he must logically maintain that science fiction art is a form of Gothic art first observed in the company of *Frankenstein*; thus, the "Introduction" to his *Science Fiction Art* (1975) begins by reproducing the Frontispiece from the 1831 edition of *Frankenstein* and asserting that "sf [literature] and Gothic are inseparably intertwined. The same holds true for sf illustration." However, he admits that the *Frankenstein* picture "is not an outstanding piece of work,"[3] and after discussing two nineteenth-century Gothic artists, he abandons any attempt to parallel his argument in *Billion Year Spree*, instead drifting into a general discussion of science fiction art in the magazines and arranging his book by artists and topics. He even says elsewhere that "before the SF magazines, there is little that can be regarded as pure generic sf illustration."[4] Aldiss thus acknowledges that his framework for a study of science fiction literature cannot usefully serve as a framework for a study of science fiction art.

I am proposing, then, to employ the history of twentieth-century science fiction literature, as I characterize it, to provisionally construct a history of twentieth-century science fiction art. To summarize a standard view of the American genre's history: first, in the 1920s, Gernsback championed and elicited a form of science fiction that featured narratives that incorporated explanations of scientific fact and detailed descriptions of proposed inventions; call this Gernsbackian science fiction. In the 1930s, writers inspired by E. E. "Doc" Smith moved to a form of science fiction that reduced science to jargon and nonsense and emphasized exciting adventures, at times mixed with adolescent eroticism; Edmond Hamilton was another of its energetic practitioners, and we now call it space opera. In the 1940s, reacting against both Gernsback's didacticism and the immaturity of space opera, John W. Campbell, Jr.'s *Astounding Science-Fiction* supported a form of science fiction that grew out of careful scientific extrapolation and logic; in the hands of later writers, this became what we call hard science fiction. In the 1950s, editor H. L. Gold of *Galaxy* and others inspired a form of science fiction that again deemphasized science, not for exciting adventure but for humor, satire, and improved writing; call this, for lack of a better term, 1950s science fiction. In the 1960s, Michael Moorcock and Harlan Ellison promoted a form of science fiction dedicated to literary quality, less attentiveness to science, and bold stylistic experiments, known as New Wave science fiction. The 1970s, engendering no new form of science fiction, became a decade of reflection, consolidation, and nostalgia that combined the lingering New Wave, a new interest in hard science fiction, and a resurgence of space opera (largely inspired by *Star Trek* and *Star Wars*); but the 1980s and 1990s witnessed the emergence of another form of science fiction, cyberpunk, that combined a fascination with new technology like computers, hard-nosed cynicism, and flashy style; William Gibson's *Neuromancer* (1984) was its exemplary text and Bruce Sterling became its major spokesperson.

Of course, caveats must be attached to any potted history of this kind. First, despite advocates' claims, each new form of science fiction was not a complete departure from tradition, but rather acknowledged and reflected to varying extents the influence of previous forms. Thus, for example, a concern for minimal scientific accuracy—Gernsback's priority—has persisted through each changing of the guard in science fiction, and cyberpunk can been viewed as an effort to simultaneously fulfill Campbell's scientific agenda and the New Wave's aesthetic agenda. Second, each type of science fiction, despite changing attitudes, has persisted in its pure form, though its texts may become less conspicuous and thus relegated to the sidelines. The proof of these observations can be found in any modern bookstore, where you can still find examples of Gernsbackian science fiction—though you may have to look in the juvenile section—along with space opera, hard science fiction, satire, New Wave science fiction, and cyberpunk. Finally, though models of this kind should be generally accurate, there will always be a few writers who refuse to fit in its pigeonholes; for example, while Cordwainer Smith might be described as a writer who produced New Wave science fiction before the New Wave, he more accurately seems *sui generis*, a writer dedicated to producing science fiction of his own unique variety, oblivious to any of the genre's trends in the past, present, or future.

If science fiction art was closely linked to science fiction literature in the twentieth century, we should be able to construct a history of science fiction art along these lines. There should be six eras of science fiction art, corresponding chronologically and thematically to the six cited eras of science fiction literature; there should probably, but not necessarily, be one artist in each era to usefully represent its character, just as figures like Gernsback, Smith, Campbell, Gold, Moorcock, and Sterling usefully represent their literary eras; each new artistic era should in part incorporate or reflect the priorities of previous eras; each form of science fiction art should be found to endure in its pure form to the present day; and there should be a few exceptional artists who fail to conform to these patterns.

As is usually the case when critics publically assign tasks to themselves, I have found that it is in fact possible to sketch a history of science fiction art along these lines.

To identify the first form of science fiction art, one must recall that Gernsback defined science fiction as a mixture of narrative, scientific fact, and prediction, designed to provide entertainment for the masses, education for young readers, and stimulating ideas for working scientists[5]; so, one asks, what form of art might best achieve these goals? First the art must be realistic or representational; some forms of abstraction—like charts or schematic diagrams—might be useful for scientists, but not the general public or youngsters. To be entertaining, the art must be colorful and imaginative; but to offer scientific education or ideas, it must be painstakingly accurate and precisely designed. Gernsback was fortunate to have the services of an artist who produced exactly this sort of art: Frank R. Paul.

To see why Paul is justly regarded as the first and greatest science fiction artist, consider one of his most renowned works: the cover painting for the August 1927 issue of *Amazing Stories* illustrating its republication of H. G. Wells's *The War of the Worlds* (1898). For entertainment, the colors are striking and well-chosen: against the background of a jarringly serene blue sky, the Martian war machines shine with reflected light from the bright red fires of the burning city; and the ingenious detail of a man fleeing from the Martians *on horseback* graphically contrasts the advanced Martians with the relatively primitive humans. For educational purposes, the machines are drafted with engineering precision, right down to their flexible knee joints, and Paul adds one feature not mentioned by Wells—gripping claws on the feet of the machines—perhaps to explain why such apparently unstable machines would not easily topple over, and perhaps to provide a helpful suggestion for an inventor planning to build such machines.[6]

Trained as both an artist and an architect, Paul skillfully depicted gigantic future cities, a visual trope that he perfected. Consider his cover illustrating Hamilton's "Cities in the Air" for the November 1929 issue of Gernsback's *Air Wonder Stories*. Highlighted by an incongruous pink background, Paul's flying New York is magnificent in its exact circularity, its multitude of yellow buildings, and tiny cylindrical airships and the Earth below to suggest its immensity. Yet Paul's triumphs are not entirely architectural; in painting "Serenis, Water City of Callisto" for the back cover of the December 1941 issue of *Amazing Stories*, for example, he offered not only arrays of white columned buildings surrounding a huge fountain, but the spectacle of nearby Jupiter filling the sky, boats on a canal of green water, and four-armed, blue-skinned aliens, including an nice image of an alien woman in the foreground tenderly feeding her iguana-like pets. Here is an alien world of evocative detail that was unhappily beyond the ability of most contemporary writers.

However, this painting—for *Amazing*'s current editor Ray Palmer—also reveals an aspect of Paul's talents that did not interest Gernsback, who primarily viewed him as an adjunct to his didactic and predictive agenda. In every Gernsback magazine, the Table of Contents page briefly described the cover—in part, no doubt, to prove that the covers were honest advertisements for stories in his magazines, but also to emphasize their educational and scientific value. In the July 1926 issue of *Amazing*, for example, the caption notes that the giant insect on the cover was "the Tse-tse fly"[7]; the caption describing the cover of the July 1929 issue of *Science Wonder Stories* says, "Mr. Paul, our artist, has shown how, under certain conditions, it is possible for a single man to lift the 60,000 ton steamship *Leviathan* without straining his muscles"[8]; and the caption on the cover of the July 1929 issue of *Air Wonder Stories* maintains that

> Mr. Paul, has cleverly portrayed in his inimitable style what one of these future aerial islands will look like.... Science will conquer gravitation sooner or later, and when that moment comes ... we will have islands like these, floating freely, suspended above our cities and important aerial crossings. They will be used not only for the regulation of air traffic, but for making emergency stops and to allow passengers to change from local to express lines without ever descending to the surface of the earth.[9]

According to other captions, the cover of the August, 1929 issue of *Science Wonder Stories* illustrated Captain Noordung's [space station].... The space house proper ... has a total diameter of about 150 feet. The wide curved surfaces are the reflectors which collect and concentrate the sun's heat. Attached to the space house by means of flexible cables, at the left is shown the observatory and at the upper right the engine house. All three objects remain fixed in space, there being no gravity to dislodge them.[10]

An aerial battle on the cover of the August 1929 issue of *Air Wonder Stories* "demonstrates the tremendous power of atomic rays once they have been developed, as they surely will"[11]; the cover of the October 1929 issue of *Science Wonder Stories* is "a graphic as well as vivid picturization by our inimitable artist Paul, of what happens when scientists of the future will make it possible for us to get a sort of television picturization of our sub-conscious memories"[12]; the cover of the October 1929 issue of *Air Wonder Stories* shows "how the special air car moves at the rate of over one thousand miles an hour, through the artificially created vacuum in the air tunnel. By electrical means the inside of the air tunnel becomes a vacuum in which the onrushing car moves free of friction"[13]; and the cover of the January 1930 issue of *Air Wonder Stories* shows "'the Thunderer' drying up one of our lakes by decomposing the water into its elements. With his airship held stationary in the air he lets down two electric cables. A spark passing between them decomposes the water."[14] Just as Gernsback's editorials taught readers how to read science fiction stories, these comments were teaching readers how to read science fiction art—not only explaining the literal meaning of the pictures, but also pointing out that they depict scientific facts involving gravity, the properties of a vacuum, and electrolysis, as well as plausible future developments—like flying cities, space stations, visualized memories, and atomic rays.

It should be noted that, from Gernsback's perspective, Paul's most frequently cited flaw—his flat or awkward people—was not really a liability. Gernsback's theory of science fiction never mentioned a need for realistic or complex characterization, because an entertaining narrative to serve as a framework for scientific education and prophecy could be achieved just as well with stock characters. Indeed, well-drawn characters, in both fiction and art, might inappropriately distract readers from the important lessons and ideas in science fiction. Thus, in both his strengths and his weaknesses, Paul perfectly reflected Gernsback's priorities.

We might call Paul's style of painting "futurist science fiction art," to acknowledge its kinship to the futurist movement in art and architecture of the early twentieth century which William Gibson pays tribute to in "The Gernsback Continuum" (1981) and which is most easily observed by modern readers in the sets of the films *Metropolis* (1927) and *Things to Come* (1936). Paul did not necessarily share the futurists' technophilia and optimism—the Wells cover reminds us that massive constructs may be sinister as well as inspirational—but there was in both futurist art and Paul's paintings an excitement about future possibilities, images of gigantic buildings laid out with stark geometry, and a sense that future developments would both dwarf individual humans and embody human desires. And the influence of Paul is visible in later science fiction art, most notably in Hubert Rogers, whose 1940s covers for *Astounding Science-Fiction* were only more somber versions of Paul's pioneering visions.

Although Paul remained active and popular in the 1930s, science fiction art began to change, reflecting changes in the era's science fiction magazines. While Gernsback had resisted making his magazines true pulp magazines by using a different size and different quality of paper, his and others' magazines were reduced during the Depression to true pulp status, and their contents began to reflect the contents of pulp magazines: writers increasingly paid little attention to scientific accuracy or logic in order to emphasize exciting adventures involving space travel, other planets, and aliens. Several artists might be chosen to represent the new style of art that emerged; but it seems fitting to discuss the artist known as the "inventor of the brass brassière," Earle K. Bergey. It is true, as Peter Nicholls and John Grant note, he "was by no means restricted to the subject matter that made him famous,"[15] and his cover for the February 1941 issue of *Thrilling Wonder Stories*, for example, is reminiscent of Paul in its cosmic perspective and stiff figures—though Gernsback would have rejected the scientific absurdity of sending a message to space by means of a huge illuminated sign on the continent of North America. However, his covers for the Winter 1946 and September 1948 issues of *Startling Stories* reveal that he did indeed often feature that singular garment. Here we quickly see departures from Paul's style: while Paul's people were often small in relation to their surroundings, Bergey's people are large and foregrounded; Bergey's characters look more realistic and natural than Paul's; Bergey's art tends to be less faithful to the stories depicted—I recall no scene of a woman in a brass brassière fleeing through space in Fredric Brown's *What Mad Universe* (1948, 1949), though Bergey's cover illustrating its first publication in the September 1948 issue of *Startling Stories* features precisely such a woman; and there is clearly little concern for scientific accuracy in Bergey's work, since the artist surely realized that a woman flying through space would have to wear more than a space helmet and brassière. We also see in these Bergey covers from 1946 and 1948 the three archetypal images of space opera, which came to be referred to as "the guy, the girl, and the goon"[16]: a handsome hero, a scantily-clad heroine, and a horrific monster (though Bergey's 1946 cover only features the guy and the girl, while the 1948 cover only features the girl and the goon). This might be termed true "pulp science fiction art," since it clearly derives from the style of other pulp magazine illustrations.

Much of this art invites or demands little critical comment, especially when artists seem to be competing to get away with exposing the greatest expanse of female flesh or to envision the most loathsome aliens. However, when the Vargas girls are omitted and a story provides an interesting idea, examples of such art can be striking. Consider Howard V. Brown, who produced one famous cover for the November 1939 issue of *Startling Stories*.[17] While it is unlikely that efforts to save Earth's animal life from disaster would so exactly mimic the iconic imagery of Noah's Ark, we can still admire this cover, with its huge spaceship in bold primary colors, pairs of exotic creatures marching up the ramp, and guards holding back angry mobs. Another Brown cover, for the April 1934 issue of *Astounding Stories*, features the familiar space opera triangle—a handsome hero and beautiful woman threatened by a bizarre alien—but the image of an immense staring eye on a box protruding from a spaceship and emitting a strange gas (or sound?) is unusually evocative. I recall this cover because when I showed some books of science fiction art to my son when he was five years old, he was especially fascinated by this picture. In the best of pulp art, then, abandoning concerns for scientific accuracy or geometric precision can generate a novel juxtaposition of the familiar and the bizarre which is, at least at first, a primary attraction of science fiction; after all, capturing the imagination of a five-year-old reader, one might argue, is what the "sense of wonder" is all about.

However, Brown is more important for his role in launching the third era of science fiction art, though the instigator of the change was Campbell, who officially assumed control of *Astounding* in 1938. To please Campbell, the style of science fiction published in his magazines had to be modified: while Gernsback was happy to see science fiction as entertainment for the masses, and that was certainly the guiding philosophy behind the space operas that he and others published, Campbell believed that science fiction should appeal only to an educated elite—"no average mind can either understand or enjoy science-fiction"[18]—and its serious purposes should be to sharpen the thought processes of budding scientists and to guide policymakers in making important decisions about future technology.[19] To create art that would appropriately accompany such science fiction, the gaudy colors of Paul's futurist art and the heroic posturings of pulp art would have to be abandoned. Campbell's priorities might be served simply by a more subdued version of Paul's art, which as noted is essentially what was provided by Rogers, the usual cover artist for *Astounding* in the 1940s; Campbell celebrated a toning-down in science fiction art as early as October 1938 when he said that "already, *Astounding* has taken the word *garish* from the description vocabulary of its covers." Instead, Campbell expressed his desire for a particular kind of serious science fiction art—one which "will add even more of the factor *reality*"[20]—and he chose Brown to create it.

The first example of this new style of art appeared on the cover of the

February 1938 issue of *Astounding Stories*, and Campbell unusually devoted most of his editorial in that issue to describing its cover:

> The cover is the first of a series—a new *mutant* field opened to science fiction.... Howard Brown and I worked over this cover, I trying to get the astronomy accurate; Brown, helping in the more difficult work of interpretation of fact to human understanding.... The Sun? It's much too large, really.... But that is where Brown's knowledge of the psychology and mechanism of human vision played its part. If he had painted that Sun as it would appear to a camera ... on Mercury—the color-plate would not have given an accurate representation of *what you would see if you were there*. Human vision is not purely a physical process; it involves physics, but is subjected to the modifying effect of psychology.... Brown has off-set that human failing of the eyes. The Sun is disproportionately large, but accurately disproportionate. And as in this first *mutant* cover, our astronomical color-plate covers will be as accurate an impression as astronomical science and knowledge of human reaction can make them.[21]

This is the first manifesto on behalf of what we now call "space art": realistic pictures of outer space or other worlds as they would appear to a human observer on the scene. Note how carefully Campbell describes the *process* of creating such art; Campbell later asserted that the science in science fiction should be more than a presentation of facts, but a detailed, logical *extrapolation* from the known to the unknown, and he discussed how Robert A. Heinlein employed that technique in his Future History stories. Here, he anticipates the same principles in describing the need for careful preparation and thought in creating science fiction art.[22]

The cover itself is not particularly impressive, but the contrast between this and previous science fiction art is dramatic enough to justify Campbell's hyperbolic praise. In a way, we have moved away from the focus on human figures in pulp art back to Paul's epic vision, but the immensities involved are not human constructs but natural wonders; and the intense black sky dominating the scene, brightened only by a stark yellow sun, conveys a sense of solemnity that Paul neither aspired to nor achieved. Brown did a better cover for the November 1938 issue of *Astounding*: the picture of a huge, partially eclipsed Jupiter dominating the sky of its moon Ganymede, watched by tiny spacesuited figures, vividly depicts frail human beings striving to master a forbidding environment—and additionally provokes emotions that had never before been stirred by science fiction art. Again Campbell devoted an editorial to the cover, which he had previously called "one of the best science-fiction covers ever published."[23]

As it happens, the *Astounding* covers of the 1940s by Brown and others were not predominantly of this type—I suspect that issues with such covers did not sell especially well—yet as painted by artists like the American Chesley Bonestell and the British Gerald Quinn, space art would become in the

1950s common in both science fiction books and magazines and in nonfiction books and articles about future space exploration. In particular, such art came to be associated with writers like Arthur C. Clarke and Hal Clement, who were producing what we now call hard science fiction. Indeed, embedded in the concept of space art is a key insight of that subgenre: that science fiction can be fruitfully directed not only at creating new constructs and mechanisms but also at envisioning and developing fantastic new natural environments. It is the difference, one might say, between Fritz Lang's Metropolis and Clement's Mesklin. And, when the object being considered is both artificial and huge enough to be regarded as a natural world, the resulting art can fuse the styles of Paul's futurist art and space art—as seen, for example, in the original paperback cover of Larry Niven's *Ringworld* (1970), painted by Dean Ellis, which combines gleaming geometry and the forbidding vastness of space in illustrating Niven's amazing construct, an alien-constructed ring around a star encountered by human space explorers.

The 1950s brought expansion and diversity to science fiction, but its key innovation is summarized in the title of H. L. Gold's first editorial for *Galaxy*, "For Adults Only." He proclaimed that

> science fiction ... has finally come of age.... GALAXY *Science Fiction* proposes to carry the maturity of this type of literature into the science fiction magazine field, where it is now ... hard to find. It establishes a compound break with both the lurid and the stodgy traditions of s-f magazine publishing. From cover design to advertising selections, GALAXY *Science Fiction* intends to be a mature magazine for mature readers.[24]

A focus on an adult audience, among other things, allowed science fiction to move towards improved literary values—as in Anthony Boucher and J. Francis McComas's *The Magazine of Fantasy and Science Fiction*, launched around the same time—or towards humor and social satire—as in Gold's *Galaxy*. And, like the stories, the artists would have to move away from "lurid" (pulp) art and "stodgy" (futurist or space) art to become more polished and versatile. Though Frank Kelly Freas would be a logical choice, the other major artist who emerged at this time, Edmund Emshwiller or "Emsh," can be examined to show how science fiction art changed in the 1950s.[25]

While Aldiss aptly called Emsh "the great all-arounder of sf art,"[26] his work is noteworthy not only for its variety but for its *ambiguity*. Previous science fiction art clearly dictated certain emotional reactions: in futurist or space art, readers are supposed to be awed by massive constructs or astronomical vistas; in pulp art, presumably male readers are supposed to identify with the handsome hero, lust after the brass-brassièred woman, and despise the repulsive alien; but we are not always sure how to react to Emshwiller's art. In his cover for the January 1953 issue of *Galaxy*, the American insignia on the spacecraft implies that we should sympathize with its occupants; but the robots emerging from the ship look strange and menacing: are these robots our allies or our enemies? Consider the three foregrounded figures in a force field on the cover of the December 1963 issue of *The Magazine of Fantasy and Science Fiction*: the human male seems handsome and admirable; the green-skinned alien man holding a machine seems sinister; but the standing alien woman seems more troubled than threatening. Are these beings heroes, villains, or victims? Each figure suggests a different answer. And his interior illustration for Eric Frank Russell's "Design for Great-Day" in the January 1953 issue of *Planet Stories* is in many ways a standard scene from pulp art—a man emerges from a spaceship to confront reptilian aliens brandishing weapons—but the man is not handsome, but fat and balding, which mitigates against our standard reaction of support for the human. Is this man a worthy fellow who will emerge as an unlikely hero? A fool, who will make us laugh at his ridiculous mistakes? Or a pompous, arrogant man, like a latter-day Nero, who will make us root for the aliens as they resist his evil plans? Overall, life in outer space or the future seems more complex than it used to be in Emshwiller's art, mirroring the greater complexity of the written science fiction of the 1950s.

As such art resists easy interpretation, it also resists easy nomenclature; but one descriptive term may be useful. Accompanying the pulp magazines had long been their more respectable cousins, the slick magazines, so named for both their higher quality paper and their greater sophistication. And much of the science fiction art of the 1950s resembled the art of the slicks more than the art of the pulps; except for its outré subject matter, Emshwiller's interior drawings seem similar to the art then appearing in *The Saturday Evening Post*. Therefore, I suggest that we call the style of art pioneered by Emshwiller and Freas "slick science fiction art."[27]

According to Grant and Nicholls, "The gritty realism of [Freas's] and Ed Emshwiller's work in the 1950s redefined sf art during that period"[28]; and these artists did continue and intensify a tradition of realism of science fiction art (but I would quarrel with the word "gritty," since much of their art was humorous in nature). However, even in the 1950s, there were harbingers of change. Richard M. Powers, who started painting book covers at this time, is the artistic equivalent of Cordwainer Smith, both an anticipation of later styles and an idiosyncratic individual creator; his covers were bold abstractions, with elongated stylized figures amidst ellipses of color and spiraling linear designs. I mention Powers because he was the first science fiction artist that I noticed: even as a twelve-year-old browsing in bookstores, I could recognize his distinctive covers for books like Kingsley Amis's *New Maps of Hell* (1960) and Leo Margulies's anthology *Get Out of My Sky* (1960), and while there were other factors involved, it happens that two of the first four science fiction paperbacks I purchased, the Fawcett Crest edition of Clifford D. Simak's *Time Is the Simplest Thing* (1961, 1962) and Donald A. Wollheim's Ace Books anthology *More Adventures on Other Planets* (1963), both had covers painted by Powers. Even without knowing his name, I could recognize at the time that these covers were painted by one unique artist.[29]

But the links between science fiction art and realism would be firmly and widely broken only during the New Wave period of the 1960s. All previous theories of science fiction at least paid lip service to the notion that science fiction should be scientifically accurate and logical, and this commitment, or pretense of a commitment, to science seemingly demanded representational portrayals of imagined wonders. But the major voices of the New Wave, Michael Moorcock and Harlan Ellison, insisted that science should not be a defining issue in science fiction; by promoting the alternative term "speculative fiction," they even sought to banish the word "science" from discussions of the genre. Instead, writers were urged to be wildly imaginative in both their ideas and their writing styles, since the abandonment of science also meant that the clear descriptive prose of much earlier science fiction was no longer necessary. And as writers responded to these calls in part by imitating the innovative styles of early twentieth century writers like John Dos Passos and James Joyce, it was only appropriate that artists would imitate the artistic styles of the early twentieth century, the first great era of abstract art. After all, with no need to provide scientific education or logical scientific predictions, why should artists have to be realistic?

To represent this new era of "abstract science fiction art,"[30] several artists might be chosen; but in America, the New Wave was most strongly associated with Harlan Ellison, and the artists most strongly associated with Ellison were Leo and Diane Dillon.[31] Again, the choice is influenced by personal reasons: while Powers was the first artist I could recognize, the Dillons were the first artists I collected. When I first saw their original covers for Terry Carr's Ace Science Fiction Specials, I was so taken by their appearance—a monochromatic background, with a box of geometric designs above the title and a box of abstract art below it—that I long purchased every book in the series, even ones by authors I otherwise would have ignored, although the artists were later instructed to abandon their geometric pattern in favor of larger abstract images.[32]

Looking at a few Dillon covers from the 1960s, we can see the double freedom that this type of science fiction art offered. Yes, the Dillons did not draw in a realistic manner and freely distorted the figures and objects they painted; but they also at times made no effort to represent the exact contents of the works they illustrated. For example, their cover for Ellison's collection *From the Land of Fear* (1967) obviously does not depict any event in its stories; rather, the mingled faces, hands, claws, animals, and objects collectively represent the essence of fear itself, or of everything that humans fear. We also note in this cover a complete absence of any reference to science or machinery; this is true Gothic art, recalling Hieronymus Bosch more than Frank R. Paul, supporting Aldiss's thesis that science fiction art had sprung from human nightmares more than scientific logic.

In other Dillon paintings, the relationship between picture and text is distant and allusive: in their cover for Clifford D. Simak's *Why Call Them Back from Heaven?* (1967), for example, we see an image of a prone body (perhaps a corpse), overshadowed by a standing human image (perhaps a ghost, a being still living after death), both connected by tentacles to some kind of gear (perhaps some type of machine keeping the corpse alive). From such clues, one might accurately guess that the novel involves cryonics, freezing dead bodies for possible future revival, which would also account for the emphasis on pale blue colors, suggesting ice; but the painting is clearly focused on conveying the emotional impact of the novel, not its contents. The Dillons's cover for Bob Shaw's *The Palace of Eternity* (1969) shows another prone body with two heads (perhaps dead, perhaps alive) beneath a colorful outburst of flowery petals and a godlike face looking down on, and perhaps caressing, the body; but it would take a prodigious imagination to deduce that the novel describes a space war with aliens that leads to the revelation that all humans are connected to a sort of group-mind that can effectively provide immortality. Again, the cover is best defended as a symbolic representation of the novel's mood: generally violent and gloomy (the predominant dark blues and violets) with an unexpected and joyous conclusion (the bright colors in the middle).

Given the power and beauty of the Dillons's work, and given the virtually unlimited freedom that this style offered artists, one might have expected abstract art to become the most common form of science fiction art. However, coincidentally around the time that the Dillons largely abandoned science fiction illustration to focus on producing children's books—1972—we see most science fiction art turning back to realism (as has remained largely true to this day). Perhaps, to paraphrase C. S. Lewis, readers found that strange worlds depicted in a strange manner represented one strangeness too many; perhaps, just as many writers raised in the liberating atmosphere of the New Wave found that they preferred the rigor of hard science fiction, many artists of the time found that they preferred the rigor of realism to the freedom of abstract art; or perhaps, from a marketing standpoint, abstract art had been found to be too esoteric to attract the mass audience that science fiction publishers increasingly craved.[33] By the 1980s, though, a distinctive new style of abstract art would become popular in science fiction.

In this period, one could say, the science fiction genre came full circle. In the 1920s, the field was dominated by one magazine, *Amazing Stories*, then the only one exclusively devoted to science fiction; in the 1980s, the field was again dominated by one magazine, *Omni*, which boasted a circulation that was larger than all of the other science fiction magazines combined. With Paul's covers, *Amazing* vigorously promoted one distinctive form of science fiction art; with its own covers—created by various artists but all seemingly produced by the same hand—*Omni* similarly promoted a distinctive form of science fiction art.[34] And just as Gernsback provided explanatory captions on his Table of Contents page to describe his covers, *Omni* also offered explanatory captions on the Table of Contents page to describe its covers—though the magazine was training its readers to appreciate an entirely different kind of science fiction art.

To understand the art of *Omni*, we recall that, as described by Howard V. Hendrix,[35] the magazine brought together three different types of material: science fiction and fantasy stories, often highly literary and not especially scientific; articles on present-day and predicted science, frequently emphasizing hard sciences like astronomy and physics like the articles in Campbell's *Astounding*, which had been renamed *Analog: Science Fiction/Science Fact*; and articles on forms of pseudoscience or mysticism, like psychic powers, ghosts, or UFOs. This combination of diverse materials seemed parallel to the agenda of cyberpunk fiction; for as Sterling observed, "what cyberpunk represents is an integration of New Wave and Hard SF."[36] In terms of the artistic correspondences I have proposed, such contradictory concerns would seem to demand a form of art that was simultaneously realistic and abstract; and there is in fact a form of art that meets that description: surrealism, defined as "a modern type of art or literature in which the painter, writer, etc., connects unrelated images and objects in a strange dream-like way."[37] In such art, "images and objects" may be depicted realistically, but the ways they are brought together may be highly unrealistic—an apt summary of the *Omni* style.

Taking the various artists responsible for the *Omni* covers collectively as a final representative artist, one can consider a typical example, the cover of the August 1983 issue. A realistic human head is cut off at the bottom by an extended geometric plane, which in the background meets a mountain range; the top of the head is also cut off and surrounded by floating globes that resemble planets. The Table of Contents page says, "Michel Tcherevkoff presents a visual interpretation of the ideational process" and speaks of "his striking, surreal images."[38] The cover of the November 1984 issue juxtaposes two hands playing a string game, Egyptian bas-relief figures, an ocean, floating polygons, and the Earth in the sky. According to the Table of Contents page, "Archetypes pervade Dickran Palulian's painting.... Hands emerge from the stones of ancient Egypt, rise above the primordial sea, and reach toward space. The cat's cradle presents a modern riddle: Will technology strip us of all individuality?"[39] Such covers both describe and embody the announced dilemma at the heart of both cyberpunk and its mainstream cousin, "postmodern" literature: we are coming to live in a world that combines bits of the past and bits of the future, but these are not smoothly integrated, but jarringly juxtaposed in a manner suggesting that all conventional categories are breaking down and can no longer be relied on; so the world indeed becomes a gigantic puzzle. Faces appear, but they are arbitrarily cut off; ancient art is next to a modern view of Earth from space. Literary critics of postmodern literature speak of its writers' use of "collage," roughly combining chunks of raw material from various sources; so it is appropriate that its characteristic art often takes the form of a surrealistic collage.

In two other *Omni* covers, we see the aspect of dichotomized modernity that is most central to science fiction: the combination of humanity and technology—as in the cyborg, or the human consciousness "downloaded" into a computer—and the consequent blurring of the lines between the two. The cover of the December 1988 issue features another woman's head, this time overlaid with various pieces of machinery; according to the Table of Contents page, "She represents the 'Venus of the future,' says artist Jean François Podevin ... an expression of technology, humanity, and nature—with a dimension of mystery."[40] And the cover of the June 1988 issue, painted by Takashi Terada, shows a woman attached to a spaceship flying through space, not even bothering to wear a brass brassière. Superficially, the cover harkens back to the eroticism of pulp art; but despite her nudity, the woman, colored cold blue, with light beaming from her eyes and metal bands on her shoulders and breasts, fails to be alluring—the touches of unreality make her seem machine-like and unappealing. The simultaneous exposure and suppression of sexuality, of course, is another aspect of the postmodern which can excite critics to rhetorical excess.

Though the word is problematic in its several meanings, I will call this style of art "surreal science fiction art,"[41] but "*Omni* science fiction art" might do just as well, to indicate both its source and its omnivorous appetite, drawing in and combining aspects of all previous science fiction art. *Omni* covers may offer at times the massive artificial constructs of Paul, the attractive human figures of pulp art, the imposing astronomical landscapes of space art, the sophisticated realism of slick art, and the unrealistic images of abstract art. The novelty here is the way these elements are starkly juxtaposed, a bringing together of opposites that is, critics say, one key characteristic of the postmodern.

There is a final comment worth adding to this section: I recall an online critique of the original version of this chapter which complained that my survey was entirely focused on American science fiction art; and just as the introduction of this book noted that it was neglecting important writers from earlier times and other countries, this chapter might have begun by noting that it would be neglecting important artists from earlier times and other countries, such as the remarkable French artist Albert Robida (1848–1926). And the chapter could have justified those omissions by arguing, in parallel with the first chapter, that in the twentieth century American science fiction art gradually came to dominate the world in the manner of science fiction literature, as the works of many American artists appeared on foreign editions and their style influenced original science fiction artwork in many countries. (Thus, the Internet Speculative Fiction Database confirms that the art of Frank Kelly Freas, for example, has been published in Croatia, Finland, France, Germany, Greece, Italy, Spain, and Sweden.)

But as was the case with science fiction novels and stories, foreign science fiction art has, in recent decades, developed its own styles and has been widely appreciated by American audiences, so that the field has also evolved into an international conversation about art. *Omni* reflected that development by regularly employing artists from other countries. Thus, considering the four artists mentioned above, both Michel Tcherevkoff and Jean François Podevin were born in France (though Tcherevkoff later moved to America), and *Omni* identified Takashi Terada as a "Japanese artist." One could also cite many other artists from countries like France, Germany, Spain, and Russia whose works have recently appeared on American magazines and books.

Overall, I have shown that we can indeed outline a history of twentieth-century science fiction art to correspond to the history of twentieth-century science fiction literature. However, to justify such an exercise, I must also explain why a history of this kind might be useful. Briefly, I would like to emphasize how this view of science fiction art might be helpful to the study of science fiction literature.

First, if this model is accurate (as summarized in Table 1), we should find a preponderance of certain styles of art at certain times, even if those styles do not suit particular writers. It is not surprising that in the 1960s, my era of abstract art, Signet Books replaced the slick realistic covers on its Heinlein novels with gaudy semi-abstract designs, or that Clarke's "documentary" novel about space flight, *Prelude to Space* (1951), was retitled *The Space Dreamers* in 1969 and provided with a colorful abstract cover, perhaps to attract the chemically-altered fans of the "trip" sequence in his and Stanley Kubrick's film *2001: A Space Odyssey* (1968). Generally, however, we should find that a certain type of writer is accompanied by one appropriate style of art: most Heinlein covers should be slick art, and most Clarke covers should be space art.[42] Thus, examining the styles of cover art could provide data to help us classify problematic writers.

As a pilot project, I surveyed the cover art of three writers to evaluate David G. Hartwell's highly debatable claim, made throughout his and Kathryn

Table 1: A Proposed True History of Science Fiction Art

Era	Style of Art	Description	Exemplary Artist(s)	Associated Literature
1920s	futurist	huge buildings, cities, geometric symmetries	Frank R. Paul	Gernsbackian sf
1930s	pulp sf	focus on humans, heroes, sexy women, monsters	Earle Bergey	space opera
1940s	space art	scenes of space, other worlds, alien landscapes	Howard Brown, Chesley Bonestell	hard sf
1950s	slick sf art	realism, variety in subject matter, ambiguity	Ed Emshwiller, Frank Kelly Freas	1950s sf
1960s	abstract sf art	semi-abstract or abstract images; no machinery	Richard Powers, Leo and Diane Dillon	New Wave sf
1980s	surreal sf art	surrealism; real objects combined in unreal manner	various *Omni* artists	cyberpunk

Table 2: Types of Cover Art for Three Science Fiction Writers

[Number (Percentage)] / (Percentages do not always total 100 due to rounding off.)

Writer	Futurist	Pulp	Space	Slick	Abstract	Surreal	Total
Hal Clement	1(3)	11(35)	11(35)	3(10)	5(16)	0(0)	31(99)
Larry Niven	4(7)	12(20)	17(28)	4(7)	21(34)	3(5)	61(101)
J. G. Ballard	0(0)	1(2)	1(2)	9(20)	30(65)	5(11)	46(100)

Writer	Total Realistic Art	Total Non-Realistic Art
Hal Clement	26(84)	5(16)
Larry Niven	37(61)	24(39)
J. G. Ballard	11(24)	35(76)

Cramer's anthology *The Ascent of Wonder: The Evolution of Hard Science Fiction* (1994), that J. G. Ballard is a hard science fiction writer. I chose two writers—Hal Clement and Larry Niven—who are universally known as hard science fiction writers, and I looked at and classified the art on every cover of their books in the J. Lloyd Eaton Collection of Science Fiction and Fantasy Literature, excluding duplicates; I did the same for Ballard's books, excluding his mainstream novels. Granted, the books in the Eaton Collection may not be complete or representative and some classifications may have been hasty or questionable; but even allowing for experimental error, my results (in Table 2) reveal a clear pattern. Both Clement and Niven attracted a large number of space art covers, exactly what we would expect for hard science fiction writers, and Ballard attracted only one such cover. If someone protests that this is simply because Ballard rarely deals with space travel in his works, there is a second pattern: the large majority of the Clement and Niven covers were realistic, displaying the various styles of art common to science fiction before 1960; the large majority of Ballard covers were non-realistic, displaying the styles of art common to science fiction after 1960. So the usual classification of Ballard as a New Wave author, not as a hard science fiction writer, is confirmed by the artwork that illustrated his novels; and these data do not represent the judgments of individual commentators with possible axes to grind, but rather a large number of separate decisions by artists and publishers who were solely interested in presenting covers that would most appropriately reflect and promote Ballard's books. To be truly meaningful, such research would have to be more thorough and could never be relied on exclusively; but it could provide useful supplementary information of a sort not otherwise available.

We may also gain by viewing science fiction art not only as an effect of, but also an influence on, the literature it accompanied. In the 1920s, Paul at times provided grand and impressive covers for petty and prosaic stories; but his persistent grandiosity may have inspired the "Thought-Variant" stories published in the 1930s by *Astounding* editor F. Orlon Tremaine, wherein writers wrestled, however ineptly, with issues more vast than marvelous new inventions or space pirates. The eroticism of the pulp art in the 1930s and 1940s at times seemed incongruous next to the pristine stories they depicted; but the recurring images of all that female flesh on the covers of magazines may have provoked writers to produce more frankly sexual stories, such as Philip José Farmer's groundbreaking *The Lovers* (1952) and the controversially erotic novels of Robert A. Heinlein in the 1960s.

Arguably, then, innovative science fiction art consistently precedes, and may eventually generate, innovative science fiction literature; thus, in my view, the space art of the late 1930s and 1940s predated by a decade the true emergence of hard science fiction,[43] and Powers was popularizing experimental art well before most writers produced experimental stories. Rather than regarding new literature simply as an outgrowth of or reaction to earlier literature, then, we might improve our understanding of science fiction history by including its accompanying art in the picture and seeing science fiction literature and art engaged in an interactive evolution, as the art endeavors to represent contemporary literature while it also influences future works of literature.

3. Artists in Wonderland 57

As a final benefit of this project, consider one predictable objection: that I am overly simplifying, even distorting, the history of science fiction art. How can I call the 1940s the era of space art, when most 1940s art was firmly in the pulp tradition? How can I call the 1980s an era of surreal art when most 1980s art was realistic? And some may complain of excluded artists: where are the names of Hannes Bok, Virgil Finlay, Vincent Di Fate, or Michael Whelan, to mention only a few of the major and influential artists who are neither represented in nor congruent with this scheme? Were they omitted simply because they inconveniently did not fit into my categories? These were exactly my own misgivings as I created this model[44]; and my projected history of science fiction art thus serves to reveal the inadequacies of our histories of science fiction literature.

For parallel objections can be made to the literary history I used as my structuring device. It is wrong to epitomize the 1940s as an era of hard science fiction; even Campbell's *Astounding* published writers like A. E. van Vogt whose works were not particularly scientific, and other major magazines—*Amazing Stories, Thrilling Wonder Stories, Startling Stories,* and *Planet Stories*—emphasized space opera. And it is wrong to describe the 1980s as a cyberpunk era, since the majority of new writers who emerged at that time could not be accurately described as cyberpunk writers. Yet critics keep mouthing glib generalizations about different eras and limiting their research with restrictive parameters—lavishing attention, for example, on 1980s writers like Gibson and Sterling and ignoring writers like C. J. Cherryh, Dan Simmons, and Michael Swanwick who did not match their preconceptions of the decade. Grafting this potted history onto science fiction art exposes its weaknesses only because histories of science fiction art have generally been more eclectic and diverse in their loosely organized surveys. My subtitle, then, allows this entire chapter to be interpreted as a satire, designed to expose the stupidity of histories of written science fiction by absurdly imposing their patterns on science fiction art.

Perhaps I would not go that far; but I now feel inspired to imagine a project precisely opposite to my original goal: how might we construct a history of twentieth-century science fiction literature that would be similar to most histories of science fiction art? As it happens, there already exists one excellent example: Paul A. Carter's *The Creation of Tomorrow: Fifty Years of Magazine Science Fiction* (1977).[45] Like historians of science fiction art, Carter does not insist upon a rigid structure for his survey; he groups discussions of stories by their topics—robots, aliens, and so on; and he does not limit himself to a few selected masterpieces, but ranges freely over the entire field, examining both major and very minor works. If Carter's book has never been influential, that may be precisely because he does not impose a tidy framework on his research and seems instead to be rambling and disorganized; yet one can argue that that is exactly the kind of study needed to truly reflect what is often, on examination, an unmanageably diverse genre.

As an ameliorative conclusion, I suggest that both science fiction literature and art in fact require two types of history. At times, no doubt, we need to establish structures, so that different eras are clearly delineated and represented by a few examples, as a good working summary and a stimulus for thought. But at other times we must be reminded that our fields of study are more inchoate and variegated than such simplified structures can convey. I began by implying that scholars of science fiction art might benefit by imitating the well-organized scholars of science fiction literature, but I conclude by suggesting that scholars of science fiction literature might also benefit by imitating the disorganized scholars of science fiction art.

I originally developed this survey of science fiction art in a paper presented at the 1995 J. Lloyd Eaton Conference on Science Fiction and Fantasy Literature, and I revised and expanded its argument for publication in the 2002 conference volume. The question I must finally address here is how, or whether, any of this analysis applies to the science fiction art of the twenty-first century.

One must first note that since the 1980s, there have not emerged, to any extent widely recognized, major new varieties of science fiction. Rather, the genre has continued to offer versions of all the varieties of science fiction that dominated earlier eras, although (as discussed below) the forces of the marketplace have increasingly foregrounded interminable series of undemanding space operas recalling the pulp science fiction of the 1930s. Still, one can also find contemporary works that resemble the stories that appeared in Gernsback's magazines of the 1920s, though they are usually more sophisticated than their earlier counterparts; examples of the hard science fiction first observed in the 1950s; stories and novels similar to the literate or satirical science fiction that characterized the 1950s; stylistically adventurous texts in the spirit of the New Wave; and stories about cynical outsiders navigating through dark future cities in the manner of cyberpunk. The corresponding observation would be that one should continue to observe covers and interior illustrations that recall all of the identified eras of science fiction art, and one can identify numerous works to support that conclusion.

There are nonetheless some novel developments that must be addressed, including the increasing international character of science fiction art mentioned above. In addition, as I noted in my contribution to the entry on "Illustration" for the online *Encyclopedia of Science Fiction*,[46] the use of computers has introduced an entirely new style of science fiction art, although there remain artists who insist upon employing the traditional technique of applying paint to a canvas. More significantly, the style of art on contemporary book covers from major publishers is now dictated almost entirely by their market research, as these companies now believe that they know both precisely what sorts of books people will want to purchase and what sorts of art will best encourage them to make such purchases. The evident consensus is that most readers are most interested in involving characters, not distinctive new ideas, so one observes on science fiction book covers a growing emphasis on portraiture—so that, for example, the cover of the most recent book in David Weber's Honor Harrington series, *Uncompromising Honor* (2018), is little more than a large picture of the titular heroine's face, painted by David Mattingly.

Today, for more variegated science fiction art, one must often look elsewhere. First, small press publishers, less concerned about market research, still offer a wide variety of styles in their covers—though there is the troubling tendency for them to sometimes rely upon the artwork of long-deceased artists. (A painting by the late Richard M. Powers, for example, incongruously adorned the cover of Jonathan Strahan's 2009 anthology *Eclipse Three: New Science Fiction and Fantasy*, while a portion of Frank R. Paul's cover for the August 1928 issue of *Amazing Stories* was used as the cover of my own *Hugo Gernsback and the Century of Science Fiction* [2007], though I was never consulted about that decision.)

Finally, increasing numbers of science fiction artists are supporting themselves by marketing their artworks, often unrelated to any specific texts, directly to consumers by selling prints and original works online or at science fiction conventions.

As book publishers increasingly resort to formulaic images or indulge in nostalgia for past artists, it may well be that the works of these independent artists, free to rely on their own imagination in crafting their strange new worlds and characters, will represent the true future of science fiction art.

Part II. The 1930s and Thereafter

4

Pulp Science Fiction
A Student's Guide

One might derive a working definition of "pulp science fiction" from a well-known fact, and a well-known opinion. As a matter of fact, science fiction magazines from the 1920s to the early 1950s (the era when science fiction emerged as a recognized genre) were generally printed on cheap yellow paper, "pulp," and hence were termed pulp magazines. As a matter of opinion, editors Ursula K. Le Guin and Brian Attebery, assembling *The Norton Book of Science Fiction* (1993), included only stories from the 1960s and thereafter because to them that represented, as stated in Le Guin's introduction, the era of science fiction's "maturity."[1] One could define pulp science fiction, then, as genre science fiction which is not mature.

To be sure, this definition's time frame must be adjusted, in part because pulp science fiction magazines (as noted) disappeared in the early 1950s, almost universally supplanted by the now-standard digest format. Furthermore, most commentators, including myself, would say the genre actually matured in the 1950s, not the 1960s, as shown by the appearance of new magazines, *Galaxy* (1950–1980) and *The Magazine of Fantasy and Science Fiction* (1949-), which explicitly sought and addressed adult readers, and by publication of many esteemed stories and novels. After all, several works from this decade—including Ray Bradbury's *The Martian Chronicles* (1950) and *Fahrenheit 451* (1953), Arthur C. Clarke's *Childhood's End* (1953), Theodore Sturgeon's *More Than Human* (1953), Robert A. Heinlein's *Starship Troopers* (1959), and Walter M. Miller, Jr.'s *A Canticle for Leibowitz* (1959)—are routinely assigned in college science fiction classes, testifying to their literary quality and, one might say, their maturity. And one naturally recoils, I think, from describing such novels as "pulp science fiction," even though portions of five of these books originally appeared in science fiction magazines.

For that reason, I will address as "pulp science fiction" only works that appeared in the science fiction magazines of the 1920s, 1930s, and 1940s, since these are usually excluded from the college curriculum, except for a few stories in retrospective anthologies, and since I argue that these works, even if some would deem them immature, do merit consideration as texts for science fiction classes. I will primarily focus on six accessible works from this era, with references to several others, including ideas for class discussions and suggestions for research projects.

One must approach the magazine science fiction of the 1920s and 1930s with an awareness of their typical readers: young Anglo males who were brighter than their peers, particularly fascinated by science, and often characterized as socially inept loners. Frustrated by a society that did not share their interests and failed to value them as people, unable to find and bond with like-minded others in their immediate vicinity, these adolescents happily turned to the fabulous world of science fiction magazines, wherein they found stories about men like themselves who made amazing discoveries in the future, conquered the universe, earned humanity's acclaim, and won the hands of beautiful women because of their intelligence and scientific acumen—heartening affirmations of their readers' true worth and glorious future. Through letters and announcements in these magazines, they also learned about a growing national network of people devoted to such fiction which many of them eagerly connected to, finally able to join a community of people like themselves. For portraits of these individuals, one might examine memoirs written by science fiction authors who grew up reading the era's pulp science fiction—such as Frederik Pohl's *The Way the Future Was* (1978), Jack Williamson's *Wonder's Child* (1984), or Clarke's *Astounding Days: A Science Fiction Autobiography* (1989)—but the best choice might be Isaac Asimov's anthology *Before the Golden Age: A Science Fiction Anthology of the 1930s* (1974), which offers both a rich selection of science fiction stories of the 1930s and lengthy commentaries on Asimov's youthful reactions to them, effectively making the book Asimov's first autobiography.

In our enlightened, multicultural age, does a population of largely male, largely white, and largely American people from 1920 to 1950 really deserve special attention? First, one must avoid stereotyping these readers: they were not, for example, virulent sexists who sought to exclude women from their all-male world of science and adventure; rather, they were desperately eager to welcome those occasional women who came to science fiction conventions or wrote science fiction stories, as documented in Eric Leif Davin's *Partners in Wonder: Women and the Birth of Science Fiction, 1926–1965* (2006). In addition, many of these young men later became the scientists and engineers who helped to build the atomic bomb and launch the American space program, meaning that, for better or worse, these were people who, as they once dreamed, would eventually have a major impact on their society. (It is a matter of record, for example, that John W. Campbell, Jr., editor of *Astounding Science-Fiction* in the 1940s, first realized that some sort of special scientific project was going on when he noticed a huge increase in subscriptions from a small town in New Mexico named Los Alamos; and there are numerous testimonials from participants in Los Alamos's Manhattan Project and America's later space program of their early interest in science fiction. How, one wonders, did the extravagant space operas read by these long-time science fiction readers affect their work?)

As a text to shed light on these readers, I personally cherish Williamson's *After Worlds End* (1938)—a particularly hallucinogenic vision of a present-day man whose identity blurs with that of an identical far-future descendant battling against an implacable robot adversary intent upon destroying humanity—but Clarke's *Against the Fall of Night* (1953) is both easier to find and a better novel. Though first published in magazine form in 1948, Clarke began writing the book in the 1930s and had completed a rough draft by 1941, when he summarized its contents in a fanzine article, "Ego & the Dying Planet."[2] Thus, despite its later publication, the story does reflect the style and concerns of the 1930s. Billions of years in the future, Alvin is a young man growing up in a fantastic city on an otherwise-deserted Earth, Diaspar, which effectively imprisons its immortal residents while benevolently providing for their every need. Although everyone else is content within its protective cocoon, the restlessly curious Alvin seeks to escape from Diaspar and learn about the outside world. With the help of an eccentric mentor, he becomes the first person in eons to leave the city and begins a journey which takes him first to the other, very different community still existing on Earth, Lys, and then into space, where he encounters a being made of pure energy and learns that everything Diaspar's citizens had been taught about their history is incorrect.

What sort of person would find this story appealing? Clearly, it would be a young man who feels he is surrounded by boring people inexplicably unexcited about the prospects of futuristic inventions and space travel; a youth anxious to discover that the dull world around him is not as it seems, or will soon be irreversibly transformed; a youth who enjoys daydreaming about becoming the one special person who will awaken the world from its complacent slumber and lead it to a new, grander destiny. (Indeed, in a way, Clarke at the time was acting out his own version of Alvin's story in his efforts to prod an uninterested world into undertaking space travel, writing articles like "We Can Rocket to the Moon—Now!" [1939] and later serving as the Chairman of the British Interplanetary Society.) *Against the Fall of Night* is not a literary masterpiece, nor is it even Clarke's best work, but it exudes undeniable energy as it speeds Alvin from revelation to revelation against the backdrop of a vast, empty universe filled with unanswered questions.

Against the Fall of Night might inspire some stimulating research projects. First, after becoming prominent in the 1950s, Clarke was embarrassed by this piece of juvenilia and extensively revised the novel to add some depth and polish, publishing the result in 1956 as *The City and the Stars*. However, while one appreciates that novel's better developed scientific ideas and more thoughtful aura, it has proved to be, overall, a lesser work, as its virtues did not compensate for a conspicuous lack of youthful vigor, and over the years *Against the Fall of Night* has been embraced as the definitive version of the story. Students might also ponder Clarke's novel and film *2001: A Space Odyssey* (1968) to explore similarities between Alvin and two other figures who embark upon lonely quests for cosmic wisdom, the prehistoric Moon-Watcher (better characterized in the novel) and astronaut Dave Bowman.

Students could further examine Gregory Benford's 1989 sequel to *Against the Fall of Night*, *Beyond the Fall of Night* (originally published in tandem with Clarke's novel as part of a purported collaboration), to observe how abysmally Benford fails to recapture the magic of Clarke's novel with a tiresome, politically-correct continuation of the story focusing on a hapless female protagonist assisted by several strange beings who stumbles through an incongruously crowded reinvention of Clarke's stark and lonely future, now cluttered with aliens and new inventions—all of which represents a betrayal of Clarke's original vision. (Benford is a productive scientist and talented author, but perhaps he spent too much time working on a college campus to be comfortable with a tale about a solitary young white man single-handedly conquering the universe, explaining his odd take on Clarke's novel. And, in a way, Benford later acknowledged that the novel was his own creation, not a true sequel to Clarke's novel, as he published a revised and expanded version of *Beyond the Fall of Night*, with all specific references to Clarke's work removed, as *Beyond Infinity* [2004], another text available for research projects).

Another novel written in the 1930s provides insight into the psychology of its readers not so much through its protagonist as through the character that is central to its concerns. In Williamson's *The Legion of Time* (1938, 1952),[3] the entire future of the universe hinges upon one action to be taken by a bright youngster in our present: if he picks up a magnet and begins playing with it, he will grow up to become a brilliant scientist whose inventions lead to a benign future utopia; if he does not pick up the magnet, he never becomes a scientist and the future devolves into a dark dystopia. Both futures now exist in quasi-real, tentative states, and combatants from each universe travel through time in efforts to ensure that the boy will either pick up or ignore the magnet and thus firmly establish the reality of their own universe and erase its rival. Here, while nerdish readers could identify with Williamson's hero from the utopian future which ultimately triumphs, they were surely more inclined to imagine themselves as the novel's child, viewed by contemporaries as insignificant but actually destined to determine the destiny of the universe. And yes, in the 1930s, magnets were common toys for science-minded youths.

Along with sociological analyses, pulp science fiction of the 1930s invites examination as the wellspring of space opera, the sort of science fiction, most prominently represented by the *Star Wars* and *Star Trek* franchises, that has long dominated popular culture. One place to begin such a study is E. E. "Doc" Smith's *Galactic Patrol* (1937–1938, 1950), first published as a serial in *Astounding Stories* and originally the first of four novels constituting the Lensman series (though Smith later revised a previously unrelated novel, *Triplanetary* [1934, 1948], to serve as the series' first installment and wrote *First Lensman* [1950] to bridge the gap between *Triplanetary* and *Galactic Patrol*, creating the six-novel series now familiar to science fiction readers). The 1937–1938 novel introduced Smith's main hero, Kimball Kinnison, who leads an alliance of humans and aliens (backed by a benevolent ancient race called the Arisians) in a galactic war against sinister pirates controlled by an implacable enemy named "Helmuth, speaking for Boskone"[4] (although, as later novels reveal, he actually works for another ancient but evil race, the Eddorians). Relying upon the mysterious Lens given to him and other Lensmen by the Arisians, which provides psychic powers, as well as his own scientific know-how and resourcefulness, Kinnison succeeds in a risky mission to gain information about his foes and eventually kills Helmuth by means of a one-man assault on his hidden base.

Students will have a field day critiquing the sometimes clunky prose, egregious sexism, and childish heroics of *Galactic Patrol*; but despite its inadequacies, they will also discern in the novel a template for the stories they have grown up watching in theatres and on television: humans allied with colorful aliens opposing evil empires; space battles involving immense starships assailing each other with amazing rays and other devices; and fierce, hand-to-hand combat on starship decks and planetary surfaces with adversaries wielding futuristic variations of ancient weapons. A question for social historians would be: why were these fantastic narratives so underappreciated in the 1930s and so popular in the 1970s and thereafter? It is not simply that advances in special effects technology were needed to make such sagas work on film, since films like Fritz Lang's *Frau in Mond* (1929) and Vasili Zhuravlev's *Kosmicheskiy Reys: Fantasticheskaya Novella* (1936) had demonstrated that, even in earlier times, filmmakers who invested time and resources in their efforts could provide persuasive renderings of space travel. Rather, there must be other reasons why cowboys and detectives have largely been supplanted by spacefaring adventurers as our larger-than-life heroes of choice.

One cannot entirely dismiss *Star Trek, Star Wars*, and similar works as mere adaptations of the space operas written by Smith and others in the 1930s, since these franchises depart from Smith's pattern in ways worth discussing. First, though he often uses the almost magical powers of the Lens—an arguable anticipation of George Lucas's mystical "Force"—Kinnison also understands the superscience of his day and employs his knowledge to solve problems; for example, stranded on an alien planet and needing energy to recharge their batteries, Kinnison and a cohort visit an alien power plant and ingeniously use "pliers, screwdrivers, and other tools of the electrician" to extract its power.[5] In contrast, the original *Star Trek* offered an appealing protagonist without such capabilities, James T. Kirk, who relied upon his subordinates Mr. Spock and Mr. Scott for technological fixes, while the *Star Wars* series almost entirely dispenses with scientifically knowledgeable characters to focus on heroes who simply make clever use of off-the-shelf technology that they may not fully understand. Perhaps, any story seeking a mass audience must foreground likeable, ordinary characters like *Star Wars*'s Han Solo instead of scientific geniuses like Kinnison.

Also, while *Star Wars* and its sequels follow Smith more closely in emphasizing armed conflict against irredeemable foes, the *Star Trek* universe prefers diplomatic intrigue and a narrative arc tending toward eventual reconciliation between bitter adversaries; thus, the chief enemies of the first series, the Klingons, later become allies, and episodes of later series regularly depict efforts to peacefully resolve conflicts with other foes like the Romulans and Cardassians. So, fittingly enough for a series that emerged in the Swinging Sixties, *Star Trek* visibly seeks viewers who prefer to make love, not war. Finally, as further material for comparison-contrast papers, students may watch the Japanese anime adaptations of Smith's series, the film *Lensman* (1984) and television series *Lensman: Galactic Patrol* (1984–1985), and decades after the project was first announced, a projected American live-action film based on Smith's novels apparently remains "under development."

In the 1940s, Campbell, who officially became editor of *Astounding Science-Fiction* in 1938, attracted and nurtured a new generation of writers who, in some cases, appealed to the nerds of science fiction in a different way: instead of presenting incredibly talented heroes who mirrored their juvenile fantasies, they offered more plausible, yet attractive visions of the mature adults they might someday become. A key transitional work is Heinlein's novel "'If This Goes On—'" (1940), later revised and published along with two other "Future History" stories as *Revolt in 2100* (1953). Protagonist and narrator John Lyle is an intelligent young man in a dystopian future America controlled by a religious dictatorship. Initially, he accepts the official religion and its government, but he begins doubting the benevolence and desirability of the regime when he falls in love with an innocent young woman recruited to become the Prophet's latest mistress, and he soon joins a vast underground movement dedicated to replacing the tyranny with a secular, democratic government. While early chapters give Lyle exciting things to do—nocturnal derring-do in the Prophet's Palace and a cross-country mission to deliver an important message—he settles into the role of a minor functionary in the revolutionary movement and is only an observer of their daring and successful *coup d'etat* (though he accidentally plays a key role in a final assault on the Prophet's palace).

To some critics, this represents a flaw in the novel, a sign of Heinlein's immaturity as a writer; wouldn't it have been better, they say, to make the leader of the revolution the story's hero? Yet I would invite students to detect a subtle agenda in Heinlein's approach. Essentially, he takes a typical science fiction protagonist from the 1930s—young, smart, and energetic—and argues that such individuals, by themselves, can never achieve significant social change; rather, unlike Kinnison—who almost single-handedly overcomes a cosmic despot—Lyle must join with many others who share his goals, help them build a large, complex organization, and ultimately serve only as one of innumerable compatriots each performing small but significant tasks that have a cumulative impact in defeating an oppressive regime. Heinlein's readers, along with his protagonist, thus receive an education in the realities of advanced civilization, wherein plucky youngsters, even if equipped with great intelligence and amazing inventions, can never conquer the universe. The contrast between *Against the Fall of Night* and "'If This Goes On—'" is illuminating: Alvin becomes the sole savior of humanity, while the similarly bright young Lyle becomes a foot soldier in a revolutionary army. (The same point surfaces in Heinlein's later juvenile novels, as discussed below.)

As one research project, students might consider "'If This Goes On—'" as a bracing comeuppance to the individualistic heroes of the 1930s by examining another Heinlein novel, *Sixth Column* (1941, 1949), which though written after "'If This Goes On—'" actually offers a story constructed well before it. In the 1930s, Campbell wrote a novella, "All" (which eventually appeared in his 1976 collection *The Space Beyond*), but deemed it unpublishable; however, to make use of his labors, he hired Heinlein to write a novel based on its story. Perhaps inspired by earlier stories about sinister Asians who have conquered America, including Philip Francis Nowlan's "Armageddon 2419 A.D." (1928) and its sequel "The Airlords of Han" (1929) (published together in 1962 as *Armageddon 2419 A.D.*), Campbell crafted a classic 1930s saga of astounding victory against daunting odds achieved by remarkable scientists: immediately after the Asians take over the United States, six geniuses conceal themselves in an isolated fortress, whip up some superscience that specifically targets people of Asian descent, and overthrow the invaders essentially all by themselves. It represents, then, how "'If This Goes On—'" might have proceeded if Heinlein had implausibly presented Lyle as a brilliant scientist who single-handedly destroys America's dictatorship with his amazing inventions. In adapting "All," Heinlein did his best to make this racist, unrealistic story palatable, but the result was unquestionably one of his lesser works. One could both understand and convey to others, then, how science fiction changed from the 1930s to the 1940s with some slightly-out-of-chronological-order reading: first, "All," a sample of the typical wish-fulfillment fantasies of 1930s science fiction; then, *Sixth Column*, to observe a reasonable man of the 1940s vainly striving to make these fantasies seem sensible; and finally, "'If This Goes On—,'" to observe that same reasonable man abandoning those fantasies and instead undertaking to describe how a successful revolution against a dictatorial government might actually be achieved.

Students particularly interested in Heinlein—one of the field's most seminal figures—might read the original magazine version of "'If This Goes On—'" and compare it to the revised, expanded version. Some changes are inconsequential: Heinlein adds a mildly salacious skinny-dipping scene for adult readers of the novel and reworks one of Lyle's thrilling escapes to make it more realistic. But one change is telling: in the original version, the rebels decide, after their revolution succeeds, to launch a propaganda campaign to persuade citizens to accept their new government, and no one objects. In the revision, upon hearing of this plan, an elderly man "who looked like the pictures of Mark Twain, an angry Mark Twain" stands up to vociferously complain: "Free men aren't 'conditioned!' Free men are free because they are ornery and cussed and prefer to arrive at their own prejudices in their own way—not have them spoonfed by a self-appointed mind tinkerer! We haven't fought, our brethren haven't bled and died, just to change bosses, no matter how sweet their motives."[6] Shamed by his passionate opposition, rebel leaders abandon their plan.

This shift in attitude defined Heinlein's later career: originally committed to the importance of working within groups to achieve social change (and once an aspiring politician before turning to writing), Heinlein initially produced stories featured individuals who, while brilliant and capable, were willing to work with others within intricate organizations to accomplish worthwhile goals. As such, he would have no quarrel with benign efforts to convince citizens to accept a new government. Later, disillusioned with society, Heinlein increasingly insisted that brilliant, capable individuals should rather abandon civilization and its annoying restrictions and seek unlimited freedom outside of society—the recurring message of his *Time Enough for Love: The Lives of Lazarus Long* (1973). That speech, then, is an early sign of a burgeoning inclination to reject socialization and embrace individualism—although, unlike the heroes of 1930s science fiction, Heinlein's later protagonists did not leave their communities to conquer the universe but rather only sought to fulfill their own personal desires.

4. Pulp Science Fiction

The other two stories in *Revolt in 2100*, however, only reinforce Heinlein's original message: "Misfit" (1939), identified by Sam Moskowitz as "Heinlein's first juvenile,"[7] anticipates the pattern of his juvenile novels by describing a troubled young man, Andrew Jackson Libby, who joins a team turning an asteroid into a space station, reveals and uses his amazing calculating abilities to save the day, and then is contentedly integrated into his society. (The character reappears in Heinlein's later novels *Methuselah's Children* [1941, 1958], *Time Enough for Love*, and *The Number of the Beast* [1980].) In "Coventry" (1940), a man unwilling to comply with the reasonable rules of his enlightened, post-revolutionary society must go where all such people are sent—a special zone where no rules are enforced—and in that lawless realm learns the desirability of abiding by social norms. (Heinlein introduced the concept of Coventry in his long-unpublished first novel, *For Us the Living: A Comedy of Customs* [2004], which his novel *Beyond This Horizon* [1942, 1948] borrows from in minor ways.)

If Heinlein in the 1940s was striving to train young nerds to function as members of society, other authors like Asimov had embarked upon another sort of training, writing stories that effectively showed young readers how to think like scientists. Like the archetypal Heinlein Hero, Asimov's protagonists were more sociable than those of the 1930s; they particularly loved engaging in conversations, leading to stories driven more by dialogue than by derring-do. But rather than seeking power, fame, or political change, Asimov's heroes primarily needed to solve puzzles—albeit puzzles linked to broader concerns. Still, in describing thoughtful individuals who carefully gathered information, considered alternatives, reasoned everything out, and finally achieved correct solutions, Asimov (then studying to become a chemist and later employed as a chemistry professor) was arguably presenting the first realistic portrayals of working scientists in genre science fiction, even if that was not always their official profession.

One useful collection displaying Asimov's approach is *I, Robot* (1940–1950, 1950), offering nine stories about humanoid robots supposedly rendered harmless by the rigid programming of the Three Laws—which famously prevent robots from harming humans or disobeying their orders while otherwise allowing them to protect themselves. Yet crises invariably arise—usually, robots representing a threat to humans—so their masters must deduce the source of the problems and devise solutions. Some stories feature space explorers Gregory Powell and Mike Donovan, who grapple with malfunctioning robots during missions on the frontiers of the solar system, but others foreground the more memorable Dr. Susan Calvin, a robot psychologist who works in laboratories to figure out why certain robots are perilously misbehaving. Asimov revised these stories in minor ways to make them consistent with each other—I have explored how, throughout the original stories, Asimov kept rephrasing and tinkering with the Three Laws until achieving a final, definitive text, then incorporated into the revisions[8]—but there is little material here for a rewarding textual study. More interesting are the later works which emerged from these stories: a trilogy of novels featuring detective Lije Baley and robot partner R. Daneel Olivaw—*The Caves of Steel* (1954), *The Naked Sun* (1957), and *The Robots of Dawn* (1983)—and a fourth novel, *Robots and Empire* (1985), which linked the robot stories to Asimov's far-future Foundation saga, also launched during the 1940s, creating a vast, multi-volume future history of which *I, Robot* is the first installment. In almost every work in the series, the focus of attention is a mystery, as the protagonists discuss the puzzle, think things through, and finally reach a satisfactory solution.

Students studying *I, Robot* might compare Asimov's book to its purported film adaptation, *I, Robot* (2004)—although the film's script originally had nothing to do with Asimov; instead, the producers who owned the script bought the rights to Asimov's title and added a few Asimovian touches to a final revision, referencing the Three Laws and using the names of two of his characters. Of course, Asimov's emphasis on thoughtful conversation and deduction could not be replicated in a money-making action film, resulting in a film that seems not only divorced from Asimov's stories but antithetical to them. A revelatory scene, discussed in my review of the film, recalls the *I, Robot* story "Little Lost Robot" (1947) in that a dangerous robot has concealed himself amidst scores of innocuous duplicates, but the story and film immediately diverge dramatically: "In Asimov's story, as one might expect, the problem sets the stage for a series of ingenious tests devised by Calvin which eventually force the robot to reveal himself. In this film, destroying any hopes for a truly Asimovian story, Spooner just pulls out his gun and starts blasting robots in the head, figuring that the frightened culprit will soon run away."[9] An intriguing analysis might also involve comparing Asimov's book to Harlan Ellison's unproduced, and reasonably faithful, adaptation of the book, published as *I, Robot: The Illustrated Screenplay* (1994). One question to ponder: if science fiction in fact matured and improved during the 1940s, why did it also, it seems, become less attractive as material for film adaptations? (Along with *I, Robot*, the sorry history of Heinlein film adaptations might be brought into the discussion.)

Even while Heinlein and Asimov established themselves as different sorts of alternatives to the extravagances of the 1930s, another new writer in Campbell's stable—A. E. van Vogt—carried the youthful exuberance of 1930s science fiction to new extremes. In the manner of the previous decade, van Vogt's stories often featured childlike loners with amazing abilities who traveled great distances, battled daunting foes, and emerged as all-powerful saviors of humanity. What he added to the pattern, first, was an abundance of ideas—one tossed out every eight hundred words, following a formula he learned from a guide to writers—that made his works seem more profound than previous space operas. Second, in keeping with this constant, dizzying assault of new concepts and perspectives, van Vogt transcended the traditional rationality of science fiction to instead generate stories that resisted logical explanation. Esteemed in his day, van Vogt is no longer well known or highly regarded, but the model of science fiction that he created—dynamic, breathless, and wildly imaginative—powerfully influenced later writers like Philip K. Dick.

To appreciate van Vogt's unique power, students might read his first novel *Slan* (1940, 1946), featuring young Jommy Cross, persecuted member of the tendrilled, telepathic race of mutants called slans. With mesmerizing energy, van Vogt rushes his hero from one deathtrap to another as he grows to adulthood, masters his late father's superscientific discoveries, and constructs weapons to wield against two relentless groups of foes: normal humans, who hunt down and kill slans, and the newly discovered "tendrilless slans," who maintain an undercover society while despising and assailing regular slans as much as, if not more than, the humans. In a final confrontation with Kier Gray, the dictator who postures as a fierce opponent of slans, Cross learns that Gray is actually a disguised slan himself, one of many actually controlling the government.

A talented writer who polished his skills in other pulp genres before tackling science fiction, van Vogt will effortlessly enthrall students who were unimpressed by Smith's less memorable prose style; but they will understand why van Vogt's kaleidoscopic approach to science fiction faded away while Heinlein's and Asimov's more subdued styles became dominant. For no matter how relentlessly van Vogt maintains his frenetic pace and keeps shocking readers with new ideas, they eventually realize that his stories fundamentally do not make sense. In contrast to Heinlein's and Asimov's meticulously planned futures, van Vogt's worlds are chaotic mixtures of mind-boggling scientific advances and anachronistic remnants of present-day life, seemingly made up while van Vogt was writing the stories. As enemies become friends and victims become victimizers, these reversals are inevitably implausible, even as van Vogt shouts out quick explanations before lurching in yet another new direction. There is no aura of reality, no sense of conviction, to van Vogt's visions; instead, they have the atmosphere, and logic, of a dream.

One scene in *Slan* is revelatory: Kathleen Layton, the young female slan inexplicably sheltered by the apparently slan-hating Gray, wakes up in the middle of the night to witness a startling confrontation between Gray and ten chief lieutenants, whose loyalties (as Layton's telepathy reveals) have gradually shifted away from Gray and toward a rebellious subordinate. Gray abruptly summons these men's assistants into the room; somehow, he anticipated this development and had previously recruited the assistants to enter at this precise moment and kill their bosses, ending the revolt. The timing of this scene gives the game away: impossible to accept as a reasonable series of events, the sequence seems more like Kathleen's dream, reflecting her subconscious fears that Gray's associates will contrive to kill her and her faith that Gray will always protect her. Even Dick, who as noted emulated van Vogt in some respects, learned enough from Heinlein and Asimov to make his future worlds passably believable, and to make his strange narrative twists ostensibly plausible. Van Vogt's imaginings, carefully examined, inexorably fall apart.

Slan also suggests several research projects. First, while van Vogt's multiple revisions of *The World of Null-A* (1945, 1948) are better known, van Vogt also revised *Slan* on two occasions, for book publication in 1946 and for republication in 1951, striving always to improve the narrative's logic while retaining its hypnotic appeal. As an effort to build upon and improve van Vogt's story, one might consider Heinlein's *Methuselah's Children*, which has an opening sequence often said to borrow from *Slan*, as citizens of a future society try to locate and capture a despised minority of unusually long-lived people; but rather than developing more and more scientific powers, Heinlein's heroes, more realistically, escape from their adversaries without overcoming them, seize a starship, embark upon a sedate interstellar journey, and finally return to rejoin humanity as equals (since their former pursuers have discovered their own method to achieve comparable longevity). Much later, Kevin J. Anderson employed van Vogt's outline and an unfinished draft of a sequel to *Slan* to produce the posthumous collaboration *Slan Hunter* (2007), endeavoring to replicate van Vogt's distinctive style while bringing the saga up to the standards of recent science fiction.

Finally, Heinlein, Asimov, and van Vogt were all regarded as Campbell's discoveries and mostly published during the 1940s in his *Astounding Science-Fiction*, universally accepted as the decade's leading magazine. Yet surveys of this era's science fiction cannot focus exclusively on Campbell, since other writers outside his circle were producing significant work and mastering their own distinctive approaches. In particular, the magazine *Planet Stories* attracted skillful writers who specialized in the subgenre of planetary romance—stories unlike space opera in that they took place almost entirely on alien worlds, with little if any space travel; and while they included genre tropes like aliens, robots, and amazing inventions, they otherwise had the style and ambience of fantasy. Since Edgar Rice Burroughs's *A Princess of Mars* (1912, 1917) first popularized the form and established its conventions, one good example of a planetary romance would be his final Mars novel, *Llana of Gathol* (1941, 1948), first published as four novelettes in *Amazing Stories*, a rousing adventure featuring the series' original hero, John Carter, returning to action one more time to assist his impetuous granddaughter. Yet newer writers in the tradition like Leigh Brackett were outdoing Burroughs in their stylish prose and impressive ambience, and an anthology of her 1940s works, *Lorelei of the Red Mist* (1943–1950, 2007), would introduce students to this unique talent, widely cherished within the genre.

Her stories, one realizes, are animated by an entirely different sensibility than previously discussed works, which focus on the future, with capable protagonists dedicated to further advancing humanity with new scientific and social achievements; even *Against the Fall of Night*, which begins with a decadent far-future civilization, concludes with reawakened ambitions and a renewed drive for progress. Brackett's narratives, like fantasies, primarily look toward the past; their protagonists are usually ordinary people, seeking to survive in alien worlds haunted by the glorious accomplishments of long-vanished civilizations and struggling to unravel their ancient mysteries. Further, rather than savoring the power to shape their own destinies, Brackett's heroes seem governed by a sort of cosmic karma that in the end rewards the virtuous and punishes the wicked. While Clarke, Heinlein, and Asimov emphasize explanations, Brackett is primarily devoted to descriptions, ignoring inner workings to illustrate surface wonders in lush, evocative prose. Consider her excellent "The Jewel of Bas" (1944)—the saga of a husband-and-wife team of thieves who fall into the clutches of aliens and robots brought by an ancient immortal who came to their world long ago but now only longs for endless sleep and pleasant dreams—and contrast her stunning description of a robot to Asimov's more prosaic efforts:

> The eyes in that face were what set Ciaran's guts to knotting like a nest of cold snakes. They were not even remotely human. They were like pools of oil under the lashless lids—black, impenetrable, without heart or soul or warmth.... It was a voice speaking out of a place where no emotion, as humanity knew the word, had ever existed. It came from a brain as alien and incomprehensible as darkness in a world of eternal light; a brain no human could ever touch or understand, except to feel the cold weight of its strength and cower as a beast cowers before the terrible mystery of fire.
>
> "Sleep," said the android. "Sleep, and listen to my voice."[10]

This passage also shows that students starved for memorable prose—rarely a hallmark of pulp science fiction—will appreciate having a writer like Brackett in the syllabus.

Lorelei of the Red Mist also usefully illustrates that 1930s and 1940s science fiction had both low points and high points. Few will admire stories like "The Blue Behemoth" (1943), a farcical tale of a tawdry space circus and its misadventures with a mammoth alien; Brackett's disappointing collaboration with Bradbury, "Lorelei of the Red Mist" (1946), a fairly lifeless exercise in planetary romance that Brackett wisely abandoned to concentrate on film work and recruited the young Bradbury to complete; and "Quest of the Starhope" (1949), the predictable saga of a selfish exploiter of captured aliens who receives his just rewards when he is killed by two beings he mistreated. But other stories powerfully linger in one's mind, like "Thralls of the Endless Night" (1943), describing descendants of a spaceship crew and the pirates that attacked them who unknowingly carry on their ancient quarrel on the barren world where their ancestors were marooned; "The Veil of Astrellar" (1944), featuring a human seduced by promised immortality into helping sinister beings from another dimension lure humans into traps so their life-forces can be drained to sustain the aliens' existence; and "The Dancing Girl of Ganymede" (1950), Brackett's sensitive exploration of a scenario later treated very differently in Dick's *Do Androids Dream of Electric Sheep?* (1968)—humanlike androids who are despised and hunted down in a future dystopia.

Seeking topics for further research, and noting that Bradbury was a one-time collaborator with, and admirer of, Brackett, students might look for signs of her influence on his fiction. For example, Bradbury's "Frost and Fire" (1946)—involving mutated descendants of stranded space travelers who aspire to reach a rocket on a mountaintop—is, despite significant differences, clearly reminiscent of "Thralls of the Endless Night." A more obvious area for study would be how Brackett's haunting stories about dying, decadent Martian cultures—some assembled in *The Coming of the Terrans* (1967)—influenced Bradbury's own visions of Mars in *The Martian Chronicles* (1950) and elsewhere. Although there are numerous antecedents for Bradbury's work, ranging back to Percival Lowell and Burroughs, students can justifiably argue that Bradbury's Mars is largely borrowed from Brackett's Mars. Students may also compare her science fiction stories to her screenplays. Finding evidence of her science fiction background in scripts for crime dramas and westerns like *The Big Sleep* (1946) and *Rio Bravo* (1959) might be challenging, but her early horror film *The Vampire's Ghost* (1946) is unusually creative, and students will be familiar with her final screenplay, for Lucas's *The Empire Strikes Back* (1980), co-written with Lawrence Kasdan. Recalling the striking descriptions in her stories, one is unsurprised that her contributions to Lucas's universe—immense "walkers" marching across an icy planet, the misty swamp home of the diminutive alien Yoda, the "cave" Han Solo retreats to that is actually the mouth of a space monster, and the elevated city of Lando Calrissian, delicately perched upon a narrow pillar—make *The Empire Strikes Back* the most *visually* imaginative and impressive of all the *Star Wars* films. One also notes her success in making Lucas's characters more rounded and complex than they were in the first film—another one of her special talents.

In choosing books to represent pulp science fiction, I have limited myself to works now in print and likely to remain in print; but other works from the era would be inspired choices if they become available. To survey its short fiction, Asimov's *Before the Golden Age*, representing the 1930s, could be paired with Campbell's *The Astounding Science Fiction Anthology* (1952), providing excellent stories from the 1940s. One might examine new retrospective anthologies featuring works by writers like Campbell, Henry Kuttner and C. L. Moore, and Murray Leinster. Along with books by writers already discussed, meritorious novels by other writers from this era include Nowlan's aforementioned *Armageddon 2419 A.D.*, which introduced the character who later starred in the *Buck Rogers* comic strip, serial, film, and television series; Edmond Hamilton's space opera *The Star of Life* (1947, 1959); L. Ron Hubbard's *Final Blackout* (1940, 1948), an evocative tale of conflict in a future world ravaged by war and disease; Clifford D. Simak's apocalyptic story cycle *City* (1944–1951, 1952); John Taine's dreamy time-travel epic, *The Time Stream* (1931, 1946); and Stanley G. Weinbaum's superman saga, *The New Adam* (1939). Also, while technically outside the realm of literature classes, no study of this subject is complete without examining the extravagant artwork that accompanied and influenced the stories in pulp magazines, displayed in compilations like Brian W. Aldiss's *Science Fiction Art* (1975) and others mentioned above.

It should also be noted that in my original survey of this era of science fiction, I felt obliged to focus on texts that could be readily found in recently published books; yet this concern is no longer relevant, since websites like the Internet Archive have now posted the entire texts of numerous science fiction magazines from the 1920s, 1930s, and 1940s, enabling enterprising students to discover and read any number of stories and serials that were once only accessible to researchers able to visit the Special Collections departments of certain university libraries; another website, Project Gutenberg, also offers the texts of numerous stories and novels from the pulp era. Hence, any number of additional projects could now be readily undertaken by motivated students. To mention two examples: though I have never had the time to satisfy my curiosity, I have long been intrigued by reports of Festus Pragnell's 1935 novel, *The Green Man of Graypec*, never republished in its complete form, which E. F. Bleiler and Richard Bleiler have described as "one of the two or three finest original novels to appear in the early s-f pulp magazines. It was praised by H. G. Wells."[11] But its entire text is now available in the July, August, and September issues of *Wonder Stories* where it first appeared at the Internet Archive. Second, after E. E. "Doc" Smith extensively revised his 1934 novel *Triplanetary* to serve as the introduction to his Lensman series, Sam Moskowitz complained that his revision "removes much of the zest from the original work."[12] Students can now investigate that claim by reading the original magazine version of the novel at Project Gutenberg. I have also found it consistently interesting to examine what editors and contemporary letter writers had to say about the stories and novels later republished in books when they first appeared in the magazines (as is evident elsewhere in this book), and this is something else that is now easy to research.

Finally, by discussing works of pulp science fiction that one might include in a standard science fiction class, I have also crafted what amounts to an annotated syllabus for a graduate-level class devoted exclusively to pulp science fiction, with ambitious research projects perhaps best assigned to graduate students. And in graduate programs focused on science fiction, such a class should definitely be offered. Why take students on a forced march through the collected works of, say, Philip K. Dick when one might better spend a semester acquainting them with some of the works that indelibly influenced Dick and countless other writers of his generation and later generations? Too many of today's publishing science fiction critics are shamefully unfamiliar with this literature, perhaps fearful of sullying their eyes with works that are not mature. But they are missing out on a lot of information, a lot of insight, and a lot of fun.

5

Beyond Logic and Literacy
The Strange Case of Space Opera

I was first inspired to examine space opera by Patricia Monk's "'Not Just Cosmic Skullduggery': A Partial Reconsideration of Space Opera," which in some respects is an admirable critical essay.[1] Monk properly addresses an important and neglected form of science fiction; she seeks to make her survey comprehensive, instead of focusing on a few "representative" works; and she usefully incorporates contemporary magazine commentaries on space opera as well as later critical judgments. This is exactly the sort of science fiction criticism I have tried to encourage, and I was delighted to see someone else doing it.

What her analysis apparently lacks, however, is an overarching knowledge of the general critical heritage of modern science fiction. This is a crucial omission, for without such an awareness, Monk is driven to what I see as a highly suspect conclusion: that space opera is "not a collection of texts but an attitudinal bias" (300). There are two problems with this statement: first, this view ignores the fact that science fiction commentators have almost universally regarded space opera as a subcategory of their literature—an easily identifiable one, at that—and such a widespread belief should not be dismissed virtually without examination. Second, the "attitudinal bias" Monk cites—"an authorial mindset which sees the extraterrestrial universe in holistic terms as both knowable and manageable" (300)—can be found in many science fiction texts that are manifestly not examples of space opera, while texts accepted as space opera do not always display that attitude; thus, the usefulness of this "bias" as a definition of space opera seems questionable. However, considering the context of the history of the idea of science fiction, I will argue, one can identify the distinctive characteristics of space opera as a subgenre, and one can explain both the widespread disapproval of the form, and its enduring popularity.

When Hugo Gernsback gave birth to the idea of science fiction in the 1920s, he imbued the genre with two highly ambitious sets of aspirations. Everyone knows of his concerns about science: writers were urged to be scrupulously accurate in their presentations of scientific fact and to be impeccably logical in extrapolating and developing their scientific speculations. In these ways, science fiction might be regarded as a truly scientific activity. However, on occasion Gernsback also articulated literary concerns: writers were urged to emulate and even surpass classic writers like Edgar Allan Poe, Jules Verne, and H. G. Wells and to improve their styles of writing.[2] Gernsback's desire for scientific accuracy and logic had an immediate impact, as readers enthusiastically embraced these goals and regularly wrote letters chastising authors who failed to achieve them, eventually engendering a new generation of writers more attentive to science; while Gernsback's desire for literary quality, not a major issue with early readers, later became prominent in the reviews and commentaries of people like Damon Knight, James Blish, Judith Merril, Michael Moorcock, and Harlan Ellison, and, of course, in the analyses of many academic critics.

Monk properly discounts definitions of space opera that focus on its obvious features—fast-paced adventures in outer space or on alien worlds—for such elements can be observed in many science fiction works, ranging from Frank Herbert's *Dune* (1965) to William Gibson's *Neuromancer* (1984), which are clearly not space operas. (I do however offer my own, broader definition in the next chapter, building upon Wilson Tucker's famous criticism of the subgenre.) However, when one considers Gernsback's priorities for science fiction, some special characteristics of space opera clearly emerge: space opera is a distinct subgenre in part because *its works not only fail to fulfill the genre's announced goals of scientific and literary excellence, but they visibly do not even attempt to fulfill those goals*. How exactly these characteristics might be cast in a rigorous definition remains problematic, but one can at least say that, recalling Supreme Court Justice Potter Stewart's famous observation on pornography, science fiction readers may not be able to precisely define space opera, but they can recognize it when they see it. And a key element in that recognition will be that the story in question has no scientific value and has no literary value. Brian W. Aldiss exactly captures these two features when he describes space opera as "a renegade sub-genre ... heady, escapist stuff, charging on *without overmuch regard for logic or literacy*."[3] With this in mind, it is no mystery why virtually all science fiction commentators have condemned space opera; they have to. That is, publicly committed to the idea of a genre which aspires to scientific rigor and literary quality, they are obliged to publicly denounce works which visibly flout those aspirations.

The process of condemnation began shortly after the true beginning of space opera with the appearance of *Astounding Stories* in 1930 (initially entitled *Astounding Stories of Super-Science*). Gernsback allowed for lots of action and adventure, but his magazines generally insisted on at least a fig leaf of scientific accuracy and respectable explanation, even in the stories he published that are now considered examples of space opera, such as E. E. "Doc" Smith's pioneering *The Skylark of Space* (1928, 1946), which endeavored to explain at length all of the author's scientific innovations. Harry Bates, the first editor of *Astounding Stories*, was less scrupulous. True, he paid lip service to the importance of science: when a reader's letter advised, "Since this magazine is about science every story must be examined to discover any false statements by the author concerning present-day science," the brief editorial reply was "We Examine All Science Very Carefully."[4] However, his hidden agenda made science a low priority: as Jack Williamson notes, "Bates was professional.... [He] wanted well-constructed action stories about strong, successful heroes. The 'super-science' had to be exciting and more-or-less plausible, but it couldn't take much space."[5] Or, as Bates himself put it, Gernsback's *Amazing Stories* was "awful stuff.... Cluttered with trivia! Packed with puerility. Written by unimaginables!"—while his *Astounding Stories* would instead emphasize "story elements of action and adventure."[6]

The popularity of this new magazine did not go unnoticed by Gernsback, whose major science fiction magazine in the 1930s was *Wonder Stories*. One editor's response to a reader who complained about scientific lapses in stories obliquely refers to *Astounding Stories* and acknowledges it as the source of such stories: "We confess that we have been carrying on a campaign against these very things that Mr. Race so soundly complains of. The difficult has been that a new element entered the field of science fiction, magazines of 'wild west fiction' in which science was of little or no consequence."[7] This may qualify as the first written criticism of space opera. However, because stories of this kind were popular, they were also creeping into Gernsback's magazines; and a year later, Gernsback (no longer involved in the day-to-day work of editing) happened to notice a forthcoming story by John W. Campbell, Jr., called "Space Rays" (1932), and he was so upset by its free-spirited creativity that he took the unprecedented step of introducing the story with a special signed editorial, the aforementioned "Reasonableness in Science Fiction," which was undoubtedly the first extended condemnation of space opera; therein, Gernsback complained that such stories were following "a policy of what I might call scientific magic, in other words, science that is neither plausible, nor possible."[8]

While Gernsback found he could justify publication of this story by inaccurately calling it a deliberate satire, he was obviously not interested in publishing similar efforts; thus, the editorial instructions to contestants in one of his "Interplanetary Plots" contests bluntly warned, "A plot submitted that simply relates a war between two planets, with a lot of rays and bloodshed, will receive little consideration."⁹ In these ways, Gernsback became the first vocal opponent of space opera because of its inattention to science.¹⁰

Around 1940, there was another wave of opposition to space opera, this time from the standpoint of literary value. In 1941, while coining the term, science fiction writer and fan Wilson Tucker described "space opera" as the "hacky, grinding, stinking, outworn space-ship yarn."¹¹ And in 1939, reacting in particular to the grotesque alien creatures often featured in such stories, Martin Alger, another prominent fan, sarcastically announced in a letter that "the cover [of the June, 1939 issue of *Thrilling Wonder Stories*] inspired me to organize the SFTPOBEMOTCOSFP (Society for the Prevention of Bug-Eyed Monsters on the Covers of Science-Fiction Publications)," thus adding "B.E.M." to the vocabulary of those denouncing space opera.¹² These complaints do not condemn space opera for its lousy science but rather for its clichéd, derivative, and monotonous stories and characters; in other words, space opera was now primarily disliked because it was lousy literature, not because of its lousy science. And such criticisms became the dominant theme of later attacks on the form, as when Frank Cioffi refers to a "story that has all the accoutrements of the 'space opera' that critics have almost unanimously cited as childish and immature" (cited in Monk 303).

A similarly critical attitude was embedded in another term for space opera that became common in the 1940s, the "thud-and-blunder story," seen in one reader's description of "the so called 'thud-and-blunder' science fiction as represented by *Planet*" in the letter column of the November 1950 issue of *Planet Stories*.¹³ Up through the early 1950s, in fact, the two terms were used interchangeably: for example, in a May 1953 review column in *Astounding Science-Fiction*, P. Schuyler Miller called *Space Hawk: The Greatest of Interplanetary Adventures* by "Anthony Gilmore" (Harry Bates and Desmond W. Hall) an example of "space opera of the old, raw, gloves-off school"; in the next issue, he said Jack Vance "has hitherto been a master of thud-and-blunder."¹⁴ That neither term is particularly complimentary goes without saying.

If space opera is defined as an effort to run away from the critical standards promulgated by Gernsback and his successors, one may reasonably ask what these writers were running towards. Here, Monk is certainly correct in claiming that space opera largely derives from "models available in the popular magazines of the nineteenth century and the very early years of the twentieth century" (300). Brian Ash makes the same point in a more critical manner when he describes space opera as "no more than unsubtle reworkings of the kind of adventure themes that have already been ground inexorably into the upper stratum of planet earth" (cited in Monk 296).¹⁵

Still, while space opera began as the cuckoo in the nest of science fiction, the form was not unaffected by developments in the genre. If nothing else, more scientifically rigorous stories provided a number of themes and ideas which were soon integrated into stories which lacked scientific rigor. A few examples: as awareness of the vast distances between stars was promulgated, space opera writers learned to insert brief references to "hyperspace" or "space warps" to justify their heroes' rapid journeys across the galaxy; Gernsback's publication of Hermann von Noordung's *The Problems of Space Flying* in 1929 brought a new awareness of space stations as a possible locale for future space adventures, and space stations began appearing in space operas of the 1930s like J. M. Walsh's *Vandals of the Void* (1931), Murray Leinster's "The Power Planet" (1931), and Manly Wade Wellman's "Space Station No. 1" (1936); more sympathetic treatments of robots in stories like Lester del Rey's "Helen O'Loy" (1938) and Isaac Asimov's robot stories made helpful robot companions a staple of space operas, beginning with Edmond Hamilton's *Captain Future* stories; and Asimov's detailed development of a collapsing Galactic Empire in his Foundation stories made this a standard background for later space operas. All of these features, by the way, can be observed in what might be regarded as the quintessential space opera, George Lucas's film *Star Wars* (1977), which features a spaceship shifting into hyperspace, a gigantic space station called the Death Star, two friendly robot companions, and the story of a group of rebel forces opposing an evil space empire. Thus, while the basic conventions and mood of the space opera may well be traced back to the nineteenth century, there are still features in the form which reveal the influence of modern science fiction.

However, these gestures of solidarity have not rescued space opera from the scorn of commentators from every era who, while continuing to criticize space opera for its weak scientific and literary values, have also found that their own particular concerns are invariably at odds with space opera. Gernsback, primarily interested in science, disliked the conspicuous lapses in scientific fact and logic in space opera; John W. Campbell, Jr., committed to science fiction as a literature for knowledgeable adult readers, disliked the overt appeal to a juvenile audience in space opera; commentators of the 1950s, determined to see science fiction address broader social issues, disliked the complete absence of such considerations in space opera; voices of the New Wave, most concerned with literary style and experimentation, disliked the monotonous prose style and unadventurous plots of many space opera adventures; and the 1980s advocates of cyberpunk, dedicated to projecting an air of knowing cynicism, disliked the innocence and naiveté of space opera. In sum, no matter what Church of Science Fiction one worships at, space opera is always the Great Heresy.[16]

Given, then, that all commentators are inclined to condemn space opera, one would expect that by the 1950s or so, with the ascendance of the more mature style of writing championed by the 1940s *Astounding* and new magazines in the 1950s like *Galaxy* and *The Magazine of Fantasy and Science Fiction*, the subgenre would virtually vanish from the written literature, although it could migrate into other media—films, television, comic books, games, and cartoons—where the impact of Gernsback's ideas was negligible and where, therefore, there would be no natural or obligatory opposition to the approach. And in fact, space opera has been for the last seventy years the overwhelmingly dominant form of science fiction in other media. And that is why, of course, modern commentators have regularly condemned science fiction in other media. Some have seen this development as a result of the colorful surface features of space opera—exotic aliens, spaceships, battles with ray guns, exploding planets—which better translate to visual media than other, more cerebral forms of science fiction. But space opera, the form of science fiction that naturally emerges from ignoring the genre's critical heritage, is also the form of science fiction most naturally produced by creators who are ignorant of the genre's critical heritage.

Thus, critics of written space opera, to be consistent, are generally critics of all science fiction in other media as well. Some comments from John W. Campbell, Jr., in the 1960s can be taken as typical:

> The major factor that distinguishes good science-fiction from fantasy is that it has a tight, logical and consistent structure that carries a sense of conviction.... What the movies and television call science-fiction isn't good science fiction, because it lacks precisely [that] element.... The movie-TV brand of "science-fiction" *isn't* science-fiction; it's fantasy, because neither the author nor the audience expects it to be believed.[17]

What one would not expect is a second development: that space opera would continue to appear in the modern written literature. And yet, as Monk's study convincingly demonstrates, there have been more than enough modern examples of the form, and she can even argue that "extensive sampling of the short stories in the science fiction magazines ... suggests that space opera has been and still is the most popular form of science fiction" (295). The question is: why has this form of writing survived—and even flourished—when it stands in overt opposition to every single principle announced and cherished by virtually all science fiction writers and readers?

To approach an answer to this question, I will first offer a personal anecdote. Recently, I found myself reading what could be taken as a pure example of space opera: "Space Mirror," by Edmond Hamilton, from the August 1937 issue of *Thrilling Wonder Stories*.[18] The one novelty in the story—and the only reason I was reading it—is its setting, a gigantic inhabited "space mirror" orbiting the Earth which is used to beam concentrated sunlight on Antarctica and generate heat and energy. Everything else in the story is unadulterated hokum: crewmen on board the mirror are dying of some mysterious ailment;

an investigator from Earth discovers that evil humanoid Mercurians, miniaturized to be only three inches high, have been surreptitiously scurrying around the mirror stabbing people with a needle containing the virus of a deadly disease; the medical officer of the mirror turns out to be a Mercurian in disguise, and he manages to vent the air out of most parts of the mirror, killing almost all of the crew; and this spy then signals a fleet of Mercurian warships to approach and seize the station, so that the Mercurians can blackmail Earth by threatening to turn the space mirror on its major cities and incinerate them. Fortunately, the investigator manages to kill the Mercurian agent with a leftover deadly needle, he revives one crewman, and together they manage to turn the mirror so that it beams reflected solar rays on the Mercurian spaceships and destroys them. From the standpoints of both scientific value and aesthetic appeal, the story is sheer, utter nonsense from beginning to end.

I cannot describe how strangely exhilarating it was to read that story.

Clearly, writing that story involved no great mental labors for Edmond Hamilton: although his accompanying remarks in "The Story Behind the Story" in that issue describe how the story was inspired by the writings of Hermann Oberth, Hamilton had obviously not bothered to work out the characteristics of his space mirror in any detail, and he was obviously inattentive to matters such as convincing characterization, realistic plotting, and eloquent prose style. He could relax and write that story. Similarly, readers of the story can relax: they understand that the story does not really demand detailed examination of its scientific issues—could science really reduce an intelligent humanoid to the size of a mouse? could a space structure as immense and unwieldy as the space mirror really be turned around quickly enough to destroy an approaching fleet of spaceships?—and the story does not really demand any thought about its deeper symbolic value, or its effective use of metaphor.

Lofty scientific and literary aspirations can function as an onerous burden, both for readers and writers; and the enduring appeal of space opera lies, I believe, in the temporary freedom from those aspirations that it sanctions. Consider two recent examples of space opera from writers who are demonstrably capable of producing more respectable examples of science fiction.

First, there is "The Crystal Spheres" (1984) by the well-known hard science fiction writer David Brin.[19] The premise of that story—that all solar systems are surrounded by an immense, invisible "crystal sphere" that can only be broken from the inside—is scientifically absurd in six different ways, and Brin knows it. But in writing this story, Brin for once does not worry about solving equations or doing the research of hard science fiction; instead, he simply accepts his implausible idea as a given and develops a charming and evocative story out of that idea.

Second, there is *The Eighty-Minute Hour* (1974) by one of the greatest of the "literary" science fiction writers, Brian W. Aldiss—a novel significantly subtitled *A Space Opera*.[20] In this story, Aldiss is for once not interested in displaying his awareness of literary values, his mastery of English prose style, or his properly profound pessimism. Instead, he simply sits down to write an exciting and amusing adventure, a mode of writing that also surfaces in his later *The Malacia Tapestry* (1976), though that novel is more of a fantasy.

Thus, "The Crystal Spheres" enabled Brin to take a break from the rigors of writing hard science fiction, and *The Eighty-Minute Hour* enabled Aldiss to take a break from the rigors of writing superior literary science fiction. And readers of those stories get to take a break as well, since they are obviously not required to closely examine the scientific logic in "The Crystal Spheres" or to admire the symbolism and subtleties in *The Eighty-Minute Hour*.

No sane people want to spend their lives on a permanent vacation, and no sane writer or reader of science fiction would want space opera to be the only form of modern science fiction. Yet everyone occasionally needs a vacation; and the chief value, and enduring attraction, of space opera is that it gives writers and readers exactly the kind of occasional vacation they need from the arduous official demands of their literature. Therefore, it is both logical and appropriate that space opera, even though it lacks "overmuch regard for logic or literacy," remains a vital and important element in modern science fiction.

6

Five Ways to Conquer the Universe
The Forms of Space Opera

Space opera is the most common, and least respected, form of science fiction. Its popularity in magazines of the 1920s and 1930s helped to establish science fiction as a recognized literary genre, and it has continued to find appreciative readers, even though it has been regularly scorned by learned commentators. To many, space opera is synonymous with science fiction itself, and to this day, average citizens asked to define science fiction might respond, "You know, the *Star Trek, Star Wars* stuff," which is to say space opera. Still, though repeatedly chastised for lacking merit and damaging the reputation of science fiction, space opera has endured, evolved, and grown, so that sophisticated writers and scholars increasingly look to the form with bemused affection, or even genuine admiration.

Despite signs of changing attitudes, space opera has garnered little critical attention; only a handful of scholars have attempted anything resembling a rigorous definition.[1] As a result, anyone discussing the nature, parameters, and history of space opera at length will necessarily break new ground.

Wilson Tucker, while coining the term in 1941, effectively presented the first definition of space opera, which can provide a useful framework for describing the subgenre:

> In these hectic days of phrase-coining, we offer one. Westerns are called "horse operas," the morning housewife tear-jerkers are called "soap operas." For the hacky, grinding, stinking, outworn space-ship yarn, or world-saving for that matter, we offer "space opera[.]"[2]

Tucker suggests that three characteristics define space opera.

First, space opera involves a "space-ship," a vehicle constructed by scientific means for traveling through space. Like the nautical fiction from which it borrows terminology and tropes, space opera depicts journeys through uncharted realms in vessels bringing humans into close contact with the mysterious stuff separating their safe harbors. Even narratives occurring primarily or exclusively on the surface of an alien planet must have nearby spaceports, creating the possibilities of departures to other worlds or arrivals from other worlds. In contrast, stories on alien worlds without access to space travel, or stories featuring travel to other planets by mystical means, should be termed planetary romances.[3]

Second, space opera is a "yarn"—an exciting adventure story. Typically positing a universe filled with human and alien space travelers—some hostile, some friendly—space opera is a literature of conflicts, usually with violent resolutions. In the year Tucker coined "space opera," a letter in *Astounding Science-Fiction* described the stories of E. E. "Doc" Smith as "scientific melodrama,"[4] epitomizing this aspect of the subgenre, and while some scholars have lauded the subgenre for its breathtakingly panoramic visions of the cosmos, most emphasize that space opera is "heady, escapist stuff" and "pure entertainment," lacking any other serious purpose.[5]

Third, space opera is all too often "hacky, grinding, stinking, outworn"—a form that, like the westerns and domestic dramas that inspired its name, tends to succumb to formulaic plots and mediocrity. Almost any well-received space opera generates a sequel or two; many spawn endless series of repetitive adventures involving the same characters in similar situations; and even stories not in a sequence may closely resemble innumerable predecessors. As early as 1932, one of Hugo Gernsback's editors announced impatience with "a plot ... that simply relates a war between two planets, with a lot of rays and bloodshed"[6]; and Tucker significantly christened the form while criticizing its staleness and abysmal quality. To remain at the forefront of science fiction, which esteems freshness and originality, space opera must continually reinvent itself and somehow make itself new. So, as one form of space opera falls out of favor and migrates to less prestigious venues—juvenile novels, films, television, comic books, cartoons, video games—another, improved form of space opera emerges to attract discriminating readers.

The origins of space opera are disputed, since many space adventures preceded the science fiction magazines, and some commentators have described texts like Garrett P. Serviss's *Edison's Conquest of Mars* (1898), Robert W. Cole's *The Struggle for Empire* (1900), and George Griffith's *A Honeymoon in Space* (1901) as progenitors of the form. However, the work that first established and popularized space opera was unquestionably Smith's *The Skylark of Space* (1928, 1946). He began writing the story in 1915 in collaboration with a friend's wife, Lee Hawkins Garby, who was recruited to handle the romantic elements and was originally credited as its co-author; but her contributions were minimal, and Smith eventually finished the novel in 1920 by himself, perhaps anticipating that his readers would not demand sensitive portrayals of men and women in love. (Further, when he revised the novel for book publication, he eliminated virtually all of Garby's prose so the novel could be justifiably attributed solely to Smith.) After Smith's original manuscript was repeatedly rejected by other publications, it found a home in Gernsback's science fiction magazine *Amazing Stories*, where it was met with tremendous enthusiasm.

To modern readers, the novel may be unimpressive, as almost half its length is devoted to preliminary shenanigans on Earth, and it includes interminable scientific doubletalk and clumsy dialogue; but some passages effectively convey the excitement of stories about spaceships hurtling into the unknown. Consider the scene when the villainous "Blackie" DuQuesne, who inaugurates human space travel by being catapulted with three passengers thousands of light years from Earth, finds his ship running out of fuel and falling toward a "dead star"—arguably the first crisis to afflict characters in space opera:

> Thus time wore on—Perkins dead; Margaret unconscious; Dorothy lying in her seat, her thoughts a formless prayer, buoyed only by her faith in God and in her lover; DuQuesne self-possessed, smoking innumerable cigarettes, his keen mind at grips with its most desperate problem, grimly fighting until the very last instant of life—while the powerless spaceship fell with an appalling velocity, and faster and yet faster, toward that cold and desolate monster of the heavens.[7]

Rescued by Dorothy's lover Seaton and his friend Crane, the humans journey to the planet Osnome, where they intervene in a conflict between a virtuous nation and its evil enemy. With such thrills available in space adventures, readers grew tired of the then-common tales of mad scientists in laboratories and demanded more of what Gernsback called "interplanetary stories"[8]—and these soon appeared, including Smith's two sequels to *The Skylark of Space*.[9] (Much later, in the 1960s, he added a fourth novel to the series.)

The 1930s proved the golden age of such "classic space opera," with stories ranging across a broad spectrum. At one extreme, stories about the solar system of the near future, positing only modest scientific advances, followed patterns long found in nautical literature, detective fiction, and westerns. Space pirates preyed upon passenger liners and cargo ships; interplanetary agents chased outlaws to uncharted moons; prospectors searched for asteroids of gold. These works might occasionally command attention—like Ross Rocklynne's stories about an interplanetary policeman pursuing a criminal that placed the friendly adversaries in intriguing scientific traps, like the "center of gravity" of a huge hollow sphere or the surface of a frictionless concave mirror[10]—but despite their numbers these stories are rarely appreciated or anthologized today. A typical example would be a forgotten story by Edmond

Hamilton, "Evans of the Earth-Guard" (1930), wherein the titular hero tracks down and captures a space pirate who was attacking spaceships traveling between the Earth and the Moon. Still, such stories served an important purpose: since space was a relatively new setting for fiction, a literary frontier as it were, writers sensibly used familiar storylines from genres dealing with frontiers, like the ocean, the criminal underworld, and the Wild West, to introduce the universe of the future to readers in a reassuring fashion and blaze a trail for works that would display more imagination.

Moving along the spectrum, one finds more ambitious stories, often reminiscent of future-war novels, with menacing aliens from nearby planets—usually humanoid in appearance but exotically hued or resembling loathsome creatures like lizards—battling against humans, who may be assisted by nicer, more attractive aliens. With mighty forces in play, entire planets might be destroyed or moved into new orbits—as in Leslie F. Stone's "The Fall of Mercury" (1935), wherein a benevolent Saturnian helps humanity defeat malevolent Mercurians by hurling their planet into the Sun. Such stories more frequently appear in nostalgic anthologies, since they can reflect the "sense of wonder" often said to define science fiction. In Jack Williamson's "Born of the Sun" (1934), for example, humans escape from Earth in a space ark when they learn that our world is only an egg, with a gigantic creature about to hatch from and destroy it.

At the opposite end of the spectrum, stories like Smith's extended into the galaxy and beyond, typically featuring heroic geniuses who, confronting vast and inimical alien empires, develop more and more powerful super-scientific weapons to thwart them. In one series inspired by Smith's Skylark novels, John W. Campbell, Jr.'s Arcot, Wade, and Morey stories, the heroes progress from adventures in Earth's atmosphere to voyages across the universe by means of "cosmic power," the ability to accomplish anything with a single thought, which eliminates any prospects for conflict and brings the series to a halt.[11] While such stories can fall victim to sheer excess, a more carefully structured epic of this kind, Smith's Lensman series, represents the crowning achievement of classic space opera. In the first of six volumes grandiosely entitled "The History of Civilization," Smith memorably begins by saying, "Two thousand million or so years ago two galaxies were colliding,"[12] and he proceeds to describe the ensuing war between those galaxies' dominant races, the virtuous Arisians and the evil Eddorians, which is eventually joined by humanity. Kimball Kinnison becomes one of many heroes armed with an Arisian "Lens" of immense powers so he can battle against various allies of Eddore until, in a final confrontation, the Eddorians themselves are conquered by Kinnison's children. Continually in print and adapted as an animated film (1984) and television series (1984–1985), this thrilling saga has been a dominant influence on innumerable literary and cinematic space operas, notably including George Lucas's *Star Wars* films and their many imitators.

Despite the accomplishments of Smith and contemporaries like Campbell, Williamson, Ray Cummings, and Clifford D. Simak, the most prolific and prominent writer of classic space operas was Hamilton. Particularly fond of stories involving planets being threatened or blown to pieces, Hamilton earned the epithets "World-Saver" and "World-Wrecker," and the reference to "world-saving" in Tucker's definition suggests that Hamilton might have been the principal target of his approbation. Yet Hamilton proved capable of producing more subdued, even wistful, varieties of space opera, like "The Dead Planet" (1946), wherein several space explorers of an alien planet listen to the holographic testimony of one member of its long-dead civilization that sacrificed itself to save the galaxy from sinister energy-beings; in the end, we learn the aliens were in fact the human race. Hamilton also crafted the first official space opera franchise in the Captain Future novels and stories mostly published in the magazine *Captain Future* (1940–1944); in a way, the series anticipated *Star Trek* in describing the numerous exploits of a heroic spaceship captain and his variegated crew—a robot, an android, and a disembodied brain.

Space operas soon made the transition to visual media: two earthbound stories about a man who hibernates for centuries and awakens in a future America conquered by Asians became the basis for a comic strip that made him a space traveler, *Buck Rogers* (1929–1967)[13]; this soon inspired two similar comic strips, *Flash Gordon* (1934–2003) and *Brick Bradford* (1933–1987); and all three were then adapted as film serials (*Flash Gordon* [1936]; *Flash Gordon's Trip to Mars* [1938]; *Buck Rogers* [1939]; *Flash Gordon Conquers the Universe* [1940]; and *Brick Bradford* [1947]). Hampered by inadequate special effects, the first four films portrayed space travel only fleetingly, with crude model spaceships, while Brick Bradford avoided space travel altogether by having its hero teleported to the Moon. Instead, the action was mostly limited to Earth, other planets, and/or spaceship interiors—like the early television series that mimicked these serials like *Captain Video* (1949–1956), *Tom Corbett, Space Cadet* (1950–1955), *Space Patrol* (1950–1955), *Rocky Jones, Space Ranger* (1954), and *Flash Gordon* (1954–1955). Science fiction films of the 1950s offered better effects, with *This Island Earth* (1955), *Forbidden Planet* (1956), and *It! The Terror from Beyond Space* (1958) qualifying as the most reminiscent of printed space operas, but further advances in special effects were needed before space opera could blossom on the screen. Since comic books faced no such limitations, however, colorful space heroes like DC's Knights of the Galaxy, Captain Comet, Space Cabby, Adam Strange, Space Ranger, Star Hawkins, the Star Rovers, and Tommy Tomorrow all made regular appearances.

However, even as classic space opera found new audiences in newspapers, theaters, television, and comic books, it was losing favor in the science fiction magazines where Campbell, now a major editor, had promoted a more mature approach to the genre. Space opera had been focused on conquering the universe; but after one achieves such a conquest, there arise new questions, such as how to govern the universe and how to make a living in the universe, and writers like Isaac Asimov and Robert A. Heinlein soon addressed these issues in stories that captivated readers not with derring-do but with thoughtful discussions and imaginative portrayals of everyday activities in the future. Further, postwar programs designed to actually send humans into orbit appeared to demand more realistic stories about space pioneers to inform and promote such initiatives, like Arthur C. Clarke's *Prelude to Space: A Compellingly Realistic Novel of Interplanetary Flight* (1951) and the film *Destination Moon* (1950), co-authored by Heinlein. Providing these important social and scientific speculations, Asimov, Heinlein, Clarke, and similar-minded authors would have recoiled at the suggestion that their works were merely space operas. Planetary romances and classic space operas still flourished in less prominent magazines of the 1940s and 1950s, most notably *Planet Stories*, and distinctive practitioners of these forms could still make an impression—like Leigh Brackett and A. E. van Vogt in the 1940s, and Alfred Bester and Cordwainer Smith in the 1950s. Yet the dominant voice of science fiction increasingly sounded practical, worldly-wise, and antithetical to space opera.

However, one type of story nurtured in this new milieu belongs to the subgenre. In settled regions of space, with worlds functioning either as independent principalities or as fiefdoms of larger empires, new sorts of adventurers could seek rewards, like a profitable bargain or an advantageous alliance, on remote planets. While physical strength might be required, these heroes would also need to be eloquent, diplomatic, and vigilant while negotiating their way through alien societies filled with shady merchants, corrupt officials, and others not to be trusted. Because tales of intrigues in imaginary European nations are called Ruritarian romances, one might call these stories "Ruritarian space opera," especially since they frequently borrow the trappings of medieval Europe for their planetary cultures (though John F. Brennan's coinage "space operetta" is a tempting alternative[14]).

While seemingly as inconsequential as the exploits of space pirates or the Star Patrol, Ruritarian space operas were distinguished by their sophisticated, ironic style and vivid descriptive detail. Of the many charming rogues soon traveling from world to world in such stories, Jack Vance's Magnus Ridolph can serve as a representative example, and the opening paragraphs from "The King of Thieves" (1949) suggest how engaging these stories might be:

6. Five Ways to Conquer the Universe 91

"There's much wealth to be found here on Moritaba," said the purser wistfully. "There's wonderful leathers, there's rare hardwoods—and have you seen the coral? It's purple-red and it glows with the fires of the damned! But—" he jerked his head toward the port—"it's too tough. Nobody cares for anything but telex—and that's what they never find. Old Kanditter, the King of Thieves, is too smart for 'em."

Magnus Ridolph ... sauntered to the port, looked out toward Moritaba.

Gollabolla, chief city of the planet, huddled between a mountain and a swamp. There were a Commonwealth Control office, a Uni-Culture Mission, a general store, a school, a number of dwellings, all built of corrugated metal on piles of native wood and connected by rickety catwalks.

Magnus Ridolph found the view picturesque in the abstract, oppressive in the immediate.

On a world where everyone carries all of their belongings around to avoid virulent thievery, Ridolph employs "near-gaseous creatures" from another planet to steal the crown from the King of Thieves, making himself King and outmaneuvering a duplicitous rival for rich profits from mining the coveted telex crystals.[15] Along with similar stories, Vance also wrote a novel entitled *Space Opera* (1965), which was actually about the experiences of an opera company traveling through space.

Another master of these stories, Poul Anderson, created two popular heroes: Nicholas van Rijn, an assertive merchant in an era of galactic expansion under the Polesotechnic League, and Ensign Dominic Flandry, who centuries later is an agent of the Terran Empire that supplanted the League.[16] Anderson also merits attention for writing the most literally medieval of all space operas, *The High Crusade* (1960), wherein alien invaders of fourteenth-century England are surprisingly defeated by Sir Roger de Tourneville's knights, who then commandeer their spaceship and soon establish a chivalrous, Christian galactic empire. Yet the most ubiquitous hero of Ruritarian space opera is Keith Laumer's indefatigable Jaime Retief of the Terran Diplomatic Corps, featured in dozens of stories and novels as he involves himself in complex disputes on various worlds. An especially Ruritarian story, "The Prince and the Pirate" (1964), takes Retief on a dinosaur hunt precisely similar to an English fox hunt before he is tossed into a dungeon.[17] While ignored by scholars and mainstream readers, these characters' adventures were cherished by many science fiction fans, who eagerly awaited each new installment of their favorite series.

While the peripatetic heroes of Ruritarian space opera were typically traders, spies, and diplomats, other professions were represented, including Vance's opera singers; Frank Belknap Long's mystery-solving botanist, John Carstairs; the handymen of Robert Sheckley's AAA Ace Interplanetary Decontamination Service; and later, Sheila Finch's Guild of Xenolinguists.[18] A noteworthy subcategory is spacefaring doctors: the master of medical science fiction was James White, whose team of physicians based on a huge space station, Sector Twelve General Hospital, treated a dizzying variety of ailing aliens at home or on expeditions to other worlds in novels and stories spanning four decades. Yet Murray Leinster wrote a similar series of Med Service stories, and a writer who was also a practicing physician, Alan E. Nourse, produced brief series of stories about Hoffman Medical Center and a future Earth dedicated to medical care, termed Hospital Earth.[19]

In the 1960s, a new generation of writers generally eschewed space opera, though they were occasionally willing to make fun of it—engendering a new form, "satirical space opera." Perhaps the earliest works of this kind are Harry Harrison's novels featuring Slippery Jim diGriz, the Stainless Steel Rat, an interstellar police officer whose missions resembled those of his Ruritarian predecessors but involved more tongue-in-cheek humor. Brian W. Aldiss especially appreciated, and quoted at length, a passage in *The Stainless Steel Rat* (1961) wherein diGriz encounters a coal-driven robot built on a backwards planet.[20] Even more openly satirical were Harrison's *Bill, the Galactic Hero* (1965) and its sequels and *Star Smashers of the Galaxy Rangers* (1973).[21] Around the same time, in Poland, Stanislaw Lem humorously critiqued western space operas in stories featuring space travelers Ijon Tichy and Pirx the Pilot.[22] After editing a collection of space opera stories, *Space Opera: An Anthology of Way-Back-When Futures* (1974), Aldiss offered his own lighthearted take on such adventures, *The Eighty-Minute Hour: A Space Opera* (1974), and a paragraph from a vignette he anthologized, Robert Sheckley's "Zirn Left Unguarded, the Jenghik Palace in Flames, Jon Westerley Dead" (1972), summarizes everything ripe for lampooning in both classic and Ruritarian space opera:

> It all began so suddenly. The reptilian forces of Megenth, long quiescent, suddenly began to expand due to the serum given them by Charles Engstrom, the power-crazed telepath.
> Jon Westerley was hastily recalled from his secret mission to Angos II. Westerley had the supreme misfortune of materializing within a ring of Black Force, due to the inadvertent treachery of Ocpetis Marn, his faithful Mnerian companion, who had, unknown to Westerley, been trapped in the Hall of Floating Mirrors, and his mind taken over by the renegade Santhis, leader of the Entropy Guild. This was the end for Westerley, and the beginning of the end for us.[23]

However, the outstanding example of satirical space opera was Douglas Adams's *The Hitchhiker's Guide to the Galaxy*, which first appeared as a radio series (1978) and led to five novels—*The Hitchhiker's Guide to the Galaxy* (1979), *The Restaurant at the End of the Universe* (1980), *Life, the Universe and Everything* (1982), *So Long, and Thanks for All the Fish* (1984), and *Mostly Harmless* (1992)—a television series (1981), and a film (2005). Adams's success demonstrated that space opera was becoming a true part of popular culture, its tropes fair game for good-natured jokes; so it is that Earth is destroyed not by malevolent design but as an inadvertent side effect of the construction of an interstellar highway, and the alien Vogons are feared not for their awesome weaponry but for their terrible poetry. The series *Red Dwarf* (1988–1993) played with space opera conventions with similar effectiveness. However, further meritorious works along these lines may be rare, as other attempts to emulate Adams's saga, like Arthur Byron Cover's novels *Planetfall* (1988) and *Stationfall* (1989), were generally dire.

Despite these sporadic satires, the most conspicuous development in space opera since the 1960s, the television series *Star Trek* (1966–1969) and its successors, traversed space in complete earnestness. To science fiction readers, the first series seemed little more than a compendium of shopworn plots from old stories, reflecting the influence of both classic space opera—in episodes like "Balance of Terror" (19660 and "The Doomsday Machine" (1967), little more than extended space battles—and Ruritarian space opera—in episodes like "Journey to Babel" (1967) and "Elayn of Troyius" (1968), featuring cloistered diplomatic intrigues. Yet *Star Trek* did contribute something new to space opera—the subject matter and sensibility of the romance novel. It was not simply that a recurring subplot in the series involved Nurse Chapel's unrequited love for Mr. Spock, nor that several episodes featured a male star falling hopelessly in love with some attractive woman; rather, it was the strong personal bond between Kirk, Spock, and McCoy that transcended the bantering, locker-room camaraderie previously characteristic of space opera (though their relationship was misinterpreted in the "slashzines" that published fan-produced stories projecting a homosexual relationship between Kirk and Spock). It is as if Smith's original plan to combine masculine scientific adventures with Garby's feminine romantic touches had finally been realized. Arguably, in fact, *Star Trek* borrowed its deep structure from the classic triangle of the romance novel, with Kirk the impetuous heroine torn between McCoy, the stolid boy next door, and Spock, the dark mysterious stranger.[24]

Whether such arguments are accepted or not, there is enough romance in *Star Trek* and its successors to warrant the label of "romantic space opera," which may have been one of the reasons why *Star Trek* became the first form of space opera to attract a significant female audience, contributing to its astounding longevity in television, films, comic books, merchandise, and the innumerable *Star Trek* novels—all qualifying as space operas—that eventually absorbed or replaced most of the run-of-the-mill space operas of previous decades. And, as if eager to attract female *Star Trek* fans ready for something new, writers after 1980 increasingly made women the protagonists of their space adventures. Anxious to show they were just as tough as their male counterparts, these women at times betrayed their softer sides in a manner reminiscent of the romantic space opera of *Star Trek*. The opening lines of

Dana Stabenow's *Second Star* epitomize this combination of bravado and tenderness:

> My full name is Esther Natasha Svensdotter but if you want to live you'll call me Star. Star is what Esther means, it was the first word I ever said, and when I'm feeling romantic, I like to say that among the stars is where I live.[25]

Others joined Star Svensdotter as the new female champions of space opera, include Melisa C. Michaels's pilot Skyrider, Chris Claremont's pilot Nicole Shea, and S. L. Viehl's physician Cherijo Grey Veil, but the major woman warrior of the era was David Weber's Honor Harrington, who in several novels re-fought the Napoleonic Wars in space with zeal and panache.[26]

In contrast to the novelty of *Star Trek*, the *Star Wars* films were less mature and innovative, straightforward transcriptions of innumerable old epics about heroic rebels opposing cruel space empires. Still, the exotic aliens, humanoid robots, and dueling starships of space opera had never looked so impressive, making the films a delight for long-time fans—pulp magazines brought to life. *Star Wars* has engendered not only several direct sequels but also a number of generally undistinguished imitations, including the films *The Black Hole* (1979), *Starcrash* (1979), and *Battle beyond the Stars* (1980), and the television series *Battlestar Galactica* (1978–1979, 2004–2009) and *Buck Rogers in the Twenty-Fifth Century* (1979–1981). Yet the stylish *Alien* (1979) and its sequels, arguably closer to horror movies than space operas, demonstrated other possibilities within the genre.

Star Wars further played a role in bringing space opera into a new medium—video games—since its space battles inspired the pioneering game Space Invaders (1978), which like the similar Galaga (1981) required players to blast unending armadas of enemy spaceships out of the sky to earn high scores. Video and computer games with more sophisticated narrative frameworks and visuals later appeared, some of them adaptations of *Star Wars* or *Star Trek* that sometimes featured the voices of actors from the franchises. A science fiction counterpart to the popular role-playing game Dungeons and Dragons was also created, appropriately named Space Opera, and it became popular as well; indeed, websites located by internet searches for "space opera" will most likely discuss that game, not the subgenre. Other visual offshoots of *Star Wars* include the space operas of Japanese anime, like the Gundam Mobile Suit series, leading to a belated but spirited American response in the animated film *Titan A.E.* (2000).

Turning to the recent literature of space opera, one finds innumerable novels based on franchised universes alongside more respected works by writers like Greg Bear, Gregory Benford, David Brin, and Larry Niven. However, during the last two decades, C. J. Cherryh and Lois McMaster Bujold have been the most noteworthy creators of traditional space opera, garnering large sales, critical approbation, and awards for series of novels set in richly elaborated future universes. Cherryh describes a region of space where Earth, the domineering Union, and the loosely structured Alliance vie for power and influence. Bujold's Miles Vorkosigan novels chronicle the adventures of a dwarfish but engaging soldier and diplomat. These authors' novels might be characterized as blends of classic, Ruritarian, and romantic space opera, with their wars in space balanced by a nuanced understanding of politics as well as persuasive attentiveness to personal relationships.[27]

If a new form of space opera is developing, it is represented by the texts occasionally called "postmodern space operas." One might tentatively characterize these works by listing some common, but not universal, features. Stories aspire to the epic scope of classic space opera but may be tempered by a hard-edged cynicism, deeper than the self-serving pragmatism of Ruritarian space opera, or even a somber pessimism about humanity's future utterly unlike the expansive hopefulness of previous space operas. Instead of populating space primarily with humans and humanoid aliens, authors embrace extreme variety in forms of intelligent life—humans, aliens, machines, or combinations thereof—crafted by evolution, technology, or bioengineering. Other heresies might include a universe where humans are not dominant, means of transportation other than starships, a rich texture of literary and cultural allusions, and an overtly serious intent juxtaposed with a lingering aura of escapist adventure. Whether these characteristics make these works truly "postmodern" as scholars define the word is problematic— here, "postmodern" may be serving primarily as a fashionable synonym for "sophisticated"—and another term to describe this embryonic form may yet emerge.

Some works arguably qualifying as postmodern space opera suggest the variety of ideas and approaches being explored. In Bruce Sterling's *Schismatrix* (1985) and *Schismatrix Plus* (1996), Mechanists seeking to transform humanity by technology struggle throughout the solar system with Shapers who wish to transform humanity through bioengineering. Michael Swanwick's *Vacuum Flowers* (1987) features rebellious spacefaring individuals, able to create and implant new personalities in themselves, battling the hive-mind that controls Earth. Dan Simmons's Hyperion series—*Hyperion* (1989), *The Fall of Hyperion* (1990), *Endymion* (1996), and *The Rise of Endymion* (1997)— envisions a vast galactic government united by a miraculous system of teleportation that must destroy this wonderful tool in order to rescue humans from the domination of artificial intelligences. Colin Greenland's Plenty trilogy—*Take Back Plenty* (1990), *Seasons of Plenty* (1995), and *Mother of Plenty* (1998)—describes the colorful exploits of a female adventurer who commandeers a vast alien spaceship and ventures into the cosmos, while John Clute's *Appleseed* (2001) offers a densely written portrait of a universe where a traveling merchant encounters artificial intelligences ("Made Minds") and, eventually, godlike aliens.

However, Iain M. Banks's Culture novels are those most frequently associated with postmodern space opera.[28] The first Culture novel, *Consider Phlebas* (1987), reads much like rousing space opera along standard lines, as a shapeshifting agent for reptilian Idirans experiences fast-paced adventures while working to retrieve a stranded artificial intelligence developed by the Culture, a seemingly utopian space empire dominated by similar sentient constructs. Yet the novel's title, taken from a stanza of T. S. Eliot's *The Waste Land* (1922) describing a corpse in a whirlpool, suggests a underlying grimness, the sense that humanity will never hold its own against superior machine intelligences, that their millennia of effort will culminate in failure, perhaps that space opera itself, founded on greater optimism about the future, faces extinction in light of these sobering realizations. As the story ends, its heroic Changer emblematically is about to die:

> The face of the man on the stretcher was white as the snow, and as blank. The features were there: eyes, nose, brows, mouth; but they seemed somehow unlinked and disconnected, giving a look of anonymity to a face lacking all character, animation and depth. It was as though all the people, all the characterisations, all the parts the man had played in his life had leaked out of him in his coma and taken their own little share of his real self with them, leaving him empty, wiped clean.[29]

Space opera has worn many faces, and novels like these, rather than culminations of a glorious tradition, might be interpreted as harbingers of the subgenre's exhaustion. Certainly, writers sometimes appear to feel that way, as indicated by the elegiac tone that creeps into not only Banks's series but also Simmons's Hyperion novels and Clute's *Appleseed*. For all the talent and creativity poured into postmodern space operas, they may as a result exude the aura of exercises, brilliantly accomplished but lacking the fervent conviction regarding humanity's manifest destiny in the cosmos that distinguished classic space opera. Yet postmodern space opera, still a relatively new form, remains capable of further evolution towards its own sort of conviction, and with readers still clamoring for traditional space operas and skillful writers pushing the boundaries of the subgenre, proclaiming the death of space opera would definitely be premature.

It may also be the case that the true future of space opera will involve writers inspired by, but outside of, the tradition of English-language science fiction. One acclaimed example is a trilogy by Chinese author Cixin Liu, *The Three-Body Problem* (2006), *The Dark Forest* (2008), and *Death's End* (2010), which after initially describing activities on Earth in response to an anticipated alien invasion from Alpha Centauri goes on to feature some stunning adventures in space, including the entrance of some space travelers into a strange "bubble" that enables them to briefly experience a four-dimensional world. While Liu was clearly influenced more by Arthur C. Clarke than by the authors more frequently associated with space opera, his epic nonetheless qualifies as a brilliant reimagining of one of the subgenre's classic themes— namely, humanity's opposition to powerful alien invaders.

Between the time space opera emerged in the early magazines and today, science fiction has associated itself with many sobering responsibilities—to guide scientists, prepare citizens for the future, analyze social problems, and emulate literary masterpieces—and works that visibly addressed such goals have received most of the attention, while seemingly inconsequential space operas, committed primarily to presenting exciting adventures for undemanding readers, have been overlooked. However, though earlier writers seeking respect disliked the label of space opera, the outstanding writers of today willingly embrace it. Perhaps science fiction is coming full circle, tacitly acknowledging the true frivolity of its portentous agendas while freshly appreciating the importance and dignity of the "pure entertainment" that space opera in all its forms provides.

Part III. The 1940s and Thereafter

7

The Tall Dark Stranger and the Boy Next Door
A. E. van Vogt and Robert A. Heinlein

Surveying the year 1939, an observer could justifiably conclude that American science fiction was doing quite well. The three major magazines from the early 1930s—*Amazing Stories, Astounding Stories,* and *Wonder Stories*—had all survived the Great Depression, though two now had modified titles (*Astounding Science-Fiction* and *Thrilling Wonder Stories*), and all three of them had new editors—respectively, Ray Palmer, John W. Campbell, Jr., and Mort Weisinger—who had undertaken in different ways to reinvigorate their publications. In addition, after a period of stagnation and false starts, new science fiction magazines were beginning to appear—*Marvel Science Fiction* (first issue: August 1938), *Startling Stories* (January 1939), *Dynamic Science Fiction* (February 1939), *Science Fiction* (March 1939), *Fantastic Adventures* (May 1939), *Famous Fantastic Mysteries* (September/October 1939), *Future Fiction* (November 1939), and *Planet Stories* (Winter, 1939)—and several others would follow in the early 1940s. By any measure, then, science fiction was more popular than it had ever been, and it had seemingly established itself as a permanent part of the magazine industry.

However, within the science fiction community, there was a growing sense that the genre was facing a crisis, as it seemed increasingly dominated by inferior, formulaic stories. Even in the letter columns of the science fiction magazines, naturally inclined to primarily print complimentary letters, signs of dissatisfaction were occasionally evident. In a 1938 letter to *Amazing Stories,* for example, science fiction fan and future physicist Milton A. Rothman archly greeted new editor Palmer by saying, "I hope that in the future you will be able to get *good* stories. By good, I am not emphasizing the thrills, heart throbs, and adventures, but the literary merits of the stories."[1] In a 1940 letter to the same magazine, Konrad Maxwell observed, "The main fault with *Amaz-*

ing Stories is the fact that few, if any, of the stories are Amazing ... nothing unusual—nothing different—nothing exceptional—NOTHING NEW. Old plots of tall heroes being accused of crimes they did not commit, or a mad nasty scientist invents a death ray and plans to rule the world."[2]

Outside of these letters columns, commentators were even blunter in their scorn for much of the science fiction appearing in magazines. In the first published book of science fiction criticism, Clyde F. Beck's *Hammer and Tongs* (1937), the author complains that the typical science fiction writer "all too often ... forgets that he is not free of men and women, that he must write of real people after all if he is to interest real people," and says that regularly featured "writers such as [Warner] Van Lorne [pseudonym of Nelson Tremaine], [Joseph W.] Skidmore, [Neil R.] Jones, and the like are continually fouling the pages of the magazines with illiterate, maudlin, or merely foolish drivel."[3] I have previously noted Wilson Tucker's attack in a 1941 fanzine on "the hacky, grinding, stinking, outworn space-ship yarn," which he named space opera, and while introducing his pioneering anthology *The Other Worlds* (1941), Phil Stong explained that he was including "no interplanetary stories, simply because in the magazines available here are not a dozen such stories with even mild originality or amusement value." He went on to condemn the "common classes" of such stories: "Scientific monsters from Mars or Sirius, attempting to conquer Earth, are frustrated" due to "a very young scientist who has made a necessary weapon just at the right moment"; the "World's first interplanetary travellers land on the moon or some planet and find the beautiful Queen Goop in desperate straits"; and "the youngest lieutenant of the Interplanetary Police has trouble with pirates." He archly summarizes these stories as a "pabulum of reiterated nonsense."[4]

In conventional histories of science fiction, this interregnum of mediocrity came to an end due to the editorial genius of John W. Campbell, Jr., who single-handedly transformed science fiction into a mature, imaginative form of literature. But this viewpoint is not entirely supported by the evidence. We know that while the September 1937 through February 1938 issues of *Astounding Stories* were ostensibly still being edited by F. Orlon Tremaine, Campbell was gradually assuming control of the magazine, and Campbell officially became its editor in March 1938, changing its name to *Astounding Science-Fiction*. By the beginning of 1939, then, he had had over a year to work his magic on the genre—but there is nothing remarkable about the early 1939 issues. The January 1939 issue, for example, does include one story by an author who became widely respected—L. Sprague de Camp's "The Incorrigible"—but the story is so weak that it has only been republished once, in Sam Moskowitz's *Futures to Infinity* (1970), an anthology specifically devoted to presenting stories by major authors which had never been republished. Of the other undistinguished stories in that issue, only two have been republished—Malcolm Jameson's "Mill of the Gods" (which appeared in a 2013 small-press collection of Jameson's stories) and the second installment of Manly Wade Wellman's "Nuisance Value" (a serial that was revised and republished as the novel *The Dark Destroyers* [1959]). One does not need to comment on the low quality of Campbell's other offerings in that issue: the notorious Warner Van Lorne's "The Blue-Men of Yrano"—described in one letter to *Astounding* as "Undoubtedly the worst story ever written"[5]—Norman L. Knight's "Saurian Valedictory," Vic Phillips's "Maiden Voyage," and Arthur J. Burks's "'The First Shall Be Last.'" Clearly, no one at the time would have scrutinized the contents of this issue and concluded that Campbell had launched "the Golden Age of Science Fiction."

In defense of Campbell, one might say that it can take a considerable amount of time to develop talented writers, and he cannot be denied credit for his major success story, Isaac Asimov—a young writer living in New York City whose first stories, published in 1939, had been uniformly unimpressive. But Campbell sensed that he had great potential and had numerous personal conversations with him, offering advice and ideas; and deeply influenced by what he heard, Asimov gradually matured during the 1940s into a major science fiction writer. But Campbell had little to do with the success of two other writers he first published in 1939 who had a more immediate impact on the field: A. E. van Vogt and Robert A. Heinlein. They were initially attracted to him not because of any appreciation of his editorial acumen, but because his magazine was paying the highest rates, making his *Astounding Science-Fiction* (and later, its companion magazine *Unknown*) the most desirable venues for professional authors of science fiction. Further, though he occasionally mandated revisions, Campbell contributed only minimally to the output of these uniquely skillful writers, who truly inaugurated the Golden Age of Science Fiction when they began publishing for Campbell in 1939 and quickly established themselves as regular contributors to his magazines and others. Their early works illustrated two, significantly different ways for science fiction to get out of its rut and improve—one generally rejected, the other almost universally embraced—and to discern their disparate approaches to the genre, all one has to do is examine the first stories that they published in *Astounding Science-Fiction*.

Based on a summary of its plot, van Vogt's "Black Destroyer" (1939) sounds precisely like the sort of story that so many science fiction readers were denouncing at the time: space explorers land on an alien planet and encounter a horrible monster, which kills several members of their crew before they are finally able to defeat it. But "Black Destroyer" differed from its precursors in some significant respects, identifying van Vogt as a writer with a new and distinctive approach to science fiction.

First, it was obvious from the start that van Vogt was a more talented writer than most of the other contributors to the science fiction magazines of the 1930s. His evocative first paragraph instantly grabs a reader's attention, arousing curiosity about who or what Coeurl is, where he is, and why he is prowling:

> On and on Coeurl prowled! The black, moonless, almost starless night yielded reluctantly before a grim reddish dawn that crept up from his left. A vague, dull light, it was, that gave no sense of approaching warmth, no comfort, nothing but a cold, diffuse lightness, slowly revealing a nightmare landscape.[6]

Van Vogt later reported that, in his first letter to the author, Campbell had advised him to emphasize "atmosphere,"[7] and the story he immediately submitted in response, "Vault of the Beast," had a similarly "atmospheric" introductory passage—though Campbell waited until 1940 to publish it.[8] As "Black Destroyer" progresses, there are a series of other well-crafted dramatic moments, and van Vogt also reveals the ability to write convincing dialogue, a skill that many science fiction writers then lacked. Further, van Vogt skillfully keeps shifting the story's point of view, smoothly alternating between the monster's perspective and that of the humans struggling to understand, and later to defeat, the formidable alien they have discovered.

Second, Coeurl is nothing like the stereotypical "bug-eyed monsters" of 1930s science fiction. He is an extremely intelligent member of a once-civilized species, though his civilization was struck long ago by an unspecified "catastrophe" that caused "a sudden vanishing of morals, a reversion to almost bestial criminality, unleavened by any sense of ideal, a callous indifference to death" (47). As readers gain access to his thoughts, they realize that he represents a tremendous threat to Earth, but they can also, to some extent, sympathize with his desperate quest to survive in the only way he can—by killing other beings and sucking all of the phosphorus out of their bodies; as a letter from Lew Cunningham commented, "Van Vogt succeeded in arousing sympathy for both Coeurl and his human enemies."[9] They can admire Coeurl's ingenuity as well, since he cleverly contrives to conceal his responsibility for the first murders and later manages, within the humans' engine room, to construct his own spaceship, which could enable him to recruit others of his race and embark on a campaign to attack and kill more humans.

Van Vogt further demonstrated from the start that he could fill his stories with interesting ideas. Coeurl breathes both oxygen and chlorine, and the tentacles on his cat-like body can monitor and manipulate any sort of "vibration," so he can penetrate even the hardest metal by "us[ing] his special powers to interfere with the electronic tensions holding the metal together" (57). The human space explorers wear transparent suits and wield weapons made of "metalite" (39), presumably a substance as strong as metal that is also lightweight; they scan the monster using a device called a "telefluor" (54); and they employ "atomic energy" to power "nonwheel machine[s]" (43). But van Vogt also presented ideas from fields other than science. The most talkative character—Korita, a "tall Japanese archaeologist" (46)—lectures about several earlier human cultures to explain how a creature like Coeurl, both intelligent and savage, might have emerged. (In "On 'Black Destroyer,'" van Vogt says that these passages were strongly influenced by his recently reading Oswald Spengler's *Decline of the West* [1918] [179]). Coeurl is ultimately defeated because he is a "primitive," and once "out in space, completely outside of his natural habitat" (62), the humans can outwit him, due to the fact that his culture, in a solar system that completely lacked any other planets or moons, never had an incentive to develop space travel and thus never learned about the "anti-acceleration" (61) that all advanced species must master to travel through interstellar space.

Overall, "Black Destroyer" certainly qualifies as both an exciting and intriguing adventure, and both Campbell and his readers immediately heralded van Vogt as a major new talent. Promoting his July 1939 issue in the June issue's "In Times to Come," he announced, "Next month, *Astounding* introduces a new author, and one of unusual promise. We rather suspect the name of van Vogt will be among those of top favorites a year or so from now."[10]

In the July issue, the blurb on the table of contents page for "Black Destroyer" proclaimed, "A new author presents a story of unusual power."[11] Campbell also celebrated "Black Destroyer" by making it the issue's cover story, a rare honor also given to van Vogt's second published story in the magazine, "Discord in Scarlet" (December 1939).

Readers seemed equally enthusiastic about van Vogt: in the September 1939 issue, Robert Jackson said that "A. E. van Vogt makes a truly remarkable entry to the science-fiction field with 'Black Destroyer'"[12]; Cunningham described it as "a masterpiece similar to [Campbell's] 'Who Goes There?' but even better written" (97); Ted Crane commented, "The tentacles are a bit unreal, otherwise a great story: it needs a sequel"[13]; and Thomas S. Gardner similarly opined that "a sequel would be appreciated."[14] In the October 1939 issue, Stanley Wells's letter identified "Black Destroyer" as his favorite story in the July issue,[15] while D. P. Bellaire said, "This yarn, written from a new angle[,] was most refreshing as a change of pace from the cut-and-dried run of alien menace yarns."[16] And in the November 1939 issue, the future critic of "space operas," Wilson Tucker (writing as Bob Tucker), contributed a letter announcing that "'Black Destroyer' is, probably, your best 1939 yarn."[17]

"Black Destroyer" largely established the course of the first decade of van Vogt's career. He would continue to write stories about strange, menacing monsters, like "Discord in Scarlet," "The Sea Thing" (1940), and "The Gryb" (1940), and there were enough of them to allow him to later publish a collection of his stories simply entitled *Monsters* (1965). But he became better known for creating various sorts of supermen with amazing abilities, as exemplified by his two most famous novels, *Slan* (1940, 1946) and *The World of Null-A* (1945, 1948). Throughout the 1940s, Campbell remained happy to publish, and praise, van Vogt's works, and he unquestionably became one of the field's most popular writers: in his "Introduction" to *Monsters*, Forrest J Ackerman notes that when science fiction fan Gerry de la Ree conducted a survey of other fans in 1947, van Vogt was voted their favorite writer.[18]

Yet not all readers were enthralled by van Vogt: as one early sign of displeasure, Wilbur J. Widmer's letter in the December 1939 issue ranked "Black Destroyer" as the only the fifth best of the seven stories in the July issue.[19] More prominently, longtime fan and future writer and editor Damon Knight reported in an influential 1945 essay, "The World of van Vogt," that "I have been progressively annoyed by van Vogt even since *Slan*," though he devotes most of his time to a detailed and devastating critique of *The World of Null-A*.[20] The reasons for uneasiness about van Vogt, which became increasingly evident in his prolific contributions to *Astounding* and other magazines, can already be observed in "Black Destroyer," and these readily explain why van Vogt's approach, and van Vogt himself, were eventually marginalized as science fiction moved into the postwar period.

One issue has already been addressed in the previous discussion of *Slan*: as Knight archly notes, "His plots do not bear examination" (60). Endeavoring to account for Coeurl's peculiar combination of intelligent and savagery, Korita can only say that "as if in one leap" his culture must have "spanned the centuries and entered the period of contending states," even while acknowledging that "there is no record of a culture entering abruptly into the period of contending states" (47). Given their advanced civilization, Coeurl's cohorts could surely have devised some better solution to their plight than having everybody become homicidal predators; even the bleakest portrayals of humanity after a global nuclear war never envision such an occurrence. Certainly, the chemical composition of a creature that breathes oxygen and chlorine and subsists on phosphorus is difficult to imagine, to say the least, and it is hard to see how Coeurl's miraculous ability to control vibrations would allow him to absorb all of the phosphorus in a human body. Van Vogt says not a word about how "anti-acceleration" works; when E. E. "Doc" Smith's Lensman novels introduced an equally dubious way to travel faster than light, dubbed the "inertialess drive," he at least tried to provide a scientific justification for the concept. Other seemingly scientific terms, like those listed above, are never really explained. If Coeurl had the power to effectively dissolve all matter by weakening their "electronic tensions," one has to wonder why he didn't immediately kill all of the humans in his vicinity and thus simplify the task of taking over their spaceship. One wearies of coming up with yet another weakness in the logic of a typical van Vogt story.

7. The Tall Dark Stranger and the Boy Next Door

The broader problem was that, despite the superficial novelties, van Vogt was not really offering readers anything new. The typical space operas of the 1930 had been about extraordinary people—stalwart heroes with amazing powers or weapons—dealing with extraordinary circumstances—such as first visits to another planet, superhumans struggling to dominate their societies, astounding discoveries in space, alien invasions of Earth—and "Black Destroyer" and later van Vogt stories perfectly match that description. As noted, stories of this sort were definitely appealing to certain sorts of readers: bright young nerds who longed for a future world that would acknowledge and reward their inherent superiority. But this would not be an effective way to appeal to a wider audience of people who did not dream about single-handedly conquering the universe as a way to validate their sadly unrecognized merit. Instead, to attract more readers, science fiction would also need to offer stories about the future involving ordinary people in ordinary circumstances; and one month after "Black Destroyer" appeared, Campbell's *Astounding* would introduce another writer, Robert A. Heinlein, who was ready and able to produce precisely those sorts of stories.

Like "Black Destroyer," Heinlein's "Life-Line" (1939) has a plot that was already familiar to science fiction readers: a solitary inventor comes up with an amazing device, refuses to reveal how it works, and ultimately dies, so that all knowledge of his breakthrough is forever lost. This was the sort of story that was common in the early magazines of Hugo Gernsback—indeed, the first name of protagonist Hugo Pinero may have been intended to pay tribute to Gernsback—and while overshadowed by the space adventures that dominated the 1930s, such stories long remained commonplace—recall Konrad Maxwell's complaint about iterative stories featuring a "mad nasty scientist." But like van Vogt, Heinlein clearly had something new to offer as well.

For one thing, in contrast to stereotypical concepts like the "death ray" mentioned by Maxwell, Pinero's invention is genuinely innovative and interesting, and it indeed conveys an almost unique perspective on time travel that I thought was unusually insightful. Building on Albert Einstein's notion that time is the fourth dimension, the story posits that people are in fact four-dimensional beings, with bodies that extend through time as well as space; as Pinero explains to a reporter,

> You are a space-time event having duration four ways. You are not quite six feet tall, you are about twenty inches wide and perhaps ten inches thick. In time, there stretches behind you more of this space-time event, reaching to, perhaps, 1905, of which we see a cross-section here at right angles to the time axis, and as thick as the present. At the far end is a baby, smelling of sour milk and drooling its breakfast on its bib. At the other end lies, perhaps, an old man some place in the 1980s. Imagine this space-time event … as a long pink worm, continuous through the years. It stretches past us here in 1939, and the cross section we see here appears as a single,

discreet body. But that is illusion. There is physical continuity to this pink worm, enduring through the years.²¹

Applying an instrument to any human body, Pinero can determine when there is a future break in this "pink worm" and thus accurately predict a person's date of death. As it happens, I was long ago persuaded by the logic behind this characterization and hence have been unwilling to embrace the conventional notion of time travel—which would by Pinero's description involve slicing one piece of a four-dimensional body, transporting it to another time, and expecting it to survive. Of course, Heinlein himself later produced several stories about the usual sort of time travel without considering the critique presented in "Life-Line." This is also, I believe, the only Heinlein story that supports John Calvin's notion of predestination, since the people Pinero examines have no ability to alter the time of death that he determines, and that must be the basis for the later assertions of George Slusser and Leon Stover that Heinlein was a Calvinist, even though both Heinlein himself and other scholars have disputed the claim.²²

But the way that Pinero uses his invention commands more attention. He is not a megalomaniac intent upon conquering the world, a recurring trope in early science fiction, or a professor at a university idly investigating future possibilities, as is the case in Edmond Hamilton's "The Man Who Evolved" (1931) and other stories. Rather, he wants to earn a living, so he sets up a business to attract paying customers who want to know precisely when they are going to die, promoting his service with advertisements and media appearances. This practical man also has to deal with a very practical problem: insurance companies which go to court to stop what he is doing, arguing that his machine is damaging the profitability of their businesses. The story thus reveals that, in contrast to the moonlighting scientists and professional pulp writers who then constituted his main competitors, Heinlein was a man who had extensive experience in the real world—as a former engineer in the United States Navy, real estate agent, and aspiring politician—and he thus could intelligently explore how an imagined invention like Pinero's might impact the real world.

To be sure, in one key respect Heinlein followed the conventions of science fiction, instead of acknowledging the realities of contemporary life, by having Pinero demand that scientists accept the effectiveness of his invention without disclosing how it works—on the stated grounds that he should not "turn over the fruits of my work for children to play with"; rather, he wishes to "keep" this "dangerous knowledge ... for the man who understands it, myself" (69). An actual inventor would have applied for a patent, thoroughly explaining the science behind the device in writing while also securing its exclusive use for a period of time, enabling him to profit from his break-

7. The Tall Dark Stranger and the Boy Next Door

through and preventing others from misusing the invention—and, not incidentally, providing the insurance companies with no incentive to murder him in order to eliminate the threat that his innovation represents, which is the way that Heinlein's story ends. It thus seems that Heinlein did not wish to fully explore, in the science-fictional manner later espoused by Campbell (and largely influenced by Heinlein), the nature of a future society in which citizens could routinely determine the dates of their deaths and live their lives with that knowledge. (However, a Heinlein story published a year after "Life-Line," "'Let There Be Light'" [1940], again features inventors—of panels that instantly converts sunlight into electricity—and while they do not obtain a patent, they do release their process to the public, charging a royalty, so that their invention, like all beneficial inventions in the real world, becomes a permanent part of human society. Since it appeared in another magazine, Campbell probably rejected the story for some reason.)

Heinlein employs other techniques to firmly place his story within the reader's everyday world. At one point, the story advances by means of a series of excerpts from popular media: two paragraphs from a newspaper story, an advertisement, a "Legal Notice" (75), and a radio announcement. In a touching vignette, Pinero meets with two clients—a young couple expecting a child—but declines to predict the time of their deaths, stating that his equipment is not functioning properly. He has actually determined that they will both be killed in an accident shortly after they leave his office, and though he strives to persuade them to remain in his office indefinitely, he cannot prevent their deaths. The contrast between this subdued moment of drama, and the thrilling exploits of heroic space adventurers, could not be clearer. This couple arguably represents the first appearance of the characters who would later be featured in some of Heinlein's stories for the "slick" magazines, such as "Space Jockey" (1947) and "'It's Great to Be Back!'" (1947)—typical married people with full-time jobs, simply trying to earn a living in the future.

One can certainly say that, in contrast to "Black Destroyer," "Life-Line" is a dull and slow-moving story; Heinlein even declines to describe the climactic murder of Pinero, ending with a scene of Pinero, after finishing his last meal, greeting the visitors who have come to kill him. And based on the evidence of what they wrote in *Astounding*, neither Campbell nor his readers initially thought of Heinlein as an especially talented writer. Campbell did not promote the appearance of "Life-Line" in the "In Times to Come" column of the preceding issue of *Astounding*, as he similarly declined to promote the third Heinlein story he published, "Requiem" (1940); and his language previewing his second Heinlein story, "Misfit" (1939), is decidedly neutral: "Robert Heinlein, who won a second place in the Laboratory with his first story. has another short, 'Misfit.'"[23] The blurbs in the August 1939 issue describing "Life-Line"—both on the table of contents page and the first page of the story—say nothing about the quality of the story, solely emphasizing that the story's idea is "startlingly plausible," which oddly represents the way that Hugo Gernsback would have defended some of the lamentable stories that he published.[24] The second Heinlein story published in *Astounding*, "Misfit" (1939), was even less popular—it finished fourth in Campbell's reader survey, the "Analytical Laboratory"—and it attracted criticism for presenting a character who can mentally perform extended mathematical calculations.[25]

Still, even though it was not voted the most popular story in the August issue, and even though it attracted less attention, "Life-Line" was praised by a few readers: a letter from Gardner echoed Campbell in stating that its concept was "Very plausible,"[26] and D. L. Dobbs commented that "'Life-Line' was as good, if not better than 'Heavy Planet' [1939, by Milton A. Rothman writing as Lee Gregor]. How about more of these?"[27] There is also this remarkable analysis from Samuel D. Russell:

> I can think of nothing to criticize in this excellent little tale, and there are several episodes of unforgettable drama, such as the death of the young couple. Pinero's character is superbly delineated, and toward the end he takes on a truly great and tragic stature. The attitudes of the scientists and insurance companies are true to life and realistically presented. My only wish is that the story had been expanded and developed to novel length.[28]

Note that Russell, unlike Campbell, says nothing about the story's premise, rather praising its qualities as a narrative, and he stresses that aspects of the story are "true to life and realistically presented." This is something that no one could ever say about a story by van Vogt.

Perhaps the most illuminating comment came from Gardner, who added that "Life-Line" was "better on the second reading." Heinlein's stories, in other words, bear examination. In retrospect readers can discern that there is some genuine substance in "Life-Line," as the story thoroughly develops an interesting scientific idea and explores how it might be introduced into a world like our own. Van Vogt, in "Black Destroyer" and other stories, is offering a boy's daydream about exciting but implausible adventures, like many other science fiction writers of the day, but Heinlein is bringing an adult perspective to the topics he addresses.

Heinlein's approach would be on display in the second and third stories that he published in Campbell's magazine. In "Misfit," a troubled young man goes into space not to battle with alien invaders or space pirates, but to participate in a construction project to transform an asteroid into a space station; and in "Requiem" (1940), another space journey is undertaken by an elderly man, whose efforts had brought about space travel, and who now longs to have the experience of walking on the Moon before he dies. Yet as was not the case with van Vogt, it evidently took Campbell a while to recognize that

Heinlein was something special, since he only began to praise him after receiving his novel, "'If This Goes On—'" (1940). But Campbell made up for lost time with his enthusiastic endorsement of Heinlein in the January 1940 issue's "In Times to Come," stating, "'If This Goes' is one of the strongest novels I have seen in science-fiction, one of the most beautifully written and carefully detailed pieces of science-fiction.... It's fiction, and it's prophecy. And it is so thoroughly different in strength and presentation from any predecessor that it wins *Astounding*'s rare Nova designation."[29]

As a result of these stories and others, Heinlein rapidly became the field's most admired writer, and one only has to look at the Guests of Honor at the first three World Science Fiction Conventions (or Worldcons) to see that a changing of the guards was in the works. The first Guest of Honor in 1939 was Gernsback's former artist Frank R. Paul, who had illustrated so many stories of the 1920s and 1930s; the second Guest of Honor in 1940 was E. E. "Doc" Smith, the man who effectively created and popularized the genre of space opera that dominated the 1930s. But Heinlein, only two years after he had started publishing science fiction, was the third Guest of Honor in 1941; van Vogt (along with his author wife, E. Mayne Hull) did not receive the same honor until the next Worldcon in 1946.

More to the point, if one examines the works of the other major science fiction writers who emerged in the 1940s—such as Asimov, Leigh Brackett, Ray Bradbury, Arthur C. Clarke, Hal Clement, and Theodore Sturgeon—it is evident that they were all, in their own distinctive ways, adopting the approach of Heinlein, not van Vogt. They were not writing stories about horrific monsters and heroic superhumans involved in exciting melodramatic adventures; rather, they also foregrounded ordinary people dealing with new inventions or strange alien environments as part of their everyday life. Unlike the feverish dreams of van Vogt, their stories seemed mature, reasonable, and realistic, and they pointed the way to the sort of science fiction that would garner wider popularity in the 1950s in science fiction magazines and books, if not films, television programs, and comic books, which continued to favor the more juvenile patterns that dominated the 1930s. If the differences between van Vogt and Heinlein are conceived of as an argument about science fiction, in other words, Heinlein had obviously emerged as the victor.

As suggested by this chapter's title, science fiction writers and readers of the 1940s effectively faced a choice that was comparable to the classic dilemma of the heroines of romance novels: should they embrace the tall dark stranger, or settle down with the boy next door? Van Vogt's stories offered thrills, mystery, and intrigue; they took readers to exotic places where they could experience stimulating adventures that defied conventional assumptions and values. Yet he was also an author who could not be trusted to deliver logical visions of future worlds and possibilities in the manner that science fiction had always promised. Heinlein's stories could seem prosaic and humdrum, as they domesticated the unknown and explained its probable effects on ordinary people. But Heinlein's speculations had a solidity and substance that made them, as Gardner noted, worth rereading, and worth remembering; he was an author, in other words, that science fiction readers could rely upon, even if his stories were not always glamorous or exciting.

Indeed, like the tortoise who raced against the hare—another analogy that might be advanced to describe these authors—Heinlein's slow and steady approach became the basis for a long and consistently memorable career: even as he sought other markets in the 1940s and 1950s, Heinlein continued to contribute occasional stories to the science fiction magazines, and despite some conspicuous lapses, the novels he wrote in the 1960s and thereafter, until his death in 1988, all received, and merited, the attention of the science fiction community, and sometimes achieved the status of best-sellers, though they were sometimes criticized as bloated and overly opinionated.

However, while van Vogt remained active throughout the 1940s, he seemed to be running out of energy, and he entirely abandoned writing science fiction in the 1950s to focus on working for L. Ron Hubbard's Dianetics and recycling previous published stories by combining them into makeshift novels that he termed "fix-ups," such as *The War against the Rull* (1959) and *The Beast* (1963), while never informing readers that the books consisted entirely of minimally revised older stories. When he returned to writing new material in the 1960s, he was a shadow of his former self, never producing any works that matched his earlier achievements, and his later sequel to *The World of Null-A* and *The Players of Null-A* (1956), *Null-A Three* (1985), was particularly scorned, condemned for example by Brian W. Aldiss and David Wingrove as "nonsense" characterized by "its essential incoherence."[30]

Further, while one can detect the influence of van Vogt in science fiction writers like Philip K. Dick and Charles L. Harness, Heinlein has manifestly had a far greater effect on the field; to this day all bookstores continue to offer several Heinlein books, while van Vogt's books appear only occasionally, and they will also be displaying many new science fiction novels that are clearly indebted to Heinlein. Like any reasonable woman facing this sort of quandary, then, science fiction chose the boy next door, Robert A. Heinlein, over the dark mysterious stranger, A. E. van Vogt, and the genre has clearly benefited from that decision.

8

The Three Golden Ages of Science Fiction

When invited to deliver a lecture to a German science fiction class on "the Golden Age of science fiction," I immediately knew what I was supposed to describe; for to members of the science fiction community, the phrase refers to the science fiction of the 1940s, and more specifically, the science fiction published during that decade by editor John W. Campbell, Jr., in his magazine *Astounding Science-Fiction* (and, to a lesser extent, its sister magazine *Unknown* or *Unknown Worlds* more devoted to fantasy). Certainly, there are many good reasons to regard these works, and their successors in the 1950s, as particularly significant and admirable, justifying the decision of most science fiction historians to make them their focus of attention. But other bodies of science fiction texts in the 1940s and 1950s, often neglected by historians, are arguably just as significant, even if their literary qualities are not quite as admirable; and, as a scholar who frequently defies conventional attitudes, I would also like to draw attention to these contemporaneous works that were outside, sometimes far outside, of the Campbell tradition.

However, before discussing "the Golden Ages" that I was not expected to discuss, I should talk about the "Golden Age" that I was expected to discuss. The standard story of this era begins with Campbell, who assumed control of the magazine *Astounding Stories* sometime in 1937 or 1938.[1] As a writer, Campbell had initially specialized in expansive space adventures, but by the time he became an editor, he was better known for the more variegated and sophisticated stories he was writing using what was widely known to be his pseudonym, Don A. Stuart, such as his evocative vision of a future humanity that has grown decadent, "Twilight" (1934), and the unusual mystery of a shapeshifting alien found in Antarctica, "Who Goes There?" (1938), which inspired three films entitled *The Thing* (1951, 1982, 2011). As a result, he had a reputation for seeking to innovate that might attract writers seeking to move beyond the formulaic space epics then featured in science fiction magazines. Thus, Clifford D. Simak, who had previously abandoned science fiction, began writing again when he learned that Campbell was editing *Astounding*, telling his wife, "I can write for Campbell.... He won't be satisfied with the kind of stuff that is being written. He'll want something new."[2]

For those unfamiliar with his reputation, Campbell announced in early editorials that he wanted new types of stories; he labeled exemplary departures from convention as "Nova" stories; and he published a special "Mutant" issue devoted to purportedly innovative works. Yet it was more happenstance than design that soon brought him, in 1939, precisely the sort of contributor that he craved in the form of Robert A. Heinlein, who sent Campbell his first story only because, he reported, another magazine had launched a contest for new writers and Heinlein shrewdly thought that he would face less competition from other neophytes if he submitted his work someplace else. Heinlein's stories would stand out for several reasons: as a man in his thirties who had worked as a United States Navy engineer, real estate agent, and aspiring politician, Heinlein could bring a knowing attitude and real-world experience to his stories, unlike the science-obsessed nerds and professional pulp writers then dominating the genre; he hit upon the idea of developing a common background for many of his stories, as displayed in his famous and often-reprinted "Future History" chart, which conveyed his unique concern for careful extrapolation and the maintenance of consistency in creating science fiction worlds; he mastered the art of conveying this background information by means of casual comments and indirect references, in contrast to the didactic "infodumps" that often slowed the pace of other science fiction stories; and perhaps most significantly, he resisted all of the common patterns of pulp storytelling, instead offering readers a variety of characters, settings, and adventures that grew from many stimulating ideas.

One of Heinlein's early masterpieces, "The Roads Must Roll" (1940), employed the background of massive, moving highways to describe an administrator who uses canny psychology to thwart a workers' strike, but even more dazzling was "By His Bootstraps" (1942), a *tour de force* in which every character is the same person at different times in his life, brought together by journeys through time; and this hero's evolution from bewildered newcomer to the future's dictatorial ruler, as H. Bruce Franklin explains, represents a fascinating critique of the notion of the "self-made man."[3] (As a variation on this theme, his later story "'All You Zombies—'" [1958] involved a similar time traveler who, by changing his gender, not only interacts with himself, but has sex with himself and gives birth to himself.) Other Heinlein stories raised provocative questions about our perceptions of reality, like "Universe" (1940), wherein a man learns that his purportedly complete world is actually a generation starship; "They" (1941), in which a man correctly deduces that the world he lives in is an illusion created to deceive him; and

"The Unpleasant Profession of Jonathan Hoag" (1942), about a man who discovers that as part of his true job, a critic of worlds, he has been assigned to evaluate the Earth, constructed as a work of art.

While he became Campbell's most popular and influential contributor, Heinlein was hardly the only major writer who first appeared, or matured, in his magazines. A young Isaac Asimov, patiently nurtured by Campbell, developed his Three Laws of Robotics in the stories published in *Astounding Science-Fiction* later collected as *I, Robot* (1950); used one of Campbell's ideas to offer a striking picture of a world where nighttime only came once every thousand years in "Nightfall" (1941); and garnered praise for a series of stories and novelettes about the impending collapse and planned revival of a future Galactic Empire, later assembled as his Foundation Trilogy (*Foundation* [1951]; *Foundation and Empire* [1952]; *Second Foundation* (1953)), which emphasized sociological speculation as much as technological speculation. Simak developed his signature style of pastoral science fiction in a series of stories assembled as *City* (1952), describing how future humans gradually surrender control of the Earth to the intelligent animals they created; the most famous of these stories, "Huddling Place" (1944), features a man who is so paralyzed by agoraphobia that he cannot bring himself to leave his home to assist a close friend, a Martian philosopher whose life can only be saved by his surgical skills. Another writer, Theodore Sturgeon, offered his own sort of sensitive, character-driven science fiction in notable stories like "Microcosmic God" (1941), involving a scientist who creates a race of miniature beings who worship him as their god, and "Thunder and Roses" (1947), wherein a compassionate man saves the human race by refusing to retaliate after a nuclear attack.

The oddest writer in Campbell's stable, A. E. van Vogt, briefly rivaled Heinlein in popularity with dazzling, fast-moving adventures like *Slan* (1940, 1946) and *The World of Null-A* (1945, 1948) which, following a pattern van Vogt had learned from a how-to-write book, strived to introduce a brand new idea every 800 words. Some of his stories for Campbell are still remembered today, like "Black Destroyer" (1939), one of many precursors to the film *Alien* (1979) in describing a vicious monster who menaces the crew of a spaceship, and "The Weapon Shop" (1942), about a future world wherein the sale of weapons becomes a tool against tyranny. Yet closely examined, van Vogt's frenetic improvisations were basically nonsensical, as first noted in a scathing review by Damon Knight in 1945, and he soon faded from prominence, his helter-skelter approach eclipsed by the superior methodology of Heinlein. Still, a later writer would figure out how to offer readers van Vogt's sort of strange, unsettling ideas in a somewhat more controlled manner, eventually earning recognition as one of science fiction's greatest writers; his name was Philip K. Dick. As one sign that Campbell's writers indeed represented the best that the decade had to offer, when the Science Fiction Writers of America voted on the best science fiction stories of all time to include in the anthology *The Science Fiction Hall of Fame, Volume I* (1970), nine of their ten stories from the 1940s had first appeared in Campbell's *Astounding* (and I have mentioned five of them).

A conventional history of science fiction, then, after focusing almost exclusively on the Campbell writers of the 1940s, would proceed to discuss the 1950s as the era when these writers fully matured and blossomed, escaping from Campbell's increasingly idiosyncratic control to write for other magazines, as well as lucrative new markets like hardcover and paperback books, juvenile fiction, and films and television programs. During that decade, veterans of Campbell's magazines produced some of their best works, like Heinlein's *Have Space Suit—Will Travel* (1958), Asimov's *The Caves of Steel* (1954), Simak's *Ring Around the Sun* (1954), and Sturgeon's *More Than Human* (1953). These were joined by memorable texts from other noteworthy authors, like Dick, Alfred Bester, Ray Bradbury, Arthur C. Clarke, and Cordwainer Smith, who in their own distinctive fashions continued to fulfill Campbell's agenda with unique and innovative works of science fiction even though they had only infrequently contributed to Campbell's magazines.

Unfortunately, by this time Campbell himself had largely abandoned his original enthusiasm for groundbreaking science fiction to instead prefer stories that promoted his own, peculiar scientific and political beliefs, most notably the predicted emergence of psychic powers as society's dominant force, and it was left to other editors to further expand the boundaries of science fiction. In magazines, H. L. Gold's *Galaxy* (1950–1980) focused on a satirical approach, while Anthony Boucher and J. Francis McComas's *The Magazine of Fantasy and Science Fiction* (1949-) emphasized literary quality. In the field of books, small presses like Martin Greenberg and David Kyle's Gnome Press led the way in republishing the science fiction classics of earlier eras and some new material, to be succeeded by larger publishers like Donald A. Wollheim, whose Ace Books would provide the first paperback editions of many esteemed science fiction novels, and Ian and Betty Ballantine's Ballantine Books, which among other works first published Clarke's thought-provoking *Childhood's End* (1953).

However, anyone researching science fiction can find many detailed histories of science fiction in the 1940s and 1950s which will emphasize Campbell's writers and Campbell's influence, rendering further discussion of them superfluous. Furthermore, I believe that such conventional chronicles of science fiction history are unfairly neglecting other traditions of this era which are just as important, and which might be cited to make an entirely different argument about why the 1940s should be considered science fiction's Golden Age.

8. The Three Golden Ages of Science Fiction 115

In standard histories, the type of science fiction that Campbell purportedly replaced was the routine, melodramatic adventures set in outer space or on other planets that were sarcastically christened by Wilson Tucker in 1941 as "space opera," or "the hacky, grinding, stinking, outworn space-ship yarn."[4] As an aside, one should note that Campbell did not entirely abandon such stories, since he continued *Astounding*'s policy of publishing the Lensman novels of E. E. "Doc" Smith, generally regarded as the progenitor of the form, and other works offering more subdued narratives about space travel with heavy doses of science, like the stories about communication in space by George O. Smith later collected as *Venus Equilateral* (1947, 1976) and the stories about antimatter, or "Seetee," by Jack Williamson that were later the basis of the novels *Seetee Ship* (1951) and *Seetee Shock* (1950). But even if Campbell was generally declining to publish the sorts of exciting space stories that previous editors had preferred, they did not vanish from sight in the 1940s. In fact, they were readily available in a magazine launched in 1939 that was expressly devoted to space opera, *Planet Stories*.

Though it was a successful magazine that lasted for sixteen years, students will be hard-pressed to find much information about *Planet Stories* in most histories of science fiction. If it is mentioned at all, it is solely because the magazine published a number of stories by two excellent writers, Leigh Brackett and Bradbury, whose not particularly scientific works were ill-suited for Campbell's *Astounding Science-Fiction*. And one should indeed celebrate a magazine for publishing Brackett's haunting planetary romances, like "Thralls of the Endless Night" (1943), wherein descendants of a spaceship crew and the pirates who attacked them unknowingly carry on their ancient feud on a barren planet, or "The Jewel of Bas" (1944), featuring a pair of thieves captured by a bored immortal and his robot. Bradbury's contributions to the magazine include "Mars Is Heaven" (1948), a tale of explorers on Mars who incongruously encounter old friends and relatives, later incorporated into *The Martian Chronicles* (1951), and "Frost and Fire" (1946), a stunning tale of mutated humans on another world who only live for eight days, bizarrely retitled "The Creatures That Time Forgot" for its appearance in *Planet Stories*.

But everyone acknowledges that such polished, original creations did not represent the usual contents of the magazine; for a picture of what its readers were typically getting, one might more fruitfully examine the contents of one randomly chosen issue, Fall 1942 (available at archive.org):

"War-Gods of the Void" by Henry Kuttner
"Space Oasis" by Raymond Z. Gallun
"Vampire Queen" by John Russell Fearn
"Stellar Showboat" by Malcolm Jameson

"City of the Living Flame" by Henry Hasse
"Quest of Thig" by Basil Wells
"The Thought-Men of Mercury" by R. R. Winterbotham
"Prison Planet" by Wilson Tucker

To be sure, three authors appearing in this issue—Kuttner, Gallun, and Tucker—have been praised for other works, though not for these stories, and the example of Bradbury illustrates that one cannot always judge a pulp magazine story by its title. Still, it seems evident that *Planet Stories* will not offer contemporary readers a treasure trove of undiscovered science fiction classics, but rather a mostly dreary series of outlandish, juvenile adventures.

Even worse, from the standpoint of literary connoisseurs, the magazine quickly spawned a sister publication, *Planet Comics* (1940–1953), which offered younger readers comic book space adventures that were even more outlandish and even more juvenile. Its standout series, The Lost World, chronicled the endless efforts of heroic Hunt Bowman and his comrades to resist the alien Voltamen who had conquered the future Earth, but its other series usually featured adventurers in outer space. Some were male, like the Space Rangers and Star Pirate, while others were voluptuous women, like Mysta of the Moon and Futura, the most fondly remembered character from the comic book. As one doesn't have to say, the melodramatic stories in *Planet Comics* foregrounded handsome men and beautiful women battling against ugly villains and loathsome aliens, employing weapons ranging from fisticuffs to atomic blasters.

At this point, my exasperated colleagues might ask, why are you wasting your time on such material, when you could be saying more about Heinlein, Asimov, and Bradbury? But my interest here, I would respond, is the history of science fiction, and one primary purpose of history, after all, is to study the past in order to better understand the present. And if one wishes to understand the books on display in the science fiction section of a modern bookstore, or the innumerable manifestations of science fiction now found in films, television, comic books, and video games, *Planet Stories* and *Planet Comics* provide far more insights than Heinlein, Asimov, and Bradbury.

I am dissatisfied, then, with the conventional view that space opera was entirely created in the magazines, comic strips, and serials of the 1930s, only to be temporarily suppressed by Campbell's more mature science fiction until it later sprang to life again in the form of countless works inspired by the earlier classics. Instead, one must recognize that after its initial emergence, space opera never really went away, and while Campbell's writers understandably command more critical attention, it actually remained the dominant variety of science fiction in the 1940s. In this respect, *Planet Stories* and *Planet Comics* are only the tip of the iceberg, so to speak, because even if their titles did not

8. The Three Golden Ages of Science Fiction

announce a focus on space opera, all of the other science fiction magazines of the decade, like *Amazing Stories, Thrilling Wonder Stories, Astonishing Stories, Startling Stories, Super Science Stories, Fantastic Adventures,* and *Captain Future*, were dominated by adventures in space. Comic books as well regularly provided space opera: *Superworld Comics* and *Target Comics* featured space heroes like those in *Planet Comics*, and when editor Mort Weisinger assumed control of the DC Comics hero Superman, he drew upon his background in science fiction to regularly have that iconic superhero travel into space and encounter alien visitors on Earth, while his like-minded colleague Julius Schwartz reinvented old superheroes in the 1950s and 1960s with new, science-fictional back stories. Even the Batman comic books of that era followed the trend by featuring stories about Batman and Robin involving amazing inventions, aliens, time travel, and space travel.

While all these stories built upon examples from the 1930s, the larger number of space adventures in the 1940s, and their usual focus on continuing characters, meant that the previously incohesive conventions of space opera were now being honed and polished to perfection, so that by the time new markets opened up for science fiction in the 1950s, a reader-tested model was available to be successfully shifted into new territories. Thus, with the sex and violence toned down for younger readers and inquisitive parents and librarians, space opera became a staple of the new field of juvenile science fiction, as best illustrated by the diverse works that appeared as the Winston juveniles; led by Donald A. Wollheim's Ace Books, recycled and new space operas became the main genre of paperback science fiction; the early days of television brought several series for children featuring intrepid space pilots battling human and alien villains, like *Space Patrol* (1950–1955), *Tom Corbett, Space Cadet* (1950–1955), and *Rocky Jones, Space Ranger* (1954); and while small budgets and crude special effects limited most science fiction films to planet Earth, there were occasional films like *This Island Earth* (1955), *Forbidden Planet* (1956), *The Angry Red Planet* (1960), and *Journey to the Seventh Planet* (1961) presenting stories about journeys to other planets that could have easily appeared in *Planet Stories* or *Planet Comics*. Later, of course, would come the *Star Trek* and *Star Wars* franchises, along with countless imitators, and ubiquitous space operas in films, television, computer games, and video games, while the spectacularly popular series of *Star Trek* novels, soon followed by the equally popular *Star Wars* novels, brought space opera back to its original home, the printed word, making it more conspicuous than ever that this was the most common form of science fiction literature. And all of these works cannot be properly appreciated without an understanding of the role that the innumerable space operas of the 1940s played in inspiring and shaping their contents.

Still, since I am perfectly happy to upset my colleagues, and since this discussion so far has probably not been upsetting enough, I must now take this argument even further to examine a third form of science fiction that originated in the 1940s and has persisted to this day—one that is even more neglected, and even more reviled, than the colorful space operas of that era. Indeed, most people would say that I will be describing a body of works that is not really science fiction at all. But their attitude, as I will discuss, reflects only their preferences, not the true nature of these texts.

Since Campbell's high-paying magazine consistently attracted the best writers of the 1940s, one would assume that his *Astounding Science-Fiction* was the most popular science fiction magazine of the era; and for much of the decade, that was the case. Yet in 1945, a different science fiction magazine actually started to sell more copies by introducing another new approach to science fiction which was able to attract even more readers than Campbell's stable of capable writers. I am referring to *Amazing Stories*, once the flagship of Hugo Gernsback's science fiction empire before declining in the 1930s under the control of his elderly successor, T. O'Conor Sloane. But in 1938, a new editor named Ray Palmer revived its fortunes with a group of younger writers based in Chicago and, predictably, an initial emphasis on thrilling space adventures. The magazine's contents, though, eventually changed because, in 1943, Palmer began receiving letters and manuscripts from a man named Richard Shaver, who had a very unusual story to tell.

According to Shaver, Earth had once been inhabited by members of an advanced alien civilization who had retreated either to other worlds or to underground cities, where these now-degenerate entities, termed "deros" or "detrimental robots" (though they were organic, not mechanical beings), caused various problems for humanity by means of monitoring devices and telepathic projection. Considered as science fiction stories, Shaver's writings had little merit as literature, and even their ideas were not particularly innovative, since they bore a vague resemblance to the Cthulhu Mythos of H. P. Lovecraft; the novelty was that Shaver, unlike Lovecraft, insisted that everything he said was absolutely true. Whether Palmer believed him or not is still debated today, but he shrewdly discerned that his readers might find this material very interesting indeed, and after some extensive revision, Palmer began publishing Shaver's stories about this "Shaver Mystery" in *Amazing Stories*, beginning with "'I Remember Lemuria!'" in the March 1945 issue. All of them were said to represent true accounts, though they were being promulgated in the form of fiction. Soon, other writers began making their own contributions to the evolving mythos of Shaver's deros, so much so that they almost took over the entire magazine.

As evidenced by the critical letters that Palmer published and heated discussions in fanzines, most members of the science fiction community utterly despised the magazine's new emphasis on these absurd concoctions, presented as fact, and they even organized letter-writing campaigns demanding an end to all Shaver-related publications in the magazine. Yet the circulation of *Amazing Stories* had also risen dramatically. The only possible explanation was that Palmer was discovering an entirely new audience of readers unrecognized by and not a part of the era's science fiction community, people with a unique interest in fantastic stories that might be true, fantastic stories that might provide more appealing explanations for aspects of the real world that conventional beliefs could not satisfyingly address. Thus, a man experiencing a number of personal setbacks might begin to discern a pattern: these misfortunes were not mere happenstance, but rather the work of those devilish deros. (As it happens, Shaver had previously been treated for psychological problems, and as many have noted, it is easy to discern signs of paranoid schizophrenia in his elaborate theories.)

In any event, if material like the Shaver Mystery stories was popular with many readers, but not with science fiction readers, there was only one logical way to respond to the situation, which played out in this series of events: *Amazing Stories* stopped publishing Shaver stories in 1948; Palmer resigned as the magazine's editor a year later; and he had launched a new magazine, *Fate* (1948–), expressly devoted to supposedly factual articles about various paranormal phenomena, which was followed by similar publications from Palmer and others. In this way, Palmer could profitably appeal to the new audience he had discovered without alienating science fiction readers, who would never pick up a magazine like *Fate*.

The magazine's first issue, unsurprisingly, featured a cover story involving the variety of science fiction purporting to be factual that was becoming far more popular than Shaver's peculiar scenario: a report on the "flying saucers" then being observed in Earth's skies, usually regarded as the vehicles of advanced aliens who were secretly spying on human civilization, occasionally kidnapping people and engaging in other sorts of mischief. Soon, many other magazines, books, and documentaries would appear that presented alleged evidence of these mysterious visitors, a tradition that has continued to the present day. (Interestingly, Palmer himself connected the Shaver hypothesis to flying saucers in a piece he officially co-authored with Shaver, "The Shaver Mystery No. 2: The Rescue of Atlantis and Lemuria by the Flying Saucers," which appeared in the January 1956 issue of another magazine that he edited, *Mystic Magazine*.)

Granted, as long as such writings restricted themselves to eyewitness accounts of flying saucer sightings, and learned consideration of possible explanations, one might justifiably regard them as nonfiction; but some examples of the form were unquestionably science fiction being published under another name. Consider the book *Flying Saucers Have Landed* (1953), by Desmond Leslie and George Adamski, which I encountered as a child at a time when libraries would sometimes mistakenly place such items on their shelves of science fiction books. It begins soberly enough, with a history of sightings of strange objects in the sky, but it then turns its attention to Adamski's account of how he was driving down a highway one day and just happened to spot a flying saucer coming to a landing nearby. He approached the vehicle and met its passenger, a friendly humanoid from Venus, who proceeded to engage Adamski in a long conversation in English about the foibles of humanity. Even at the age of ten, I realized that I was reading a work of fiction, and from later encounters with works of a similar nature, I know that such transparent fabrications are still being published.

Decades later, for example, while visiting a bookstore, I glanced through a book, whose title I do not recall, that purported to contain translations of captured alien documents; in one passage, the supposed alien author scornfully noted that we primitive humans were still seeing the world in terms of dualities, having not yet recognized that, in reality, everything breaks down into threes. I'm sorry, but if you want to convince me that you are presenting the wisdom of an advanced alien civilization, you will have to do better than that. Yet when such material does not extend to such outright fraud, it can serve as palatable entertainment, like another book in that section that I actually bought, read, and enjoyed, Don Wilson's *Secrets of Our Spaceship Moon* (1979), which earnestly argues that our Moon is actually an enormous alien spaceship, parked in Earth orbit and abandoned many millennia ago. Wilson seemed quite sincere in his belief, and I found his evidence and arguments surprisingly persuasive, though recent discoveries would appear to invalidate his startling thesis.

What Palmer launched with his Shaver stories and later magazines, then, has grown into a vast body of writings about secretive aliens now monitoring our planet and other, related phenomena not recognized by scientists—such as the Bermuda Triangle, Bigfoot, the Abominable Snowman, the Loch Ness monster, the lost continent of Atlantis, Erich von Däniken's ancient aliens, and so on—which are effectively forms of science fiction, since no reasonable person can believe what these texts are reporting, even though they present themselves as factual accounts of real events that for various reasons cannot be officially acknowledged. Since most readers of science fiction abhor such dubious pseudoscience, these texts are never placed alongside science fiction books, where they arguably belong, so they must be shelved in another category—"New Age," perhaps, or "Paranormal Literature"—along with books about more venerable but similarly discredited subjects like astrology, ghosts, palmistry, witchcraft, and voodoo.

Granted, most of this material has no literary value whatsoever; but if one attraction of science fiction is its myth-making power, any observer must admit that this extensive body of works is, among other things, collectively presenting an intricate and fascinating portrait of a world much like our own which is influenced by powers that governments refuse to recognize, and is inhabited by various strange beings lurking just out of sight, prominently including the intelligent aliens who have covertly shaped human history and continue to control our destiny. The television series *The X-Files* (1993–2002, 2016–2018), one of the few works of science fiction to draw upon this constructed mythology, provides one sign of its evocative allure, and this brilliant and expertly produced series suggests that these works merit more critical scrutiny than they have previously received.

We find, then, that there are actually three reasons to regard the 1940s as the Golden Age of Science Fiction: there are the noteworthy writers of Campbell's *Astounding Science-Fiction*, who crafted the form of science fiction that remains most admired by connoisseurs and critics; the lesser writers of 1940s space opera, who perfected what has now become the most popular form of science fiction in all major media; and the even lesser writers like Richard Shaver, purporting to reveal hidden truths about our world, who engendered another, very popular form of science fiction that happens to go by another name. Only works in the first tradition are likely to be cited or praised in histories of science fiction, or assigned as readings in a science fiction class, which is perhaps as it should be; but I still feel that the other two traditions are important as well, and that they will reward those few people who choose to examine them.

It is interesting to consider, for example, the very different attitudes toward human abilities and proclivities that are embedded within these three traditions. In classic works of science fiction, one typically finds that humans in the future can both control and change their worlds, which is simultaneously uplifting and disturbing. It is exciting to imagine, for example, that a person might engender a race of tiny beings who would look up to their creator as a god, as in Sturgeon's "Microcosmic God," or that a man might leave behind his mundane job and employ time travel to transform himself into the dictator of a future world, as in Heinlein's "By His Bootstraps." But if people are someday able to completely transform themselves and their world, the results may also be disquieting and disheartening, as is perhaps best conveyed by Clarke's *Childhood's End*, wherein alien overseers help humanity evolve into a form of group intelligence which a surviving human perceives as repugnant and incomprehensible. (Another Clarke story from this period, "The Sentinel" [1951], later inspired another unsettling tale of future human transformation, the film and novel *2001: A Space Odyssey* [1968].)

Second, in the space operas that have dominated science fiction from the 1930s to the present, humans are easily able to control their future worlds, but they seem unable to change those worlds; they may have faster-than-light spaceships, force fields, and ray guns, they may travel to other solar systems and interact with various aliens, but they still seem to talk, think, and act precisely the same way that people talk, think, and act today, and they face the same sorts of problems that people face today, like cunning criminals, violent assailants, unsympathetic bosses, impetuous youth, malfunctioning equipment, and natural disasters. By taking typical conflicts from westerns, detective fiction, war stories, and romance novels, and transplanting them into futuristic settings, space opera (despite its surface novelties) thus provides a very comforting and familiar form of entertainment, which helps to explain why it is always the form of science fiction that is most appealing to a mass audience, if not always to critics and scholars.

Finally, in the literature of flying saucers and related paranormal phenomena, we observe an imagined version of our present-day and future world which humans are both unable to control and unable to change. Rather, as in the past (or so these works assert), humans will always be subject to unacknowledged forces, unseen aliens, and human co-conspirators that have all covertly dictated important developments in our history. For example, as various books and magazine articles solemnly testify, aliens helped the Egyptians build the pyramids, destroyed Sodom and Gomorrah, erected the statues on Easter Island, and killed Marilyn Monroe; and they meet with every new American president to ensure his complicity in their secret mastery over the Earth. Further, with their magically advanced technology, they will surely maintain their grip on humanity for decades or centuries to come, which may after all be for the best, given our uneven track record in managing our own affairs.

Indeed, perhaps it is not the crudity and absurdity of these theories, but their assertion of essential human impotence, that is most offensive to readers of science fiction; for they, like Heinlein, would rather believe that ornery humans will always be able to prevail in any conflict, and are therefore destined to conquer the universe, overcoming any obstacles in their way, including mischievous deros or domineering aliens. They embrace, in other words, the doctrine most delightfully expressed at the end of Heinlein's *Have Space Suit—Will Travel*, when a boy defiantly tells the advanced aliens who are threatening to destroy Earth's sun, "All right, take away our star—You will if you can and I guess you can. Go ahead! We'll *make* a star! Then, someday, we'll come back and hunt you down—*all of you!*" "That's telling 'em, Kip!" his friend enthusiastically responds,[5] and most science fiction readers, I suspect, would echo her enthusiasm.

As it is interesting to contemplate what divides these three forms of science fiction, it is equally worthwhile to consider what they all share, which I believe would include the following: a belief that humans are not alone in the universe, that there exist countless other intelligent species we will someday interact with; a confidence that human technology, if not human nature and human society, will keep advancing to higher and higher levels in the future; and a conviction that things are going on right now, and things will be going on in the future, that most people today are unable or unwilling to discern, imbuing all science fiction readers with a slight sense of superiority over those people who opt for mundane diversions while refusing to acknowledge that everyone's world, and everyone's perceptions of the world, are destined to someday change.

For now, at least, I have given up the game of trying to define science fiction, but I have criticized other definitions for focusing exclusively on the works of science fiction that their creators admire, that is, texts that fulfill Campbell's desire for provocative, innovative science fiction. Yet while one might reasonably describe the works of Robert A. Heinlein and Philip K. Dick in Darko Suvin's words as a *"literature of cognitive estrangement,"*[6] this appellation is nonsensical when applied to, say, the contents of *Planet Stories* or *Flying Saucers Have Landed*, which are cognitively reassuring, not estranging. Some critics are perfectly happy to assert that such texts, and others not meeting their high standards, are not really science fiction at all; but it is surely more reasonable and productive to instead seek a broader definition of science fiction which would apply to all of its texts.

So, while my own scholarly pursuits keep moving in peculiar directions of their own, I hope that this survey might inspire some scholars and students to examine not only the works of science fiction they are expected to examine, but also the works of science fiction they are not expected to examine. Like other explorers who stray from the beaten path to go where no one has gone before, they are likely to be surprised, and enlightened, by what they might find.

9

Assemblers of Infinity:
The Early History of Science Fiction Anthologies

Histories of American science fiction in the twentieth century typically focus on two types of publications. Surveying the 1920s, 1930s, and 1940s, scholars primarily discuss the science fiction magazines, which published numerous short stories along with occasional serialized novels by the era's major authors. Moving into the 1950s and 1960s, they mostly turn their attention to the original hardcover and paperback novels that emerged at that time to become the most profitable work for writers to pursue, and hence increasingly their major avocation, although they still acknowledge a few significant magazines of the era, like H. L. Gold's *Galaxy*, J. Francis McComas and Anthony Boucher's *The Magazine of Fantasy and Science Fiction*, and Michael Moorcock's *New Worlds*, that continued to provide attractive markets for short stories. When scholars reach the 1970s and thereafter, they usually limit their scrutiny to novelists, while pausing occasionally to note the works of a few idiosyncratic talents who continued to specialize in short stories for magazines, like Harlan Ellison and Ted Chiang. Yet in addition to the magazines and original novels, there is a third type of science fiction publication that is consistently marginalized in these histories: science fiction anthologies.

Of course, they are not entirely ignored: science fiction historians will explain that along with novels, science fiction anthologies also became prominent in the 1940s, and they might mention a few pioneering anthologies like Donald A. Wollheim's *The Pocket Book of Science-Fiction* (1943), Groff Conklin's *The Best of Science Fiction* (1946), and Raymond J. Healy and McComas's *Adventures in Time and Space* (1946). While describing later decades, they may devote a little space to a few heralded series of original anthologies, like Frederik Pohl's *Star Science Fiction* anthologies, Harlan Ellison's *Dangerous Visions* anthologies, and Damon Knight's *Orbit* anthologies, and some will pause to vilify Roger Elwood and his prodigious production of mostly mediocre anthologies during the 1970s, said to have brought about a devastating reduction in the numbers of published anthologies. Yet the vast majority of the countless science fiction anthologies that appeared from the 1940s to the 1970s, and the still numerous anthologies that have continued to appear up to the present day, have virtually been erased from the history of science fiction.

To my knowledge, only one researcher has undertaken to study science fiction anthologies at length, the late Bud Webster, who published a series of articles about various types of anthologies, under the umbrella title of "Anthropology 101," and later collected these articles in a book, *Anthropology 101: Reflections, Inspections, and Dissections of SF Anthologies* (2010). However, while his research and careful attention to numerous anthologies make his book a valuable resource, there are three crucial limitations to his study. First, he examined anthologies following no particular order, in articles for several publications, and his book simply presents those articles in chronological order according to their date of publication, so that he made no real effort to craft a genuine history of science fiction anthologies. Second, he limits his studies to anthologies that he actually examined, citing in his introduction the valid concern that "it's not just a matter of what stories are in which book, there are editors' introductions and headnotes, as well as occasional authors' notes, to be considered."[1] This meant that he was excluding anthologies that might be difficult to find yet are accessible to researchers with access to an efficient interlibrary loan service or specialized collections like the University of California, Riverside's J. Lloyd Eaton Collection of Science Fiction and Fantasy Literature; thus, while he mentions J. Berg Esenwein's pioneering *Adventures to Come* (1937) several times, and even described it in vague terms for the "Curiosities" series of *The Magazine of Fantasy and Science Fiction* (2004), his comments make it evident that he never actually examined a copy of the book. Finally, Webster fails to present a strong defense of the importance of anthologies; in keeping with his title, he does assert that anthologies merit attention primarily as "artifacts that exemplified the times in which they are created" (2), yet this actually strikes me as their least interesting feature, and indeed this is an aspect of the anthologies that Webster himself rarely seems interested in. Even a cursory look at Conklin's *The Best of Science Fiction* and Healy and McComas's *Adventures in Time and Space* reveals that humanity's newly discovered ability to unleash atomic power was inspiring both extreme anxiety, and great hope, in the year they were published, 1946, but one can learn this from innumerable other documents; the questions that can only be answered by these anthologies involve the ways that they influenced, and have continued to influence, the history of science fiction.

I would argue, then, that science fiction anthologies are significant for three different reasons, two of them relatively obvious, one less so. In the first place, they represent the way that growing numbers of science fiction readers were exposed to short stories, novelettes, and novellas. Growing up in the 1950s and 1960s, I was part of the first generation of readers who grew to love science fiction but never read science fiction magazines. Certainly, I was aware of their existence, and I sometimes read anthologies that consisted entirely of stories from one magazine, like two of the first paperbacks I ever purchased, H. L. Gold's *The Fourth Galaxy Reader* (1959) and *Bodyguard and Four Other Short Science Fiction Novels from Galaxy* (1960). But the magazines, I thought, were generally offering inferior stories, and I was better off waiting for the editors of retrospective anthologies to select and provide me with only their best offerings. In reaching this judgment, I may have been overly influenced by reading one science fiction magazine that was given to me, the December 1958 issue of *If*. Its cover did not convey that its contents were impressive—an image of a humanoid robot's head, cut away to show that its thoughts were being controlled by a rat inside its head (illustrating Rog Phillips's aptly named story "Rat in the Skull")—and I was particularly appalled by one story that seemed insufferably silly, about the projected creation of a series of increasingly powerful bombs designated by different letters, culminating with the "S-Bomb" (designed to destroy the solar system), the "G-Bomb" (to destroy the galaxy), and the "U-Bomb" (to destroy the entire universe). After later research, I was astounded to discover that the story in question, "Null-O," had been written by none other than Philip K. Dick, now enshrined as one of the genre's giants, though even his most ardent admirers would admit that this story, rarely if ever mentioned in critical studies of Dick, was one of his least distinguished efforts. (Admittedly, I might have appreciated the story a bit more had I realized that it was satirizing A. E. van Vogt's *The World of Null-A* [1945, 1948], but I did not read that novel until its second revised version was published in 1970.) In any event, the young Westfahl concluded that it would be much better to spend all of his time reading anthologies, which generally featured only the best stories that had appeared in the magazines.

Anthologies have also played a role in building and maintaining awareness of memorable stories by the genre's lesser-known writers. Isaac Asimov, Arthur C. Clarke, Robert A. Heinlein, and other renowned authors could bring their previously published stories to wide audiences by publishing collections of their own works, but stories like Jerome Bixby's "It's a *Good* Life" (1953) and Tom Godwin's "The Cold Equations" (1954) have been enshrined as classics solely because they have repeatedly appeared in anthologies featuring stories by many writers. Some anthologies have even had the announced goal of bringing meritorious works overlooked by other anthologists to readers' attention, such as Sam Moskowitz's *Futures to Infinity* (1970) and Piers Anthony, Barry N. Malzberg, Martin H. Greenberg, and Charles G. Waugh's *Uncollected Stars* (1986), wherein I encountered two remarkable stories that I still remember vividly, Bixby's "Little Boy" (1954) and Howard L. Myers's "The Creatures of Man" (1968).

Finally, by means of the stories chosen for inclusion, the way they are arranged, and the editorial commentaries that usually accompany the stories, anthologies are offering their own definitions, histories, and defenses of science fiction, and while they may have had less impact than the comparable arguments of commentators like Hugo Gernsback and his many successors, they nonetheless have undoubtedly influenced their readers' perceptions of the genre. Some anthologies are descriptive, focused on bringing attention to representative science fiction works of the past and present, such as the small but growing number of anthologies specifically designed for use in high school or college classrooms; others are prescriptive, presenting in their stories and commentaries the editor's vision of what science fiction should be in the future. Occasional anthologies of both types have been demonstrably influential: in Isaac Asimov's *Before the Golden Age: A Science Fiction Anthology of the 1930s* (1974), a prominent author provided modern readers with superior examples of science fiction from a period that many had long dismissed as inferior, arguably leading to a better representation of stories from the 1930s in later anthologies; and Harlan Ellison's *Dangerous Visions* (1967) inspired many American writers and editors to explore new possibilities in science fiction beyond what was then acceptable in the magazines. One anthology, Robert Silverberg's *The Science Fiction Hall of Fame, Volume I* (1970), seemed to encapsulate the modern history of science fiction so well that critic John Huntington employed its stories as the exclusive basis for his study of twentieth-century science fiction stories, *Rationalizing Genius: Ideological Strategies in the Classic American Science Fiction Short Story* (1989).

Needless to say, it would be impossible to examine all of the innumerable anthologies published in the last century to assess their overall effects on the genre; however, the first six science fiction anthologies—Esenwein's *Adventures to Come*, Phil Stong's *The Other Worlds* (1941), Wollheim's *The Pocket Book of Science-Fiction* and *The Portable Novels of Science* (1945), Conklin's *The Best of Science Fiction*, and Healy and McComas's *Adventures in Time and Space*—can be usefully analyzed as templates for most of the anthologies that would follow and as indications of how later editors would seek to characterize the genre and influence their readers.

Adventures to Come represents a pioneering example of a type of anthology that, understandably, only rarely attracts the attention of regular science fiction readers and scholars: a collection of stories aimed at younger readers with no particular attachment to the genre. Since publishers long believed that books of this kind would be purchased exclusively by parents and librarians, not the children who would actually be reading them, their major concern was the product's packaging, not its quality, and hence they might recruit someone without any background in science fiction to oversee the preparation of a book of science fiction stories—like Esenwein, otherwise noted for authoring books about writing and editing other anthologies for children. It was especially appealing that this former English professor could be presented on the title page of *Adventures to Come* as "J. Berg Esenwein M.A. Litt.D." to assure parents that their children's reading material was being handled by a capable and responsible expert. Presumably, some editor at McLoughlin Brothers had noted the popularity of the *Buck Rogers* and *Flash Gordon* comic strips and the first *Flash Gordon* serial (1936) and decided to ask Esenwein, one of their regular contributors, to add a book of similar stories to their "World of Adventure Series." As Webster notes, the book "has far more in common with the 'boys' series' books written under the house-pseudonyms of Victor Appleton and Roy Rockwood than with the magazine SF of even a decade earlier" (194).

The book's nine stories are uniformly undistinguished—none of them have ever been reprinted—and Webster repeatedly states that his "research," not described, indicated that Esenwein had written most or all of the stories himself. I suspect that Webster simply endeavored to obtain biographical information about the eight credited authors and found that six of them had never published anything else, suggesting that the names were pseudonyms. (Webster also offers the theory that Esenwein recruited some former students in his correspondence classes to write stories, but since he stopped teaching such classes in 1928, and since students in correspondence classes rarely forge close relationships with their instructors, it seems extremely unlikely to me that Esenwein would be employing students from a decade or more in the past to contribute to his publications.) Even the two stories attached to recognizable names were probably not written by those authors: in 1937, future science fiction film director Jack Arnold was working as an actor on Broadway, so one has to doubt that that he would be moonlighting as a story writer for an editor based on Massachusetts, and it also improbable that Esenwein would have been in a position to recruit the obscure British author Norman Leslie to contribute to his collection. These names, then, might have simply been two other pseudonyms randomly created by Esenwein that happened to coincide with the names of actual people living at that time.

The book has two interesting features. First, although there is no editorial introduction, and there are no introductory comments preceding individual stories, the interior dust jacket flap does offer this unattributed description of the book's contents:

> For sheer entertainment of an adventurous type, "Adventures to Come" can be highly recommended. The book contains a group of imaginative tales of the future, fantastic yet plausible. They are based on the latest scientific inventions and discoveries and the things that people dream of today which may become realities in the future.
>
> Space ships, the stratosphere, and television figure in the astonishing events, but the characters who experience these adventures are the kind of everyday people whom we know in real life. The story of how a life is saved from a distance of thousands of miles by means of television is most dramatic.
>
> The book has been planned and written in such a way that it will be readily visualized and understood by any young person with an adventurous spirit.[2]

The first thing to notice is that by stating these stories are "based on the latest scientific inventions and discoveries" and present "things that people dream of today which may become realities in the future," the introduction demonstrates that Gernsback's innovative arguments in favor of science fiction—that it provides a scientific education and offers predictions of the future—had by 1937 percolated sufficiently into popular culture as to be referenced in a description written by someone who, almost certainly, had never seen any of Gernsback's magazines.

However, while many later anthologies would seek to explain how science fiction differs from other forms of literature, this description does not dwell upon the unique features of science fiction at length, but rather takes pains to emphasize how similar these stories are to other stories for young readers: they offer "sheer entertainment," they involve "the kind of everyday people whom we know in real life," and they are accessible to "any young person with an adventurous spirit." Except for its scientific and futuristic content, the book thus asserts, science fiction is exactly like all of the other sorts of fiction that young readers enjoy, exemplified by other Esenwein collections like *Sport and Adventure Stories for Boys* (1937) and *Field and Campus Stories for Girls* (1937). To further emphasize the book's quotidian nature, the dust jacket only briefly refers to space travel—long regarded as the most thrilling aspect of science fiction—while singling out for special praise a story about the more modest innovation of television, perhaps in an effort to appeal to more conservative parents and librarians. (For the record, this is what occurs in that "most dramatic" story, Arnold's "A Life by Television": the life of a gunshot victim can only be saved by one eminent surgeon; unfortunately, he lives a considerable distance away, and he cannot fly because the airplane he planned to employ has been grounded due to inclement weather; a resourceful police officer recalls, and obtains, some experimental television apparatus; and a successful operation then occurs under the supervision of the surgeon, observing everything by means of television.)

The book was also published with two different covers. The cover displayed at the Internet Speculative Fiction Database, with no identified artist, shows a flying man in a red suit brandishing a ray gun, an image that strikingly recalls the famous Frank R. Paul illustration on the cover of the August issue of *Amazing Stories*—presumably the cover that Webster described as "a Buck Rogers-inspired jacket" (though that cover was actually illustrating, as noted above, the first installment of E. E. "Doc" Smith's *The Skylark of Space* [1928, 1946]).[3] Language at booksellers' websites indicates that this cover in fact adorned the first edition. But Webster reports that the book was republished in 1940 with a different cover, and that must be the edition I examined in the J. Lloyd Eaton Collection of Science Fiction and Fantasy Literature at the University of California, Riverside, with a cover illustration, signed by artist Charles Zingaro, showing a boy on board an orbiting spaceship or space station who is looking through a porthole at the planet Earth below him. Perhaps the original illustration was deemed overly similar to trashy pulp magazines and comic books, prompting the decision to republish the book with a more subdued image of a boy sedately staring at Earth, accompanied by an illustration on the spine showing a boy looking through a telescope.

When science fiction books for younger readers emerged as a standard publishing category in the 1950s, publishers normally commissioned original novels, but they produced some anthologies as well. Since she had already written several juvenile science fiction novels, Andre Norton was commissioned by the World Publishing Company to edit three juvenile anthologies—*Space Service* (1953), *Space Pioneers* (1954), and *Space Police* (1956)—featuring carefully selected stories from science fiction magazines deemed suitable for younger readers, though these occasionally required some editing; for example, characters in James Blish's "Beep" (1954) were not allowed to drink alcohol when the story appeared in *Space Police*. An author named Richard M. Elam, Jr., wrote two volumes of original stories for Lantern Press, *Teen-Age Science Fiction Stories* (1952) and *Teen-Age Super Science Stories* (1957); like the stories in Esenwein's collection, none of Elam's stories have ever been reprinted, except for two that surfaced in another anthology for young readers, Marjorie Barrow's *Science Fiction and Reader's Guide* (1954). Whether they are original or reprinted, the stories in these anthologies are usually inferior, with rare exceptions like Theodore R. Cogswell's "The Specter General" (1952) in *Space Service* and Robert A. Heinlein's "The Black Pits of Luna" (1948) in Barrow's anthology; and this is incongruous, since any number of science fiction novels for young readers have been acknowledged as classics. Perhaps, only when science fiction stories for youngsters are given ample space to develop their ideas can they overcome the limitations imposed by their audience to produce superior work.

More broadly, Esenwein's book is the first example of what might be termed the ameliorative science fiction anthology, designed to appeal to readers with no special interest in the genre and focused on emphasizing how

9. Assemblers of Infinity 131

science fiction is similar to, not different from, other forms of popular fiction. The intent of such anthologies may be best conveyed by the title of Terry Carr's 1966 anthology, *Science Fiction for People Who Hate Science Fiction*. If science fiction readers and scholars pay little attention to such collections, then, that may only reflect the fact that they do not represent their target audience.

The second science fiction anthology—Stong's *The Other Worlds*—has been unduly criticized because of four words in the book's "Foreword"— "pabulum of reiterated nonsense"[4]—which, Webster reports, represents Stong's opinion about "most magazine science fiction" (60). In fact, it does not. In the first place, the descriptive phrase comes at the end of a passage wherein Stong explains why his anthology contains "no interplanetary stories, simply because in the magazines available there are not a dozen such stories with even mild originality or amusement value" (74), and he goes on to describe some of their clichéd plots. Hence, the quoted phrase applies exclusively to the genre's outer space adventures, and as it happens, this is precisely the sort of complaint that science fiction fans were then making regarding the low quality of the space operas appearing in the pulp magazines of the 1930s; after all, it was also in 1941 that Wilson Tucker famously coined the term "space opera" as a way to condemn "the hacky, grinding, stinking, outworn space-ship yarn."[5] Furthermore, the phrase occurs in a statement that is otherwise praising science fiction:

> In this palubum of reiterated nonsense, however, there appear with almost incredible frequency, stories that are original, stories that are brightly written, stories that present extensions of engaging philosophies, and neatly constructed stories of dramatic impossibilities.
> For the curious reader, the lode is very well worth working [14].

Stong thus asserts that excellent works of science fiction do "appear with almost incredible frequency" in the science fiction magazines that Webster claimed he was lambasting. And although Webster emphasizes that Stong drew many of his stories from *Weird Tales*, *The Other Worlds* also contains stories from *Amazing Stories*, *Astounding Stories*, *Thrilling Wonder Stories*, and John W. Campbell's fantasy magazine *Unknown*. Stong, clearly, was not hostile toward science fiction; however, he did have and express strong views about what constituted the ideal sort of science fiction, which was related to what he regarded as the ideal sort of fantasy, and he chose numerous stories from *Weird Tales* only because they best represented his prescription for superior fantastic fiction.

Stong's "Foreword" begins with two anecdotes involving apparently genuine acts of precognition, and he then concludes that scientists may soon demonstrate the validity of these reports, with findings establishing that some people actually do have the power to see into the future. One might expect that he is laying the groundwork for an argument, recalling Gernsback, that the stories in his book will similarly deal with apparently fantastic phenomena that might someday prove to be, or become, realities. In fact, he ends the discussion by announcing that "because such matters are still in the center, or at least the suburbs, of sober philosophy or research, I have neglected them altogether in the collection that follows" (5), and he proceeds to explain why he has done so: "The first requirement of a good fantastic story—and half the magazines who specialize on these things neglect the fact—is that it should not be even remotely possible ... a fantastic story should be consistent within its own definitions but ... these definitions should be incredible" (5). In contrast to Hugo Gernsback, Stong thus asserts, stories that might come true someday should be condemned, not admired. Stong identifies three other ingredients of superior fantastic fiction: "The fantasy for my money, as we purists say, is one in which the fantastic premise is known to the reader from the start of the story" (8). He further states, "Nor must the fantasy run completely wild. The story in which all things are possible seems to me extraordinarily dull because there is no conflict" (8)—and he proceeds to criticize E. E. "Doc" Smith's *Skylark* novels and the *Superman* comic books for the reason that their predictions are excessively extravagant. Finally, as already indicated, he values stories with "a delightful and original turn" (5), as opposed to stories that merely follow conventional formulas.

Indeed, the way that Stong chose to organize his collection conveys a message about the priorities that should govern the writing of non-realistic fiction. His first section, "Strange Ideas," features "short story notions involving the fantastic that I had never heard of before"; the second section, "Fresh Variants," contains "ideas of origin" that "are of earlier use, though pleasantly and ingeniously diverted into new channels and conclusions"; and the third section, "Horrors," consists of "the old quivery or shivery story in its best new presentations" (11). The primary value of this form of literature, then, is that it offers new ideas, or new approaches to old ideas, thus startling and stimulating their readers; there is also some special merit in employing such novelty in a frightening story. Emphasizing these qualities more than conventional considerations such as plotting, character development, and prose style seems to be perfectly in keeping with one of the oldest clichés about science fiction, that it is "a literature of ideas."

Since these observations are part of an introduction that is rambling and conversational in its tone, it is hard to read Stong's "Foreword" as an impassioned polemic; nonetheless, *The Other Worlds* can be properly regarded as the first anthology with an agenda, designed to persuade authors to produce, and to persuade readers to seek out, the particular sort of story that the editor prefers. The book's espousal of stories featuring "notions involving the fantastic that I had never heard of before," in a way, anticipates Harlan Ellison's later efforts to promote stories offering "dangerous visions."

Stong's anthology was reviewed in several science fiction and fantasy magazines, generally receiving qualified praise—it did represent, after all, the first time that stories from these magazines had been republished in a hardcover book—although even a supportive review in *Thrilling Wonder Stories* commented that "the trained science fiction fan will soon note, during his delightful journey through this book, that some of his favorite types of stories are missing, and that some of the stories included are not properly representative of the fantasy field."[6] A scathing review in *Stirring Science Stories* even more strongly condemned Stong's choices: "Mr. Stong states that he considers the only criterion of good fantasy the condition that the story should be utterly impossible. Since no fantasy writer can take such an attitude and continue to sell, obviously he is expressing a private opinion which must arrive at the conclusion that since these stories are impossible nonsense, why worry about good writing?" The reviewer concludes,

> We do not mind saying that in general this book makes us feel slightly nauseated. It could have been so great; it is so utterly incapable. The anthologist deliberately turned down virtually all the great weird and science-fiction, to parade a set of inferior material. The average would be passable for a single issue of a magazine but for permanent book publication, no. Someday, the classics of fantasy fiction will get their due. That day is not yet.[7]

One has to agree that the reviewer has a point; after all, the criteria that Stong employed ended up excluding virtually all of the science fiction stories from the 1930s that have now been enshrined as classics and repeatedly anthologized, like Edmond Hamilton's "The Man Who Evolved" (1931), C. L. Moore's "Shambleau" (1933), Stanley G. Weinbaum's "A Martian Odyssey" (1934), John W. Campbell, Jr.'s "Twilight" (1934), Raymond Z. Gallun's "Old Faithful" (1934), Lester del Rey's "Helen O'Loy" (1938), and Robert A. Heinlein's "Life-Line" (1939). In contrast, while some significant authors are represented in the collection, the chosen stories are not regarded as their author's best work, like Murray Leinster's "The Fourth-Dimensional Demonstrator" (1934), Weinbaum's "The Adaptive Ultimate" (1935), and del Rey's "The Pipes of Pan" (1940). As it happens, the author of that review, Donald A. Wollheim, would soon get the opportunity to present a couple of those excluded stories, and a few others from their milieu, in his own, very different, science fiction anthology.

Looking at the contents of Wollheim's *The Pocket Book of Science-Fiction*, one might imagine that it was compiled by two different editors; certainly, it appears to represent a compromise between two different visions of science fiction. The first five stories are all written by well-known authors with respectable literary reputations—Stephen Vincent Benét, Ambrose Bierce, John Collier, H. G. Wells, and T. S. Stribling—including two Pulitzer Prize winners (Benét and Stribling). The last five stories are all written by science fiction writers, known only to science fiction readers, who at the time had only published in science fiction magazines—Wallace G. West, Stanley G. Weinbaum, John W. Campbell, Jr. (as "Don A. Stuart"), Theodore Sturgeon, and Robert A. Heinlein. To explain why Wollheim included "these five" stories from outside the pulp magazines, Webster offers these "possible reasons": "to make the book more 'respectable'; to expose the genre readers to stories of which they would otherwise be ignorant; or to enhance his own image by choosing a table of contents designed not only to entertain, but also to make him look considerable more cosmopolitan than he would if he chose only pulp yarns" (72). However, Webster's second theory seems dubious; after all, the stories by Wells—"In the Abyss" (1896)—and by Stribling—"The Green Splotches" (1920)—had been republished in Gernsback's *Amazing Stories*, so many "genre readers" were already aware of them, and it is even possible, if not probable, that that is where Wollheim first encountered those stories. A story by Ambrose Bierce, "The Damned Thing" (1893), had also been reprinted in the September 1923 issue of *Weird Tales*, so his name would be familiar to many science fiction readers as well. Fans at the time were also beginning to compile bibliographies of science fiction including stories that had not appeared in the magazines. And Webster further fails to note that Wollheim probably saved his publishers some money by including the stories by Wells and Bierce ("Moxon's Master" [1899]), since they probably did not have to pay any money to republish stories that first appeared in the nineteenth century.

My own theory would be that the stories from outside the genre were suggested in Wollheim's original proposal as a device to persuade editors with little background in science fiction to publish his book, since they might prefer to publish a book including some names that they recognized. Webster observes, "In his autobiographical *The Futurians*, Damon Knight indicates that Wollheim took advantage of the fact that both publishers [Pocket and Viking] might be open to adding a science fiction novel to their series and leapt in to pitch the books [this one and *Portable Novels of Science*]" (70). And while Webster points out that Pocket editor Philip Van Doren Stern already had some familiarity with "fantastic literature" (70), Wollheim may not have been aware of that.

In addition to offering two different types of science fiction stories, Wollheim also intermingles in his introduction two very different perspectives on science fiction. It begins by identifying science fiction as merely one modern variety of an ancient tradition:

9. Assemblers of Infinity   135

> There are two kinds of adventure: first, that which actually happened—the discovery of America, for example; and second, that which took place only in the mind of its narrator—and this second variety has variously been known through the ages as "myth," "legend," "fable," "whopper," "fish story," "extraordinary voyage," and also as "science-fiction."
>
> But whether it is called "myth" or "science-fiction," whether it deals with a goddess with snakes where her hair ought to be, or with a voyage to the moon, it is still the same fascinating thing—the unalloyed figment of a curious, speculative, and ingenious imagination.[8]

Later, again emphasizing how similar science fiction is to other forms of literature, Wollheim states that the stories in his anthology "are stories—pure fiction, fabulous, exciting, stimulating, incredible—written for pleasure and enjoyment" (x).

But at other times, Wollheim also echoes Gernsback in suggesting that works of science fiction might be fruitfully regarded as predictions of the future—though he simultaneously downplays the notion. In one general statement—"take these stories as you find them—as prophecy, as embroidery, as exaggeration, as possibility, as inconceivability, as romance, or as shadow on the wall" (ix)—Wollheim acknowledges that some readers may regard a story as a "prophecy" depicting an actual "possibility." He goes on to say that "so many of the things today that we believe, but cannot logically or scientifically say we know, will some day be comprehended, and will pass out of the realm of science-fiction and into the body of human knowledge, and proved, scientific fact" (ix). But he immediately and specifically refuses to defend the selected stories on those grounds: "This introduction is not to be construed as meaning that the editor believes that any of these stories actually holds the key to a great riddle. The unknown is unraveled nowadays by unexciting and hard-working technicians—a very prosaic business" (ix). Still, unwilling to entirely deny that some stories might prove to be prophetic, he elliptically concludes, "But don't forget, strange things have come to pass in this world—and one of our hardest-working figures of speech is 'What on earth!'" (x).

Considering both the stories he chose and his introduction, one has to conclude that Wollheim had two goals in editing *The Pocket Book of Science-Fiction*: to persuade readers who knew nothing about science fiction that it included the work of renowned authors they were aware of and that it was merely one recent variety of a form of entertaining and imaginative literature that had existed since ancient times. Second, he wished to valorize the modern genre by presenting some of its best authors to this new audience and by gently intimating that its stories might have some special value as prophetic visions.

In the decades to come, there would be innumerable anthologies dedicated to the second goal, foregrounding the authors who emerged from the twentieth-century pulp tradition and celebrating the unique qualities that make science fiction a special form of literature; but there would also be occasional anthologies that continued to seek readers who would ordinarily, in Carr's words, "hate science fiction," but might be attracted by noteworthy authors who are not associated with the genre. For example, the anthology edited by Ray Bradbury, *Timeless Stories for Today and Tomorrow* (1952), announces the "three reasons" Bradbury prepared the book in the first paragraph of its introduction: "to locate stories by authors who rarely write fantasy; to find stories heretofore not used in other fantasy anthologies; and, most important of all, to publish stories of quality."[9] And David G. Hartwell described in an essay how he was approached by "two editors of the Book-of-the-Month Club" and told the following:

> We've decided we really want a science fiction anthology; however, not one of your specific proposals—what we want to do is put a science fiction book into our *World Treasury* series.... Clifton Fadiman is general editor of the series, and he is enthusiastic about including science fiction. But you have to make sure it emphasizes the literary quality of the stories and writers, and it's a *world* treasury, so you have to use a lot of translations. This was their recipe for marketing success in the *World Treasury* series: emphasize the high literary quality of the contents, include name writers (including those not generally known for their science fiction), and use as many translations from as many languages as possible.[10]

Like *Adventures to Come*, then, these books might be described as ameliorative anthologies, designed to make science fiction seem similar to other forms of literature; but the strategy here is to make science fiction seem like great literature, not everyday entertainment. Such anthologies may not be popular with science fiction fans, who can recognize that their own favorite stories and authors are being marginalized in favor of luminaries from outside the genre, but they can succeed in reaching large audiences and having an impact; Hartwell boasted in 1996, for example, that "to my knowledge" *The World Treasury of Science Fiction* "is the largest-selling science fiction anthology of all time" (44).

To many commentators, large volumes that gather together complete novels are not anthologies but "omnibuses," and for that reason they would not consider Wollheim's *The Portable Novels of Science* to be relevant here, since its contents consist of three novels—Wells's *The First Men in the Moon* (1901), John Taine's *Before the Dawn* (1934), and Olaf Stapledon's *Odd John: A Story Between Jest and Earnest* (1935)—and one novella—H. P. Lovecraft's "The Shadow Out of Time" (1936). Still, Wollheim himself presents the book as an anthology, a successor to his own *The Pocket Book of Science-Fiction*, described in Wollheim's "Introduction" as the first science fiction anthology; "This present volume," he proceeds to say, "is therefore the first comprehensive selection of the science-fiction story in its most powerful form, the novel."[11]

9. Assemblers of Infinity

Commentators have noted that the book did not contain the term "science fiction" in its title—which may have been a decision by the publisher beyond the editor's control—but as the above quotation shows, Wollheim had no hesitation about repeatedly discussing science fiction by that name in his introduction. On the first page, in fact, he states that his introduction "must also serve to introduce a branch of literature which has been curiously neglected by anthologists and other students of world literature," and immediately gives its name: "Science-fiction is a branch of literature that is as old as *Gulliver's Travels*.... Yet up to a couple of decades ago, it lacked even a name for itself" (vii). Then, after again identifying the genre as a specific form of fantastic literature, he offers this succinct definition: science fiction "brings all the books together that base their fantasy upon any extrapolation of science. Hence, the generic term of science-fiction" (viii).

It is also interesting that Wollheim, on this second occasion, says little about the potential value of science fiction as prophecy—perhaps because none of the four works he was presenting could have been plausibly regarded as predictions of events that might someday occur. Instead, he offers two other defenses of the genre that would later become commonplace: first, "the fact that" science fiction "has now come to the fore is a product of our times, for we live in an era of constantly accelerating change, when the margin between what is and what will be has drawn so close as to force speculation and prognostication upon even ordinarily unimaginative persons" (vii). Science fiction, in other words, is said to represent the characteristic mindset of the contemporary world. It is an early version of an argument that would later be associated with writer and scholar James Gunn, who said in *Alternate Worlds: An Illustrated History of Science Fiction* (1975) that

> we live, indisputably, in a science fiction world. All around us we see evidences of a new order: life is not what it was for our fathers and certainly not what it was for their fathers. Life moves faster, and we move with it. We are on the back of galloping technology, and we cannot dismount without breaking our necks.[12]

Wollheim also asserts that "no literature has any lasting value unless its main theme is man.... The ideal science-fiction novel is ... the book which manages to combine a sound imagination and believable prognostication with a sincere desire to get the reader thinking along concepts vaster than his own petty life, concepts as large at least as the movement of Earth's inhabitants as a whole" (xii–xiii). The notion that science fiction could be uniquely thought-provoking was later emphasized by John W. Campbell, Jr., who said that science fiction was "a way of considering the past, present, and future from a different viewpoint, and taking a look at how else we *might* do things ... a convenient analog system for thinking about new scientific, social, and economic ideas—and for re-examining old ideas."[13]

While Wollheim's introduction lacks anything resembling a capsule history of science fiction—a task that subsequent anthologists would address—he does contrive to mention a number of authors and works that collectively demonstrate the long history and large scope of science fiction: along with general references to H. G. Wells, Edgar Rice Burroughs, E. E. "Doc" Smith, John W. Campbell, Jr., Robert A. Heinlein, and A. E. van Vogt, the introduction mentions Thomas More's *Utopia* (1516), Mary Shelley's *Frankenstein, or, The Modern Prometheus* (1818, 1831), Jules Verne's *Journey to the Center of the Earth* (1864), Edward Bellamy's *Looking Backward: 2000–1887* (1888), M. P. Shiel's *The Purple Cloud* (1901), Hilaire Belloc's *The Man Who Made Gold* (1930), Aldous Huxley's *Brave New World* (1932), and C. S. Lewis's *Out of the Silent Planet* (1938). Displaying a desire to set boundaries for the genre, however, Wollheim specifically excludes Lewis's sequel *Perelandra* (1943) as science fiction on the grounds that it strays into fantasy. Each of the four works was also preceded by an "Editor's Preface," and these provided Wollheim with the opportunity to name additional science fiction texts, including numerous books by Wells, Taine, Lovecraft, and Stapledon, Verne's *From the Earth to the Moon* (1865), Wollheim's own "The Man from Ariel" (1934), and several stories about superhumans: J. D. Beresford's *The Hampdenshire Wonder* (1911), Philip Wylie's *Gladiator* (1930), Stanley G. Weinbaum's *The New Adam* (1939), Norvell Page's "But Without Horns" (1940), and van Vogt's *Slan* (1940, 1946).

Another statement about science fiction is conveyed by the works Wollheim chose to present, and they command attention because it is hard to envision any knowledgeable reader in 1945, asked to select four science fiction novels to appear in a representative collection, deciding upon these particular texts. With the possible exception of the Lovecraft novella, none of these can be considered their author's finest work, and there are literally scores of other science fiction novels from this period that were more esteemed then, and are more esteemed now, than any of the novels in this collection. It is possible, of course, that Wollheim could not obtain permission to republish several other novels that he would have preferred, forcing him to settle for these unlikely candidates.

Perhaps, though, one can discern a logic to Wollheim's selections; for if someone tried to make a list of major themes in the science fiction of the era, four prominent items would be space travel, time travel, aliens, and future superhumans—and Wollheim's book offers one example of each type. True, the "time travel" in Taine's novel is of an unusual variety—a "time viewer" that enables present-day scientists to observe the life of a dinosaur in the late Cretaceous Period—and Lovecraft's ancient aliens, staying alive by inhabiting the bodies of other intelligent beings, are hardly typical of the genre; but considered as an illustration of the typical subject matter of the twentieth-century genre, *The Portable Novels of Science* could be defended as a satisfactory compendium. In two cases, Wollheim's own language suggests that the novel's contents did in fact influence his choice, since he comments in his "Editor's Preface" to *The First Men in the Moon* that it was Wells's second interplanetary story, and the only one that actually took its protagonists to another world, and the "Editor's Preface" to *Odd John*, as indicated, offers what amounts to a short history of the literature of superhumans. But the feature of Taine's novel that Wollheim emphasizes is its strong scientific content, not its innovative form of time travel, as he notes that the book was originally published by a publisher who specialized in science books, and Lovecraft's novella is cited as a superior example of science fiction horror; also, since the "Editor's Preface" calls Lovecraft "the Edgar Allan Poe of this century,"[14] it is apparent that Wollheim laments this author's relative obscurity at that time and would like to heighten awareness of his work, clearly another reason for this selection.

More broadly, we can only guess about the many considerations that might have led Wollheim to these selections. Evaluating Stapledon's works, most readers and scholars would agree that *Last and First Men* (1930) and *Star Maker* (1937) are superior to *Odd John*, but Wollheim might have feared that their vast, cosmic perspectives, and lack of individual characters, would be too disconcerting for inexperienced readers of science fiction. In selecting a Wells novel, Wollheim might have viewed the implications of *The Time Machine* (1895) and *The Island of Dr. Moreau* (1896) as too disturbing, and *The War of the Worlds* (1898) was at the time unfortunately associated with Orson Welles's disastrously misinterpreted radio adaptation of the novel in 1938. Taine's novel, which limits itself to an apparently realistic account of the activities of ancient dinosaurs, might have been deemed a "safe," even educational choice, and Wollheim's most daring selection—the Lovecraft novella—might have resulted from another concern: Wollheim had surely been advised to limit his collection to a certain length—he comments that "length of story was a factor" in his decisions (xii)—and since "The Shadow Out of Time" was actually a novella, it could serve as the book's fourth "novel" without taking up too much additional space. Finally, though *Before the Dawn* has now been relegated to the status of a minor, forgotten work, Wollheim's other three choices are still admired today as excellent science fiction, even if they would not be regarded as the very best the genre had to offer in 1945.

Although there have been many collections of science fiction novellas, and many omnibuses presenting three or more novels by the same author, very few books have emulated *The Portable Novels of Science* by presenting three or more novels by different authors. E. F. Bleiler and T. E. Dikty did publish, from 1952 to 1954, three volumes entitled *The Year's Best Science Fiction Novels*, but these consisted of novellas, not true novels, and the two

"Twayne Triplets" edited by an uncredited Fletcher Pratt in 1952 included both novels and novellas. The only other books of this type I can currently identify are Wollheim's *Ace Science Fiction Reader* (1971), a collection of three novels; two anonymously edited books—*The Paranoid Fifties: Three Classic Science Fiction Novels* (1995) and *The First Science Fiction Novel Megapack: Featuring Six Great Science Fiction Novels* (2016); I. F. Clarke's eight-volume compilation *British Future Fiction: 1700–1914* (2001); and Gary K. Wolfe's Library of Congress compilations, *American Science Fiction: Four Classic Novels, 1953–1956* (2012) and *American Science Fiction: Five Classic Novels, 1956–1958* (2012). In light of Wollheim's claim, which would be echoed by many commentators, that the novel represents the "most powerful form" of science fiction, it seems surprising that so few anthologists have endeavored to collectively publish related science fiction novels by different authors

Conklin's *The Best of Science Fiction* is both the first, and the second, major science fiction anthology. It appeared first in 1946; however, since he only began working on the book after Healy and McComas had launched their own project, and since he was unable to use any of the stories they had already chosen, it can also be considered the second major anthology. The fact that Conklin, despite starting later, was able to complete and publish his anthology first was an early sign that he had a natural aptitude for such editing work—as was demonstrated in the decades to come, as he became one of the field's most prolific anthologists.

The first thing one notices about Conklin's *The Best of Science Fiction* is its unusually extensive introductory material: in addition to Conklin's thorough "Introduction," there is also a lengthy preface by John W. Campbell, Jr., entitled "Concerning Science Fiction." Unlike earlier anthologies which seemed primarily focused on addressing readers who were unfamiliar with science fiction, Conklin clearly was striving to appeal to two different audiences: Campbell's name would help to attract experienced science fiction readers, and Conklin knew he would vigorously argue that science fiction was a uniquely challenging, and uniquely valuable, form of literature. In contrast, Conklin's own introduction could speak to general readers and emphasize the genre's similarities to other forms of literature.

It is also interesting that Conklin is the first anthologist to explicitly refer to another anthologist, as his introduction, like Stong's, announces that it is excluding routine space adventures, and he even quotes Stong while denouncing "the run-of-the-mill S-F pulpsters, those highly prosperous producers for juveniles who are responsible for Phil Stong's denunciation of most science fiction as a 'pabulum of reiterated nonsense.'"[15] While Conklin thus endorses Stong's desire for fresh and original material, another aspect of Stong's argument is indirectly referenced—and refuted—near the end of Campbell's preface:

9. Assemblers of Infinity   141

> Some while ago, I was trying to figure out why it was that a friend who very much liked fantasy—(as distinct from science fiction, fantasy embraces only the "ghoulies and ghosties and things that go boomp in the night")—could not abide science fiction.
>
> The reason was hard to find. He didn't lack imagination, or have a stereotyped mind; if that were the case, he wouldn't have enjoyed fantasy stories so wholeheartedly. Eventually, it worked out to this:
>
> In fantasy, the author knows it isn't true, the reader knows it isn't true, knows it didn't happen, and can't ever happen, and everybody is agreed. But in science fiction, this man felt an overwhelming pressure on the part of the author to convince him that the story was possible, and could happen, a driving sincerity that oppressed and repelled him. The author was trying to convince him that the story—which he knew perfectly well was utterly "fantastic"—*could, and quite probably would, happen.*
>
> In effect, he didn't like science fiction because the author was sincere, highly competent, and had put into his story such a feeling of certainty and reality that it almost forced the reader to accept its message against his own "better judgment":
>
> The story we were discussing—in 1942—was *Solution Unsatisfactory*.[16]

Campbell's friend shared Stong's preference for stories that were undeniably impossible—indeed, it is slightly possible that the friend was Stong himself, since both men lived in the New York City area and were connected to the publishing industry, and hence might have met—but the problem with this friend's attitude was illustrated by his rejection of Robert A. Heinlein's story "Solution Unsatisfactory" (1941, published as by Anson MacDonald), the first story in Conklin's collection, which Campbell had just defended as "uncannily accurate prophecy" (vi). Campbell therefore enthusiastically embraces the argument that Wollheim tentatively presented and backed away from, the argument that science fiction is meritorious because its stories can sometimes predict the future.

Still, as another aspect of Conklin's twofold strategy, his own introduction, while also offering examples of science fiction's successful predictions, follows Wollheim in de-emphasizing its prophetic aspects, noting that "science fiction, despite its treading on the toes of nuclear physics, has no business claiming the robes of the prophet" (xvi)—since their stories merely make use of already available scientific knowledge—and later announcing that

> for fun, after all, is the primary import of science fiction, which, like the detective story and the fairy tale as well, has one purpose, clear and simple: the purpose of entertaining you. It is first as entertainment that *The Best of Science Fiction* is offered, with only a slight and faintly uneasy salaam to the writers who have put their imaginations to the practical problem of what nuclear fission might involve in the way of social and political change [xviii].

Surveying Campbell's and Conklin's introductions and the contents of the book, one detects a recurring desire to classify—both to establish science fiction as one specific variety of fantastic literature in general, and to divide science fiction itself into subcategories. While Wollheim's *The Pocket Book of Science-Fiction* noted that science fiction was merely one modern type of story "that took place only in the mind of the narrator," Conklin offers a more precise taxonomy: "Under the broad heading of fantasy, there are four primary types: the utopia, the fairy tale, the supernatural story, and science fiction" (xix). While discussing the three other forms, he indicates how they differ from science fiction: utopias "often have science-fiction overtones in the mechanics of their construction," but they are distinguished by their "purposefulness.... They always have a moral, an end in view, a line to sell, a philosophy to put across. In this resides much of their dullness" (xix). Science fiction can be distinguished from supernatural tales because their happenings "all have rational explanations" (xxi). And though Conklin never specifies precisely how fairy tales are unlike science fiction, his list of their typically magical contents—"Mice wear tophats and talk Oxford English; beautiful girls spout jewels instead of words; jackasses change into handsome princelings; and ogres nearly, but not quite, devour harmless little children" (xix–xx)—provides ample support for his conclusion that "fairy tales are wonderful, but they are not science fiction" (xx). Campbell's introduction employs a similar strategy to distinguish science fiction from fantasy—describing their fantastic content—with his parenthetical remark that "as distinct from science fiction, fantasy embraces only the 'ghoulies and ghosties and things that go boomp in the night.'"

In a sense, Stong's anthology had already divided science fiction (and a great deal of fantasy) into idiosyncratic groups—stories with new ideas, stories with new approaches to old ideas, and frightening stories—but *The Best of Science Fiction* makes more of an effort to offer comprehensive categories based on a single organizing principle. Campbell describes "three broad divisions of science fiction" essentially based on the authors' different intents:

1. Prophecy stories, in which the author tries to predict the effects of a new invention.
2. Philosophical stories, in which the author presents, in story form, some philosophical question using the medium of science fiction simply to set the stage for the particular point he wants to discuss.
3. Adventure science fiction, wherein the action and the plot are the main type [vi].

Yet Campbell also acknowledges that "no story can be purely one or the other of these" categories (vi), weakening its usefulness as a taxonomy, and he is also contradicting Conklin who, after all, excluded utopias from the genre of science fiction on the precise grounds that a typical author of utopias is solely focused on "the particular point he wants to discuss."

Conklin's table of contents endeavors to subdivide science fiction in a different way, according to its subject matter. He says in his introduction that "the present collection makes no pretense of being comprehensive," but "I think I have represented most of the major types [of science fiction], one way or another. As you will see if you study the table of contents, the species has only a few important divisions; though within these divisions the varieties, the sports and mutants are infinite" (xxv). Conklin divides his anthology into six sections: "The Atom," stories about atomic energy; "The Wonders of Earth," stories about strange phenomena found on Earth; "The Superscience of Man," stories about scientific advances that do not take the form of new inventions; "Dangerous Inventions," requiring no explanation; "Adventures in Dimension," including time travel; and "From Outer Space," the book's longest section, which despite its title mostly features stories about space travel, not stories about visitors from outer space. Ignoring the special category of stories involving "The Atom," a reflection of one specific concern that dominated America in 1946, one could say that, according to Conklin, science fiction is primarily about these things: amazing discoveries in our own world; posited scientific advances, including new inventions; time travel and travel into other dimensions; and travel into outer space. One cannot say that the list is comprehensive—if nothing else, one might wish to add the characteristic subjects of humanity's distant future, robots and artificial intelligence, and fantastic events in Earth's past—but Conklin is undoubtedly identifying the most common themes in the science fiction of his era.

And, in fact, Conklin is the first science fiction anthologist to indicate that his collection is designed to be representative of the entire genre: "I have tried to make it an adequate cross-section of the whole field, historically as well as contextually." Indeed, he employs versions of the word "represent" four times on a single page: "no one anthology can actually represent [science fiction], without taking on the dimensions of an unabridged dictionary"; "I have represented most of the major types"; "All I have been able to do is to present a few of the choicer representatives of each division"; and "Beyond simple representation, the first and most obvious standard for an anthology of short stories is that it shall contain no long stories" (xxv). And while using a form of "represent" the fifth time, Conklin seems to criticize his most immediate predecessor, *The Portable Novels of Science*, and its choices, with this remark concluding his defense of his work: "at least I have not packed in half a dozen novels and called the result a representative anthology" (xxv).

Another distinguishing feature of Conklin's book is that it is the first anthology to include a capsule history of science fiction, which makes up the fourth section of his introduction. Although he begins by saying that "it is impossible to say ... when the first science-fiction story was written," he then indicates that it originated at the time of "the beginning of the industrial revolution and the growth of interest in the physical sciences," presumably the nineteenth century, although he also describe one eighteenth-century text, Jonathan Swift's *Gulliver's Travels* (1726), as "certainly one of the greatest science-fiction stories of all time" (xxi). Conklin proceeds to discuss, roughly in chronological order, a number of nineteenth-century authors and works: Richard Adams Locke's *The Moon Hoax* (1835); Edgar Allan Poe's "stories of the mind"; Fitz James O'Brien's "tales of super-microscopes, invisible men, and the like"; the "adventurous machinery" of Jules Verne; Arthur Conan Doyle, Ambrose Bierce, and Jack London, who all "dabbled in the field"; H. Rider Haggard "and others of his fictional school," who "developed the sciences of exploration and geographical prospecting with a fine disregard for the petty limitations of the known world"; Frank Stockton's *The Great War Syndicate* (1889); and Mark Twain's *A Connecticut Yankee in King Arthur's Court* (1889) (xxi–xxii). "Finally," around the beginning of the twentieth century, "the elder statesmen of modern science fiction began making their appearance: H. G. Wells, George Allen [sic] England, Charles B. Stilson, Austin Hall, Homer Eon Flint, Garrett P. Serviss, Julian Hawthorne, and a number of other writers, most of whom you no doubt have never heard about" (xxii). He concludes with a page about the rise of the science fiction magazines, beginning with Gernsback's *Amazing Stories* and ending with Campbell's *Astounding Science-Fiction*. Later, he also mentions several recent authors: S. Fowler Wright, David Lindsay, Edwin Balmer, Philip Wylie, A. Merritt, C. S. Lewis, Olaf Stapledon, and J. U. Giesy. While some might complain about the exclusion of several British authors, ranging from Mary Shelley to Aldous Huxley, Conklin's overview of science fiction history is reasonably comprehensive, and many later critics would agree with Conklin that the genre primarily emerged in the nineteenth century.

Of course, while the anthology itself included an edited version of *The Great War Syndicate* and stories by Poe, Doyle, and Wells, all of the other luminaries that Conklin lists were excluded from his "representative" anthology, something that Conklin feels obliged to explain. He identifies three problems with their works: first, some of them are simply inferior—*The Moon Hoax* is "dreary and prolix reading" (xvii), and the efforts of Doyle, Bierce, and London did not achieve "great success"; second, O'Brien's stories fall short of the standards of modern science fiction because "he neglected to arrange any scientific mumbo-jumbo to 'explain' their happenings" (xxii); and finally, "many outstanding science-fiction writers have written chiefly in the novel form" (xxv) and hence could not be included.

While this history of science fiction was a novel feature, Conklin's anthology may be most noteworthy for laying the groundwork for the thematic anthology, consisting entirely of stories about a single subject. Conklin himself edited several of these, including three that covered two of the topics that were the focus of sections of this book: dimensional travel (*Science Fiction*

Adventures in Dimension [1953]) and space travel (*Enemies in Space* [1962] and *Great Stories of Space Travel* [1963]). He also edited anthologies devoted to subjects that he failed to foreground here, like alien invaders (*Invaders of Earth* [1952]), robots (*Science-Fiction Thinking Machines* [1954]), mutants (*Science Fiction Adventures in Mutation* [1955]), and medical advances (*Great Science Fiction about Doctors* [1963] with Noah D. Fabricant). Further, while these are only some of the innumerable retrospective anthologies that were devoted to certain topics, it has also become increasing common to assemble anthologies of original stories based on one theme, sometimes a very specific theme, like Kevin J. Anderson's *The War of the Worlds: Global Dispatches* (1996), featuring new stories taking place during the Martian invasion of Wells's *The War of the Worlds*. Thus, while only the most naïve definitions of science fiction would assert that the genre can be identified by certain sorts of subject matter, that is precisely the perspective on the genre that is embedded in many science fiction anthologies.

In beginning their introduction to *Adventures in Time and Space*, Healy and McComas address the same issue that Wollheim wrestled with while introducing *The Pocket Book of Science-Fiction*: should they argue that science fiction is uniquely valuable because it can predict the future, or merely emphasize its other qualities as worthwhile reading material? They quickly decide that making that choice is not really necessary:

> Science-fiction concerns itself with the world of the future, a world whose political, social and economic life has been shaped by the expansion of scientific knowledge. In depicting this world, science-fiction very nearly falls between two stools. Is it literature? Or is it prophecy?
> We contend that it is both.[17]

Still, like Wollheim, they also partially retreat from defending science fiction as prophecy: "more important to us than either of these aspects of science-fiction in offering this collection is our conviction that this field offers readers an entirely original and enjoyable adventure in reading" (xi). Throughout these early anthologies, then, only Campbell does not seem to fear that some potential purchasers and readers might be put off by special claims for science fiction, inspiring editors to include bland assertions that these stories merit attention solely because they are "enjoyable."

Healy and McComas also convey a certain ambivalence toward the history of science fiction. Like Conklin, they claim that the genre has a long history, identifying one example—Johannes Kepler's *Somnium* (1634)—that dates back to the European Renaissance:

> Science-fiction reaches further back in the past than one might imagine. From the very beginning of astronomy man has dreamed of checking his theories by actual visits to the other planets of his universe. Among its many other attributes, that

lovely satellite, the moon, has been a perpetual challenge to the would-be voyagers of space. One of the first science-fiction novels was written (in Latin) by the great astronomer, Kepler [xii].

Describing two other obvious progenitors of the field, Healy and McComas surprisingly discount the works of Jules Verne on the grounds that "Verne's emphasis, however, remained on the adventure aspect and science-fiction as such was never quite realized in his writings." The true father of science fiction, they assert, was Wells: "It is to the imagination and intellect of Herbert George Wells that science-fiction owes its initial establishment as a mature form of literature" (xii).

Although they later mention Shelley's *Frankenstein* while discussing robots, Healy and McComas do not provide the sort of detailed survey found in Conklin's introduction, probably deeming it unnecessary, because they also announce, as is evident from their table of contents, that "our aim has been to introduce *modern* science-fiction taken almost exclusively from the magazine field" (xv). In fact, only one of their stories—S. Fowler Wright's "Brain" (1932)—did not originally appear in an American science fiction magazine. One could say that it was only logical to emphasize this contemporary material, since many readers outside the genre were already familiar with classic writers like Verne and Wells; yet by "almost exclusively" presenting these recent stories, the editors were also implicitly conveying the opinion that these works were actually central to science fiction, and were superior to their venerable precursors, thus relegating the long history of science fiction to a secondary status.

Another innovative aspect of this anthology is that it presents, along with 33 stories, two works of nonfiction—even though, in their introductory remarks preceding Willy Ley's "V-2 Rocket Cargo Ship" (1945), Healy and McComas note that "it was not the editor's original plan to include any nonfiction articles in this volume" (344). In this way, the anthology seems to extend the boundaries of science fiction in two ways. First, it had long been the habit of Campbell's *Astounding Science-Fiction*—and occasionally, other science fiction magazines—to include articles about cutting-edge or speculative science, suggesting that such works could be considered part of the genre, and by featuring one work of this type, Ley's essay, the editors convey a similar attitude. The other nonfictional piece in the anthology, A. M. Phillips's "Time Travel Happens!" (1939), is an apparently factual report of an actual instance of time travel, and this falls into the category of another type of nonfiction sometimes associated with science fiction—purportedly true accounts of events and phenomena that are rejected as false by the scientific community. Campbell's predecessor, F. Orlon Tremaine, had serialized in several 1934 issues of *Astounding Stories* a renowned compilation of such reports, Charles Fort's *Lo!* (1931), and at the time this anthology appeared, the current editor of *Amazing Stories*, Ray Palmer, was publishing material, presented as nonfictional, describing the fantastical "Shaver Hypothesis" discussed in another chapter. Within a few years, as noted, such works would be permanently exiled from science fiction by disgruntled fans, but they would forever remain a vibrant, if unacknowledged, form of science fiction.

Finally, and perhaps appropriately, *Adventures in Time and Space* was the first science fiction anthology to anticipate vast numbers of future science fiction anthologies: "There will be, we hope, many more collections of these stories that challenge both the imagination and the intelligence; that portray logically and well man's existence" (xv). Although Healy and McComas personally did not match Wollheim and Conklin in their later efforts, editing only a few more anthologies, one can certainly say that their hope for additional anthologies was more than fulfilled in the decades that followed their first anthology.

No one can deny that *The Best of Science Fiction* and *Adventures in Time and Space* were milestones in the history of the genre; unlike the overwhelming majority of anthologies, they have been republished on several occasions, sometimes in shorter versions, and so have long continued to attract readers; Webster reported that he consistently recommended these anthologies as two of the five books that could best acquaint someone with the genre. They also established a model for a type of anthology—the comprehensive anthology offering the genre's best stories—that has endured to this day, although some of these, like *The Wesleyan Anthology of Science Fiction* (2010), are specifically designed to be used as textbooks in college classes, instead of seeking a broader audience.[18] And the last time I visited a bookstore, its science fiction section included one recent addition to this tradition, Ann and Jeff VanderMeer's *The Big Book of Science Fiction: The Ultimate Collection* (2016), still attracting readers seeking a convenient, one-volume overview of the genre's history.

Any effort to continue a comprehensive survey of all of the science fiction anthologies ever published would require a book in itself—perhaps several books, since even Webster's *Anthropology 101* is far from complete, and anthologies have continued to appear since he completed his research. Yet surveying the history of the science fiction anthology since 1946, one can discern two patterns: first, a steady increase in the numbers of the anthologies published during the 1950s, 1960s, and 1970s, and a significant decline in their numbers in the 1980s and thereafter. Any attempt to explain these trends must consider the science fiction anthology's relationship to its most obvious competitor, the science fiction magazine.

As already suggested, as vehicles for publishing short stories, anthologies apparently were superior to magazines in several ways. In contrast to frail, ephemeral magazines, which most readers quickly discarded, hardcover and paperback books provided a more durable and permanent home for stories worth remembering. Retrospective anthologies allowed editors to provide readers only with superior stories, whereas magazines facing regular deadlines were often obliged to publish the best material they had on hand, even if it was less than outstanding. Editors might prefer to work on anthologies, free from the pressure of producing several magazines a year on a regular schedule and happy to trade the security of a monthly salary for the prospect of ample royalties and additional earnings from foreign editions and later republications of their collections; and authors often found that the payments for stories in anthologies exceeded the payments available from the magazines. Since the 1950s, books had demonstrated the power to attract far more readers than the magazines, and in the 1960s and 1970s, there began appearing numerous series of original anthologies seemingly designed to replace magazines, like John Carnell's *New Writings in SF* anthologies, Knight's *Orbit* anthologies, Terry Carr's *Universe* anthologies, Robert Hoskins's *Infinity* anthologies, Robert Silverberg's *New Dimensions* anthologies, Harry Harrison's *Nova* anthologies, Samuel R. Delany and Marilyn Hacker's *Quark* anthologies, and Judy-Lynn del Rey's *Stellar* anthologies. At the same time, the numbers of science fiction magazines were precipitously declining. One has to ask, then: why didn't the anthologies simply replace the magazines?

As it happens, I long ago addressed this issue in a 2000 column for the science fiction magazine *Interzone*, entitled "What Is a Science Fiction Magazine? (And Why on Earth Are They Still Around?)." I noted therein that unlike anthologies, which usually include only an editor's introduction and stories, magazines offer a plethora of other features: editorials, nonfiction articles about science and science fiction, interviews, book reviews, film and television reviews, poetry, interior artwork, readers' letters, and advertisements. The experience of reading a science fiction magazine, then, is like going to a science fiction convention: "magazines have served as the waterholes of science fiction, where fans gather not only to enjoy the latest stories from old masters and rising stars, but also to sample its associated products and overhear another portion of the fascinating extended conversation that has accompanied science fiction ever since it was first recognized as a genre."[19] While a few series of anthologies have endeavored to offer a similarly eclectic mixture of features—like Jerry Pournelle and John F. Carr's *Endless Frontier* anthologies, which provided readers with stories, poems, and articles about space travel—they generally could not duplicate the stimulating variety of the science fiction magazines, which would explain why all of the series of anthologies listed above eventually ceased publication, while a small number of science fiction magazines from the 1960s have endured to this day.

The precipitous decline in science fiction anthologies is usually attributed to Roger Elwood, who flooded the market with innumerable and usually inferior anthologies in the 1970s, as described by Kathryn Cramer and others.[20] Yet after the publication of innumerable and often unmemorable science fiction novels in the 1950s, the market for science fiction novels eventually recovered, and one would have expected the same to occur with science fiction anthologies. The issue, I think, is that readers who prefer anthologies of short stories, by their nature, must crave constant originality; yet since the 1980s, with the emergence of *Star Trek* novels and similar series of novels based on other media or original franchises, the science fiction marketplace has been driven by readers who desire familiarity: new stories, yes, but new stories featuring characters and settings that they know very well from watching films and television programs or reading previous novels. This preference for the familiar extends to favoring the single extended story of a novel to the irregularity of reading several different stories, although there have been a number of original anthologies featuring stories based on media franchises or various sorts of devised shared worlds, like David A. Drake and Bill Fawcett's *The Fleet* anthologies. However, since the authors contributing to such anthologies are bound by rigid guidelines and, sometimes, a specified story arc, the stories by different authors invariably seem very similar to each other.

The other question to ask, then, is: if short stories in magazines are retaining an audience, and traditional sorts of original and retrospective anthologies are not, why haven't the magazines replaced the anthologies? Part of the answer relates to the three original arguments I presented regarding the importance of anthologies: to this day, no doubt, there remain readers like the young Westfahl who like reading science fiction stories but prefer anthologies to magazines; anthologies remain the best place to find excellent stories from less prominent writers; and aside from their stories, anthologies also provide valuable statements about the nature and history of science fiction to readers with an interest in the genre. So, if someone wants to learn more about the history of science fiction, they can always read books like Adam Roberts's *The History of Science Fiction* (2016); but they might prefer instead to read the VanderMeers' *The Big Book of Science Fiction*, wherein a century of excellent stories illustrating the development and growth of the genre are conveniently arranged in chronological order.

Two other types of retrospective anthologies, that chronicle science fiction history in a piecemeal fashion, have also proven to have lasting appeal. First is the thematic anthology offering the best representatives of one particular type of science fiction story; for example, in the early 2000s, Harry Turtledove collaborated with Martin H. Greenberg to edit three such volumes: *The Best Military Science Fiction of the 20th Century* (2001); *The Best Alternate History Stories of the 20th Century* (2001); and *The Best Time Travel Stories of the 20th Century* (2002). Second is the anthology of the year's best science fiction stories: significantly, in every single year since the early 1950s, there has always appeared at least one such anthology, and sometimes several such anthologies, that were all installments of ongoing series of year's best anthologies that, in some cases, endured for a decade or more. There are obvious reasons why readers seek out such anthologies: even though their numbers have declined, most people simply do not find it possible to read all of the science fiction magazines, and while intense competition has increased the quality of their offerings, they continue to include some mediocre products. An experienced and knowledgeable reader of science fiction, then, provides a valuable service by reading all of the magazines published in one year, selecting their best stories, and presenting an edited volume of those stories in one convenient volume. I recently read a short article by a veteran science fiction scholar that described a few recent science fiction stories, and I noticed that all of them had appeared in one of Gardner Dozois's *The Year's Best Science Fiction* anthologies. Clearly, this busy and productive scholar did not have the time to read science fiction magazines, but he regularly read Dozois's anthologies as his way to keep up with developments in the field.

As for original anthologies, the type that emerged in the 1960s, offering unrelated stories, have now become rare, as magazines are now viewed as better venues for such material; but editors have been able to come up with original and stimulating ideas for original anthologies that can be given to authors with no restrictions as to how they develop their ideas, and these ideas can inspire worthwhile stories that otherwise would have never been written. Indeed, some stories written for such original anthologies have been nominated for, and even won, major awards, such as Larry Niven's Hugo Award-nominated "The Return of William Proxmire" from Gregory Benford's and Greenberg's *What Might Have Been, Volume 1: Alternate Empires* (1990), devoted to alternate history stories involving empires; Nicholas A. DiChario's Hugo Award-nominated "The Winterberry" from Mike Resnick's *Alternate Kennedys* (1993), alternate history stories featuring John F. Kennedy; Gregory Feeley's Nebula Award-nominated "The Crab Lice" from Resnick's *Alternate Tyrants* (1997), alternate history stories about famous people who become dictators; Bruce Holland Rogers's Nebula Award-winning "Thirteen Ways to Water" from Greenberg and John Helfers's *Black Cats and Broken Mirrors* (1999), devoted to stories about superstitions; and Neil Gaiman's Hugo Award-winning "A Study in Emerald" from Michael Reaves and John Pelan's *Shadows over Baker Street* (2004), stories that confront Arthur Conan Doyle's Sherlock Holmes with the world of H. P. Lovecraft. As long as editors can continue to come up with attractive concepts, these sorts of anthologies are also likely to keep appearing in the future.

Overall, then, one cannot say that science fiction anthologies are thriving—when I visited a Barnes and Noble bookstore in 2018, the science fiction section had only two shelves devoted to anthologies, and 94 shelves devoted to novels—but they have retained a niche in the science fiction marketplace and will undoubtedly continue to appear. For if nothing else, preparing an anthology that represents the genre represents an attractive challenge. My chapter title, borrowed from Kevin J. Anderson and Doug Beason's 1993 novel about alien nanotechnology on the Moon, epitomizes the arduous but stimulating task that such anthologists face: surveying a virtually infinite array of stories and carefully choosing the ones best suited to their purposes. It will surprise no one to hear that on two occasions, I myself have endeavored to create and publish an anthology of science fiction stories, like many other scholars, and some day, when other tasks do not occupy my time, I may be able to make my own contribution to the long and distinguished tradition of science fiction anthologies.

PART IV. THE 1950S AND THEREAFTER

10

Invasion of the Saucer Men
How the Universe of Science Fiction Expanded in the 1950s

Prior to 1945, virtually all works of science fiction—at least, those that went by that name—were stories, novels, and art published in science fiction magazines, and one might also mention the innumerable fanzines that mostly featured articles, letters, and cartoons related to science fiction as well as occasional science fiction stories. But as is commonly noted, the explosion of the atomic bomb in 1945, and the subsequent establishment of the well-publicized American space program, generated a larger interest in futuristic fiction that enabled the genre to expand beyond the magazines into several new areas: science fiction stories in "mainstream" or "slick" magazines; science fiction hardcover and paperback books for adults; juvenile science fiction books; science fiction comic books; science fiction art appearing outside the magazines; and science fiction merchandise. However, these new forms of science fiction have received varying degrees of attention, and here they will receive varying degrees of attention in inverse proportion to the amount of attention that they have received elsewhere.

Three generalizations about all of these developments can be provisionally advanced. First, since powerful individuals with no background in science fiction, but desiring to dabble in the field, often felt unsure about how to approach the genre, they tended to recruit people who had experience in writing for science fiction magazines and engaging in other fan activities to guide or assist in their initiatives. Second, even as they focused on work outside of the genre's traditional venues, these writers and fans remained in touch with the science fiction community, and members of that community were attentive to, and supportive of, what they were doing; those in worked in other media, then, functioned as ambassadors of science fiction, not as immigrants to another genre, and one could even characterize them, as suggested in this chapter's title, as invaders, determined to bring science fiction into areas where it had heretofore been absent. Third, even though they were well aware of how science fiction was evolving and changing in the 1940s and 1950s, and even though writers working outside the magazines were advancing alongside those who continued to focus on magazines, the people working in fields other than literature tended to favor the sort of science fiction that had been popular when they first became involved in the genre—namely, the science fiction of the 1930s—probably because they perceived (correctly) that such adventures would be most pleasing to people who were unfamiliar with science fiction and generally disinclined to examine it; indeed, despite their own proclivities, they probably felt compelled to emulate the science fiction of their youth.

The results of their work were paradoxical: on one hand, science fiction readers were excited to see works recognizably part of their genre appearing in other media, they knew many of their creators, and they appreciated their efforts to enlarge the science fiction audience. On the other hand, readers worried especially that the stories in films, television programs, and comic books, largely replicating older forms of science fiction that magazines and publishers of the 1950s would have generally rejected as naive and immature, were reinforcing the popular belief that science fiction was nothing more than "kids' stuff," not meriting the attention of adults.

In a way, what happened in the late 1940s and 1950s was a larger version of science fiction's initial foray outside the magazines—into the comic strips of the 1930s. The first of these, *Buck Rogers in the 25th Century* (1929–1967), was initially written by an author from the science fiction magazines, Philip Francis Nowlan, based on two stories he had published in 1928 and 1929 in *Amazing Stories*. Its protagonist Buck Rogers's early comic strip adventures were earthbound, as in the stories, featuring a contemporary man who awakens 500 years in the future to confront a foreign dictatorship controlling America; however, the strip soon ventured into outer space and came to resemble many of the space operas that were being published in the magazines of the 1930s. Once Nowlan had promulgated a pattern for this sort of science fiction, comic strip imitations of *Buck Rogers* soon appeared, most notably *Brick Bradford* (1933–1987) and *Flash Gordon* (1934–2003), and these inspired adaptations as radio series, film serials, and Big Little Books. Dedicated fans were happy to observe stories about outer space appearing outside the magazines, but they were concerned because these works did not reflect the maturation of science fiction that occurred in the 1940s. The main architect of that maturation, John W. Campbell, Jr., summed up this attitude in his 1946 introduction to Groff Conklin's anthology *The Best of Science Fiction* (1946), "Concerning Science Fiction": "Science fiction has, definitely, been a misunderstood type of material. In the public mind, 'Buck Rogers' is the standard science-fiction character; the comic strip has tended to be accepted as representative of the field. It is—precisely to the extent that Dick Tracy is representative of detective fiction."[1]

In examining the various invasions of science fiction figures into other areas in the 1950s, I will with relative haste cover the topics of science fiction in mainstream magazines, science fiction hardcover and paperback books, and science fiction films and television programs before moving on to examinations of science fiction comic books, science fiction art outside of the magazines, and science fiction merchandise; the topic of juvenile science fiction will be addressed in a later chapter. As it happens, my discussions of these new forms of science fiction in the 1950s will have autobiographical resonances, since my initial exposure to the genre almost entirely involved these forms.

In retrospect, though it attracted attention at the time, probably the least significant expansion of science fiction during this period was the appearance of several genre authors in mainstream, or "slick" magazines. After all, such magazines had long published occasional stories that could be classified as science fiction, including Stephen Vincent Benét's "By the Waters of Babylon" (*The Saturday Evening Post*, 1937), and Nelson Bond's *Exiles of Time* (Blue Book, 1940), and stories by authors more strongly associated with the pulp magazines did not necessarily have the effect of increasing the visibility of the genre, although it is possible that some readers, impressed by stories from, for example, Robert A. Heinlein and Ray Bradbury, might have sought out some of their books. Heinlein is widely celebrated as the first science fiction writer from the magazines who broke into these more prestigious markets, beginning in 1947 with "The Green Hills of Earth," which appeared in *The Saturday Evening Post*. However, he was hardly the only science fiction writer who published in that magazine: Gerald Kersh, an author who had specialized in writing science fiction and fantasy stories for mainstream magazines, eschewing the pulps, regularly published there, and *The Saturday Evening Post* also presented stories by other writers whose names were more familiar to readers of science fiction magazines, such as Ray Bradbury, John Christopher, Murray Leinster (whose *Post* stories credited his real name, Will F. Jenkins), Ward Moore, and Philip Wylie. In fact, that magazine had published enough science fiction and fantasy stories by 1963 as to generate an anthology, credited solely to "The Editors of *The Saturday Evening Post*," entitled *The Post Reader of Fantasy and Science Fiction* (1963).

Yet *The Saturday Evening Post* was not the only "mainstream" magazine that was publishing science fiction stories after World War II. During the postwar period, Heinlein stories appeared in *American Legion Magazine*, *Argosy*, *Blue Book*, *Boys' Life*, *Senior Prom*, and *Short Stories Magazine*, while in Great Britain, Arthur C. Clarke stories were published in non-genre magazines such as *The Heiress, King's College Review, Lilliput,* and *Sketch*; a bit later, I recall being thrilled to encounter another Clarke story, "The Secret" (as "The Secret of the Men in the Moon"), in the pages of the August 11, 1963, issue of the *This Week* magazine included in the Sunday newspaper received by my parents and many other newspapers. None of these publications outside of the science fiction magazines should be considered surprising, for authors are naturally attracted to the markets that pay the highest rates for their fiction, especially if they suspect that those publications might be more inclined than usual to include science fiction due to recent events.

Still, such publications outside of the genre magazines were becoming increasingly less significant primarily because, due to competition from paperback books and television, mass-market magazines primarily devoted to short fiction were gradually beginning to disappear. But one of the few magazines that still published and paid high rates for fiction, Hugh Hefner's *Playboy*, did become one of Clarke's favorite markets in the 1960s and early 1970s, and under the supervision of editor Ray Russell, the magazine also published stories by other noted authors such as J. G. Ballard, Robert Bloch, Ray Bradbury, Frederik Pohl, Robert Sheckley, Theodore Sturgeon, and others, who were all represented when *Playboy* published its own anthology of science fiction stories from the magazine, *The Playboy Book of Science Fiction and Fantasy* (1966), edited by an uncredited Russell. Later, the magazine published two award-winning science fiction stories, Ursula K. Le Guin's "Nine Lives" (1969) and Clarke's "A Meeting with Medusa" (1971) (reflecting the era's sexism, though, *Playboy* concealed Le Guin's gender by crediting her as "U. K. Le Guin").

In the postwar period, while major publishers were willing to publish occasional anthologies of science fiction, they initially remained disinclined to publish science fiction novels, so this task was left to the publishers of small presses specializing in science fiction. While a few small presses had already been established (most notably Arkham House, founded in 1939 and initially dedicated to republishing the works of H. P. Lovecraft), their numbers significantly increased after 1945. One reason is that by that time, many science fiction fans who had encountered the genre as youngsters in the magazines of the 1920s and 1930s were now mature adults who had accumulated enough experience and financial resources as to enable them to set up and run small businesses to print hardcover science fiction books; their usual priority was republishing fondly remembered serials and anthologies of stories that had originally appeared in earlier magazines. A typical example is Gnome Press, founded in 1946 by science fiction fan David A. Kyle and Martin Greenberg (not the Martin H. Greenberg who later edited innumerable anthologies); its noteworthy publications (all from the magazines) included the collected Conan stories of Robert E. Howard, Isaac Asimov's Foundation trilogy, and books by Robert A. Heinlein and Arthur C. Clarke. But these books, generated by and marketed primarily to the science fiction community, did not really represent an expansion of science fiction into other areas.

But gradually, larger publishers aimed at general audiences did begin to publish science fiction books. Doubleday began publishing hardcover science fiction books in January 1950 with Isaac Asimov's *Pebble in the Sky*, soon followed by several others, including Ray Bradbury's collection *The Martian Chronicles* in May 1950, and other publishers soon began publishing science fiction novels as well. Major authors still might turn to small presses on some occasions—as late as 1959, Heinlein published two anthologies from Gnome Press—but they generally migrated to major publishers because they were more prestigious, promoted their products widely and effectively, and thus enabled writers to heighten their visibility and, not incidentally, to earn much more money.

However, the most significant breakthrough came with the establishment of two companies with a special interest in publishing science fiction paperbacks: Ballantine Books, founded in 1952 by Ian and Betty Ballantine, and Ace Books, founded in 1953 by long-time writer and fan Donald A. Wollheim. Of the two, Ballantine quickly became noted for publishing some outstanding works of science fiction, including Clarke's *Childhood's End* (1953), Bradbury's *Fahrenheit 451* (1953), and Frederik Pohl's *Star Science Fiction* anthologies (1953–1959), while Ace Books published a dizzying variety of books from small presses (such as the first mass-market editions of Asimov's Foundation trilogy), other serials from the pulp magazines, and original novels by noteworthy new authors like Philip K. Dick and John Brunner.

Science fiction paperbacks were important because hardcover books were too expensive for typical consumers, and while they could be found in libraries, those in operation in the 1950s and early 1960s often had little interest in science fiction; I do not recall exactly when or where, but as an inveterate visitor to libraries around that time, I regularly went to one library that offered precisely two shelves of science fiction books. (I read every one of them, even a few books that really didn't belong there, such as Desmond Leslie and George Adamski's *Flying Saucers Have Landed* [1953].) But paperback books were cheap, and they were sold almost everywhere—newsstands, drug stores, grocery stores, and convenience stories—so anyone with an interest in science fiction could begin assembling their own collection of science fiction books, as I did starting in 1962. By that time, virtually every paperback publisher offered at least occasional science fiction books, so when I first purchased them, my earliest acquisitions came from Fawcett Crest Books, Bantam Books, Ace Books, and Pocket Books. I was especially pleased because virtually all major science fiction works of the twentieth century were occasionally republished, so that I was able to obtain virtually every book published by the five authors I most enjoyed at the time—Asimov, Bradbury, Clarke, Heinlein, and Clifford D. Simak. Other exciting acquisitions included all of the Skylark and Lensman novels of E. E. "Doc" Smith, Edgar Rice Burroughs's eleven Mars novels, C. S. Lewis's space trilogy, and—the paperbacks that everyone was purchasing in the 1960s—J. R. R. Tolkien's *The Hobbit* (1937) and *The Lord of the Rings* (1955–1956). And by buying many of the numerous anthologies then being published, I was able to read key stories by virtually all of the major writers who had appeared in the science fiction magazines from the 1920s to the present, further broadening my knowledge of the genre's history.

Also, while historians of science fiction understandably focus on the science fiction novels, collections, and anthologies that were being published during this period, a few science fiction writers profited by writing different sorts of books for general readers—nonfiction about space travel and other scientific subjects. One pioneering work of this kind was John W. Campbell, Jr.'s *The Atomic Story* (1947), but the first science fiction writer to specialize in books about space was Arthur C. Clarke, whose first published book was *Interplanetary Flight: An Introduction to Astronautics* (1950), soon followed by *The Exploration of Space* (1951), *The Exploration of the Moon* (1954), and *The Young Traveller in Space* (1954); at the time, in fact, these books were making more money for Clarke than his science fiction novels and stories. While he wrote two more books of this kind during the 1950s—*The Making of a Moon: The Story of the Earth Satellite Program* (1957) and *The Challenge of the Spaceship: Previews of Tomorrow's World* (1959)—he largely shifted his attention to writing another sort of nonfiction, books about the undersea world and his skin diving adventures, beginning with *The Coast of Coral* (1956), and he continued to produce nonfiction books until the 1990s, albeit with less frequency, as his science fiction novels were now more profitable.

Later, other science fiction writers also wrote books about outer space; as a child, I was thrilled to purchase three of their books in the Golden Library of Knowledge series for young readers: two by Otto Binder (who wrote science fiction as Eando Binder), *The Moon: Our Neighboring World* (1959) and *Planets: Other Worlds of Our Solar System* (1959), and one by Lester del Rey, *Space Flight: The Coming Exploration of the Universe* (1957). In addition to another book about space travel, *Rockets through Space* (1957), del Rey also wrote about other scientific subjects: *It's Your Atomic Story* (1951), *The Mysterious Earth* (1960), *Rocks and What They Tell Us* (1961), and *The Mysterious Sea* (1961). Other science fiction writers did the same: I purchased two of their books, Poul Anderson's *Is There Life on Other Worlds?* (1963), which included an introduction by Isaac Asimov, and Robert Silverberg's *Lost Cities and Vanished Civilizations* (1962). L. Sprague de Camp was also active in this field, contributing *Engines* (1961), *Man and Power* (1961), and *Energy and*

10. Invasion of the Saucer Men

Power (1962) to the Golden Library series and publishing *Lands Beyond* (1952, co-authored by Willy Ley), *Lost Continents: The Atlantis Theme in History, Science, and Literature* (1954), and other nonfiction books in the 1960s and thereafter, including a 1975 biography of H. P. Lovecraft.

Of course, the science fiction writer who became most devoted to writing nonfiction was Isaac Asimov, who began publishing occasional nonfiction works in the 1950s, mostly related to the field in which he earned a Ph.D., biochemistry: *Biochemistry and Human Metabolism* (1952, with Burnham S. Walker and William C. Boyd), *The Chemicals of Life* (1954), *Races and People* (1955, with Boyd), *Chemistry and Human Health* (1956, with Walker and M. Kolaya Nicholas), *Inside the Atom* (1956), *Building Blocks of the Universe* (1957), and *Only a Trillion* (1957). But the Russian launch of the Sputnik satellite in late 1957 inspired widespread concern that the United States was falling behind in its scientific education, and Asimov announced that he would do his part to address the problem by focusing exclusively on scientific nonfiction; soon, however, during the 1960s and 1970s he expanded his work in this area to cover an amazing variety of subjects, and though he did write two more novels and occasional stories, he did not return to full-time fiction writing until the 1980s.

A previous chapter discussed another sort of book that first appeared during this period, officially published as nonfiction but better considered science fiction, that offers purportedly solid evidence of aliens currently visiting Earth, usually by means of flying saucers, and interacting with human beings, and other accounts of events not accepted by the scientific community. To my knowledge, the only figure from the science fiction community who produced such material was Ray Palmer, who as editor of *Amazing Stories* had earlier promoted Richard Shaver's "Shaver hypothesis" that unseen underground beings were secretly influencing human behavior; his contribution to this growing body of literature was *The Coming of the Saucers* (1952), co-authored by Kenneth Arnold, the pilot whose 1947 observation of an apparent flying saucer first inspired interest in the alleged phenomena.

One should also mention the appearance during this period of several nonfiction books about science fiction. There were three collections of essays: Lloyd Arthur Eshbach's *Of Worlds Beyond: The Science of Science Fiction Writing* (1947), Reginald Bretnor's *Modern Science Fiction: Its Meaning and Its Future* (1953), and Basil Davenport's *The Science Fiction Novel: Imagination and Social Criticism* (1959). There were also some books about science fiction: J. O. Bailey's *Pilgrims through Time and Space: Trends and Patterns in Scientific and Utopian Fiction* (1947), Marjorie Hope Nicolson's *Voyages to the Moon* (1948), L. Sprague de Camp's *Science-Fiction Handbook* (1953), Basil Davenport's *Inquiry into Science Fiction* (1955), and Damon Knight's *In Search of Wonder: Essays on Modern Science Fiction* (1956). These books probably did little to increase awareness of science fiction outside of the science fiction community, with the possible exception of the one such book written by a major author, Kingsley Amis's *New Maps of Hell* (1960).

It is hard to say whether these other books by science fiction writers had any effect on the growth and development of science fiction. One could argue that they harmed the genre by diverting authors who might have written more science fiction into spending their time on other projects; yet these books brought the names of science fiction writers to a larger audience of readers who had never read science fiction, who perhaps were then inspired to seek out their works of science fiction. But I personally doubt that this was the case: for the record, I purchased *Lost Cities and Vanished Civilizations* solely because I was interested in its subject and, at the time, did not know that Silverberg was a science fiction writer; as he grew prominent in the late 1960s, I became aware of his work in other ways and only noticed later that I happened to own his third published work of nonfiction.

Overall, by the 1960s, hardcover and paperback science fiction books had emerged as the most important venue for new works in the genre, both novels and series of original anthologies, eclipsing the science fiction magazines that had then diminished in both their numbers and their influence. Indeed, aside from a few stories, Heinlein only appeared in science fiction magazines of the 1950s and 1960s when he serialized several of his forthcoming novels to earn a little additional income from them. Yet the magazines also profited from the burgeoning market for science fiction books by regularly publishing collections of stories from their magazines. The editors of *Galaxy* during that era, H. L. Gold and Frederik Pohl, were especially energetic in recycling their best products in this form, and I still own copies of five paperback editions of their anthologies (all officially edited by Gold, though Pohl was usually their actual editor): *The Third Galaxy Reader* (1958), *The Fourth Galaxy Reader* (1959), *The World That Couldn't Be and 8 Other Novelets from Galaxy* (1959), *Bodyguard and Four Other Short Science Fiction Novels from Galaxy* (1960), and *Mind Partner and 8 Other Novelets from Galaxy* (1961).

Still, although changes in the system of magazine distribution were also a factor that diminished their viability, increasing competition from books, films, television programs, and comic books in the 1950s brought about a precipitous decline in the numbers of science fiction magazines, a perceived crisis addressed in Earl Kemp's Hugo Award-winning fanzine *Who Killed Science Fiction? An Affectionate Autopsy* and discussed in a later chapter. In the late 1950s and 1960s, even the news media emerged as a competitor of sorts to the magazines as newspapers, news magazines, and television news programs devoted an enormous amount of attention to the actual American and Russian space programs and their various accomplishments. Yet as previously noted, a few science fiction magazines have been able to survive until the present day, and they are constantly joined by newcomers, though the new magazines mostly publish online instead of print editions.

Before the 1950s, science fiction was not an established film genre, so that during the first fifty years of cinema, one observes only occasional films about space travel or humanity's future alongside numerous horror movies featuring mad scientists creating monsters and other menaces that stalwart heroes must oppose. But postwar film producers were developing an interest in the genre, and one of their usual habits was to either approach working writers to work on forthcoming projects or adapt previously published stories and novels as films. Any effort to document how frequently they sought out science fiction authors is handicapped by one obvious problem: then and now, the overwhelming majority of efforts to produce films never have any results. One anecdote that surfaced in Sam Moskowitz's "The Return of Hugo Gernsback" is probably illustrative of other unsuccessful initiatives: in 1953, prominent science fiction fan Forrest J Ackerman was approached by filmmaker Ivan Tors and asked to suggest some science fiction stories that might make good films; as Ackerman reported in a letter to Hugo Gernsback, he responded in this fashion:

> along with [A. E.] Van Vogt's *Slan* [1940, 1946], Homer Eon Flint's "Nth Man" [1928] (I represent his widow), and two others, the next day I laid down on the producer's desk a copy of your novel *Ralph 124C 41+* I have given him quite a pep talk about it.
>
> If you approve of the negotiations I have instituted on your behalf, and wish me to consummate the transaction if *Ralph* is the lucky winner, please wire me authorization to close the deal for you "if and when," stipulating that my fee is to be 15%.[2]

In the end, of course, no Tors films based on any of these works were produced, as Tors instead decided to rely upon himself and other screenwriters (such as Curt Siodmak) to write original screenplays for his films *The Magnetic Monster* (1953), *Riders to the Stars* (1954), and *Gog* (1954). It is very possible, then, that other writers became involved in proposed film projects that never came to fruition.

This much is known about the science fiction writers who contributed to films and television: Heinlein was asked to work on a major film, officially based on his novel *Rocket Ship Galileo* (1947) but very different in most respects, that was released in 1950 as *Destination Moon*; he then unsuccessfully struggled to launch another film project, to be entitled Abbott and Costello Move to the Moon, and a television science fiction anthology series that only yielded a pilot film released as the film *Project Moonbase* (1953). Science fiction writers Isaac Asimov, James Blish, Damon Knight, Robert S. Richardson (who published stories as Philip Latham), Robert Sheckley, and Jack Vance wrote episodes of *Captain Video and His Video Rangers* (1953,

1954).[3] Although he wrote no scripts for that series, Arthur C. Clarke did contribute as an advisor and set designer, and he also wrote a script for an episode of the anthology series *Tales of Tomorrow*, "All the Time in the World" (1952), which he also published as a short story. Other science fiction writers who wrote episodes of *Tales of Tomorrow* are Fredric Brown, Max Ehrlich, C. M. Kornbluth, S. A. Lombino (who published science fiction as Richard Marsten and was better known for mainstream novels as by Evan Hunter and Ed McBain), and Frederik Pohl, while Theodore Sturgeon wrote episodes for both *Tales of Tomorrow* and another anthology series, *Out There* (1951–1952). Murray Leinster wrote another episode of *Out There*, and it is further reported that Nelson Bond wrote episodes of the lost television series *Rod Brown of the Rocket Rangers* (1953), while Henry Kuttner, C. L. Moore, an uncredited Jerome Bixby, and Curt Siodmak collectively wrote the pilot episode for a rejected series, released as the short film *Tales of Frankenstein* (1958). Siodmak, who had begun his writing career in Germany with science fiction stories and novels, continued to produce occasional novels even as he came to focus primarily on screenplays, first in Germany and later in the United States.

By the late 1950s and early 1960s, some science fiction writers were, like Siodmak, shifting their careers to focus primarily or exclusively on writing for film and television, including Bixby, Charles Beaumont, David Duncan, Harlan Ellison, Richard Matheson, and Jerry Sohl, although they also worked outside the genre; during the late 1950s and early 1960s, for example, in addition to several genre films, Matheson wrote episodes of the television series *The D.A.'s Man* (1959), *Buckskin* (1959), *Markham* (1959), *Wanted: Dead or Alive* (1959), *Have Gun—Will Travel* (1960), *Bourbon Street Beat* (1960), *Cheyenne* (1960), *Lawman* (1960–1962), and *Combat!* (1962). Ellison's work outside the genre in the 1960s included the film *The Oscar* (1966) and episodes of the television series *Route 66* (1963), *Ripcord* (1963), *Burke's Law* (1963–1964), and *Cimarron Strip* (1968).

The 1950s science fiction films that were faithfully or loosely based on published works of science fiction included *When Worlds Collide* (1951, based on Philip Wylie and Edwin Balmer's 1933 novel); *The Thing (from Another World)* (1951, based on John W. Campbell, Jr.'s "Who Goes There?" [1938]); *The Day the Earth Stood Still* (1951, based on Harry Bates's "Farewell to the Master" [1940]); the serial *Mysterious Island* (1951, based on Jules Verne's 1874 novel); *Donovan's Brain* (1953, based on Curt Siodmak's 1942 novel); *Four-Sided Triangle* (1953, based on William F. Temple's 1949 novel); *The Twonky* (1953, based on Kuttner and Moore's 1942 story); *The War of the Worlds* (1953, based on H. G. Wells's 1898 novel); *The Beast from 20,000 Fathoms* (1953, based on Bradbury's "The Fog Horn" [1951]); *Target Earth* (1954, based on Paul W. Fairman's "Deadly City" [1953]); *20,000 Leagues under the Sea* (1954, based on Verne's 1870 novel); *This Island Earth* (1955, based on Raymond F.

10. Invasion of the Saucer Men 163

Jones's 1952 novel); *Invasion of the Body Snatchers* (1956, based on Jack Finney's *The Body Snatchers* [1955]); *1984* (1956, based on George Orwell's *Nineteen Eighty-Four* [1949]); *The Electronic Monster* (1957, based on Charles Eric Maine's *Escapement* [1956]); *She Devil* (1957, based on Stanley G. Weinbaum's "The Adaptive Ultimate" [1935]); the film referenced in the chapter title, *Invasion of the Saucer Men* (1957, based on Fairman's "The Cosmic Frame" [1955]); *The 27th Day* (1957, based on John Mantley's 1957 novel); *The Incredible Shrinking Man* (1958, based on Matheson's *The Shrinking Man* [1956]); *The Fabulous World of Jules Verne* (1958, based on Verne's 1896 novel *Facing the Flag*); *The Fly* (1958, based on George Langelaan's 1957 story); *From the Earth to the Moon* (1958, based on Verne's 1865 novel); *Journey to the Center of the Earth* (1959, based on Verne's 1864 novel); *On the Beach* (1959, based on Nigel Shute's 1957 novel); and *The World, the Flesh and the Devil* (1959, based on M. P. Shiel's *The Purple Cloud* [1901]). There are also films regularly described as unofficial adaptations of science fiction stories, such as *The Brain Eaters* (1958), which is very reminiscent of Heinlein's *The Puppet Masters* (1951), and *It! The Terror from Beyond Space* (1958), which recalls A. E. van Vogt's "Black Destroyer" (1939), as well as numerous episodes of television anthology series that adapted published stories; *Tales of Tomorrow*, for example, presented adaptations of stories by Campbell, Raymond Z. Gallun, Raymond F. Jones, Robert Sheckley, William Tenn, Weinbaum, and Wylie; *Out There* adapted three of Heinlein's stories; and a 1955 episode of *Studio One* offered another adaptation of Siodmak's *Donovan's Brain*. Granted, not all of these films' source material came from writers strongly associated with the science fiction community, and granted, the adaptations sometimes bore little resemblance to their source material. Nonetheless, the list does indicate that both science fiction writers and science fiction stories were well represented in the era's films and television programs.

As an aside, it should be mentioned that at least one science fiction writer contributed to another sort of science fiction film that first appeared in the 1950s: documentaries about the coming age of space travel, which regularly included fictional sequences (either animated or live-action) depicting the activities of future astronauts. The first of these was a 1955 episode of *Disneyland*, "Man in Space," featuring excerpts from an interview with Willy Ley, the German-born writer best known for his articles and books about science who wrote one science fiction novel and four science fiction stories as Robert Willey. (Ley also served as a technical advisor for the television series *Tom Corbett, Space Cadet* [1950–1955].) This was followed by two similar *Disneyland* documentaries, "Man and the Moon" (1955) and "Mars and Beyond" (1957), while in Russia, director Pavel Klushantsev produced a documentary depicting an early space flight with the English title *Road to the Stars* (1957) which included a brief biography of space visionary and science fiction author Konstantin Tsiolkovsky; its sequel, *Luna* (1965), involves a pioneering lunar colony.

Another relevant development during the postwar period is the appearance of science fiction cartoons from the Warner Brothers studio. Although a few of their earlier cartoons were parodies of horror films with science-fictional elements, their first cartoon about space travel was "Haredevil Hare" (1948), wherein Bugs Buggy battles against the combative Marvin the Martian on the Moon; the Martian went on to bedevil Bugs Bunny in three later cartoons: "The Hasty Hare" (1952), "Hareway to the Stars" (1958), and "Mad as a Mars Hare" (1963). Marvin the Martian was also the villain in a parody of the Buck Rogers comic strip and serial, "Duck Dodgers in the 24½ Century" (1953), featuring Daffy Duck and Porky Pig as space adventurers. Needless to say, none of these cartoons could be described as scientifically accurate, as characters are regularly observed functioning perfectly well in outer space or on alien worlds while not wearing spacesuits. It is also worth noting that the humor in Warner Brothers' Road Runner cartoons of the 1950s and 1960s usually involved the ravenous Wile E. Coyote haplessly deploying some piece of futuristic technology that invariably malfunctions when he attempts to capture and eat the Road Runner, such as rocket launchers and invisible paint, and in the early 1960s there was one animated series from Hanna Barbera featuring a family in a Hugo Gernsback–like future of advanced technology but no social advances, *The Jetsons* (1962–1963), who later appeared in several film and television revivals.

Despite the input of numerous science fiction writers, however, the overall effects of the science fiction community on films and television arguably remain inconsequential, though certain ideas and tropes from the genre did penetrate into these media. In regards to television, series like *Tales of Tomorrow* (1951–1953), *Science Fiction Theatre* (1955–1957), and *Men into Space* (1959–1960) had their moments, but science fiction television during the 1950s was infrequent and largely unmemorable, and the one relevant series still popular today, Rod Serling's *The Twilight Zone* (1959–1964), more often than not offered fantasies instead of science fiction. In contrast, the science fiction films of the 1950s constitute a fascinatingly complex and variegated body of works that has justifiably attracted an enormous amount of critical attention, and they remain a powerful influence on the science fiction films produced in later decades, but they bear little resemblance to the written science fiction that preceded them and accompanied them. Instead, science fiction films and television programs were evolving in their own fashion to eventually become entirely separate domains, because of the very nature of these media: unlike literature, which consists of the products of individual imaginations only minimally altered by editorial input, films and television programs are crafted and controlled by corporate entities, so that the writers themselves, unless they attain positions as producers (like Serling), have little power to influence the stories that are filmed. Though he worked in the 1960s and 1970s, not the 1950s, Harlan Ellison provides an object lesson in the problems faced by science fiction writers working for television, as he documented instance after instance when his scripts were infuriatingly altered, sometimes to the extent that he withdrew permission to use his name and had them credited to his farcical pseudonym Cordwainer Bird. The less vocal science fiction writers who focused on writing film and television screenplays doubtless had similar stories to tell, but discreetly chose not to tell him.

During the 1950s, I had no opportunities to watch science fiction television, but I did cajole my parents into taking me to see several science fiction films, including the very disappointing *War of the Satellites* (1958) and *First Man into Space* (1959). But I voraciously watched television during the 1960s, and I was very pleased to find that innumerable science fiction movies from the 1950s were being shown on television, sometimes as weekly features under an outré umbrella title like the series I watched in Minneapolis, entitled *Chiller*. It was at this time, I believe, that the films of the 1950s truly became a part of many young people's education in science fiction and led to all of the remakes of, and homages to, those films that began appearing in the 1970s and 1980s.

Due to the enormous popularity of Jerry Siegel and Joe Shuster's superhero Superman, who first appeared in 1938, the number of comic books being published quickly increased enormously, creating opportunities for imaginative writers, so it is not surprising that several science fiction writers began writing stories for comic books in the 1940s, including such luminaries as Alfred Bester, Otto Binder, Edmond Hamilton, and Henry Kuttner and C. L. Moore (and in some cases continued to do so in the 1950s and 1960s). However, as a rule, their stories in the 1940s were not particularly science-fictional, though there were some recurring devices in stories about superheroes such as serums or rays that provided people with amazing powers and the dangerous inventions of various villains. The first comic book to feature science fiction was Hugo Gernsback's *Superworld Comics* (1940), which only published three issues, though not all of its stories were science-fictional; some stories were written by the former editor of Gernsback's *Wonder Stories*, Charles Hornig, and the comic also included the work of Gernsback's favorite science fiction artist, Frank R. Paul.[4] There was also *Planet Comics* (1940–1953), an offshoot of the magazine *Planet Stories* (1939–1955), that primarily featured space adventures, often foregrounding voluptuous women, though the authors of its typically undistinguished stories mostly remain unidentified.

One should mention *Weird Science* (1950–1953), the comic book from Educational Comics (E. C. Comics) that featured science fiction stories, for although it employed no science fiction writers other than comic book veteran Gardner Fox (primarily noted for his later contributions to DC comics and a few novels), the stories it published regularly appeared to be unauthorized adaptations of stories by science fiction writers like Anthony Boucher, Charles L. Harness, Henry Hasse, Katherine MacLean, Theodore Sturgeon, and Donald Wandrei. When Ray Bradbury noticed and complained about a story in another E.C. comic that seemed based on one of his stories, he reached an agreement that allowed *Weird Science* to publish authorized adaptations of other Bradbury stories. A companion comic book, *Weird Fantasy*, also included some science fiction stories, most notably the often-discussed "Judgment Day" (in issue No. 18, March-April 1953), wherein a visiting astronaut decides that an alien world is not yet ready to join the Galactic Republic because of its racist policies; a final panel stunningly reveals that the astronaut is an African-American.

The two men who would become central to the new prominence of science fiction in comic books of the 1950s, Mort Weisinger and Julius Schwartz, initially did little to display their familiarity with the genre. Both were young science fiction fans who had co-edited, with Forrest J Ackerman, a pioneering science fiction fanzine, *The Time Traveller* (1932–1937), and they had dabbled in writing science fiction stories, but they first became prominent after establishing an agency to represent other science fiction writers, and in the 1940s they were hired to work as editors for DC comic books. After overseeing the adventures of other DC superheroes, including Batman and Aquaman, Weisinger came to work exclusively on the growing numbers of comic books featuring Superman, and as is regularly noted, his tenure was distinguished by an increasing emphasis on science fiction. Among other assignments, Schwartz launched and edited DC's major science fiction comics of the 1950s, *Strange Adventures* (original series 1950–1973) and *Mystery in Space* (original series 1951–1966), and in the late 1950s and early 1960s he was responsible for reviving and refashioning several DC superheroes from the 1940s to have science-fictional origins and engage in science fiction adventures, including the Flash, Green Lantern, the Atom, Hawkman, and the superhero team the Justice League of America. Later, Schwartz also assumed control of Batman and (after Weisinger's retirement) Superman.

As originally presented by Siegel and Shuster, Superman had always been a science-fictional character, an alien from the destroyed planet Krypton who, due to Earth's lower gravity, developed super-strength and a prodigious leaping ability once on Earth (perhaps reflecting his creators' memories of Edgar Rice Burroughs's John Carter, who similarly became a superman of sorts when he was teleported from Earth to the smaller world of Mars). But Superman's early adventures otherwise tended to be rather mundane, aside from the menacing creations of mad scientists like Lex Luthor. Siegel and

Shuster were also writing stories for a character who was then appearing in only three comic books, *Action Comics* (1938-), *Superman* (1939–2011), and *World's Finest Comics* (1941–1986), so they only had to devise a limited number of new stories. As Weisinger assumed control of the character, however, Superman was being featured more and more frequently: the superhero's adventures when he was a teenage Superboy, which debuted in 1945 in *More Fun Comics* (1935–1947), were soon regularly appearing both in *Adventure Comics* (original series 1938–1983) and *Superboy* (1949–1977), and the 1950s brought two additional titles featuring Superman but starring *Superman's Pal Jimmy Olsen* (1954–1974) and *Superman's Girl Friend Lois Lane* (1958–1974).

To understand the challenge that Weisinger faced, consider the situation in 1959, the year when I first began to regularly read Superman comic books. *Action Comics* and *Adventure Comics*, published every month, each featured one 12- to 13-page story respectively starring Superman and Superboy, while *World's Finest Comics*, published eight times a year, featured one 12- to 13-page story starring Superman, Batman, and Robin. Four other comics—*Superboy, Superman, Superman's Girl Friend Lois Lane*, and *Superman's Pal Jimmy Olsen*—appeared eight times a year, typically including three 8- to 9-page stories featuring Superman or his younger self. What that meant is that during that calendar year, Weisinger and his writers and artists had to come up with different plots for 96 8- to 9-page stories and 32 12- to 13-page stories starring Superman or Superboy—a total of 128 stories in one year, though it should be noted that *Superman* and *Superboy* occasionally offered two-part or three-part stories that would have slightly reduced that number.[5] In having to come up with new ideas for so many stories in this and other years,[6] Weisinger quite understandably turned to the form of literature that he had long known the best, science fiction.

So it was that I and innumerable other young readers were first introduced to many of the tropes of science fiction by means of Superman's comic book adventures.[7] Employing the advanced science of Krypton, Superman constructed a team of Superman robots who looked exactly like him and shared his powers, so that they could substitute for him when necessary, and he constructed as his headquarters an underground Fortress of Solitude in the Arctic (an idea stolen from pulp hero Doc Savage) which included a Kryptonian supercomputer. While he encountered many lost worlds on Earth, such as a remote island governed entirely by women in "The Super-Prisoner of Amazon Island" (1957), the most memorable of these was the lost continent of Atlantis, whose inhabitants had scientifically transformed themselves into mermaids and mermen when their homeland sank into the sea so they could maintain their civilization in an underwater city. Some of his friends also developed their own super-powers: his teenage girlfriend Lana Lang received a device from a visiting alien that enabled her to replicate the abilities of various insects, allowing her to occasionally function as the heroic Lana Lang, Insect Queen; a scientist's serum periodically transformed Jimmy Olsen into a hero resembling Plastic Man, the infinitely flexible Elastic Lad; and other cohorts of Superman, including his human father Jonathan Kent, Lois Lane, and Perry White, briefly acquired super-powers. A scientist's invention that created imperfect, stupid duplicates of Superboy and Superman, both named Bizarro, eventually inspired a separate series of humorous adventures featuring the innumerable similar residents of the square Bizarro World.

It was established that, by flying faster than light, Superman could travel through time, providing a springboard for stories that brought him into contact with various historical and quasi-historical figures, including Samson, Hercules, Cleopatra, King Arthur, Robin Hood, Benjamin Franklin, George Washington, and Abraham Lincoln. Less frequently, he would venture into the future, though Superboy later would regularly visit the 30th century to serve as one member of that era's Legion of Super Heroes. Even when he remained in the present, Superman might encounter adversaries from the future—such as the "Futuremen," criminals from the future who pretend to be law enforcement officers seeking Superman's arrest for future crimes, and the members of the evil counterpart to the Legion of Super Heroes, the adult Legion of Super Villains.

Also, since he was invulnerable and did not need to breathe, Superman could fly throughout the cosmos to have adventures on other planets. As a quibble, since his increasing range of abilities, such as invulnerability, x-ray vision, heat vision, telescopic vision, and microscopic vision, could not be accounted for by referencing the different gravities of Krypton and Earth, it was explained that Superman's abilities were actually caused by exposure to radiation from our yellow sun, contrasting with Krypton's red sun, so that stories occasionally stipulated that Superman in all his travels through interstellar space would scrupulously avoid approaching any red suns, which presumably would have rendered him mortal and led to his instantaneous death in the vacuum of space. Superman's most famous foe, scientist Lex Luthor, began visiting an alien world where he romanced a beautiful woman and became regarded as that planet's superhero. Adversaries who came from other worlds were commonplace, most prominently the sinister scientist Brainiac, originally presented as a green-skinned alien but later re-imagined as an advanced computer.

Despite its inconvenient destruction, Superman's home planet of Krypton also became a frequent setting for stories. On at least two occasions, Superman traveled into the past to visit Krypton and interact with his parents and other Kryptonians, Jimmy Olsen also experienced a sojourn on Krypton, and an imaginary story described what would have happened if Krypton had escaped destruction and Superman had grown up on that world. Although

Superman was originally said to have left Krypton as a baby, it now was claimed that he lived there until he was a toddler, and a series of Superboy stories involved a device that stimulated his brain and enabled him to remember various experiences during his early years on Krypton. Most notably, when Superman first encountered Brainiac, he learned that the villain had the habit of shrinking cities from various planets and keeping them in bottles, and one of them just happened to be Krypton's former capital city, Kandor. Retrieving the city from Brainiac, but unable due to contrived circumstances to restore it to its original size, Superman brought the bottle to his Fortress of Solitude, and by means of temporary shrinking he could periodically visit Kandor to spend some time in a Kryptonian city. On a few occasions, he brought his friend Jimmy Olsen along, so that they could serve as Kandor's costumed heroes Nightwing and Flamebird.

In addition, although Superman was originally described as the sole survivor of the planet's destruction, stories in the 1950s and 1960s introduced a growing cast of other survivors in addition to the innumerable citizens of Kandor. These included several animals, such as Krypto the Super-Dog, Beppo the Super-Monkey, a super-gorilla, and a super-dragon; a robot teacher programmed to teach the young Superman how to use his super-powers; and various villains who had survived by being exiled to outer space or transported into another dimension termed the Phantom Zone. A fragment of Krypton improbably preserved intact after its destruction was also the original home of Superman's cousin Supergirl, who eventually was sent to Earth and appeared in her own adventures after the other residents on the fragment died (although Supergirl's parents also survived by transporting themselves into another ethereal dimension, the Survival Zone). Perhaps the silliest Kryptonians who made regular appearances were the members of the Supermen Emergency Squad, a group of male Kandorians who all happened to look exactly like Superman and by scientific means could temporarily enlarge themselves to the size of dolls, so that during a crisis a swarm of miniature Supermen could appear to save the day.

Though portrayals of Krypton were not rigorously consistent, the planet was always depicted as being more scientifically advanced than Earth, and their scientists' achievements included a machine that controlled the weather, a healing ray to cure diseases, a device that determines which professions people are best suited for, and several types of robot laborers. Yet to maintain the basic legend, the Kryptonians had to be ignorant in two key respects: first, though they employed rockets to travel to different places on their planet, they never mastered space travel, explaining why its citizens did not save themselves by fleeing into space; and second, they never figured out that their planet was about to explode, and when Superman's father, the scientist Jor-El, finally discovers and announces the impending crisis, his scientific colleagues ridicule him, forcing him to work in isolation to build a spaceship to save his immediate family (though when he did not have time to complete a large enough spaceship, he and his wife La-Ra were obliged to place their son in a smaller spaceship to send him to Earth).

Weisinger's numerous excursions into science fiction are regularly mentioned, but it should be noted that his Superman also ventured into the realm of fantasy, in two ways. First, since Superman's ever-increasing powers were making it difficult to fashion credible opponents for the superhero, it was stated that he had two vulnerabilities—to kryptonite, fragments from his home planet, and to magic. This opened the door to stories in which Superman was attacked by various magical opponents, such as the fifth-dimensional imp Mr. Mxyzptlk and the ancient Greek sorceress Circe, who temporarily transforms Superman into a lion-headed man in "The Lady and the Lion" (1958) and later turns the centaur Biron into Supergirl's pet Comet the Super-Horse.[8] Second, to escape the confines of the established continuity of Superman's life, Weisinger began to present a series of "Imaginary Stories" describing various events that could not have occurred within that history, including the death of Superman, his marriages to both Lois Lane and Lana Lang, a story about Lois Lane traveling to Krypton to become a superhero, and the splitting of Superman into two beings—Superman-Red and Superman-Blue—who respectively marry Lois Lane and Lana Lang as the first Superman and his wife relocate to a re-created Krypton while the other continues to serve as Earth's guardian.

While they have been frequently republished, and thoroughly chronicled by websites, Weisinger's Superman stories are routinely denounced as juvenile, and vastly inferior to the more sophisticated superhero adventures being presented in the Marvel comic books of the 1960s. Yet one occasionally finds fascinating stories that explore the character of Superman in surprising depth. In "Superman's New Power" (1958), for example, an encounter with an alien spaceship deprives Superman of his own powers but enables him to create a miniature Superman with the same abilities who can perform heroic acts. If Superman's sole motivation is altruism, assisting others in distress, this situation should not bother him at all, yet his inability to personally intervene to rescue people makes him unhappy, and as if sensing his distress, his tiny counterpart soon sacrifices his own life so that Superman can regain his own powers.[9] "The Menace of Metallo" (1959) introduces a revelatory doppelgänger to Superman, a criminal resembling Superman whose brain is transplanted into a robot body after a car accident, literally making him a "Man of Steel"; while he is endeavoring to romance Superman's girlfriend Lois Lane, she opens a fortune cookie that reads, "Neither false heart nor faint heart e'er won a fair maid"—aptly summarizing the reasons why she never settled down with either man: the sinister Metallo clearly has a "false heart," while Superman has a "faint heart," insufficiently enamored of Lois Lane to assertively pursue her lifelong companionship.[10] Hamilton contributed an evocative adventure, "Under the Red Sun" (1963), wherein Superman is stranded on a far-future Earth, now abandoned by humanity, that has a red sun depriving him of his super-powers and forcing him to make a lonely trek across a deserted Earth in search of some means of returning to his own time, his only companions being a few surviving robots from his Fortress of Solitude. Despite their apparent simplicity, in other words, there are a number of stories published under Weisinger's supervision that invite detailed critical analysis, and perhaps a reevaluation of his editorial skills.

Still, around the time that I stopped reading comic books in 1964, there were signs that Weisinger and his writers were running out of ideas, as stories appeared that blended together previously used elements, sometimes in a bizarre fashion. There are two peculiar adventures that I vividly remember: "Superman Meets the Goliath-Hercules" (1964) takes Superman to a parallel world where he meets a Hercules who resembles Goliath (both heroes he had already encountered) and helps him when he is threatened by red kryptonite (which to him is equivalent to deadly green kryptonite). And in "King Superman Versus Clark Kent, Metallo" (1964), the unpredictable red kryptonite has had the effect of splitting Superman and Clark Kent into two people (which had already happened long ago), and when the apparently villainous Superman establishes himself as the world's dictatorial king, the heroic Clark Kent becomes the world's second Metallo so he can attack Superman with the green kryptonite that fuels his robotic body. Weisinger also became notorious for simply reusing the plots of previously published stories, figuring that his usually young readers would never be familiar with stories published before they were born; in fact, Craig Shutt's *Baby Boomer Comics* (2003) includes a list of 53 recycled Superman stories.[11] Despite obvious signs that a fresh perspective on Superman was becoming necessary, Weisinger soldiered on as Superman's principal editor until 1970; and though subsequent Superman reboots eliminated some of the science-fictional elements that Weisinger had added to the Superman saga (such as the Superman robots and bottled city of Kandor), others have endured, testifying to his permanent impact on the Man of Steel.

As for Schwartz, his devotion to science fiction was immediately evident in the two titles he launched, *Strange Adventures* and *Mystery in Space*, both primarily devoted to unrelated science fiction adventures though some recurring characters were featured. No effort was made to achieve any sort of consistency in the future worlds that the stories in these comics presented, but they can be generally characterized as the sorts of science fiction stories that were prevalent in the 1930s. The people in their future worlds were capable of regular travel to other planets in the solar system, and occasional interstellar journeys, but society was otherwise essentially unchanged; thus, in one early series in *Mystery in Space* set in the thirtieth century, Knights of the Galaxy, it was considered shocking when a woman sought to become a member of the team, and in "It's a Woman's World" (1952), a future world where women are dominant sees the errors of its ways and it is resolved that "we women ran things long enough.... It's time you men took over again."[12] It was further assumed that all planets in the solar system were habitable homes of alien races who resembled humans except for superficial differences like skin color and attributes like large ears and antennae.

Perhaps the archetypal protagonist featuring in the stories of *Strange Adventures* and *Mystery in Space* was the latter's hero Space Cabby, sometimes rendered as Space Cabbie. The series' naive premise was that as travel to other planets and moons in the solar system became commonplace, there would emerge a need for small spaceships to transport individual passengers to various worlds in the manner of taxicabs transporting passengers to various destinations in a city. Thus, in one story, "Follow the Space-Leader," the unnamed Space Cabby faces the challenge of informing the authorities that he is traveling with a criminal, though his success in doing so is entirely accidental.[13]

The individual stories presented in the Schwartz comics can be generally characterized as naive and juvenile, but interesting ideas would sometimes surface; I have noted elsewhere, for example, that the first American work of science fiction to predict a televised moon landing was a 1955 story in *Mystery in Space*, written by Bill Finger, entitled "The Last Television Broadcast on Earth," which concludes by showing how scientists, after an encounter with a comet prevents television broadcasts, enable people to continue enjoying television by transforming the Moon into a gigantic television screen. Such extravagant visions, long exiled from the now-sophisticated science fiction magazines, could also strike a chord with younger readers. Thus, I still recall my first encounter with a science fiction comic edited by Schwartz: in 1958, I purchased and read a copy of *Mystery in Space* No. 48 (July 1958), which presented the story "The Amazing Space-Flight of North America," written by Otto Binder, with a cover image of North America being lifted into outer space by a flying saucer. Even though I no longer possess a copy of this issue, the fact that I vividly remember this cover testifies that these comic book stories, despite their indefensible science, could have an evocative power. Another story with an awesome concept, "The Immortality Seekers!" in *Strange Adventures* No. 157 (October 1963), implausibly posited that the shapes of Earth's continents represented a formula for an immortality serum, carved into the planet by an ancient alien visitor; later aliens attempting to find the secret formula must physically reinsert the lost continents of Atlantis and Mu to complete the formula.

Even at the time when I was gradually shifting my focus to written sci-

10. Invasion of the Saucer Men

ence fiction instead of comic books, I recall being particularly impressed by the contents of *Strange Adventures* No. 159 (December 1963): in "The Maze of Time" (written by Gardner Fox), aliens transport astronauts to the distant past and, to assess their acumen, present them with puzzles they must solve to return to their own time; "Yes, Virginia, There Is a Martian," also by Fox, is the sentimental tale of a young girl and her encounter with a friendly man who is actually a Martian, yearning to find a way to travel back to his home planet; and "Will the Star Rovers Abandon Earth?" features the recurring characters the Star Rovers, who had recently moved from *Mystery in Space* into *Strange Adventures*—two men, Homer Gint and Rick Purvis, and one woman, Karel Sorensen—who seek adventures on other worlds in their own spaceships and invariably discover, as in this story, that the separate problems—here, in returning to Earth—are intriguingly interwoven.

I should also mention the other regular series in these magazines at the time when I began to purchase and read them. The Adam Strange stories, which long served as *Mystery in Space*'s star attraction, are essentially adaptations of Burroughs's Mars novels, although the human who is teleported to another world, archaeologist Adam Strange, reaches a scientifically advanced planet orbiting Alpha Centauri, Rann, instead of Mars, and after staying long enough to deal with some menace he is automatically returned to Earth until another "zeta beam" again transports him to Rann. In the early 1960s, there were three alternating series in *Strange Adventures*: the Atomic Knights are a group of men—and one woman—who strive to deal with problems following a devastating nuclear war by donning suits of armor that protect them from radiation and venturing forth on horses (later motorcycles) to deal with various crises. Star Hawkins is a perpetually down-and-out detective in Earth's future who must periodically pawn his faithful robot assistant to address his financial difficulties while solving futuristic mysteries. In the Space Museum stories, a father regularly takes his son to the eponymous institution to examine one exhibit and relates the story behind it. To recall my own youthful reactions to these series, I was never particularly enamored of Adam Strange, and found the Star Hawkins stories too farcical for my taste, but I enjoyed and looked forward to adventures involving the Atomic Knights, the Star Rovers, and the Space Museum.

Of Schwartz's contributions to superheroes, his most impressive science-fictional achievement was the re-creation of Green Lantern as one member of an intergalactic organization of crusaders for justice, the Green Lantern Corps, that have later figured in numerous DC adventures. He also re-imagined Hawkman as a police officer from the planet Thanagar, equipped like his colleagues with wings and bird-like attire, who visits Earth and decides to remain in order to learn from our experiences in dealing with criminals, a new phenomenon on his planet; later, conflicts between Thanagar and Adam Strange's second home Rann would regularly figure in several DC comics. Schwartz's Flash employed a special treadmill to travel into the future and faced adversaries from the future such as the Reverse-Flash and Abra Cadabra. The Justice League of America adventures written by Gardner Fox and edited by Schwartz regularly sent its members into outer space to confront powerful alien villains like Despero and Kanjar Ro, and one story involved a visit to a microscopic world named Starzl, a tribute to author R. F. Starzl, who had written one of the first stories about such worlds, "Out of the Sub-Universe" (1928). Schwartz's superhero the Atom, who obtained his shrinking powers by finding a meteor from a dwarf star, also visited microworlds on several occasions and traveled into the past by means of a scientist's "Time Pool"; his name, Ray Palmer, referenced the long-time science fiction magazine editor who was renowned for his diminutive stature.

It should be noted that another DC editor, Jack Schiff, was also in charge of comic books that regularly published science fiction stories, including *Challengers of the Unknown* (original series 1958–1971), *Rip Hunter, Time Master* (original series 1961–1965), and *Tales of the Unexpected* (original series 1956–1968), which featured the adventures of Space Ranger, a future space hero more than a little reminiscent of Asimov's Lucky Starr. Schiff also oversaw the adventures of Batman at the time when he was regularly encountering aliens and traveling through time by means of a professor's device. However, Schiff lacked a background in science fiction and his stories were consistently less interesting than those overseen by Schwartz; indeed, when he inherited *Mystery in Space* and *Strange Adventures* from Schwartz in 1964, they rapidly declined in quality until he retired in 1967.

In the 1950s, generally unmemorable comic books featuring science fiction stories were also published by Marvel Comics and Charlton Comics, again written by authors who had no connections to the science fiction community. Even in the 1960s, when Marvel's Stan Lee and co-creators Jack Kirby and Steve Ditko revolutionized comic books with innovative new superheroes, their stories were not particularly interesting if considered as works of science fiction, as they mostly involved heroes and villains who develop amazing powers after being exposed to some sort of "radiation," though Lee's attentiveness to realistic settings, and more complex and better developed characters, made them more appealing than the more science-fictional adventures being offered by Weisinger and Schwartz, whose settings seemed unrelated to the real world and whose characters were generally bland.

Finally, just as the tropes of science fiction found their way into the cartoons of the 1950s, they also figured in some of the era's "funny animal" comic books, including two that I happened to have purchased at the time: *Mighty Mouse in Outer Space* (Dell Giant No. 43, 1961), wherein the rodent superhero helps a scientist build a spaceship and travels to the Moon, Venus, Mars,

Jupiter, and Saturn, and *Rocky and His Friends* No. 1275 (December-February 1962), which features a cover showing the moose Bullwinkle standing on the Moon while his friend the flying squirrel Rocky takes a photograph (though there is no story in that comic involving such an achievement). The Disney comic books featuring Donald Duck also introduced a character, Gyro Gearloose, a chicken and brilliant scientist noted for his numerous inventions that invariably lead to comically disastrous consequences. Another avian scientist, the duck Ludwig von Drake, first appeared on *Walt Disney's Wonderful World of Color* television series in 1961 but later made numerous appearances in comic books as well.

Overall, I believe that the role played by comic books in educating children about science fiction, and encouraging them to read science fiction novels and stories, has been underrated. If nothing else, I can identify myself as one young reader who first had a primary interest in science fiction comic books and gradually shifted my reading habits—and purchases—to science fiction books as I matured during the 1960s, and surely I am not the only person who made a similar transition. One irony is that, because few readers at the time valued these comic books, they have become cherished collectors' items; the early Marvel comics of course earn the highest prices, but even DC comic books from that era like *Superman* and *Strange Adventures* are regularly offered in the online auctions of the major company specializing in that activity, Heritage Auctions. In a way, this can be construed as evidence that the comic books of the 1950s and 1960s were important works of science fiction, far more important than most scholars of science fiction have been willing to acknowledge.

As science fiction expanded beyond the magazines, it was accompanied by science fiction art, since book publishers regularly turned to experienced artists from the magazines to paint their book covers; Ed Emshwiller, who had started his career doing covers for science fiction magazines, was soon asked to paint a number of covers for Gnome Press, Wollheim's Ace Books, and other paperback publishers like Ballantine and Pyramid. Other artists from the magazines who moved to books include Hannes Bok, who produced memorable covers for Shasta Press and other publishers; Edd Cartier, who did several covers for Gnome Press and Fantasy Press; and Alex Schomburg, who did covers for many of the Winston juveniles. Other examples of artists from the science fiction magazines who went on to produce book covers could be provided, and one could further mention that veteran science fiction artist Frank Kelly Freas painted a number of covers for *Mad* magazine and paperback collections of articles from *Mad*, though only one of them—the cover for *Mad in Orbit* (1962), showing a spacesuited Alfred E. Newman flying away from a square Earth—could be considered science-fictional.

However, the general public was primarily exposed to science fiction art by means of colorful posters for science fiction films, and while it is notoriously difficult to establish which artists were responsible for creating them, one gets the impression that studios generally relied upon their regular poster artists instead of bringing in science fiction artists. A few iconic artists from earlier eras have been identified, such as Heinz Schulz-Neudamm, who created a poster for Fritz Lang's *Metropolis* (1927), and Alfred Hermann, who produced the poster for Lang's *Frau im Mond* (1929). We know the name of one artist, Reynold Brown, who briefly drew a comic strip but is best noted for his memorable posters for 1950s science fiction films like *Creature from the Black Lagoon* (1954), *Tarantula* (1955), *This Island Earth, The Land Unknown* (1957), *Attack of the 50-Foot Woman* (1958), and *The Atomic Submarine* (1959), while Saul Bass is responsible for the poster advertising the Alfred Hitchcock film that involved reincarnation, *Vertigo* (1959), and later painted the poster for Stanley Kubrick's horror film *The Shining* (1980). There is also scattered information about the painters of later film posters, such as Drew Struzan, who painted the posters for, among numerous other films, *Food of the Gods* (1976), *Empire of the Ants* (1977), *Blade Runner* (1982), *The Thing* (1982), and *E.T.: The Extra-Terrestrial* (1982), and Bob Peck, who painted the posters for *Rollerball* (1975), *Superman* (1978), *Star Trek: The Motion Picture* (1979), and the next four *Star Trek* films.

Still, one science fiction artist contributed to the era's science fiction films in another way—Chesley Bonestell. He had initially specialized in producing artwork for a variety of films in the 1940s, notably including *Citizen Kane* (1941), but he developed an interest in astronomical art and began painting covers for *Astounding Science-Fiction* in 1947. He therefore was a natural choice to assist Heinlein and his colleagues in preparing realistic lunar sets for *Destination Moon*, and his work is also observed in other films such as *When Worlds Collide, The War of the Worlds, Cat-Women of the Moon* (1953), *Conquest of Space* (1955), and the television series *Men into Space* (though his contributions to the undistinguished *Cat-Women of the Moon* were unauthorized and, one gathers, greatly resented).

Perhaps the most important role that Bonestell played in expanding awareness of science fiction art, though, involved his memorable artwork for a series of eight articles in *Collier's* magazine (1952–1954) devoted to scientific plans for space travel; the first was Wernher von Braun's "Crossing the Space Frontier" in its March 22, 1952, issue, accompanied by five related articles, and the series concluded with Fred L. Whipple's "Is There Life on Mars?" and von Braun and Cornelius Ryan's "Can We Get to Mars?" in its April 30, 1954, issue. Since the magazine was comparable to *The Saturday Evening Post* in its prestige and large readership, one can say that, just as Heinlein first brought science fiction stories to general readers, Bonestell was the first to bring science fiction art to those readers, with his painstakingly accurate and beautiful paintings of various sorts of space vehicles traveling into and through outer space. Bonestell also illustrated several books about space and space travel during this period, beginning with Willy Ley's *The Conquest of Space* in 1949.

As interest in science fiction and space travel increased during the 1950s, science fiction art began appearing in other places as well. One interesting example is the covers of vinyl record albums. In 2000, marketing professors Morris B. Holbrook and Barbara Stern published a fascinating study of jazz albums that displayed science fiction themes. After noting that "many jazz albums issued as 33 rpm LPs during the 1950s, 1960s, and 1970s did in fact conspicuously feature rocket-ship or space travel imagery on their covers," they describe the results of a statistical study of "eighty-three examples of jazz recordings issued between 1950 and 1980 whose album covers (graphics, pictures, names, or song titles) included conspicuous references to space travel, rocket ships, or other aspects of interplanetary science fiction."[14] Their conclusion is that "the statistical tests of our hypothesis show that the use of space-travel or rocket-ship imagery does appear to coincide with a shorter longevity or lower endurance in the appeal of jazz recordings," though they emphasize that the correlation does not illustrate a clear cause and effect: "Perhaps rocket-travel themes brand the music as faddish or low-brow. Perhaps commercial music inspires the use of sci-fi covers" (60). Holbrook and Stern do not discuss whether recognized science fiction artists painted any of these covers—the companies probably relied upon artists they had worked with previously instead of seeking out science fiction artists—but when musicians gained more control over their cover art, they sometimes sought out science fiction artists to paint their album covers. A website, Album Cover Artists: The Master List, include examples of album covers from several artists who also painted science fiction book or magazine covers, including Neal Adams, Richard Corben, Roger Dean, Philippe Druillet, Frank Frazetta, the Brothers Hildebrandt, Dave McKean, Moebius, Michael Whelan, and Patrick Woodroffe.[15] Yet the list omits the artist responsible for the most famous science fiction album cover: Frank Kelly Freas, who was hired to paint a new version of his iconic cover for the October 1953 issue of *Astounding Science Fiction* for the Queen album *News of the World* (1977).

Science fiction art also began appearing in magazine advertisements; among other examples that can be found online, Joachim Boaz's website Science Fiction and Other Suspect Ruminations posted a series of vintage magazine advertisements with science fiction themes.[16] There is also Megan Prelinger's *Another Science Fiction: Advertising the Space Race 1957–1962* (2010), an interesting compilation of advertisements specifically designed to attract qualified workers to the many companies becoming involved in space initiatives, and these were produced by at least one experienced science fiction artist, Paul Calle, who did several covers for science fiction magazines and books in the early 1950s and was later responsible for a drawing of an orbiting satellite in an advertisement published in the December 18, 1961, issue of *Aviation Week*. Yet the other artists that Prelinger is able to identify had no background in science fiction art, suggesting that the iconography of science fiction was now becoming familiar to artists outside of the genre.

The appearance of merchandise inspired by science fiction was first noted in a 1953 editorial in *Science-Fiction Plus* by Hugo Gernsback, "The Science-Fiction Industry," which noted after mentioning other manifestations of science fiction that "in recent years, a new form has been added: *the third dimensional world of science-fiction*":

> These new three-dimensional forms of science-fiction which are now beginning to swamp our stores consist of toys, games, gadgets, scientific instruments of all kinds, wearing apparel for youngsters, and countless other constantly-evolving, ingenious devices.
>
> Space helmets of every description, space-suits, space guns, space shooting ranges, Space Cadet modelcraft, space viewer picture guns, "Buck Rogers Sonic Ray Gun," "Official Space Patrol Watch," "Space Patrol Monorail Train," "Meteor Express" (imported), dozens of space rockets and space ships—these are only a small part of the large catalog of this type of merchandise now to be found in thousands of stores.
>
> *Remember, this is only a modest beginning....* So far, little has been produced for the youngsters from ten years upward. This easily may become the most lucrative three-dimensional market.[17]

To indicate how ubiquitous such merchandise might have been at that time, I searched eBay for items related to *Tom Corbett, Space Cadet*—one of several science fiction television series of the early 1950s—and found listings not only for books and comic books but also for lunch boxes, watches, puzzles, binoculars, thermos bottles, bags, pocket knives, a toy "space gun," a "cadet ring," a paper doll book, and coloring books. The similar series *Space Patrol* (1950–1955) also inspired a number of items for sale, including "Space-a-Phones," toy guns, and watches. As a child, however, I do not recall seeing such items in stores, since by the time I was old enough to desire certain sorts of toys, all of the early science fiction series for young viewers like *Tom Corbett, Space Cadet* had long been cancelled, and the toy shelves I remember in the late 1950s were dominated by western items. I do vaguely recall purchasing and assembly a Revell model spaceship, and I undoubtedly acquired a few other science-fictional toys as well, but today I can identify only a few relevant items among my own possessions: a collection of tiny plastic airplanes includes several that look like spaceships, and I sent away to DC Comics to receive a button and a certificate, signed by Clark Kent, attesting that Gary Westfahl had become one of the "Supermen of America."

I can uncover no evidence that anyone directly associated with science fiction was responsible for any of this merchandise, and I doubt that they were, since companies would undoubtedly rely upon individuals who had previously worked for them to produce items that involved science fiction. Yet I can provide an anecdote indicating that such merchandise was proving more popular than manufacturers of that era had anticipated. In the late 1950s, while we were living in West Germany, my parents relied upon catalogs to order products that were not readily available in local stores, and I was very excited to observe in one of those catalogs, and to request as a Christmas present, pajamas that featured science-fictional images such as spaceships and the planet Saturn. I was very disappointed to instead receive pajamas displaying the imagery of westerns, accompanied by a note explaining that the company had run out of science fiction pajamas and hence was substituting western pajamas. Clearly, the science fiction pajamas had proven to be unexpectedly popular, in contrast to the western pajamas, indicating that I was not the only child who was unimpressed by the numerous western films and television programs then flooding the market and preferred the less frequently encountered science fiction films and television programs.

Two conclusions can be reached about science fiction in the 1950s. First, in large part due to the efforts of science fiction writers and fans, the genre expanded beyond the magazines into a variety of new venues and generally enjoyed a significant amount of success. One can observe the long-term results of this expansion at any contemporary science fiction convention by entering the dealers' room. There, one will find on sale not only copies of old science fiction magazines, but also science fiction books, ranging from rare first editions from the small presses of the 1940s to new copies of recently published novels, and science fiction comic books. There will also be videocassettes and DVDs of numerous science fiction films and television programs, as well as film posters; original and reproduced works of science fiction art; and various items of merchandise and memorabilia, ranging from vintage toys to new creations. In each category, the earliest available products will generally date to the 1950s, and with the exception of the old magazines, none of these items would have been available to science fiction fans during the 1940s.

Second, although science fiction did establish itself as a distinct presence in popular culture in the 1950s, it did not become a dominant force, and the genre would remain marginalized until the enormous popularity of the *Star Trek* and *Star Wars* franchises brought the genre to the forefront in the 1970s and thereafter. Still, it is hard to see how science fiction would have become so popular then had it not been for the pioneering efforts observed in the 1950s, and the works of this decade have remained a powerful influence on all forms of science fiction in subsequent decades.

11

Hard Science Fiction
An Overview

In its very name, science fiction announces a special concern for, and a special connection to, science. Repeated campaigns to eliminate or deemphasize that concern and that connection by renaming the genre "speculative fiction" have met with ignominious failure; and a broad range of commentators have agreed that, at the very least, science fiction must display a basic respect for the principles and laws of science. Works that utterly fail to meet this standard—by depicting, say, a breathable atmosphere on the Moon or rapid spaceflight to other stars without reference to the limitation of the speed of light—have been universally castigated and delegitimized as science fiction, and as a result are now extremely rare. So it is entirely justifiable to describe the genre as "science fiction."

Approaching the task of defining "hard science fiction," one might begin by calling it a form of science fiction that displays an especially heightened concern for, and an especially heightened connection to, science. Precisely how one might characterize works in that category, predictably, is a matter of ongoing debate. Undoubtedly, certain features in a text would seemingly qualify it as hard science fiction: thorough explanations of scientific facts and/or lengthy expository passages providing evidence of a scientific thought process at work in the creation of an imagined innovation or world. This is the essence of Allen Steele's commonsensical definition of hard science fiction: "the form of imaginative literature that uses either established or carefully extrapolated science as its backbone."[1]

In addition, some would identify a certain sort of narrative voice—detached, objective, cold, clinical—as a defining characteristic. These are the grounds on which David G. Hartwell idiosyncratically classifies J. G. Ballard as a hard science fiction writer, arguing that "hard sf is, then, about the emotional experience of describing and confronting what is scientifically true."[2]

Finally, my own efforts to define hard science fiction have primarily appealed to extra-textual evidence: texts can be considered hard science fiction if their authors energetically promote themselves as hard science fiction writers, if they mostly publish in venues known to favor hard science fiction, such as the magazine *Analog: Science Fiction/Science Fact* or publisher Baen Books, and/or if their stories become the basis for discussions between authors and readers regarding the soundness of their scientific ideas and reasoning.[3]

Just as there are disagreements about the best way to define hard science fiction, there are disparate views regarding the subgenre's value and significance. Aficionados often describe hard science fiction essentially as a stimulating but frivolous "game," as writers enjoy the process of developing wildly imaginative but scientifically defensible concepts and readers enjoy the process of analyzing and critiquing the fruits of their labors. Looking especially at hard science fiction stories set in the near future, one might also defend the subgenre, in the manner of Hugo Gernsback, as a productive database of ideas for possible future inventions—the premise of the European Space Agency's Innovative Technologies from Science Fiction Project, which hired scholars like myself to examine hard science fiction stories in search of ideas for possible initiatives that the ESA might undertake in the future. From such prosaic and utilitarian perspectives, hard science fiction stories might be viewed more as intellectual exercises than as literary works, equivalent to the narrativized mathematical puzzles by Martin Gardner that once appeared regularly in *The Magazine of Fantasy and Science Fiction*.

At the other extreme, some see the scientific foundation of hard science fiction as an effective way to develop and project a uniquely inhuman perspective on the universe and humanity's place in that universe. This virtue in some science fiction stories was recognized long ago by C. S. Lewis:

> It is sobering and cathartic to remember, now and then, our collective smallness, our apparent isolation, the apparent indifference of nature, the slow biological, geological, and astronomical processes which may, in the long run, make many of our hopes (possibly some of our fears) ridiculous.[4]

As John W. Campbell, Jr., explained in a 1956 article, science fiction can provide not only the opinions of people, but "the opinion of the universe."[5] The story Campbell employed to make his point, Tom Godwin's "The Cold Equations" (1954), has since that time been frequently advanced as the archetypal hard science fiction story, as the human desire of its spaceship pilot to rescue his female stowaway is overridden by the unbending laws of science which require her death. Such principles suggest that hard science fiction, far from embodying an extraliterary or excessive concern for science, in fact represents the purest, most central form of the genre, the attitude conveyed by the alternate term sometimes used to describe the subgenre, "hardcore science fiction."

Definitions and defenses of hard science fiction are sometimes marred by two tendencies which must be politely but firmly resisted. First, hard science fiction is best approached as a relatively small and distinct subgenre, not as one of two large categories encompassing the entirety of science fiction. Some commentators assume that the existence of "hard science fiction" necessarily requires the existence of an opposing form, "soft science fiction," and that all science fiction can accordingly be classified as either "hard" or "soft." Yet this is about as logical as classifying all science fiction as either "space opera" or "non-space opera," or "cyberpunk" or "non-cyberpunk." In fact, few if any authors have ever described themselves as "soft science fiction writers," and there has never existed anything resembling a community of soft science fiction writers or an audience clamoring for soft science fiction. Instead, the texts that fall outside the parameters of hard science fiction are numerous, diverse, and badly mischaracterized as monolithic or unified in their nature.

It is also disquieting to see the term "hard science fiction" employed not as a description, but as a criticism or praise. Some tend to associate hard science fiction only with makeshift plotting, cardboard characterization, and a clumsy prose style, as if all literary considerations were being sacrificed for the sake of scientific content—a description that is arguably suitable for, say, the works of George O. Smith or Robert F. Forward but is nonsensical when applied to the novels and stories of Gregory Benford or Octavia E. Butler, all authors who are routinely characterized as hard science fiction writers. In truth, vastly differing qualities of writing are found both within and outside of hard science fiction.

Conversely, others present hard science fiction as the most rigorous and intellectually demanding form of science fiction, implying that those who do not produce it are somehow failing to realize the true potential of science fiction. This is objectionable as well; writers like Chad Oliver and Ursula K. Le Guin, for example, have brought to their writing a background in anthropology that makes their extrapolated aliens and future societies every bit as fascinating and intellectually involving as the technological marvels and strange planets of hard science fiction. Because anthropology is a social science, not a natural science, it is hard to classify their works as hard science fiction, but one cannot justly construe this observation as a criticism. In addition, there is much hard science fiction which reflects little in the way of deep thought, such as Hal Clement's "Fireproof" (1947), which is little more than an extended explanation of the principle that a fire cannot be sustained in weightless conditions. Overall, both unfavorable and favorable generalizations about hard science fiction rarely withstand thoroughgoing examination.

Even in the absence of a clear consensus regarding how to properly define and defend hard science fiction, commentators are usually in agreement as to which authors best represent the subgenre; the names of Benford, Clement, Arthur C. Clarke, and Larry Niven come up most frequently in critical discussions, and any number of authors—including Poul Anderson, Stephen Baxter, Greg Bear, Ben Bova, David Brin, Butler, Greg Egan, Forward, Jerry Pournelle, Charles Sheffield, Joan Slonczewski, and others who emerged in the 1980s and thereafter—have been universally accepted as practitioners of the subgenre. One might say, as has been said of science fiction as a whole, that hard science fiction is difficult to define in abstract terms but easy to recognize in particular cases.

In attempts to trace the origins and development of hard science fiction, one irony becomes apparent: all of the authors most strongly identified with hard science fiction became prominent in the 1950s or later decades, yet all of the critical ideas that are central to hard science fiction were promulgated much earlier. Hard science fiction, then, is a subgenre created by critical commentaries, as future authors exposed to those commentaries matured with a determination to produce science fiction that actually practiced the serious devotion to scientific laws and thought that the genre's advocates had long been preaching.

Arguably, one can trace the priorities of hard science fiction back to two of the field's most celebrated pioneers, Jules Verne and H. G. Wells, who both contributed key principles. While Verne famously criticized Wells in a 1903 interview, he described his basic techniques, in contrast to Wells's techniques, more respectfully and usefully in a subsequent interview:

> I have always made a point in my romances of basing my so-called inventions upon a groundwork of actual fact, and of using in their construction methods and materials which are not entirely without the pale of contemporary engineering skill and knowledge.... The creations of Mr. Wells, on the other hand, belong unreservedly to an age and degree of scientific knowledge far removed from the present, though I will not say entirely beyond the limits of the possible.[6]

Verne's attentiveness to current progress in a given area, and his impulse to cautiously envision how it might be advanced in the near future, would later lie at the heart of some works of hard science fiction, set in the near future, that offered meticulous portrayals of pioneering space flights, space stations, and colonies on the Moon and Mars.

As for Wells, though he spoke disparagingly about his science fiction in later years, he did convey a desire to follow a process of logical extrapolation and develop his ideas in detail. In his 1921 "Preface" to *The Sleeper Awakes*, he says,

> The present volume takes up certain ideas already very much discussed in the concluding years of the last century, the idea of the growth of the towns and the depopulation of the country-side and the degradation of labour through the higher

organisation of industrial production. "Suppose these forces to go on," that is the fundamental hypothesis of the story.[7]

And in his 1933 "Preface" to *The Scientific Romances* (published in America in 1934 as *Seven Famous Novels*), he notes that in imaginative fiction, "Touches of prosaic details are imperative."[8] These principles of extrapolation and detailed development would later govern the more extravagant and futuristic forms of hard science fiction that provide visions of bizarre worlds, massive constructs in space, and remarkable scientific advances.

Still, having acknowledged their contributions, one cannot appropriately classify Verne and Wells as hard science fiction writers, since science was so visibly neither man's chief interest. Both wrote novels emphasizing broader social and political concerns (often obscured in Verne's case by expurgated translations), and neither worried a great deal about detailed scrutiny of the validity of their scientific projections. Verne did not expect or receive readers' letters criticizing flaws in the engineering of his moon cannon in *From the Earth to the Moon* (1865), just as Wells did not expect or receive readers' letters questioning the scientific logic of his antigravity element Cavorite in *First Men in the Moon* (1901).

An author who did make science his chief interest, Hugo Gernsback, would in the 1920s create a true genre of science fiction by devising and promulgating the term "science fiction," editing the first science fiction magazine, *Amazing Stories*, and describing the characteristics of science fiction in his magazine's editorials, story introductions, and responses to readers' letters. Science fiction, he asserted, was a combination of narratives, explanations of scientific facts, and predictions of future inventions[9]—a definition that presumably would lead naturally to stories that were both scientifically researched and rigorously reasoned. Yet Gernsback's own stories, and those he published, rarely met such expectations. While stories did include presentations of scientific knowledge, to make science fiction educational, and imagined inventions, to make science fiction prophetic, the two features usually were not closely connected to each other. Gernsback's typical strategy, as observed in his novel *Ralph 124C 41+: A Romance of the Year 2660* (1911–1912, 1925), is to first explain current progress in an area, then announce the future discovery of some element or ray with almost magical properties—"Arcturium," "F-9 rays," and so on—and describe how this miraculous material or radiation enabled scientists to achieve a breakthrough. He makes no effort, then, to carefully extrapolate from known science to unknown science in the manner that would later characterize hard science fiction.

Similar procedures were followed to varying extents by the popular authors who dominated the early science fiction magazines, such as E. E. "Doc" Smith, Campbell, Edmond Hamilton, and Jack Williamson. Their works, though sometimes laden with scientific or pseudoscientific jargon, instead epitomized another distinctive subgenre of science fiction, space opera, which offered thrilling adventures in space but displayed little evidence of disciplined scientific thinking. Indeed, Gernsback ridiculed one of Campbell's stories, "Space Rays" (1932), as a parody of some writers' tendencies to offer what he termed "scientific magic, in other words, science that is neither plausible, nor possible."[10]

At one point, Gernsback did attempt to identify and celebrate stories that adhered very closely to current scientific progress, stories that would later be considered one variety of hard science fiction. In a 1930 editorial, "Science Fiction vs. Science Faction," he defined the proposed subgenre of "science faction" as

> science fiction in which there are so many scientific facts that the story, as far as the scientific part is concerned, is no longer fiction but becomes more or less a recounting of fact.
> For instance, if one spoke of rocket-propelled fliers a few years ago, such machines obviously would have come under the heading of science fiction. Today such fliers properly come under the term science *faction*; because the rocket is a fact today ... the few experimenters who have worked with rocket-propelled machines have had sufficient encouragement to enable us to predict quite safely that during the next twenty-five years, rocket flying will become the order of the day.

Such stories were contrasted with standard science fiction, in which "the author may fairly let his imagination run wild."[11] Needless to say, there were precious few stories in Gernsback's magazines, or other magazines of the day, that would have qualified as "science faction," and Gernsback made no efforts to subsequently popularize the term, which quickly faded from view.

However, one important precedent was established during the 1930s: the role of magazine letter columns in responding to and debating the scientific issues that were raised in stories. This was particularly evident in the "Brass Tacks" letter column of *Astounding Stories*, then edited by F. Orlin Tremaine. In 1934, for instance, Campbell published a story using the pseudonym Karl Van Campen, "The Irrelevant," which describes a purported method for evading the law of conservation of energy; during the next year, "Brass Tacks" printed numerous letters attacking the story's logic, met by fiery responses from its author. Campbell's idea was essentially indefensible, but the whole experience made a point: there was indeed an audience of science fiction readers who were eager to read and argue about innovative scientific ideas, and the lengthy controversy could be considered a preview of the debates that would follow the publication of later classics of hard science fiction like Clement's *Mission of Gravity* (1953) and Niven's *Ringworld* (1970). In fact, letters with this sort of content eventually became so common that in the February 1937 issue, Tremaine renamed the letters column "Science Discussions," although Tremaine's successor Campbell would soon retitle the column "Brass Tacks and Science Discussions" and eventually reverted to "Brass Tacks." Reading all of these letters focused on scientific arguments was undoubtedly one factor that encouraged authors to produce stories containing meatier material for readers' informed analyses.

When Campbell officially became editor of *Astounding Stories* in 1938 and renamed it *Astounding Science-Fiction*, his editorials placed more emphasis on science fiction generated by scientific extrapolation, insisting in theory upon the thought process of hard science fiction. Initially, however, the new authors he discovered and promoted did not entirely fulfill that agenda: writers like Robert A. Heinlein, Isaac Asimov, and Theodore Sturgeon were attentive more to exploring future social developments than to devising future inventions, while others like A. E. van Vogt and Henry Kuttner flaunted a wild, unfettered imagination that had little to do with scientific thinking.

Still, there were signs throughout the first decade of Campbell's editorial career of authors attempting to build their stories upon sound scientific principles. Ross Rocklynne, who contributed stories to Campbell's *Astounding*, had already pioneered the form that became known as the "scientific problem story," mimicking the structure of the detective story, in three adventures featuring space policeman John Colbie and criminal Edward Deverel, who joined forces to reason out the answer to some scientific puzzle, such as how to get off the surface of a huge frictionless mirror. As noted, George O. Smith wrote a series of stories about a space station equidistant from Venus and Earth, later collected as *Venus Equilateral* (1947), to explore the various problems of communication across space, and space opera veteran Williamson, using the pseudonym Will Stewart, offered his own contributions in this vein, several stories involving antimatter, termed contraterrene matter or "Seetee." The results of these authors' ruminations were not always scientifically flawless—for example, Rocklynne's "At the Center of Gravity" (1938) falsely posits that people inside a hollow sphere would be attracted to its center, while George O. Smith needlessly overcomplicates the difficulties involved in sending a radio message to a spaceship—but they came closer to the ideals of hard science fiction than previous stories.

Astounding in the 1940s also published early stories by two authors, Clement and Clarke, who would become central figures in hard science fiction. Their early stories for Campbell included Clement's "Proof" (1942), a persuasive description of life forms that might have emerged within the Sun, and Clarke's "Hide and Seek" (1949), which cleverly demonstrates that a man running across the surface of the Martian moon Phobos could plausibly outmaneuver a pursuing spaceship. All of the editorials about the importance of science, and all of the readers' letters complaining about sloppy or dubious science, were starting to have an effect on the stories published in the magazines alongside those editorials and letters.

11. Hard Science Fiction

Nevertheless, only in the 1950s did two texts that would truly define hard science fiction finally appear. Not surprisingly, both of them came from already noteworthy writers, both were highly popular in its day, and both were accompanied by an influential article from their authors, published in *Astounding*, explaining how the works were created. What is surprising is that one of the texts was not a story or novel, but rather a film.

Destination Moon (1950) was directly inspired by an important event outside of the realm of science fiction: the establishment of an American space program after World War II, initially headed by the German scientists like Wernher von Braun who had built the V-2 rockets, and devoted to the announced goal of human flight into outer space. Suddenly, what was then science fiction's most prominent trope—space travel—loomed as a real possibility in the near future; and this naturally led practical writers like Heinlein to ponder how space travel might actually be achieved, and to create narratives that were sufficiently grounded in current research as to qualify as plausible predictions of future space flights. Thus, although Heinlein was originally hired to write a film script based on his juvenile novel *Rocket Ship Galileo* (1947), he and producer George Pal quickly decided to abandon its silly plot—three teenagers help an engineer build a rocket, they all fly to the Moon, and they discover renegade Nazis plotting to establish the Fourth Reich—and instead made a film that would depict a first flight to the moon in a painstakingly realistic manner. Now, a rocket to the Moon would be constructed by teams of industrialists headed by a retired general, not an isolated genius and three youngsters, and moon explorers would battle only the harsh conditions of space, not contrived villainy.

When the film was released, Heinlein published an article in *Astounding*, "Shooting *Destination Moon*" (1950), which described the priorities and activities of everyone involved in producing the movie:

> By the time the picture was being shot the entire company—actors, grips, cameramen, office people—became imbued with enthusiasm for producing a picture which would be scientifically acceptable as well as a box office success. Willy Ley's "Rockets and Space Travel" was read by dozens of people in the company. [Chesley] Bonestell and Ley's "Conquest of Space" was published about then and enjoyed a brisk sale among us. Waits between takes were filled by discussions of theory and future prospects of interplanetary travel.
>
> As shooting progressed we began to be deluged with visitors of technical background—guided missiles men, astronomers, rocket engineers, aircraft engineers. The company, seeing that their work was being taken seriously by technical specialists, took pride in turning out an authentic job.

Heinlein also emphasizes that "realism is compounded of minor details" and that "most of creating the illusion of space travel lay ... in constant attention to minor details."[12] Writers and readers could sense from Heinlein's article that it could be exciting and rewarding to be meticulously attentive to all aspects of science in crafting near-future narratives.

Heinlein's film and article, as it turns out, had little influence on Hollywood: while a few other films about space travel did aspire to the documentary-style realism of *Destination Moon*, such as Heinlein's own *Project Moonbase* (1953), *Riders to the Stars* (1954), *Conquest of Space* (1955), and the television series *Men into Space* (1959–1960), science fiction films generally turned to more colorful and escapist stories featuring aliens, mutants, and monsters. But science fiction writers energetically responded to the challenge of portraying humanity's future space ventures more carefully and scientifically in prose, rather than on film, leading to the first real outpouring of hard science fiction.

One of the most prominent and capable chroniclers of humanity's early steps into space was Clarke: in 1951, he published the first novel about a pioneering flight to the Moon that matched the persuasive authenticity of *Destination Moon*, *Prelude to Space: A Compellingly Realistic Novel of Interplanetary Flight*, with a subtitle added to the American edition to emphasize its verisimilitude. Later, Clarke wrote another serious depiction of a first lunar expedition, "Venture to the Moon" (1956), as well as realistic portrayals of life in space stations (*Islands in the Sky* [1952] and "The Other Side of the Sky" [1957]), lunar colonies (*Earthlight* [1955] and *A Fall of Moondust* [1961]), and Martian settlements (*Sands of Mars* [1952]). Countless authors provided similar stories, often in novels aimed specifically at juvenile audiences: veteran writers Murray Leinster and Lester del Rey, for example, each produced trilogies of juveniles that successively described building a space station, flying to the Moon, and colonizing the Moon (Leinster's *Space Platform* [1953], *Space Tug* [1953], and *City on the Moon* [1957]; del Rey's *Step to the Stars* [1954], *Mission to the Moon* [1956], and *Moon of Mutiny* [1961]). My research for the book *Islands in the Sky: The Space Station Theme in Science Fiction Literature* (1996, 2009) revealed numerous other stories and novels in the 1950s about building space stations; even Tom Swift, Jr., constructed his own space station with a reasonable degree of plausibility in *Tom Swift, Jr., and His Outpost in Space* (1955). Engineer G. Harry Stine, writing as Lee Correy, emphasized the nuts and bolts of space travel in a series of stories published in *Astounding* during the 1950s, such as "And a Star to Steer Her By" (1953) and "The Plains of St. Augustine" (1955). Other hard science fiction writers who debuted at that time, often in the pages of *Astounding*, include Dean McLaughlin, Alan E. Nourse, and Gordon R. Dickson. Overall, while historians of science fiction in the 1950s generally emphasize the emergence of satirical science fiction in *Galaxy*, and of a more literate brand of science fiction in *The Magazine of Fantasy and Science Fiction*, most stories and novels of the decade probably fell into this category of near-future hard science fiction—works largely forgotten because they were overlooked by contemporary critics and have rarely been examined by later scholars.

A second, more ambitious form of hard science fiction came to the forefront in 1953 with the appearance of Clement's *Mission of Gravity*, first serialized in *Astounding* before being published as a book in 1954. In contrast to cautious extrapolations like those in *Prelude to Space*, which I termed "microcosmic hard science fiction" in my *Cosmic Engineers: A Study of Hard Science Fiction* (1996), one might describe the expansive visions of *Mission of Gravity* and similar works as "macrocosmic hard science fiction." Like Heinlein, Clement wrote an article about his achievement for *Astounding*, "Whirligig World," which began by describing its creation as a "game":

> Writing a science fiction story is fun, not work.... The fun, and the material for this article, lies in treating the whole thing as a game. I've been playing the game since I was a child, so the rules must be quite simple. They are: for the reader of a science fiction story, they consist of finding as many as possible of the author's statements or implications which conflict with the facts as science currently understands them. For the author, the rule is to make as few such slips as he possibly can.[13]

This is probably the first description of the friendly but combative relationship between careful authors and nitpicking readers—regularly referred to as "the game" by hard science fiction writers like Anderson and Benford—which would always be closely associated with hard science fiction stories.

The article goes on to describe how Clement, building upon recently discovered evidence of a large planet circling the star 61 Cygni, crafted a huge, rapidly-spinning, pancake-shaped world named Mesklin that became the unique setting of *Mission of Gravity*. Never before had an author described developing an imagined world in such extreme scientific detail. At one point, after Clement decided that he must provide his world with moons and a ring, he says,

> I checked the sizes of the rings against the satellite orbits, and found that the inner moon I had invented would produce two gaps in the ring similar to those in Saturn's decoration. The point never became important in the story, but it was valuable to me as atmosphere; I had to have the picture clearly in mind to make all possible events and conversations consistent [109].

He also recounts how Asimov helped him develop the methane-based aliens that would necessarily inhabit this strange planet, giving readers a glimpse of the collaborative thought processes often involved in hard science fiction, and he emphasizes the unexpected and creative results that can stem from the process: "The rest of the detail work consists of all my remaining moves in the game—finding things that are taken for granted on our own world and would not be true on this one" (113). The outgrowth of all of these efforts was one of the most stunningly original environments ever seen in science fiction:

a world of wildly varying gravity, inhabited by small crustaceans with shells hard enough to resist the powerful gravity at its center, yet a sort of world that scientists would have to concede might actually exist. Also, as would become characteristic of such creations, scientifically trained readers carefully examined Clement's work and discovered flaws: as he later reported in an interview, "I was a little unhappy when the MIT science fiction people buckled down and analyzed Mesklin and found that I was wrong, that it would actually have come to a sharp edge at the equator."[14]

This variety of hard science fiction—demanding writers with a strong scientific background, infinite patience, and a mind constantly open to unexpected consequences—proved harder to emulate than the near-future realism of *Destination Moon*, so there were initially fewer authors who endeavored to follow in Clement's footsteps. But some were up to the challenge. Anderson made himself an expert in the art of concocting imaginary but scientifically plausible planets; later in his career, he first created a planet he called Cleopatra as an exercise to illustrate his techniques for an essay, "The Creation of Imaginary Worlds: The World Builder's Handbook and Pocket Companion" (1974),[15] and then employed that same world as the setting for an anthology, *A World Named Cleopatra* (1977, co-edited with Roger Elwood). Another writer who regularly published in *Astounding* during the 1950s, Frank Herbert, presented a landmark achievement of world-building in his novel *Dune* (1965) and its sequels. While some were not impressed by the novel's derivative palace intrigues, recalling stock images of medieval Arabia, everyone could admire its setting, the magnificently developed and hauntingly austere desert world of Arrakis. In 1975, Herbert was asked by Harlan Ellison to join other hard science fiction writers, including Clement, Anderson, and Niven, in collaboratively creating a distinctive alien planet to serve as the setting for some original science fiction stories, which were later published in Ellison's anthology *Medea: Harlan's World* (1985).

This is not to say that the construction of innovative alien worlds was the only sort of extravagant speculation figuring in hard science fiction. Clement, for example, had distinguished himself before *Mission of Gravity* with another novel, *Needle* (1950), which presented a strange protoplasmic alien, capable of entering into and communicating with a human body, who visits Earth searching for an escaped criminal from its home world. Another unusual alien, an immense sentient cloud that drifts toward the Earth, appeared in the first of several science fiction novels written by esteemed astronomer Fred Hoyle, *The Black Cloud* (1957). Clarke dusted off an early novel about a city in Earth's far future, *Against the Fall of Night* (first published in *Startling Stories* in 1948), and rewrote it as *The City and the Stars* (1956), beefing up its scientific underpinnings while retaining its boldly imaginative portrayal of humanity's eventual destiny. He also garnered critical acclaim for *Childhood's End* (1953), in which an alien race conquers Earth in order to prepare humanity to evolve into a group intelligence. Anderson played with expansive ideas in *Brain Wave* (1954), which posits a future Earth that emerges from a cosmic intelligence-dampening cloud, transforming humans into vastly superior intellects, and *Tau Zero* (1970), which takes a spaceship traveling near the speed of light countless millennia into the future until it survives through the end of our universe and a second Big Bang that launches a new universe. Larry Niven first impressed his peers with a dramatic and realistic story about a man's close encounter with a "Neutron Star" (1966).

As more and more works of hard science fiction appeared, a term was needed to describe them. Throughout the 1940s and 1950s, several terms for forms of hard science fiction were proposed—the aforementioned "scientific problem story," "gadget story," "heavy science story," "engineers' story," and "Campbellian science fiction"[16]—but like Gernsback's "science faction," none of these terms became common. It was not until 1957 that P. Schuyler Miller, then the regular book reviewer for *Astounding*, properly christened the subgenre. One priority that Miller brought to his reviewing was a determination to identify the subgenre to which a work belonged, so readers who preferred a particular type of science fiction could be guided to what they liked and could avoid what they did not like; as one consequence, he constantly needed terms to describe various subgenres of science fiction. He became the first person to use the term "hard science fiction" in his column "The Reference Library" in the November 1957 issue of *Astounding*, while reviewing Campbell's recently republished novel, *Islands of Space* (1957):

> It was a world-beater in those days [the 1930s]. Although it has been carefully modernized, it's old-fashioned now. It is also very characteristic of the best "hard" science fiction of its day.[17]

In applying the term to what would now be regarded as a colorful space opera, not a controlled work of hard science fiction, Miller reflected what would become a recurring fallacy in later discussions of hard science fiction: namely, the notion that hard science fiction was the typical sort of science fiction seen in the 1920s and 1930s and not a more recent invention. In subsequent reviews, Miller kept featuring the term, and by the 1960s other commentators like James Blish, Algis Budrys, Ellison, and Fritz Leiber were also using it.

A key development in the growth of hard science fiction came in 1960, when editor Campbell changed the name of *Astounding* to *Analog: Science Fact/Science Fiction*, announcing his intent to divide the magazine equally between science articles and science fiction stories. While that plan was abandoned—the magazine was soon retitled *Analog: Science Fiction/Science Fact* and reverted to *Astounding*'s policy of only one or two science articles per issue—Campbell's magazine had been officially designated as a publication emphasizing science, and throughout the turmoil of the British New Wave and its aftermath, it remained a safe haven for hard science fiction writers devoted to careful scientific speculation and uninterested in literary experimentation. When Campbell died in 1971, *Analog* was taken over by Bova, who had already made a name for himself as a hard science fiction writer with near-future thrillers like *The Weathermakers* (1965), and he maintained the magazine's focus on science, as did his successors Stanley Schmidt and Trevor Quachri. Almost all of the authors of the 1960s, 1970s, and 1980s who earned the label of hard science fiction writer did so primarily because of their contributions to *Analog*; even Orson Scott Card, now better known for space adventures and fantasies, was initially pigeonholed as a hard science fiction writer after publishing stories in the magazine.

During the 1960s and 1970s, translations were gradually increasing American awareness of scientifically interesting texts being written outside of North America and Britain: among others, one might mention, from Japan, Kōbō Abe's *Inter Ice Age 4* (1959), a complex story of scientists confronting the anticipated submersion of Japan; from Poland, Stanislaw Lem's *Solaris* (1959), a haunting portrayal of an enigmatic sentient planet, filmed in 1971 and 2003; from France, Pierre Boulle's *Planet of the Apes* (1963), a portrait of an alien world where apes have become intelligent while humans are savages that went on to inspire numerous film and television adaptations; and from Russia, Arkady and Boris Strugatsky's *Roadside Picnic* (1971), a striking account of an investigation of puzzling debris left by alien visitors, filmed as *Stalker* (1979). These foreign-language writers, despite their intriguing ideas, were rarely considered hard science fiction writers, although two chapters on Lem were included in George Slusser and Eric S. Rabkin's critical anthology *Hard Science Fiction* (1986). But the major English-language hard science fiction writer to emerge in this era was Niven, whose early works included both documentary-style space adventures ("The Coldest Place" [1964] and "Becalmed in Hell" [1965]) and a number of stories (like "Neutron Star") set in a well-developed future universe called Known Space. The greatest work in that series, and another milestone in hard science fiction, was the novel *Ringworld* (1970), which envisioned a huge inhabited ring circling a star, somehow constructed by ancient aliens. Incredibly, Niven could demonstrate that it was all technically feasible, and despite some resistance to its mind-boggling concept—Niven first published the novel as a paperback original, unable to get it accepted as a magazine serial or hardcover—the novel won the Hugo Award and Nebula Award as the best science fiction novel of 1970.

Niven's construct also inspired an unprecedented torrent of reactions from readers who were anxious to critique and expand upon the basic design, as Niven later reported in his anthology *N-Space* (1990):

A Florida high-school class determined that all of the Ringworld's topsoil will end up in the oceans in a few thousand years.... In Philadelphia, a member of the audience pointed out that, mathematically, the Ringworld can be treated as a suspension bridge with no endpoints. Simple in concept; harder to build.... At the 1970 World Science Fiction Convention, students in the halls were chanting, "The Ringworld is unstable! The Ringworld is unstable!" Yeah, it needs attitude jets. Ctein and Dan Alderson, computer wizards working independently, took several years to work out the *exact* instability. Ctein also worked out data on *moving* the Ringworld. (*Yes,* for fun. Isn't that how you have fun?).... Dan Alderson, making proper use of playground equipment, designed a system with four Ringworlds. Three are in contact with each other, spinning orthogonally to each other on frictionless bearings. But the fourth was built by Mesklinites (see Hal Clement's *Mission of Gravity*). It's the size of Jupiter's orbit (Mesklinites like it cold) and to maintain hundreds of times Earth's surface gravity, it spins at an appreciable fraction of lightspeed.[18]

Niven's novel perhaps qualifies as the quintessential work of hard science fiction precisely because it proved capable of sparking such creative responses, some of which influenced Niven's sequels to the novel, *The Ringworld Engineers* (1980), *The Ringworld Throne* (1996), *Ringworld's Children* (2004), and (with Edward J. Lerner) *Fate of Worlds: Return from the Ringworld* (2012).

Ringworld also became the chief representative of a new sort of hard science fiction gradually being recognized, devoted to developing and describing what critic Roz Kaveney has called "Big Dumb Objects." Many of these massive structures were directly derived from the work of professional scientists. Freeman Dyson envisioned advanced aliens constructing massive structures to surround a star and gather all its energy, a concept that was misinterpreted as a huge solid sphere enclosing a star—called a Dyson Sphere—and such a structure was the centerpiece of Bob Shaw's *Orbitsville* (1975) and its sequels *Orbitsville Departure* (1983) and *Orbitsville Judgement* (1990). The space habitats designed by Gerard O'Neill—huge hollow spheres or cylinders rotating to simulate gravity for people living on the interior side of their surfaces—became settings for countless novels, such as Bova's *Colony* (1978), Mack Reynolds's *Lagrange Five* (1979), and William John Watkins's *The Centrifugal Rickshaw Dancer* (1985); and Clarke described a similar structure functioning as a mysterious alien starship in *Rendezvous with Rama* (1973), which later engendered three sequels co-written by Gentry Lee. In 1979, space elevators—the concept developed independently by Yuri Artsutanov and John Isaacs of an immense tower physically linking the surface of Earth to a space station in orbit—burst upon the scene in two novels, Clarke's *The Fountains of Paradise* and Sheffield's *The Web Between the Worlds*. But hard science fiction writers could add their own ideas as well; Clarke, for example, concluded *The Fountains of Paradise* by envisioning six space elevators, positioned around the Equator, with terminal bases leading up to six connected structures in space to form an inhabited "Ring City" around the Earth.

Throughout the 1960s and 1970s, new authors kept stepping forward to fill the pages of *Analog* with hard science fiction. Some, like Donald Kingsbury, P. J. Plauger, Tom Purdom, and W. T. Quick, never achieved prominence outside the magazine, but others like Vernor Vinge and Dean Ing made names for themselves with published novels. Jerry Pournelle was best known for his collaborations with Niven, including *The Mote in God's Eye* (1974), a space adventure filled with scientific ideas, and *Lucifer's Hammer* (1977), a near-future thriller about a large comet that strikes the Earth with disastrous consequences. Pournelle's solo works included a series of stories about political intrigues in Earth orbit that were collected in *High Justice* (1977). Benford, who long worked as a physics professor at the University of California, Irvine, published numerous stories and an impressive juvenile, *Jupiter Project* (1975), inspired by Heinlein's juveniles. John Varley, after earning praise for several stories collected in *The Persistence of Vision* (1978), launched a trilogy about a vividly realized, and intelligent, artificial world with *Titan* (1979), first serialized in *Analog*, to be followed by *Wizard* (1980) and *Demon* (1984). James P. Hogan attracted attention with an intriguing novel about scientists examining evidence of ancient aliens in the solar system, *Inherit the Stars* (1977), which inspired three sequels about actual alien encounters: *The Gentle Giants of Ganymede* (1978), *Giants' Star* (1981), and *Entoverse* (1991).

In 1979 and 1980, several landmark publications served in a way to signal hard science fiction's coming of age. After Clarke's *The Fountains of Paradise* earned both the Hugo Award and Nebula Award in 1979, Benford won the Nebula Award in 1980 for *Timescape*, an involving portrait of scientists at work in an imperiled future who manage to send a warning to scientists in the past by means of tachyons, particles that travel faster than light. Correy was maintaining the tradition of near-future space adventures with *Shuttle Down* (1980), involving the problems faced by a space shuttle which makes an emergency landing on Easter Island, while Clement returned to prominence with *The Nitrogen Fix* (1980), an impressively nuanced portrayal of a future Earth with a poisoned atmosphere.

However, newer writers were also having an impact. *The Web Between the Worlds* established Sheffield as a noteworthy new voice, and George Zebrowski drew upon the visionary ideas of Dandridge M. Cole to produce *Macrolife* (1979), an expansive saga of humanity gradually evolving, by means of space colonies constructed out of asteroids, into an enormous collective intelligence. Scientist Forward made an impressive debut with his novel *Dragon's Egg* (1980), daringly and persuasively positing strange life forms living on the surface of a neutron star. First novels by two other hard science fiction writers, Bear's *Hegira* (1979) and Brin's *Sundiver* (1980), were largely overlooked, but both authors would become major figures after publishing more acclaimed works in the 1980s: Bear's *Blood Music* (1985), in which genetic engineering gone awry chillingly transforms humanity into a group intelligence, and Brin's *Startide Rising* (1983), a rousing saga of spacefaring humans accompanied by the animals they have endowed with intelligence, or "uplifted." And, showing that hard science fiction was not necessarily a man's game, women writers were also starting to produce their own carefully extrapolated scientific visions, such as Butler's *Wild Seed* (1980), Slonczewski's *Still Forms on Foxfield* (1980), and C. J. Cherryh's *Downbelow Station* (1981).

Around this time, then, there was a growing feeling that hard science fiction had risen to a higher level, as an exciting subgenre distinguished by fresh ideas and an improving literary style. Even authors who had previously disdained the form began to express interest in joining their ranks; for example, Brian W. Aldiss, known as a New Wave writer in the 1960s, successfully ventured into scientific world-building with his well-received Helliconia trilogy (*Helliconia Spring* [1982], *Helliconia Summer* [1983], and *Helliconia Winter* [1985]), though he needed to rely on several scientists for assistance in developing his strange alien planet.

Despite signs of its growing stature, however, hard science fiction in the early 1980s had still not risen to the highest level of science fiction, as its writers rarely received extended critical attention or recognition as major talents. It would require another new generation of hard science fiction writers, with their own distinctive styles, to further advance the reputation of hard science fiction and inspire what David G. Hartwell and Kathryn Cramer termed in the title of their 2002 anthology *The Hard SF Renaissance*.[19]

It is difficult to summarize all significant works of hard science fiction that have appeared in recent decades, but a few comments might be offered. While veterans like Ben Bova and newcomers like Allan Steele would carry on the tradition of near-future hard science fiction in series of novels about the exploration and colonization of the solar system, writers like Stephen Baxter, Greg Egan, and Charles Stross dazzled readers with their ingenious, bold, and sometimes almost incomprehensible new scientific ideas. Another new writer living in China, Cixin Liu, demonstrated that the principles of hard science fiction were now being embraced throughout the world, as he became famous for a trilogy of novels—*The Three-Body Problem* (2006), *The Dark Forest* (2008), and *Death's End* (2010)—that were clearly inspired by the works of Arthur C. Clarke but featured several breathtaking concepts that went beyond anything Clarke had created, such as unknown alien invaders who destroy most of humanity by collapsing the solar system into two dimensions. In a 1986 volume of essays about hard science fiction, David Brin had lamented that the subgenre of hard science fiction might be "Running Out of Speculative Niches,"[20] but writers like Liu suggest that imaginative writers will always be able to develop genuinely novel and stimulating concepts by building upon and extending contemporary scientific knowledge in the classic manner of hard science fiction.

12

The "Big Three" Approaches to Juvenile Science Fiction and Why One Worked and the Others Did Not

In the 1950s, a number of experienced science fiction authors were recruited to write for the new subgenre of science fiction for children and young adults, and it is hardly surprising that these included the writers who came to be identified as the "Big Three" of science fiction: Isaac Asimov, Arthur C. Clarke, and Robert A. Heinlein. Writing as "Paul French," Asimov produced juveniles for Doubleday featuring a recurring character, David "Lucky" Starr, beginning in 1952 with *David Starr, Space Ranger*, soon followed by *Lucky Starr and the Pirates of the Asteroids* (1953) and four other titles. Clarke was one of many experienced science fiction writers—including Poul Anderson, Lester del Rey, Raymond F. Jones, Robert W. Lowndes, Chad Oliver, Jack Vance, and Donald A. Wollheim—invited to publish contributions to what was officially named the Winston Science Fiction series but generally known as the "Winston juveniles"; his novel *Islands in the Sky* appeared in the same year as Asimov's first juvenile. Eleven years later, Clarke authored another juvenile for a different publisher, *Dolphin Island: A Story of the People of the Sea* (1963). And Heinlein was hired to produce a series of juveniles for Scribner's that began with *Rocket Ship Galileo* (1947) and *Space Cadet* (1948) and continued with ten more annual novels until Scribner's rejected the thirteenth juvenile he submitted, published elsewhere as *Starship Troopers* (1959), and ended the relationship; one later Heinlein novel, *Podkayne of Mars* (1963), can also be classified as a juvenile.

Everyone knows how these books were received. Asimov's Lucky Starr novels and Clarke's two juveniles have been republished on a few occasions, but they quickly fell out of print again and now are largely forgotten; this is also true of almost all the juveniles published by other major authors. (Indeed,

12. The "Big Three" Approaches to Juvenile Science Fiction 197

at least one of them—Hal Clement's *The Ranger Boys in Space* [1956]—has solely been republished as a 2016 audiobook, despite the acclaim the author has earned for other novels.) However, Heinlein's juveniles have long been celebrated as a major contribution to science fiction, garnering widespread praise, frequent new editions, numerous scholarly analyses, and explicit homages from other writers. One of Heinlein's juveniles—*Space Cadet*—almost immediately inspired the television series *Tom Corbett, Space Cadet* (1950–1955); another—*Red Planet* (1949)—was adapted as an animated television miniseries (1994); and *Starship Troopers* has inspired three animated films (1988, 2012, 2017), a major 1997 film that was followed by two direct-to-video sequels (2004, 2008), an animated television series (1999), and a video game (2005). Since Asimov, Clarke, and Heinlein were equally effective in writing science fiction novels for adults, one has to wonder why Heinlein was the only one who was so spectacularly successful in writing science fiction novels for children.

In my view, based on a close reading of the three authors' first two juveniles, the reason for this is that Asimov and Clarke chose patterns for their young adult fiction that only imperfectly addressed the typical interests of younger readers, while Heinlein, after an initial stumble, hit upon a pattern that offered precisely the sort of story younger readers of the 1950s were looking for. In the 1960s and 1970s, there were relatively few science fiction juveniles, but the subgenre came to life again in the 1980s with a new generation of writers that were largely unconnected to the science fiction community and had no reason to cherish Heinlein's example; and by the twenty-first century, writers had developed a new pattern that represented a fascinating variation on the Heinlein pattern, and one that explains much about changing attitudes toward young people and their proclivities.

As background information, it should be noted that these three sets of juveniles arose from different circumstances. Asimov was specifically asked to write novels that could serve as the basis of a television series, so he knew that he needed to focus on developing an appealing hero who could appear in numerous television episodes and subsequent novels. Clarke had only contracted to write a single juvenile, since Winston preferred to hire a series of different authors, so he was free to create a story that would not necessarily lead to sequels or establish a template for other juvenile novels. Heinlein initially intended to employ recurring characters in his juveniles, but Scribner's granted him the freedom to abandon those plans and develop new characters and settings for each of his juveniles. However, while these factors may have influenced their works, the differences between their juveniles must be primarily attributed to differences between their authors.

In recent years, whenever I reexamine the works of the "Big Three" authors, I usually find that Asimov most conspicuously fails to impress upon rereading—and that was definitely true of *David Starr, Space Ranger* and *Lucky Starr and the Pirates of the Asteroids*; bluntly, I found the novels were more irritating than entertaining, which can explain why they have failed to garner appreciative attention in recent decades.

It should first be noted that Asimov, whose stories characteristically consist primarily of extended conversations, visibly struggles to come up with story lines that would interest young readers. Consider the central crisis in *David Starr, Space Ranger*: food items imported from Mars are mysteriously causing the deaths of many people on Earth; after observing someone die while sitting in a restaurant, Starr resolves to investigate who might be poisoning these foods by anonymously traveling to a Martian farm and taking a job as a laborer. None of this, to say the least, sounds particularly exciting. Asimov promises more thrills in the second novel by pitting Starr against pirates lurking in the asteroid belt, but his hero still spends far more time talking to pirates than fighting them, and he finally does not defeat them in a spectacular battle; instead, after one man kills the pirate he was pursuing, Starr explains in a long speech to his colleagues that the murderer is actually the pirates' leader, leading to his arrest.

In addition, Asimov regularly set his stories in the distant future, when humanity has traversed the galaxy and made numerous wondrous discoveries, and that is what he did for his juveniles; *David Starr, Space Ranger* announces early on that it is taking place "ten thousand years after the pyramids were built and five thousand years after the first atomic bomb had exploded."[1] Readers then learn that almost all the planets and moons of the solar system have been explored and colonized, and mastering faster-than-light travel has also enabled people to journey to other stars, though Asimov chose to limit Starr's adventures to nearby worlds, each identified in subsequent titles: *Lucky Starr and the Pirates of the Asteroids*, *Lucky Starr and the Oceans of Venus* (1954), *Lucky Starr and the Big Sun of Mercury* (1956), *Lucky Starr and the Moons of Jupiter* (1957), and *Lucky Starr and the Rings of Saturn* (1958). (A seventh novel in the series, *Lucky Starr and the Snows of Pluto*, was planned but never written, due to Asimov's decision in 1958 to focus exclusively on writing nonfiction.) The first novel stipulates that Earth's enormous population now depends upon food grown on Martian farms; a form of antigravity keeps space travelers and the colonists of other worlds comfortable; force fields are employed as tables in restaurants; advanced robots bound by Asimov's Three Laws of Robotics appear in *Lucky Starr and the Big Sun of Mercury*; and aliens from the distant star Sirius are humanity's recurring adversaries. This is a setting, then, which is far removed from the experiences of readers in the 1950s, who knew that, even assuming astounding scientific progress, Lucky Starr's world would never be a world they could someday inhabit.

12. The "Big Three" Approaches to Juvenile Science Fiction   199

To further diminish the interest of young readers, they immediately learn that Asimov's hero Starr is an adult: the second paragraph of the first novel states that he is in a restaurant to enjoy "his first real celebration now that he had obtained his degree and qualified for full membership in the Council of Science" (9). The next chapter further identifies his "degree" as a Ph.D., as he "managed to do original work in bio-physics on the graduate level" (20), establishing that he is a precocious genius that few youngsters could readily identify with. Even though he is described as "the youngest man ever to be accorded full membership in the Council of Sciences" (20), his maturity is emphasized when one of the men who raised him speaks of seeing "David Starr ... suddenly and magically grown up" (17). Although both Clarke and Heinlein would unfailingly follow the convention of employing younger protagonists—usually teenagers—there have been other young adult novels with adult heroes, but they typically at least have a youthful sidekick, which was also the case in the early 1950s television series that Asimov had been instructed to emulate; however, while David Starr's eventual colleague Bigman Jones is short in stature, he is also an adult man. One can say that Asimov was only being logical, recognizing that any future society would never rely upon youths for important missions, yet the complete absence of any characters of the same age as the book's target audience remains striking.

The odd thing is that although Starr is described as a mature adult, he consistently acts like an impetuous and irresponsible child: his recurring habit is to suddenly rush off on an individual mission without telling anybody what he is doing, hoping that he can somehow improvise a way to conceal his identity, infiltrate suspicious organizations, and locate dangerous adversaries. In *David Starr, Space Ranger*, he dashes off to Mars by himself, chooses one of its many farms, and successfully applies to work there using a pseudonym; and the farm where he decides to work just happens to be the residence of the man ultimately revealed as the mastermind behind the sinister plot to poison Martian food. In *Lucky Starr and the Pirates of the Asteroid*, he stows away on a spaceship bound for the asteroid belt hoping that he can encounter pirates and persuade them to recruit him as a colleague, and he just happens to run into the man ultimately revealed to be the chief pirate. Frankly, the things that he does simply seem silly, and the successes he achieves as a result would undoubtedly be regarded, even by undemanding younger readers, as wildly improbable. This is simply not the way that an adult acts, and in offering such tales, Asimov indicates that he did not have a great deal of respect for his projected audience, assuming that they would be unable to appreciate that his hero was being rash and foolish. Granted, Asimov liked to structure his stories as mysteries, so keeping readers in the dark as to what Starr was doing and why may have struck him as a good strategy; yet it remains the case that Lucky Starr could never be recommended to any youth as a model for how they should behave.

Even more distressing is the way that Starr acts in *David Starr, Space Ranger* when he decides to investigate, for the first time, the interior of Mars (improbably, no other human ever thought about doing this during the five thousand years that people had lived on Mars). As another amazing stroke of luck, he immediately encounters ancient Martians who have long ago converted themselves into beings of pure intellect and devoted themselves to intellectual and philosophical pursuits instead of the conquest of the universe. One of these beings, developing an illogical fondness for the human interloper, gives him a "mask" that enables him to conceal his appearance and protect himself from harm so he can secretly serve as the solar system's "Space Ranger" in addition to his duties as a member of the Council of Science. Starr keeps all of this a secret, which is utterly bizarre. After all, he is described as a scientist, and true scientists are always supposed to share their findings with others; surely, he should have immediately reported to colleagues what he had discovered and given them the device so they could analyze it and perhaps figure out how it works, so it could usefully advance scientific progress. If Asimov himself, who once worked as a professor of chemistry, had been visited by aliens who gave him a sample of their advanced technology, one doubts that he would have kept it all a secret.

In essence, Starr does not act like a scientist, but rather like a comic book superhero, since they regularly obtain access to some scientific marvel providing them with amazing powers and, instead of sharing it with the world, resolve to individually employ their new abilities to battle against various foes. In defense of Starr's actions, Asimov does say in *Lucky Starr and the Pirates of the Asteroids* that the mask "was the development of a science that had continued for a million years longer than the science known to Mankind and along alien paths. It was as incomprehensible to him as a spaceship would be to a cave man, and as impossible to duplicate."[2] Still, if Starr had allowed fellow scientists with diverse areas of expertise to carefully examine the device, they might have been able to deduce *something* that would be valuable to human science.

Overall, the success of Asimov's series would appear to reflect the fact that in the 1950s, virtually any story involving spaceships and aliens was likely to be successful, given that many young people were keenly interested in science fiction and space travel; but I fail to detect anything particularly appealing about Asimov's works that would inspire other writers to closely follow his example. Indeed, though my knowledge of juvenile science fiction is not encyclopedic, I fail to recall any other series of novels that strike me as similar to the adventures of Lucky Starr. About the only texts that seem indebted to his flawed works, appropriately enough, are the comic book stories featuring

DC hero Space Ranger, introduced in 1958, who also fought against villainy throughout space in the future, had the last name Starr, concealed his face with a mask, and had a diminutive assistant (albeit an alien, not a human being).

Like Asimov, Arthur C. Clarke is not renowned for writing thrilling adventure stories, yet he seems to make more of an effort to do so in his two juveniles, which after a number of more prosaic incidents do conclude with the same sort of genuine crisis—a colleague in urgent need of medical assistance—so that their protagonists are involved in serious business; and their heroes do so without engaging in lengthy conversations. Further, Clarke works harder than Asimov to describe and explain the modest wonders of his future worlds, so that his detailed descriptions of the workings of a space station, and an island facility establishing contact with intelligent dolphins, are genuinely interesting, if not packed with action and excitement.

In contrast to Asimov, Clarke often wrote stories set in the relatively near future, which is the case with his two juveniles. An early announcement in *Islands in the Sky* that "in 2054 ... the United States, like all the other members of the Atlantic Federation, signed the Tycho Convention" does establish that the story takes place sometime after that date,[3] yet while Earth has constructed inhabited space stations and is in the process of colonizing Mars, this future world otherwise seems very similar to the world of today, as established by the mundane nature of young protagonist Roy Malcolm's life before he journeys to a space station. Further, because Clarke carefully based his space station on the actual plans then being developed by scientists, there is little that seems strange or futuristic about much of its technology and social structure, though there are provocative asides like one comment about the future Earth: "agriculture moved out to sea at the end of the twentieth century" (15). *Dolphin Island* similarly takes place in the near future—its hero Johnny Clinton is described as a "boy of the twenty-first century,"[4] and the novel depicts hovercrafts that transport passengers across both land and sea, but nothing else about the paradisiacal island where young Johnny Clinton comes to reside seems particularly futuristic, despite the revelation of dolphins' human-like intelligence. Clarke foregrounds some novelties, in other words, but much about the worlds of these novels would have seemed very familiar, perhaps overly familiar, to their contemporary readers.

Clarke also employs protagonists who are close to the age of his projected readers. Roy Malcolm, the protagonist and narrator of *Islands in the Sky*, reports in the first chapter that "I was sixteen when all of this happened" (13). *Dolphin Island*'s Clinton also happens to be sixteen, as the narrator reports that "twelve years ago, when he was only four, both his parents had been killed in an air crash" (8)—though near the end of the novel his scientist mentor comments that "you're seventeen now" (137). Despite their youth, both teenagers seem more mature than Lucky Starr: while at the Inner Station, Malcolm obeys all orders and causes no trouble, and Clinton is similarly cooperative and well-behaved when he joins the scientists and others at the research station on Dolphin Island.

Yet nothing happens in the novel to alter the protagonists' status as teenagers in need of additional training before they can truly become full members of the communities they interact with. True, when he becomes a part of a mission to transport an imperiled astronaut that becomes a crisis when it accidentally enters a dangerous orbit, Malcolm makes an important contribution by detecting a satellite containing dangerous radioactive material that will have to be dealt with; yet for most of the novel he functions merely as an observer of others' actions. To obtain needed medical assistance for Professor Kazan, the adult scientist he has bonded with, Clinton allows himself to be transported by dolphins on a dangerous journey to Australia; but he is otherwise nothing more than a young boy being supervised and supported by adults. The lack of appreciation for their minimal heroism is communicated at the end of both novels, as the protagonists only earn promises of future rewards for their exploits: the commander of the Inner Station merely tells Malcolm that "I've kept my eye on you in the last few weeks and have noticed how you've been shaping up. If when you're old enough—that will be in a couple of years, won't it?—you want to put your name down [to work at the station], I'll be glad to make a recommendation" (133). Kazan says to Clinton, "What I'm suggesting ... is that we get you into the University of Queensland next semester.... You have the skills and enthusiasm we need badly.... What you lack is discipline and knowledge—and you'll get both at the University" (137). Thus, Clarke's heroes both begin and end their adventures as insufficiently experienced and insufficiently educated teenagers, which of course was the status of most readers of these novels, though not the status that they were dreaming of.

Generally, Clarke's juveniles today are more readable than Asimov's, inasmuch as they persuasively describe near-future worlds wherein youthful heroes have realistic if not impressive accomplishments; and they arguably had more of an impact on other writers than the Lucky Starr novels, since many later novels for young readers would similarly deal with humanity's near future in a realistic manner (though Clarke's novels for adults were probably just as influential). Yet then and now, Clarke's juveniles never matched the enormous popularity of the juveniles of Robert A. Heinlein.

In Heinlein's first juvenile, *Rocket Ship Galileo* (1947), Heinlein generally follows the pattern later observed in Clarke of focusing on youthful protagonists in the near future: after a lengthy prologue involving preparations for a flight to the Moon, occasionally disturbed by apparent attempts at sabotage, Heinlein provides excitement by having his lunar pioneers—an adult and

12. The "Big Three" Approaches to Juvenile Science Fiction   203

three teenagers—encounter renegades from Nazi Germany plotting to establish the Fourth Reich from a secret base on the Moon. His descriptions of the technology and navigation of space flight is reasonably interesting, and he is prescient in anticipating that the complexities involved in flying to the Moon will require an onboard computer—referred to as "Joe," though he has no personality—to figure out most of the maneuvers. Still, the entire premise of the novel—that a solitary engineer, assisted by three youths, could construct and fly the first rocket to the Moon—is absurd, and Heinlein knew it, as it is pointed out by one of Heinlein's own characters, the father of one of the teenagers: "space flight is not a back-yard enterprise. When it comes it will be done by the air forces, or as a project of one of the big corporations, not by half-grown boys."[5] Yet Heinlein energetically struggles to make it all seem plausible: engineer Donald Congraves first attempted to interest a corporation in his plans for space flight, but with no success; since Heinlein established as his setting a future world which regularly employs rockets for terrestrial flights, it is reasonable that Congraves can obtain most of the equipment he needs by purchasing it instead of building it; and the minimal labor of transforming one used rocket into a spaceship only requires a few individuals who are knowledgeable about rockets—and the teenagers, all members of a rocketry club, have already built and launched several small rockets of their own.

In Heinlein's near future, while readers learn that the United Nations now maintains peace by means of its military forces, and that rockets are commonplace, little else about the environment seems unusual at all. Everything about American society seems about the same; indeed, although Heinlein regularly described future worlds that granted equality to women and racial minorities, virtually every character in the novel appears to be a white male. (Perhaps Heinlein cautiously assumed that it would be safest to begin with such characters before experimenting with more diversity in his later juveniles.)

Heinlein further emulated Clarke in foregrounding teenage men as his heroes, though the three young rocketeers seem bland and largely interchangeable; yet having Cargraves build his rocket solely with the assistance of one strong protagonist would have made the story even less plausible. The use of three main characters may thus have seemed essential. However, although they provide Congraves with capable assistance, and although they play key roles in confronting and outwitting their Nazi adversaries, they remain subordinate to their adult mentor, and at the end of the novel, there is every reason to believe that, after they land on Earth and receive acclaim for their flight, they will return to their families and their schools to continue their education. Like Clarke's novels, then, *Rocket Ship Galileo* is about adolescents who remain adolescents, despite their remarkable accomplishments.

Overall, the novel remains a surprisingly entertaining example of Heinlein's skills at storytelling, but it is weakened by his plot's obvious improbabilities, and the available evidence indicates that Heinlein himself was dissatisfied with his work. Indeed, he conspicuously repudiated the novel in two ways. First, his original plan had been to continue featuring the trio of teenagers from *Rocket Ship Galileo* as the protagonists in a series devoted to the "Young Atomic Engineers," but he abandoned the idea and, as his second juvenile, wrote an unrelated and very different novel, *Space Cadet*. Second, although the film he soon worked on with George Pal was officially an adaptation of *Rocket Ship Galileo*, Heinlein agreed to abandon its story of a single individual working in his backyard with teenagers to reach the Moon and battle against Nazis, and he instead co-authored a more realistic screenplay for *Destination Moon* (1950). In the film it is a coalition of businessmen, not a man and three teenagers, who construct and launch humanity's first spaceships; its workers and its crew are all mature adults (though an ignorant radio technician became a last-minute addition to the crew to provide comic relief); and once on the Moon, the astronauts must deal solely with an entirely realistic problem: the urgent need to reduce the weight of their spacecraft so that it can successfully take off with unexpectedly limited fuel.

Space Cadet shares one characteristic with *Rocket Ship Galileo*: it is about young men who travel into space. Yet in order to provide a more realistic picture of how young men might become space travelers, the novel is set farther into the future, as the novel begins with hero Matt Dodson receiving a letter inviting him to be tested for entry into the "Interplanetary Patrol ... on or before One July 2075."[6] By this time, space travel has become a regular activity; to assist space travelers and combat villains, the world has logically established a quasi-military force to maintain peace throughout the solar system; and like the American armed forces, this organization has an academy to train qualified young men to join its ranks. The novel has an air of plausibility because Heinlein could draw upon his own experiences at the United States Naval Academy; and once Dodson and other young cadets are finally allow to serve on a mission, a series of unlikely—but not wildly improbable—events puts them in a position where they must deal with a crisis on Venus.

The setting of *Space Cadet* seems to strike a good balance between the relatively mundane innovations of Clarke's near-future juveniles and the extravagantly advanced science of the far-future Lucky Starr novels. The Earth of the year 2075 is different enough from the present day to be interesting, but its wonders were not inaccessible, since it was possible to imagine that, during the lifetimes of young readers in the late 1940s and early 1950s, humanity would reach the point of routinely traveling to other worlds and establishing a cadre of space soldiers that someone now living might become a part of. Unlike Clarke and Asimov, Heinlein also envisions a future that has

12. The "Big Three" Approaches to Juvenile Science Fiction 205

advanced socially as well as scientifically; the last names of various past and present cadets indicate that they come from many different races but are all accepted as equals. This is confirmed late in the novel when one of Matt's comrades says, "Matt hasn't got any race prejudice and neither have I. Take Lieutenant Peters—did it make any difference to us that he's as black as the ace of spades?" (171). At a time when racism was still prevalent in American society, it was courageous of Heinlein to present a future world where it no longer existed. And while his Interplanetary Patrol does not include any women, the novel strikes a mild blow against sexism because the Venerians (the term Heinlein uses for the native inhabitants of Venus) that assist Dodson and the others are all women; while Venerian men are said to exist, they are never observed, and it is the women who clearly dominate their society.

The most significant thing about *Space Cadet*, however, is that it is not a story about adults who remain adults, like Asimov's juveniles, or a story about adolescents who remain adolescents, like Clarke's juveniles and *Rocket Ship Galileo*; it is rather a story about adolescents who become adults. At the beginning of the novel, Dodson and his friends are raw recruits without any status at all who must obey everyone else around him and constantly worry that they will be found unsuitable in some respect and expelled from the academy. Gradually, they prove themselves capable of advancement, and they progress through further levels of training until they are finally permitted to join the crew of an actual space mission. And having successfully handled the problems they faced on Venus, Dodson is, at the end of the novel, on the verge of officially becoming an officer of the Patrol, as he learns during a meeting with the Commandant:

> The Commandant paused for a moment as if thinking, then went on, "When will you be ready to be commissioned, Mr. Dodson?"
> Dodson strangled a bit, then managed to answer, "I don't know, sir. Three or four years, perhaps."
> "I think a year should suffice, if you apply yourself" [219].

Afterwards, though Dodson had hoped for an immediate commission, "he felt curiously elated rather than depressed" by that meeting, for reasons he understands while talking to his friend and colleague Tex Jarman who also "feel[s] wonderful":

> "I feel the same way, and yet I can't remember that he had a kind word to say. The whole business on Venus he just tossed off."
> Matt said, "That's it!"
> "What's what?"
> "'He just tossed it off.' That's why we feel good. He didn't make anything of it because he didn't expect anything else—*because we are Patrolmen!*"
> "Huh? Yes, that's it—that's exactly it. Like he was thirty-second degree and we were first degree, but members of the same lodge" [221].

In other words, even though he will need to undergo a little more training, Dodson has been accepted by the Commandant as a fellow adult, and as a fellow Patrolman.

And this, I submit, is what makes *Space Cadet* precisely the sort of story that young readers of the 1940s and 1950s would prefer. Of course they were interested in adults (like Lucky Starr), since they controlled all aspects of their lives and could engage in many exciting and worthwhile activities; of course they were interested in other young people (like Roy Malcolm and Johnny Clinton), who they could relate to and identify with. But they were most interested in learning about how they might become adults—a process that clearly involved more than simply growing older. And Heinlein describes the process very well: you first must learn a great deal; you must gradually master various skills; as you do so, you will be granted more and more responsibility; and then you will finally be accepted as a true adult.

Further, with his military background, Heinlein understood, unlike Asimov, that genuine heroism is always a matter of teamwork: young people must learn to work well with others and will always need some support in accomplishing significant results. Matt Dodson does not single-handedly save the day in the absurd manner of Lucky Starr: while stranded on Venus, his friend Oscar (who grew up on Venus) proves essential in building a working relationship with the Venerians and obtaining their assistance, and his other friend Tex helps out in various ways. In contrast, a former cadet, "Stinky" Burke, disastrously goes off by himself without any preparation to seek valuable metals on Venus—which is of course what Lucky Starr would have done—but he misunderstands and mistreats the natives, who capture and imprison him, and his rash actions threaten to inspire an ongoing conflict that Dodson, Oscar, and Tex must strive to prevent. Thus, Burke demonstrates the folly of individuals trying to handle complex problems all by themselves. Overall, in *Space Cadet*, Heinlein capably addresses the two tasks that all authors of juveniles in his era faced: to please young readers (by offering them an exciting story about someone like themselves becoming an adult) and to please the parents and librarians who purchase books (since they can recognize Dodson as an excellent role model for their children).

Space Cadet established a pattern that Heinlein followed in most of his later juveniles, although in some of them he ventured much farther into the future. *Red Planet* (1949) features a young man on Mars who matures while assisting his father and others in achieving Martian independence and establishing peaceful relations with the native Martians, while in *Farmer in the Sky* (1950) a teenager accompanies his father, stepmother, and stepsister to confront and learn from the grim difficulties of colonizing the Jovian moon Ganymede. A teenager in *Between Planets* (1951) becomes part of a rebellion to achieve Venusian independence; in *Starman Jones* (1953), a boy longing to become a space navigator stows away on a starship and eventually becomes its commander due to his unique knowledge of astrogation; *The Star Beast* (1954) features an young man with an alien "pet" (actually one member of a highly intelligent species) who later becomes humanity's ambassador to the aliens; in *Tunnel in the Sky* (1955) a teenager is first teleported to a distant planet as part of an "Advanced Survival" class and is finally observed as the adult leader of a group of colonists being teleported to another world; in *Citizen of the Galaxy* (1957), a young boy originally sold as a slave later inherits and takes control of a large corporation; and in *Have Space Suit—Will Travel* (1958) a teenager is taken into outer space and eventually (though unconventionally) successfully convinces some advanced aliens to allow the human race to survive. The novel most explicitly modeled on *Space Cadet* is *Starship Troopers* (1959), another story about a young man who joins a space force and, after a long period of training, goes on a space mission, though this one involves waging a long war against fierce alien adversaries.

There were a few exceptions to the pattern: *The Rolling Stones* (1952) features two teenage boys who remain supervised by their family as the group travels farther and farther into space; the young protagonist of *Time for the Stars* (1956) does mature in the course of an interstellar journey but never assumes adult responsibilities; and in *Podkayne of Mars* (1963), not officially published as a juvenile, Heinlein innovates both by featuring a female protagonist and by having the novel end not with her maturation but with her death. Though he changed the ending in response to pressure from his publishers, the original version of the novel has subsequently appeared.

One sign of the influence of Heinlein's juveniles is that there have been several works by other authors that are explicitly modeled on them. Alexei Panshin, after writing a critical study of Heinlein, *Heinlein in Dimension: A Critical Analysis* (1968), wrote a novel, *Rite of Passage* (1968), that precisely mimics his juveniles by featuring a young woman and a male companion who literally undergo a "rite of passage" when they are required, like other young people living in an immense spaceship, to survive for thirty days on their own on a planet in order to prove themselves worthy of being accepted as adults. The novel so impressed his fellow writers that it earned the 1968 Nebula Award as Best Novel, triumphing over two other novels now regarded as classics: John Brunner's *Stand on Zanzibar* (1968) and Philip K. Dick's *Do Androids Dream of Electric Sheep?* (1968). Gregory Benford has reported that his 1975 novel *Jupiter Project* "was a direct homage to *Farmer* [*in the Sky*], a sort of prequel to its events," featuring as its "protagonist, seventeen year-old Matt Bohles,"[7] who makes an important discovery after living on a satellite orbiting Ganymede. (In a personal conversation, Benford further revealed that he wrote the novel because he "wanted to see the Heinlein Hero get laid," something that Heinlein himself of course could never have described in his juveniles.) And in the 1990s, writers Charles Sheffield and Jerry Pournelle launched a series of Jupiter novels that were specifically designed to be updated versions of Heinlein's juveniles; the one I read, James P. Hogan's *Outward Bound* (1999), involves a young delinquent who is offered the opportunity to train to work in outer space and eventually straightens himself out to become a productive member of society.

Yet the most significant development in juvenile science fiction during later decades was a novel not originally published as a juvenile (though later republished as a juvenile)—Orson Scott Card's *Ender's Game* (1985)—which introduced a significant variation on the Heinlein approach. Like *Starship Troopers*, it involves a young man who is being trained to fight in a war against insect-like aliens, but Ender Wiggin gains the status of an adult, and indeed unknowingly becomes humanity's most important combatant, *while remaining a child*. This novel was the progenitor of several young adult science fiction novels in the twenty-first century that similarly featured youthful protagonists who do not have to undergo years of training to become accepted as adults; instead, they are recognized as extraordinarily capable and valuable members of society while they are still teenagers.

A few prominent examples—that I read in order to provide informed reviews of their film adaptations—will suffice. In Suzanne Collins's *The Hunger Games* (2008) and its sequels, young Katniss Everdeen becomes renowned as a brilliant warrior after she triumphs in a staged duel to the death against other young opponents, and she then emerges as the most prominent and influential member of a movement to overthrow the repressive government that created the Hunger Games. In James Dashner's *The Maze Runner* (2009) and its sequels, some young people represent the only hope for the survival of humanity, as they are singled out to undergo stressful experiences because it is believed that it will enable scientists to develop a cure for a devastating plague. In Alexandra Bracken's *The Darkest Minds* (2012) and its sequels, certain young people who have developed amazing powers as the result of another plague that killed most of Earth's population are threatened by an oppressive government that seeks to either slaughter or exploit them. And in Rick Yancey's *The 5th Wave* (2013) and its sequels, some teenagers who survive a virulent disease and other alien assaults on humanity are unknowingly trained to kill other humans before they realize what is going on and instead begin working to defeat the alien invaders. In all cases, the young protagonists become significant and empowered figures without any need to become adults, a pattern that can also be observed in fantasy novels like J. K. Rowling's Harry Potter books, in which a magically gifted teenager is the only person capable of defeating an evil wizard who threatens the entire world.

All of this, I think, speaks to the ways that American society has changed since Heinlein wrote his juveniles in the 1950s. At that time, adults were the experts on everything; children knew nothing and were forced to rely on adults for guidance and instruction; and parents, teachers, and other adults maintained effective control over children until they became adults. Today, however, because they are more informed about, and better able to use, all of the new technology that has entered and now dominates society, like computers and smartphones, youngsters are often considered the experts, as parents approach them for help in dealing with their devices, and teenagers can largely control their own lives, with minimal attention to the dictates of parents and educators. For these reasons, it is only to be expected that young readers might regard themselves, not their elders, as the true masters of the world, and that they would prefer stories that similarly present their peers as the true masters of their worlds.

The problem with these stories is that they conflict with reality: as I have noted elsewhere, there has never been a society in human history which placed a teenager in charge of their armed forces in a war, as occurs in *Ender's Game*, or a revolution that was primarily led by a teenager, as occurs in Collins's Hunger Games novels. In order to become an effectual and influential member of society, it remains necessary for young people to first undergo a long period of maturation, education, and training, and nothing about the increasing influence and autonomy of young people has changed that. With that in mind, one can conclude that, in regards to the way the world actually works, Heinlein's juveniles were right while contemporary juveniles are wrong.

Still, one can argue that the business of science fiction writers is to provide entertaining fantasies, not lessons about inevitable requirements, and there is nothing wrong with fiction that provides an escape from reality: as C. S. Lewis noted, "My friend Professor Tolkien asked me the very simple question, 'What class of men would you expect to be most preoccupied with, and most hostile to, the idea of escape?' and gave the obvious answer: jailers."[8] Still, I must report that I originally purchased *Outward Bound* as a gift to my teenage son, yet I never would have given copies of works like those of Collins, Dashner, Yancey, and Bracken to any teenage child, since I continue to believe that Heinlein and his emulators have something important to say to young people.

Epilog. The 1960s and Thereafter

13

After Things Fell Apart
The Fragmentation of Science Fiction in the 1960s and 1970s

For the record, this chapter's title is taken from a 1970 novel by Ron Goulart, *After Things Fell Apart,* which I purchased and read because it was part of Terry Carr's series of Ace Science Fiction Specials that I was then collecting. It describes a future United States that no longer has a functioning central government, but has rather split into a number of smaller nations with divergent policies. Based on my memories of the novel, I think it is highly unlikely that Goulart was commenting on the state of science fiction in 1970, but his title nonetheless provides an apt summary of how the genre had changed since the 1950s.

It should first be noted that prior to the 1960s, the science fiction community had not always been harmonious, as is discussed in the introductory editorial of a special issue of *Extrapolation* that I guest-edited on the topic of "Contentiousness in Science Fiction."[1] For further details about various feuds that erupted in science fiction fandom from the 1930s to the 1950s, one can also consult the histories of fandom in those eras by Sam Moskowitz and Harry Warner, Jr.[2] Yet all of these disputes and arguments tended to fade away over time, so that the community as a whole remained relatively united. It is my contention that more serious, and more lasting divisions only emerged during the 1960s.

As an early indication of what was going to happen, one can examine a special issue of longtime science fiction fan Earl Kemp's fanzine *SaFari Annual,* published in 1960, provocatively entitled *Who Killed Science Fiction?,* sometimes subtitled *An Affectionate Autopsy.* As one sign of its widespread impact, it earned the Hugo Award as the Best Fanzine of that year, and a revised and expanded version of the original text has been available online since 2006. Kemp's specific concern at the time was the recent and visible decline in the numbers of science fiction magazines, and along with some ancillary material, the issue consisted of the sometimes brief, sometimes lengthy responses of numerous science fiction writers, editors, and others connected to the genre to a survey Kemp had sent out with these five questions:

1. Do you feel that magazine science fiction is dead?
2. Do you feel that any single person, action, incident, etc., is responsible for the present situation? If not, what is responsible?
3. What can we do to correct it?
4. Should we look to the original paperback as a point of salvation?
5. What additional remarks, pertinent to the study, would you like to contribute?[3]

The respondents included two authors who initially chose to remain anonymous—Robert A. Heinlein and Philip Jose Farmer—along with other prominent writers and editors such as Poul Anderson, Isaac Asimov, Alfred Bester, James Blish, Robert Bloch, Ray Bradbury, Marion Zimmer Bradley, John W. Campbell, Jr., L. Sprague de Camp, Hugo Gernsback, James Gunn, Damon Knight, Fritz Leiber, Andre Norton, Mack Reynolds, Eric Frank Russell, Robert Silverberg, E. E. "Doc" Smith, Kurt Vonnegut, Jr., Jack Williamson, and Donald A. Wollheim.

While the survey's focus on magazine science fiction might strike some contemporary readers as parochial, it should be recalled that, from 1926 to the 1950s, the magazines had represented the primary—almost the exclusive—venue for the publication of science fiction under that name; and as even science fiction spread into the realms of mainstream magazines, hardcover and paperback books, films, television, and comic books during the late 1940s and 1950s—as documented above—many still regarded the magazines as the genre's primary home, inasmuch as they not only published new stories and serialized novels but also offered articles, book and film reviews, reports on conventions, and readers' letters. As I said in another context, the added features in science fiction magazines

> reflect, and to an extent replicate ... the characteristic ambience of a science fiction convention.... Like conventions, magazines have served as the waterholes of science fiction, where fans gather not only to enjoy the latest stories from old masters and rising stars, but also to sample its associated products and overhear another portion of the fascinating extended conversation that has accompanied science fiction ever since it was first recognized as a genre.[4]

A few of Kemp's respondents made the same point: Farmer commented that "we can't look to the original paperbacks as a point of salvation. There are no lengthy letter columns in the paperbacks to create a sense of togetherness,

13. After Things Fell Apart

to stimulate a controversial and at the same time a brotherly feeling. This sense and feeling will have to be carried on by the fanzines, which means that only a very small group will have them." And Wollheim said, "if science fiction is reduced to nothing but paperback novel publishing, it will mean the end of fandom. Because readers of paperbacks do not write letters—not to the editors and certainly not to each other." Thus, a significant decrease in the number of science fiction magazines, and the prospect of their coming extinction, represented a serious concern for anyone committed to the genre of science fiction.

Kemp himself found it difficult to summarize the results of his survey, but a few observations can be made. There was a general consensus that the science fiction magazines were not really dead, though some respondents agreed that they were imperiled. A number of respondents largely attributed the decline in the numbers of science fiction magazines to factors that were beyond the control of anyone in the genre, such as changes in the system of distributing magazines and the fact that fiction magazines of all kinds were steadily losing readers. But what I found most interesting about the responses was their indications that the field of science fiction, which as previously noted had expanded into several new areas during the 1950s, was now beginning to split into factions.

One conspicuous difference of opinion involved the relative quality of science fiction magazines and science fiction paperbacks, suggesting that the readership of science fiction was dividing into people who preferred the magazines and people (like the young Gary Westfahl) who preferred the paperbacks. Several people commented that the problem with science fiction magazines was the low quality of the material they were publishing: longtime fan C. L. Barrett complained that "whole magazines were published of second-rate material from good authors. People buying this stuff, if they read that crud would have choked, which they did, and they didn't buy again." Another fan and fanzine editor Gregg Calkins said that "as for the death of the other science fiction magazines.... The market was overstocked—and with poor quality science fiction to boot!—and eventually supply exceeded demand with the characteristic drastic results as far as the suppliers were concerned." Small-press publisher and fanzine editor Gerry de la Ree claimed that "frankly, I think the main fault with magazine science fiction is that the product is inferior. The quality of the writing is poor, but quite in keeping with the rates being paid." Philip Jose Farmer noted that he had stopped buying the magazine *Galaxy*: "It hurts me not to buy one; I feel like a traitor. But why buy a magazine I will throw down in disgust, half read?" Writer Dean McLaughlin observed that "even the best magazines seem to be publishing a large proportion of drab, uninteresting, and unstimulating stuff." According to another fanzine editor, Edmund S. Meskys,

> The booms, especially that of 1952, produced so much gorsh dern awful crud that it must have driven a number of people from the field. If someone had picked up the second issue of *Spaceway* or any issue of *Cosmos*, out of curiosity, I doubt that anything could convince him to ever try science fiction again. These are the only real crudzines I remember, but there must have been others (many of which I never read).

Smith reported that "I personally am still buying them all [science fiction magazines]; but I don't know how much longer even I will keep on buying crap that I simply can not read."

Yet other respondents instead complained about the low quality of the science fiction hardcovers and paperbacks that were being published in the 1950s. Bloch archly commented, "Should we look to the original paperback as a point of salvation? For an answer to this one, I suggest you just look *at the original* paperbacks which have been published. When you stop vomiting, then rephrase your question." The former editor of *The Magazine of Fantasy and Science Fiction*, Anthony Boucher, claimed, "'The original paperback as a point of salvation?' Well, economically it's been a help to writers, but the standards of editing have been so low as to encourage writers to turn out crap for a fast sale." Writer and fan Robert Coulson observed,

> At the Detroit World Science Fiction Convention someone mentioned that paperback publishers should be better informed about science fiction and cited Donald A. Wollheim of Ace Books as one publisher who really knew his business. If that's true, I'd like to know why Ace publishes such crud and the only paperback publisher which regularly puts out above-average material is Ballantine Books.

And according to writer Andre Norton, "I do feel that my field—that of teenage science fiction—was badly hit by very poor editorial selection of books which happened in a rush about four or five years ago. Librarians who admittedly knew little of the field bought heavily of this poor stuff and now fight shy of the whole genre, not being able to tell one type of book from another."

Another repeatedly expressed concern was that the rise of science fiction films and television programs, mostly of a very low quality, was harming the science fiction magazines by both competing for potential readers' attention and diminishing the genre's reputation. British magazine editor John Carnell wrote that

> basically, however, I agree with John Campbell's feelings that one of the main contributions to the present low in science fiction is the mess that Hollywood movies have made by labeling weird and horror films as science fiction. Potential new readers of the genre, appetites whetted by both American and Russian space probe successes, must receive a severe jolt when viewing a movie labeled "science fiction" which, apart from the appallingly poor dialogue and mediocre acting, is based mainly upon some monstrosity from outer space or the depths of the ocean.

13. After Things Fell Apart

According to Leiber, "Television and other forms of mass-media entertainment are cutting deeply into the *reading*-for-escape habit. Considerable fantasy and science fiction of varying quality is available on television, in the movies, etc." Bookseller Stephen Takacs said that "the dozens of horror (science fiction) films released by Hollywood during the past few years, have so turned the public (intelligent public) from science fiction that the publishers are moving heaven and earth to take off the words 'science fiction' from their titles of their magazines." Williamson further cites competition from the science fiction comic books: "There are a good many reasons for the present unsatisfactory state of magazine science fiction. It has been hurt in a triple squeeze between television, the comics, and the paperbacks."

One other recurring theme is that news coverage of the emerging Russian and American space programs was drawing people away from science fiction. Asimov claimed that "obviously, Sputnik and all that followed bears a major share of responsibility for the decline of magazine science fiction. The newspapers are so science fictiony now that there is scarcely any urge to continue looking for more science fiction in the magazines." Another writer, Alfred Bester, said that "the tremendous strides that science has made in the past decade fill the public with so much wonder and amazement that the headlines of the daily newspaper now provide what science fiction used to offer. Fiction has been supplanted by fact." Leiber commented that "progress and speculation in space flight, atomics, robotics, and similar fields are no longer under a general editorial taboo. We can read this stuff in the mass media; we no longer have to get this information from science fiction stories." McLaughlin speculated that "the recent developments toward space flight may well be providing the imaginative stimulation which people once sought in science fiction," and Williamson observed that "as escape fiction, [science fiction] is to some extent the victim of the events and inventions that it has most often prophesied—the Russians, for example, are busy removing the moon from the domain of the free imagination."

Overall, Kemp's fanzine provides early evidence of how the expanding field of science fiction would be changing in the 1960s: it was going to fall apart, as perhaps was inevitable when a genre grows larger and more diverse. Two sorts of divisions can be discussed: first, one observes the beginnings of separate communities of creators and fans dedicated to forms of science fiction other than books and magazines, including films, television programs, comic books, games, art, and other fan activities. Second, the people who were still most interested in written science fiction also began to split into different groups, based on their different preferences. There would continue to be readers who focused their attention on the magazines, but there would also be a new generation of readers (like me) who primarily if not exclusively read science fiction in the form of paperback books. Some writers would grow tired of science fiction and seek new careers writing in other genres, and there were also writers with no connections to the genre who began producing works that could be considered science fiction, both realistic portrayals of the current space program and inventive works of literature. There was an ongoing series of books about UFOS and other types of pseudoscience which I have argued are best regarded as science fiction under another name. Some scattered academic scholars studying science fiction began to coalesce into a separate community of readers whose analyses often irritated longtime fans. A new movement in science fiction—termed the New Wave—would generate fierce arguments between readers who were supportive of its substantive and stylistic innovations and readers who preferred the sort of the science fiction published in earlier decades. Finally, and unsurprisingly, the events that were dividing Americans as a whole—the Vietnam War and the rise of a "counterculture" of young people—were also causing divisions within the science fiction community.

At the science fiction conventions of the 1950s and 1960s, and at the science fiction conventions of today, one could encounter attendees with an interest in various forms of science fiction—novels and stories, films, television programs, comic books, and art. Yet it is not surprising that factions of fans with a special attachment to only one of those forms were gradually being forged. One key figure was Forrest J Ackerman. As a young science fiction fan in the 1930s, Ackerman was like all of the others initially focused on the science fiction magazines and science fiction fanzines, as he became well known for contributing numerous letters to magazines and fanzines and writing occasional science fiction stories for those publications. But he was becoming especially interested in the science fiction films of the 1930s and 1940s, which mainly featured various sorts of horrific monsters, and as someone who lived in Los Angeles, he found it easy to start visiting the sets of science fiction films, getting to know various science fiction filmmakers, and developing a collection of props and other memorabilia from their films; eventually, he also was regularly invited to play small roles in science fiction films. In 1958, he significantly launched the first magazine specifically devoted to the films that he cherished, *Famous Monsters of Filmland*, which attracted readers who shared his devotion to them. One young man who read the magazine, Bill Warren, soon became acquainted with Ackerman and eventually wrote a definitive book about the science fiction films of the 1950s, *Keep Watching the Skies!* (1982, most recently revised in 2016).

While various science fiction films and television programs were moderately successful in the 1960s, the most important development was the appearance of the series *Star Trek* (1966–1969), which during its original run and later appearances in syndication would attract the attention of both many science fiction fans and others with no previous interest in the genre. One individual previously focused on science fiction of all kinds, Bjo Trimble, would become noted for her special devotion to *Star Trek*: she visited its sets, got to know its actors and behind-the-scenes personnel, and was later one of the people who in 1972 organized and ran a science fiction convention, specifically focused on *Star Trek* and other science fiction films and television programs, called Filmcon; it was soon combined with another series of conventions, called Equicon, that came to focus primarily on *Star Trek*. (Trimble also authored the first authoritative reference book on the original series and its animated successor, *The Star Trek Concordance* [1976]). As it happens, the one time that I actively participated in fan activities was as one volunteer working for the 1976 Equicon/Filmcon convention, having been recruited by a fellow graduate student at Claremont Graduate University, Cliveden Chew Haas, who had long been a science fiction fan. At that convention, which provided me with an opportunity to observe and listen to iconic figures like Gene Roddenberry, Majel Barrett Roddenberry, and Leonard Nimoy, I became well aware that there was a growing body of fans who had little interest in the written science fiction I preferred and were rather enamored of *Star Trek* and other science fiction films and television programs.

In the 1970s and thereafter, in addition to conventions primarily focused on science fiction films and television in general, there were many other conventions devoted to *Star Trek*, as well as conventions focused on other popular media franchises such as *Star Wars* and *Doctor Who*. As is regularly observed, such films and television programs attracted some fans who were otherwise not interested in science fiction, such as my niece Laura Bright, who joined the official *Star Wars* fan club in the late 1970s and provided me with copies of its newsletter, *Bantha Tracks*. One other key development should be noted: Donald A. Reed's founding in 1972 of the Academy of Science Fiction, Fantasy and Horror Films, dedicated to supporting such films, and the creation of the organization's Saturn Awards, given each year to outstanding achievements in several relevant categories, including science fiction films and television programs.

As devotees of science fiction films and television programs were evolving into distinct communities, the authors of those films and television programs also had fewer and fewer connections to the written genre. The science fiction writers who scripted films and television programs in the 1950s, for the most part, either returned to primarily writing stories and novels or came to specialize in writing for film and television. Only occasional science fiction films of the 1960s involved individuals familiar with science fiction, including *Fantastic Voyage* (1966) whose authors included Jerome Bixby and David Duncan, and *2001: A Space Odyssey* (1968), famously co-authored by Arthur C. Clarke. There also seemed to be fewer films based on science fiction novels and stories, though prominent exceptions include *First Men in the Moon*

(1964, based on Wells's 1901 novel), *The Terrornauts* (1967, based on Murray Leinster's *The Wailing Asteroid* [1960]), *The Power* (1968, based on Frank M. Robinson's 1956 novel), *Planet of the Apes* (1968, based on Pierre Boulle's 1963 novel), and two other films mentioned below.

Further, the major creative forces behind science fiction television in the 1960s—Rod Serling, Irwin Allen, and Gene Roddenberry—all had no real background in science fiction. It is true that Serling's series *The Twilight Zone* (1959–1964) and *Night Gallery* (1969–1973) employed a few veteran writers like Richard Matheson and Ray Bradbury and occasionally adapted science fiction stories, while Roddenberry made a determined effort to recruit noteworthy science fiction writers like Robert Bloch, Bixby, Harlan Ellison, Norman Spinrad, and Theodore Sturgeon to write episodes of *Star Trek* (1966–1969). Yet a majority of the episodes of these series were written by specialists in writing for other television series, not writing science fiction. As for Irwin Allen, he only rarely used science fiction writers for his films and television programs, and he alienated Ellison after he reworked the one script Ellison provided for the series *Voyage to the Bottom of the Sea* (1964–1968), "The Price of Doom" (1964), so ruinously that the writer insisted on being credited as his farcical pseudonym Cordwainer Bird. Similarly, the major British television series of the 1960s and 1970s—*Doctor Who* (1963–1989), *The Prisoner* (1967–1968), and various puppet and live-action productions from Gerry and Sylvia Anderson—were entirely written by screenwriters with no background in science fiction.

Some major science fiction writers, however, did profit from the growing prominence of science fiction in the media by writing novelizations of films and television series. Murray Leinster wrote a collection of stories based on the television series *Men into Space* (1959–1960), though he had no access to and did not adapt any specific episodes of the series; Sturgeon novelized the film *Voyage to the Bottom of the Sea* (1961); Isaac Asimov wrote the novelization of *Fantastic Voyage*; James Blish wrote a series of twelve books adapting episodes of *Star Trek*, beginning with *Star Trek* (1967); in 1969 Thomas M. Disch wrote the first of three novelizations of *The Prisoner*; and a few minor science fiction writers, such as John T. Phillifent, J. Hunter Holly, Robert Coulson, and Gene DeWeese, contributed to a long series of novels based on the television series *The Man from U.N.C.L.E.* (1964–1968).

In the 1970s and thereafter, though, as "tie-ins" based on science fiction films, television programs, and video games became an increasingly prominent part of the industry, there would still be some veteran writers who produced *Star Trek* novels and similar products along with standalone novels, but this form of writing would largely become the domain of a separate community of writers who specialized in the form, prominently including the prolific Alan Dean Foster. Eventually, these writers would form their own organization, the International Association of Media Tie-In Writers, and bestowed annual Scribe Awards on outstanding works of this type.

The 1960s also witnessed the emergence of science fiction fans who were primarily interested in superhero comic books. Two major figures in this development were Jerry Bails and Roy Thomas. There had been a few fanzines launched in the 1950s that focused on comic books, including two edited by prominent fans who also became writers: Ted White's *The Facts Behind Superman* (1952), a one-issue pamphlet White produced while in ninth grade, and Richard A. Lupoff's *Xero* (1960–1963, with his wife Pat credited as co-editor), Still, Bails is generally considered the founder of the first fanzine exclusively devoted to comic books, *Alter-Ego*; after debuting in 1961 as a cheaply reproduced fanzine, the publication has evolved into a true magazine and is still publishing in 2019. Bails also established in 1961 an organization of comic book enthusiasts, soon named the Academy of Comic-Book Fans and Collectors, and the group began to present their own version of science fiction fandom's Hugo Awards, the Alley Awards, to the year's outstanding comic book stories.

As for Thomas, another comic-book enthusiast, he came into contact with Bails in the 1960s, contributed to *Alter-Ego* and Bails's other publications, and joined the Academy of Comic-Book Fans and Collectors. He and Bails also wrote regular letters to the letters columns in comic books (then a standard feature because having two pages of text qualified comics for reduced mailing rates). One *Justice League of America* story, "The Cavern of Deadly Spheres" (1962), involved a hypothetical scheme to destroy the Justice League that was sent to the superheroes by a concerned fan, and author Gardner Fox paid tribute to Bails and Thomas by naming the fan "Jerry Thomas." A few years later, Thomas became a writer for Marvel Comics and later served as Marvel's chief editor and as a writer for DC Comics. While an informal gathering at Bails's house in 1964 is considered by some the first comic book convention, a more significant development was the first major convention focused on comic books, initially entitled the Golden State Comic Book Convention and held in 1970, which evolved into San Diego's ComicCon, now the largest science fiction convention of them all, and officially devoted to science fiction films, television programs, and games as well as comic books.

There have remained some occasional connections between comic books and science fiction literature: several writers who initially specialized in comic books, ranging from Gardner Fox in the 1960s to Chris Claremont in the 1980s and Neil Gaiman in the 1990s, shifted to writing science fiction novels, and a number of prominent science fiction writers like Harlan Ellison and William Gibson have scripted stories for comic books. There have also appeared books featuring major comic book characters, such as Elliot S. Maggin's novels *Superman: Last Son of Krypton* (1978) and *Superman: Miracle*

Monday (1981), and Martin H. Greenberg's anthology *Adventures of the Batman* (1995), wherein various science fiction writers—including Robert Silverberg and Dan Simmons—contribute original stories about the DC superhero. Numerous books have also featured Marvel superheroes such as the Fantastic Four, Iron Man, Spider-Man, and the X-Men.

There was little evidence of an interest in science fiction games during the 1960s, but one practitioner of war games, Gary Gygax, did establish the first convention devoted to table-top gaming, Gen Con, in 1968, and he created the popular role-playing game Dungeons and Dragons in 1974. It also became a standard practice for science fiction conventions to include a room set aside for games—initially, card games and board games, since there were then several games that had been inspired by science fiction works. I recall there being such a room at the 1976 Equicon/Filmcon that I helped to organize and attended, and there has been a similar room at every science fiction convention that I visited in the 1990s and thereafter. Examples of board games derived from science fiction include one based on Serling's *The Twilight Zone*, released in 1964; a game about Irwin Allen's television series *Voyage to the Bottom of the Sea* (1964–1968), which also appeared in 1964; a board game based on Allen's *Lost in Space* (1965–1968), marketed in 1965; a 1966 game featuring the superhero Batman, who had just debuted in a popular television series (1966–1968); a *Star Trek* game that appeared in 1967; an adaptation of the film *Planet of the Apes* (1968) that was introduced in 1974; a game based on Heinlein's *Starship Troopers* (1959), first marketed in 1976; and a game featuring the comic book superhero the Incredible Hulk, released in 1978, that I once owned. In 1966, Whitman also introduced card games featuring Superman and Batman. Whether such games were truly popular must remain debatable; for with the exception of the aforementioned game that I acquired, I learned about the existence of these games only by means of internet searches in 2019. Yet the fact that all of these games can now be purchased on eBay indicates that at least some people were purchasing and playing these games.

However, science fiction games would only become widely popular as computers gradually entered popular culture. I first encountered such a computer game while I was a mathematics major at Carleton College in the early 1970s and employed the department's bulky computers to play a text-based game based on *Star Trek*; the player assumed the role of starship captain James T. Kirk and, in response to written comments from other crew members, would have to decide how to deal with alien opponents. Whenever I played, I invariably failed to achieve victory, and the game would end with the message, "A Captain Kirk you're not!" However, games would not become a serious rival for the attention of science fiction fans until the 1980s and the rise of video games, both large boxes available in arcades and home video systems that were attached to television sets. Some of these, like the pioneering arcade games Asteroids (1979) and Galaga (1979), were explicitly science-fictional in involving spaceships that were required to annihilate various obstacles in space, and video games featuring characters from *Star Trek*, *Star Wars*, superhero comic books, and other media franchises would soon become commonplace. Still, it must be noted that a hastily produced video game based on Steven Spielberg's film *E.T.: The Extra-Terrestrial* (1982) proved to be a notorious disaster, and other games based on films and television programs, in the 1980s and 1990s, would be regularly denounced, engendering the perception that all games of this type were inferior to games involving imagined worlds and characters that had originated in video games.

It would take a long time for a separate community dedicated to science fiction art to coalesce, but the Association of Science Fiction and Fantasy Artists did emerge in the 1980s and began in 1985 to present its own awards for outstanding science fiction artworks, the Chesley Awards. But even in the 1960s, some artists were beginning to recognize that there were science fiction fans with a particular interest in their work, especially paintings that became book or magazine covers, and there was also some interest in entirely original art that had never been published. Soon, many artists were successfully marketing their works at science fiction conventions, so much so that an "art show," separate from the dealers' market, became a standard feature of such conventions, including the aforementioned Equicon/Filmcon 1976 that I worked for. Indeed, particularly since items in the art show were often sold by means of a silent auction, some artists began to earn significant amounts of income by selling their paintings to a growing number of collectors of science fiction art, who prominently included Jane and Howard Frank, a husband-and-wife team of collectors who accumulated a massive collection of original art and made use of it in publishing several books about science fiction art, such as Jane Frank's *Science Fiction Artists of the Twentieth Century: A Biographical Dictionary* (2013). To my knowledge, there have never been science fiction conventions exclusively devoted to art, but paintings, sculptures, jewelry, clothing, and other original merchandise have been a very visible element in virtually every science fiction convention that I have attended, displayed either as items in its art show or as merchandise for sale in the dealers' room.

There was also a growing realization that the science fiction art presented in magazines and on book covers constituted a genre that merited separate attention, most clearly evidenced by a series of books devoted to such art that began appearing in the mid–1970s: Jacques Sadoul's *2000 A.D.: Illustrations from the Golden Age of Science Fiction Pulps* (1973), Anthony Frewin's *One Hundred Years of Science Fiction Illustration* (1974), Brian W. Aldiss's *Science Fiction Art* (1975), Lester del Rey's *Fantastic Science Fiction Art 1926–*

1954 (1975), and Janet Sacks's *Visions of the Future* (1976). A few science fiction artists also began to earn recognition outside the genre: the paintings of Richard M. Powers, for example, were annually exhibited at New York's prestigious Rehn Gallery, and original works of space art by Chesley Bonestell were regularly appearing in works of nonfiction like Willy Ley's *The Conquest of Space* (1949) and *Beyond the Solar System* (1964), Robert S. Richardson's *Mars* (1965), and Arthur C. Clarke's *Beyond Jupiter: The Worlds of Tomorrow* (1972). A younger specialist in space art, Don Davis, would contribute to Carl Sagan's series *Cosmos* (1980) and prepared artwork for Sagan's books *Comet* (1985), *The Dragons of Eden* (1977), and *Pale Blue Dot* (1994).

While one can observe the embryonic development of conventions specifically devoted to science fiction films and television programs, comic books, and games in the 1960s, it should also be noted that these fields remained a part of standard science fiction conventions—though usually in separate areas. Thus, in adding to several rooms set aside for panel discussions and presentations, a convention would typically have one room devoted to continuously showing old science fiction movies and television programs—by the 1990s, anime from Japan was the most popular feature—one room devoted to playing games, and one room for the aforementioned art show. Old comic books were always on sale in the dealers' room and, along with films and games, were occasionally the topics of the panel discussions that have remained the major activity at science fiction conventions.

But conventions had other distinctive offerings that were increasingly attracting certain sorts of fans. One room would be dedicated to "filking"— fans singing original or satirical folk songs involving science fiction themes— while a standard highlight of one evening would be a costume parade, featuring people portraying science fiction characters in colorful costumes of their own devising, an activity now referred to as "cosplay." Some rooms at conventions were devoted to celebrating the history of fandom, displaying copies of old fanzines for visitors to examine or a gallery of photographs of famous writers and fans taken at past conventions. It remains unusual for there to be a convention solely for these certain aspects of fandom, though one now-defunct convention in San Diego that I sometimes attended, Conjecture/Conchord, was as its name implies a merger of one typical science fiction convention and a convention devoted to filking. There is also a website, Cosplay Convention Center, to inform interested parties about upcoming conventions involving a special emphasis on cosplay. As if to rebel against the increasing diversity of science fiction conventions, an annual convention in Boston launched in the 1980s, Readercon, defiantly focuses entirely on science fiction stories and books, as was standard at conventions during the 1940s.

Overall, science fiction conventions remain to this day a place for people with an interest in various sorts of science fiction to come together, and anyone attending a convention will have the experience of suddenly running into someone they know in its crowded hallways; but due to the wide variety of events to choose from—sometimes, over a dozen at the same time at larger conventions—it is also entirely possible for members to never see most of the other attendees, as they focus on their favorite offerings while others attend different events. One could say, then, that science fiction fandom has not entirely fallen apart, though it is becoming increasingly splintered and increasingly variegated.

Turning to divisions between those who still preferred science fiction literature, the split in the science fiction community between readers of magazines and readers of paperback and hardcover books is the one most difficult to document, for two reasons. First, although I can provide myself as one example to demonstrate that there were many science fiction readers in the 1950s and 1960s who only read books and avoided the magazines, the people who read the science fiction magazines undoubtedly purchased and read science fiction books as well—so that there was only a blurry division between people like myself who only read books, people who read both books and magazines, and perhaps a few people who still only read magazines. Further, while magazine readers could send letters to magazines that, when published, permanently conveyed their opinions of the genre, those who only read books had no public outlet to express their opinions, since as noted the books they purchased had no letter columns and they had no way to connect to the science fiction community and communicate by means of fanzines. Thus, although I had regularly read science fiction since the late 1950s, my first published comments on the genre came in my 1986 Ph.D. dissertation, and there were surely many others like me who never found any way to offer their personal input about the science fiction books they were reading at the time, other than purchasing decisions that undoubtedly had some cumulative effect on the genre. (For example, I was keenly interested in purchasing paperback republications of science fiction classics that I had heard of, and I was evidently not the only one, since they long continued to periodically appear.)

There are only two available sources of information about the people who were solely interested in the science fiction that appeared in paperback books: personal testimonies, and surveys of the materials that were published in the 1950s and 1960s, presumably reflecting the proclivities of most of their purchasers. In my own case, these are the priorities that governed the beginnings in the early 1960s of my collection of science fiction books: I would purchase every book from the major authors that I liked; Isaac Asimov, Ray Bradbury, Arthur C. Clarke, Robert A. Heinlein, and Clifford D. Simak were my perennial favorites (the first book I bought was Simak's *Time Is the Simplest Thing* [1961]), though other writers occasionally enjoyed the same status in my estimation, including Brian W. Aldiss, Edgar Rice Burroughs, Hal Clement, R. A. Lafferty, and A. E. van Vogt. Books related to science fiction television series attracted my attention, as the second book I purchased was Rod Serling's *More Stories from the Twilight Zone* (1961), and I later obtained his other two collections of stories based on *Twilight Zone* episodes as well as all of James Blish's collections of stories based on *Star Trek* episodes, beginning with *Star Trek* (1967), and Thomas M. Disch's first novelization of the British series *The Prisoner* (1969). I purchased numerous anthologies of science fiction, such as the fourth book I purchased, Donald A. Wollheim's *More Adventures on Other Planets* (1963), as well as any novels that struck me as interesting based on their covers and descriptions, such as the third paperback I purchased, Rex Gordon's *First Through Time* (1962). Later, I purchased almost all of Terry Carr's Science Fiction Specials in the 1960s and early 1970s, attracted by both the assurance that they were books of a high quality and their distinctive Leo and Diane Dillon covers. Overall, the paperback books published during the 1960s suggest that my interests were not atypical, as they prioritized major authors and anthologies while also offering potentially interesting novels by less esteemed writers.

While Heinlein and other science fiction writers, as previously noted, sought to expand their audience and influence by publishing in mainstream magazines, they generally remained part of the field and continued to publish stories in science fiction magazines and science fiction novels. Yet there were also writers who visibly sought to distance themselves from the genre. The phenomenon was not entirely new: Paul A. Carter has documented how Nat Schachner, a prolific contributor to science fiction magazines in the 1930s, later sought to reinvent himself as the respected author of biographies of prominent early Americans like Alexander Hamilton and Thomas Jefferson.[5] An early contributor to *Amazing Stories*, G. Peyton Wertenbaker, abandoned science fiction in the 1930s to work on other novels, but he later contributed to documentaries about space travel and wrote speeches for NASA. Bernard Wolfe wrote one science fiction story and one science fiction novel, *Limbo* (1952), before moving into writing mainstream novels and screenplays, though he later wrote a few more stories. John D. MacDonald, after writing three science fiction novels and numerous short stories, decided that he would rather focus on detective fiction, producing a well-received series of novels featuring investigator Travis McGee. And Bester, after writing numerous stories and two highly-praised science fiction novels, long chose to do his only writing for the magazine he worked for, *Holiday*.

Yet another recurring theme in the responses to Kemp's survey is that economic factors inevitably were and would be driving science fiction writers away from the genre. Bibliographer and commentator Robert T. Briney wrote that "the biggest problem faced by the field (and the one that will eventually deliver the *coup de grace*) is the economic vicious circle: dwindling readership leads to dwindling rates, which cause the full-time writers (the ones who write for a living, not for fun) in the field to look elsewhere for markets; as the authors desert the field, the editors find it more and more difficult to fill their issues with readable material, thus their circulations drop even more," and De Camp claimed that "it will not be possible to make a living by writing such [imaginative science fiction] stories, just as you can't make a living writing ghost or weird stories today." Farmer noted that "the writers are not paid a penny more than they were ten years ago, and prospects are that they will not in the future. So, even if a writer loves science fiction dearly and would rather write science fiction than anything, he still turns to westerns or detectives or mainstream. He has to make a living." According to McLaughlin, "The ugly fact is, science fiction writing is not, on the average, a very remunerative business. To the best of my knowledge, only one man has been able to make a comfortable living writing science fiction. For all the others, their science fiction writing must be supplemented by writing in other fields, or by other income." Editor Larry T. Shaw was the most blunt: "You can't make a living writing science fiction."

Another respondent made the same point, but in a flippant manner:

> The pulp writers can't make a living any more? Tant pis. They made intelligent readers want to throw up.
>
> Anybody who announces that he is a science fiction writer is announcing that he is in damn bad company financially and artistically.

As it happens, this author would soon become the era's most prominent defector from science fiction: Kurt Vonnegut, Jr., initially noted in the 1950s for his science fiction novels and stories. Even in 1960, he must have still felt a part of the genre, since he was sent and responded to Kemp's survey about the status of science fiction; but in the 1960s he shifted to publishing novels outside the genre and developed a reputation as a respectable mainstream novelist. Even though some of his novels could still be considered science fiction, they were never labeled as such, he refused to identify himself as a science fiction writer, and he maintained no further connections with the science fiction community. As indicated by the reference to "bad company financially and artistically," Vonnegut was motivated a desire to both enhance his reputation and earn more money.

We now know that another major writer who emerged in the 1950s fervently longed to emulate Vonnegut, as Philip K. Dick repeatedly attempted and failed to move away from science fiction by publishing mainstream novels, but his works of this sort only appeared long after his death. Like Vonnegut, Dick was interested in both broader recognition and a higher income, but at least one contributor to Kemp's survey, Robert Silverberg, after surveying the bleak economics of the field, indicated that he was largely giving up science fiction for purely financial reasons, and he pessimistically predicted that others would do the same:

> it's an unpleasant situation, both for the fans and for the people who, like me, once earned most or all of their living from writing science fiction. After a nasty period of conversion, I'm now busily at work in other fields, and will be writing science fiction—only when and if I have some free time and an irresistible idea. (I'll continue to write science fiction novels, though.) I think science fiction has reached the peak of its curve of popularity, and, strangely by the distributors, will drop back to become once again the arcane thing it was in 1948—except for the crud so-called science fiction in the movies and on television, which will remain to haunt us. From a fan's point of view, the best thing to do seems to be to retire to the study and spend the rest of their days with back issues; the science fiction magazines of the future, bouncing along with their penny-a-word rates, will only attract amateur writers, and the prospect of future classics is thin.

I previously mentioned one product of Silverberg's decision to mostly leave science fiction that I happen to own, the nonfictional *Lost Cities and Vanished Civilizations* (1962); but as he promised, he did continue to write occasional novels and completely returned to writing science fiction in the late 1960s and thereafter.

Other defectors from science fiction in the 1960s had different motives: as noted, Isaac Asimov reported that he felt obliged to focus almost exclusively on nonfiction after the launch of Sputnik, though he must have found work in that area both personally and financially fulfilling, since he went on to branch out into areas of nonfiction—such as *Asimov's Guide to Shakespeare* (1970)—that bore no relation to his original announced goal of improving the scientific education of America's young people. And Ray Bradbury, having secured his fortune by becoming an author widely known and respected outside of science fiction circles, chose in the 1960s to mostly devote his energies to forms of writing that were less lucrative, such as poetry and plays. Overall, surveying the science fiction of the 1960s, any observer would notice that a number of acclaimed authors from the 1950s were no longer writing much, or any, science fiction, validating predictions that many authors would be abandoning the genre.

Still, their absence was not regarded as a crisis because many talented new writers did enter the field in the 1960s, though some of them took new approaches to science fiction that aroused controversy. There was also the emerging phenomenon of writers with no connection to the genre who were writing books that could be regarded as science fiction. For one thing, ongoing attention to the American space program, regularly chronicled in magazine articles, in nonfiction books, and on television, inspired some writers to produce novels that were closely based on the nation's actual space endeavors, so much so that they might be regarded as realistic fiction, not science fiction, though as I have repeatedly argued elsewhere, such stories are still usually classified as science fiction. One major figure in this movement was Martin Caidin: although he had previously written a near-future thriller about a nuclear war, *The Long Night* (1956), his first major success came with *Marooned* (1964), the saga of an American astronaut stranded in Earth orbit, filmed in 1969; a similar novel, *Four Came Back* (1968), concerned a crisis on a pioneering space station. Another writer with an interest in the space program, Hank Searls, first wrote a novel about the pioneering test pilots later celebrated in Tom Wolfe's *The Right Stuff* (1979), called *The Big X* (1959), then wrote a novel about a desperate American endeavor to beat the Russians to the Moon, *The Pilgrim Project* (1964), filmed in 1968 as *Countdown*. A third writer, Jeff Sutton, specialized in books about the American space program for young readers, including one that I happen to own, *Apollo at Go* (1963), though his other similar books escaped my scrutiny.

While science fiction readers occasionally noticed and commented on these novels, they were generally not impressed; yet there were also writers renowned for their literary talents who began to produce occasional novels that could be considered science fiction. Two examples of such novels— William S. Burroughs's *Nova Express* (1964) and Thomas Pynchon's *Gravity's Rainbow* (1973)—were even recognized by being nominated for the Science Fiction Writers of America's Nebula Award for best novel. Eventually, works by writers outside the genre that seemed to combine science fiction tropes with elements of other genres would be christened "slipstream" fiction by writer Bruce Sterling. One could celebrate the fact that respected writers of traditional fiction were now dabbling in their own sort of science fiction and producing distinctive and impressive works of fiction; but these writers also lacked an awareness, or appreciation, of the traditional expectations of science fiction that, for many, created the peculiar tensions that generated memorable examples of the genre. Hard science fiction writer Gregory Benford would say that these writers were playing "tennis with the net down."[6]

There were also increasing numbers of books appearing devoted to purported aliens visiting Earth and other forms of pseudoscience, and a few of these books undoubtedly attracted the attention of science fiction readers, even if they were generally inclined to be skeptical about such matters; for example, I purchased one acclaimed book about UFOs, Frank Edwards's *Flying Saucers—Serious Business* (1966). Yet I was more impressed by another book on the subject that I also purchased, *Final Report of the Scientific Study of Unidentified Flying Objects, Conducted by the University of Colorado under Contract to the United States Air Force* (1968), which soberly considered all of the evidence before concluding that the phenomena did not merit serious scientific investigation. Erich von Däniken opened up a new front in the business of pseudoscience with another book that I also purchased, *Chariots of the Gods?: Unsolved Mysteries of the Past* (1968), dubiously asserting that various artifacts from past civilizations represented clear evidence of ancient alien visitors—a theory that would inspire several subsequent books, by Däniken and others, as well as numerous documentaries, including the long-running series *Ancient Aliens* (2009-). But I remain one of the few who would classify such books as a form of science fiction, since they are abhorred by almost all aficionados of the genre, and while as noted above a few books of this sort once found their way into the ranks of science fiction, by the 1960s they were universally appearing solely in separate sections of bookstores and libraries devoted to paranormal phenomena.

The 1960s further witnessed the first signs of a growing interest in science fiction within academic circles. One pioneering scholar and long-time literature professor, Thomas D. Clareson, launched in 1959 a journal for critical studies of science fiction, *Extrapolation*, and he and others formed the Science Fiction Research Association in 1970, which among its other activities sponsored an annual science fiction conference. These gatherings were unlike science fiction conventions, dominated by panel discussions, as they mostly featured scholars reading prepared papers, but organizers did make an effort to invite prominent writers to attend, and they would usually contribute by serving on occasional panels during the convention. The attendees at these conferences, mostly literature professors and graduate students, would have bristled if they had been described as "science fiction fans," but effectively that is what they were, a new sort of fan devoted to scholarly analyses of science fiction novels, stories, films, and television programs. Yet despite their outreach to writers and other members of the science fiction community, these scholars were often resented by writers and fans who questioned their priorities and the genuine value of their work. (And those feelings have endured to the present time: over a decade ago, I was obliged to remove myself from a listserv because its founder posted a vicious personal attack on me, fueled solely by his manifest disdain for anyone with a Ph.D. who dared to write about science fiction.) By the 1980s, there were three annual science fiction conferences—the others sponsored by another organization established in 1979, the International Association for the Fantastic in the Arts, and by the J. Lloyd Eaton Collection of Science Fiction and Fantasy Literature at the University of California, Riverside. It also became common for the World Science Fiction Convention to include an "academic track" devoted to the presentation of critical studies in the manner of a conference, suggesting an emerging degree of acceptance for scholarly endeavors among science fiction fans.

The most famous division in science fiction during the 1960s involved the movement referred to as "the New Wave," dedicated to promoting forms of science fiction that deemphasized science and foregrounded experimental writing techniques and the freedom to explore sexuality and other subjects previously unwelcome in science fiction. This is not the occasion to provide a detailed history of the movement, particularly since scholar Rob Latham has long promised to provide such a history, but a few facts can be offered: the first reference to newer science fiction writers as a "new wave" occurred in 1961, when book reviewer P. Schuyler Miller while discussing British writers spoke of "the 'new wave'—[E. C.] Tubb, [Brian W.] Aldiss, and to get to my point, Kenneth Bulmer and John Brunner"[7]; an effort to promote a new sort of science fiction was then primarily associated with Michael Moorcock, who employed the British magazine he edited from 1964 to 1969, *New Worlds*, as a forum for polemical editorials and wildly experimental works like Brian W. Aldiss's novels *Report on Probability A* (1968) and *Barefoot in the Head* (1969); and his campaign soon attracted two prominent American advocates, Harlan Ellison and Judith Merril, who respectively edited the anthologies *Dangerous Visions* (1967) and *England Swings SF* (1968) to promote their own visions of New Wave science fiction.

Of these figures, I am most familiar with the writings of Harlan Ellison, one of the subjects of my doctoral dissertation, and I can offer two observations about his contributions to this debate. First, he regularly employed language suggesting that his New Wave represented youth and the future while previous forms of science fiction represented old people and the past; for example, in his "Introduction: Thirty-Two Soothsayers" to *Dangerous Visions*, he wrote that

> even more heinous is the entrance on the scene of writers who won't accept the old ways. The smartass kids who write "all that literary stuff," who take the accepted and hoary ideas of the speculative arena and stand them right on their noses.... And all them smartass punks keep emerging, driving the old guard out of their jugs with frenzy. And lord! how the mighty have fallen; for most of the "big names" in the field, who dominated the covers and top rates of the magazines for more years than they deserved, can no longer cut it, they no longer produce. Or they have moved on to other fields.[8]

Yet Ellison also offered conciliatory language indicating that he only wanted to add to, and not replace, older forms of science fiction: "no one is suggesting that the roots of science fiction be ignored or forgotten or cast aside. Solid plotting, extrapolation, trends and culture, technology—all of these things are staples that are necessary to keep the genre electric and alive."[9] It should also be noted that, despite his rhetoric, the stories Ellison presented in *Dangerous Visions* were for the most part not that much different from the stories then available elsewhere; and when he publish a successor volume with more idiosyncratic and more experimental stories, *Again, Dangerous Visions* (1972), it noticeably proved less popular than its predecessor.

Epilog. The 1960s and Thereafter

It would be easy to see the controversies aroused by the New Wave as yet another sign of the "generation gap" then being perceived throughout American society, and as evidence, one might also point to the way that science fiction community divided over the issue of the Vietnam War. This was displayed in the form of two petitions that appeared as advertisements in the June 1968 issue of the science fiction magazine *Galaxy*: one had the heading, "We the undersigned believe the United States must remain in Vietnam to fulfill its responsibilities to the people of that country"; the other had the heading, "We oppose the participation of the United States in the war in Vietnam."[10] Predictably, many defenders of traditional science fiction like Poul Anderson, John W. Campbell, Jr., and Jack Williamson identified themselves as supporters of the war, while champions of the New Wave like Harlan Ellison and Judith Merril placed themselves in the other camp. Yet the writers did not always split along those lines: some writers who emerged in the 1960s, like R. A. Lafferty and Thomas Burnett Swann, supported the Vietnam War, while other figures who dated back to the 1930s, like Forrest J Ackerman, Isaac Asimov, and Donald A. Wollheim, were opposed to it.

In addition, unlike the other forces that were creating disharmony in the science fiction community, these debates in the 1960s did not seem to have any lasting effects. For example, it is certainly significant that in the early 1970s, two works that could be regarded as obvious criticisms of the Vietnam War—Ursula K. Le Guin's "The Word for World Is Forest" (1972) and Joe Haldeman's *The Forever War* (1975)—both won Hugo Awards (Haldeman's novel also won that year's Nebula Award), suggesting that opposition to the war had faded as an issue. More broadly, as the extreme experimentation embraced by Moorcock became less common in the 1970s, one could argue that there had occurred a gradual merger of science fiction's Old Wave and New Wave, as the genre was now more open to sexual content and stylistic variety while remaining committed to traditional concerns about scientific accuracy and careful extrapolation. Yet the cyberpunk movement of the 1980s would introduce a new era of factionalism, as Bruce Sterling championed William Gibson, himself, and similar writers as the avatars of a generational shift in science fiction toward an embrace of new technologies, countercultural lifestyles, and generally being cooler than everybody else. But this is also a story better told more fully elsewhere.

Another source of conflict within the science fiction community emerged in 1965, when writer, editor, and reviewer Damon Knight founded the Science Fiction Writers of America, later renamed the Science Fiction and Fantasy Writers of America. There was nothing objectionable about an organization of writers dedicated to promoting their craft, but the group promptly decided that it should vote on and present its own awards, called the Nebula Awards, to honor the best science fiction stories and novels published each year. This was implicitly a criticism of, and challenge to, the Hugo Awards that for over a decade had been awarded to outstanding science fiction works by the fans who attended the World Science Fiction Conventions; presumably, working science fiction writers regarded themselves as better able than fans to identify and celebrate the best works of science fiction. And indeed, in its early years, the Nebula Awards regularly diverged from the fans' choices, most conspicuously in the category of Best Novel: in 1966 and 1967, the Hugo Awards went to two widely popular novels, Robert A. Heinlein's *The Moon Is a Harsh Mistress* (1966) and Roger Zelazny's *Lord of Light* (1967), while the Nebula Awards recognized two less acclaimed novels by a young Samuel R. Delany, *Babel-17* (1966) and *The Einstein Intersection* (1967). The next year produced an even more questionable choice, as the writers overlooked two novels now acknowledged as masterpieces, John Brunner's *Stand on Zanzibar* (1968) (which won the Hugo Award) and Philip K. Dick's *Do Androids Dream of Electric Sheep?* (1968), in order to recognize Alexei Panshin's routine pastiche of the Heinlein juvenile, *Rite of Passage* (1968). Yet sometimes the writers and fans reached the same conclusions, as in 1969 and 1970, when both the Hugo Award and the Nebula Award for best novel respectively went to Ursula K. Le Guin's *The Left Hand of Darkness* (1969) and Larry Niven's *Ringworld* (1970).

In the 1970s and thereafter, several other groups established their own annual awards, so much so that the early months of each year are now referred to as science fiction's "awards season," as one organization after another announces its awards for the previous year. Today, there are separate awards for science fiction works by writers from Canada, Australia, Great Britain, other countries, and regions of the United States like the Pacific Northwest; separate awards for science fiction stories that deal with gender issues or offer alternate histories; separate awards for works of fantasy and horror; and separate awards for stories published in particular magazines. The Science Fiction Awards+ Database, maintained by Mark R. Kelly as part of the Locus Online website, now lists over one hundred different awards bestowed by various organizations around the world.[11] Predictably, the varying perspicacity of each set of choices regularly inspires controversies within the science fiction community, especially when it appears that one faction of voters is exerting a disproportionate influence on the results; thus, in the last decade, there have been great concern and resentment over peculiar nominations for both the Hugo Awards and Nebula Awards that visibly were mostly determined by one small group of active voters.

This chapter, no doubt, has not discussed all of the issues that were functioning to divide the science fiction community during the 1960s; but enough has been said to prove the point that the genre, at the end of the decade, was clearly less unified than it was at the beginning of the decade. In part, this is simply a reflection of the growing popularity of science fiction: movements that attract few adherents tend to remain small and monolithic, while movements that bring in large numbers of outsiders tend to become more diverse and divided as they expand. Yet all of these divergent interests and opinions would eventually become irrelevant, as the genre gradually became subject to a force that none of them could resist—namely, the publishing industry, and the priorities that it would gradually impose upon the science fiction that it marketed.

14

Science Fiction Today
The Triumph of the Marketplace

Although science fiction was created in the marketplace, and always seemed comfortable in that milieu, most of its leading figures, paradoxically, constantly struggled against the natural pressures that the marketplace exerts upon the literature that it publishes; however, after several decades of successful resistance, they have finally lost that battle. Many have lamented this outcome, but there are also reasons to celebrate this triumph of the marketplace.

The story of science fiction and the marketplace begins with Hugo Gernsback, who introduced science fiction in his science magazines with his serialized novel *Ralph 124C 41+: A Romance of the Year 2660* (1911–1912, 1925), found that readers of those magazines enjoyed similar stories by other authors, and finally launched the first magazine entirely devoted to science fiction, *Amazing Stories*, in 1926. Though not officially a pulp magazine, *Amazing* soon adopted that format, and it was later joined by other science fiction pulps which employed garish covers to attract readers who were mostly young males.

Gernsback recognized that the stories he was presenting, which he initially christened "scientifiction," represented a new form of popular fiction, as announced in his first editorial: "There is the usual fiction magazine, the love story and the sex-appeal type of magazine, the adventure type, and so on, but a magazine of 'scientifiction' is a pioneer in its field in America."[1] He promoted his new genre by distinguishing it from other varieties of popular fiction: unlike the less scientific stories published elsewhere, which Gernsback dismissed as "fairy tale[s]" that "have no place in *Amazing Stories*,"[2] scientifiction was solidly based upon scientific facts, so stories could educate young readers and provide scientists with useful ideas; and unlike the "'sex-appeal' type of story," scientifiction offered wholesome entertainment "that appeals to the imagination, rather than carrying a sensational appeal to the emotions."[3] In 1929, providentially forced by bankruptcy to abandon *Amazing Stories* and its copyrighted term and devise another term to describe the stories in his new magazines, Gernsback renamed his genre "science fiction," but his arguments on its behalf remained the same.

In defining science fiction, Gernsback stipulated no particular patterns for stories to follow; as long as their science was correct and their predictions were scientifically defensible, any sort of narrative was apparently suitable. In this respect, the genre that he described defied standard expectations that popular fiction should feature stock characters in formulaic plots, like detectives tracking down murderers, beautiful heroines romanced by mysterious strangers, cowboys battling rustlers and outlaws, or explorers trekking through African jungles in search of treasures. As Walter Nash notes, "in popular fiction the conventions are simplified and more or less fixed ... pop-fiction is nothing if not predictable."[4] When writers submitting stories to Gernsback realized that science-based content was his only requirement, with no other conditions imposed, they usually relied upon patterns from other pulp genres, so that issues of *Amazing Stories* included comic tales of inept inventors, globe-spanning adventure stories, detective fiction involving cutting-edge science, and horror stories with a scientific patina. Believing that two of these hybrid forms might be especially appealing, Gernsback launched new magazines to feature them: *Air Wonder Stories* (1929–1930) for futuristic aviation stories, and *Scientific Detective Monthly*, later *Amazing Detective Tales* (1930), for scientific detective stories.

Yet his efforts to promote these forms of science fiction based on other generic models were unsuccessful, as they were overshadowed by another sort of story modeled upon a novel that Gernsback had published as a 1928 serial in *Amazing Stories*: E. E. "Doc" Smith's *The Skylark of Space*. Its bold story of interstellar space travel, with heroic scientists in conflict with both alien and human villains, proved enormously popular, inspiring many other writers to produce similar tales, ranging from the renowned John W. Campbell, Jr., Edmond Hamilton, and Jack Williamson to the now-forgotten Frank K. Kelly, Leslie F. Stone, and Harl Vincent. By the 1930s, such adventures, which Wilson Tucker derisively labeled "space opera" in 1941, were so common, and so formulaic, that Gernsback's *Wonder Stories* held contests encouraging readers to offer new "Interplanetary Plots" that professional authors could turn into stories; instructions warned contestants that "a plot submitted that simply relates a war between two planets, with a lot of rays and bloodshed, will receive little consideration." Instead, the magazine wanted stories with "some original 'slant' on interplanetary travel."[5]

Yet it seems that Gernsback was fighting a losing battle against a generic pattern that remained ubiquitous in science fiction magazines and was gain-ing a toehold in other media aimed at the same young men who read the science fiction pulps. Although Philip Francis Nowlan's stories in 1928 and 1929 about Anthony Rogers, a present-day man who awakens in the future, involved no space travel, they soon became the basis for a comic strip, *Buck Rogers in the 25th Century* (1929–1967), that evolved in a standard space opera; it was followed by two similar comic strips: *Flash Gordon* (1934–1992), which also inspired a short-lived pulp magazine, *Flash Gordon Strange Adventure Magazine* (1936), and *Brick Bradford* (1933–1987). All three characters went on to appear in film serials that were destined to become models for several films and television programs in the 1950s and thereafter.

By the end of the 1930s, then, science fiction was apparently settling into the sorts of narrative conventions that characterized other forms of popular fiction: its central trope was space travel; its typical protagonists were heroic space pilots; and its standard plots were battles in space, or adventures on other planets, involving evil adversaries ranging from space pirates to loathsome aliens. It is not surprising that a new magazine specializing in stories along these lines, *Planet Stories* (1939–1955), debuted in 1939, or that it spawned a similar comic book, *Planet Comics* (1940–1953), in the following year. Another magazine launched in 1940, *Captain Future* (1940–1951), took the subgenre's formulaic plotting to its next logical step, with space adventures starring a set of recurring characters: a brilliant scientist flying through space, accompanied by a robot, an android, and a "living brain," and confronting various menaces in the course of their journeys. There was every reason to believe, then, that science fiction in the 1940s and thereafter would predominantly consist of such "predictable" products.

Yet this did not occur, and while Great Men theories of history are inherently suspect, the best explanation for that development is that one man single-handedly prevented science fiction from gelling into a conventional generic pattern. After saying that "the true history of the field can be written as the story of that dialectic between creative impulses and market forces," Norman Spinrad argues that "the battle began when John W. Campbell, Jr. became editor of *Astounding Science-Fiction*"[6]; for Campbell struck the first effective blow against the growing standardization of science fiction.

Although Campbell first became known in the 1930s for writing expansive space operas in the manner of Smith, he garnered more praise for the innovative stories he wrote as "Don A. Stuart" (since his true identity was widely known), including the aforementioned "Twilight" (1934) and "Who Goes There?" (1938). Thus, when Campbell was named the new editor of *Astounding Stories* in 1937, he not only inherited the practical advantage of editing the science fiction magazine with the highest rates, but his reputation could attract writers whose interests ranged beyond routine space adventures, like Clifford D. Simak.

Indeed, Campbell immediately signaled his desire for "something new" in science fiction: he retitled the magazine *Astounding Science-Fiction* to suggest a shift into new directions; early editorials aggressively solicited new writers with scientific backgrounds, presumably best equipped to come up with new ideas; borrowing a device from F. Orlon Tremaine, who labeled especially inventive works as "Thought-Variant" stories, he promoted unusual narratives as "Nova" stories for other writers to emulate; and he published a special "Mutant" issue to suggest that his brand of science fiction was evolving in novel ways. Soon, he was presenting stories by contributors with new and distinctive approaches to science fiction, including Simak, who developed a unique style of gentle, pastoral science fiction; A. E. van Vogt, who enthralled readers with fast-paced, hallucinogenic adventures; Theodore Sturgeon, who specialized in emotional, character-driven narratives; Hal Clement, a pioneering master of hard science fiction; and Isaac Asimov, who became noted for stories involving the solution of scientific mysteries.

But one writer, more than any other, enabled Campbell to achieve his goal of publishing new and different forms of science fiction: Robert A. Heinlein. Using his own name and three pseudonyms, Heinlein appeared almost continuously in *Astounding Science Fiction* and its sister magazine *Unknown* (later *Unknown Worlds*) from 1939 to 1942, impressing readers with his streetwise characters, well-developed backgrounds, skill at imparting information through casual references, and insights garnered from his diverse experiences in engineering, the military, the real estate business, and politics. Most significantly, Heinlein recognized that Campbell did not want formulaic work and accordingly provided him with a wide variety of disparate stories. These included a few space adventures—one occurring in the asteroid belt ("Misfit" [1939]), and three on generation starships traveling to other stars ("Universe" [1941], "Common Sense" [1941], and *Methuselah's Children* [1942]); other space stories more idiosyncratically focused on oppressive labor conditions on Venus ("Logic of Empire" [1941]), a dying entrepreneur's poignant trip to the Moon ("Requiem" [1940]), and a company devoted to solving odd problems on other planets ("'We Also Walk Dogs'" [1941]). His Earthbound stories were a cloistered tale of an inventor and his amazing discovery, a device that determines how long people will live ("Life-Line" [1939]); adventures taking place in a future Earth involving a bureaucrat thwarting a strike that threatens its society's moving roads ("The Roads Must Roll" [1940], a nuclear power plant about to explode ("Blowups Happen" [1940]), rebels opposing totalitarian governments ("'If This Goes On—'" [1940], *Sixth Column* [1941]), and unique utopias ("Coventry" [1940], *Beyond This Horizon* [1942]); innovative treatments of time travel ("By His Bootstraps" [1941]), travel into other dimensions ("Elsewhen" [1941]), and psychic powers ("Waldo" [1942]); a comic excursion into the fourth dimension ("—'And He Built a Crooked

House—'" [1941]); what we would now term a near-future technothriller about the predicted outcome of World War II ("Solution Unsatisfactory" [1941]); a strange encounter with enigmatic aliens ("Goldfish Bowl" [1942]); a paranoid, solipsistic vision anticipating Philip K. Dick ("They" [1941]); and fantasies developed with a rigorous logic that recalled science fiction ("Magic, Inc." [1940], "The Unpleasant Profession of Jonathan Hoag" [1942]).

Inspired by Heinlein's example, Campbell was soon arguing that "science-fiction is the freest, least formalized of any literary medium,"[7] and he described "*Astounding*'s policy" as "free and easy—anything in science fiction that is a good yarn is fine."[8] He maintained that science fiction writers, driven solely by scientific ideas, could take stories into unpredictable territory: "the plotting is as nearly 100% uninhibited as anything imaginable ... because the author feels that freedom, he can let the story have its head, let it develop in any direction that the logic of the developing situation may dictate."[9] Such stories, by following premises to their logical conclusions, could then offer guidance to scientists and policymakers who needed to anticipate and deal with future advances. And while these thoughtful works might not appeal to young readers, who gravitated in the 1940s toward magazines like *Planet Stories* and *Captain Future* that offered more juvenile fare, Campbell maintained his high circulation by attracting scientifically-trained adult readers. (As early as 1938, Campbell boasted that "over thirty percent of *Astounding*'s readers are *practicing technicians*—chemists, physicists, astronomers, mechanical engineers, radio men—technicians of every sort."[10])

Ironically, just as he was promulgating the ideas that would long shape science fiction, Campbell was about to lose his status as the field's dominating editor; for coming revolutions in science fiction publishing would first marginalize Campbell, and would later marginalize all magazine editors like Campbell.

Initially, these changes were not harmful to Campbell's goals, since his commitment to a variegated genre was shared by some of the people involved in these new developments. First, during the 1950s, all of science fiction's pulp magazines either vanished or, like *Astounding*, converted to the smaller digest format, which looked more dignified and, unlike the science fiction pulps, implicitly sought adult readers who were presumably not interested in routine space operas. Reflecting such an intent, H. L. Gold, editor of the new digest magazine *Galaxy* (1950–1980), entitled his first editorial "For Adults Only" and went on to publish a wide variety of sophisticated stories. Another new digest, Anthony Boucher and J. Francis McComas's *The Magazine of Fantasy and Science Fiction* (1949–), similarly sought to attract adult readers with diverse stories of a high literary quality. Since these magazines paid just as well as *Astounding*, they could draw major writers away from Campbell, who also began alienating readers and writers as he became obsessed with psychic powers and other forms of pseudoscience. By the 1960s, having renamed his magazine *Analog: Science Fact/Science Fiction* (soon changed to *Analog: Science Fiction/Science Fact*), Campbell largely turned away from championing originality to refashion the magazine as a home for hard science fiction—the role it has continued to play to this day—even as others were promoting the different, less scientific, and more literary sort of science fiction associated with the New Wave.

Another development—the rise of paperback books—would undermine the status of all magazine editors by providing an alternative, and more profitable, market for science fiction writers. Yet Campbell's influence remained pervasive, since paperback companies were often controlled by strong-willed editors who were in their own ways equally committed to avoiding generic formulas. Thus, while Donald A. Wollheim's Ace Books did reprint many space operas from the 1930s and 1940s, and published original novels along similar lines, he also nurtured distinctive new talents like Dick, John Brunner, Samuel R. Delany, and Ursula K. Le Guin; and Ian and Betty Ballantine's Ballantine Books became renowned for publishing highly regarded works like Arthur C. Clarke's *Childhood's End* (1953) and Frederik Pohl's *Star Science Fiction* anthologies (1953–1959).

As an additional force influencing science fiction, reviewers and commentators, publishing in professional magazines, fanzines, and books, became more numerous and prominent in the 1950s, and they tended to support Campbell's view that science fiction should be variegated and far-ranging in its speculations. In a compilation of his reviews, *In Search of Wonder* (1956, 1967), Damon Knight called science fiction "the last stronghold of independent thought" and a genre that was "more fruitful and various than we generally (in our biased impatience) imagine."[11] Fanzine writer Norman Siringer, after approvingly noting "the decline of the space opera in the late thirties," acknowledged that "under the able guidance of John W. Campbell, *Astounding Science-Fiction* has rescued science fiction from the formula type action story." Siringer also pioneered in calling for science fiction to be freed from "confinement to the pulp magazines," since "even the better American pulps are subject today to the same codes and taboos that restricted the writer for the *Golden Argosy*, *Hoffman's Adventure*, *All Story*, and *Blue Book*."[12] This desire to break taboos became central to science fiction's "New Wave" in the 1960s: Michael Moorcock dedicated his magazine *New Worlds*, in Spinrad's words, to "stylistic and formal experimentation,"[13] and Harlan Ellison did the same in his anthology *Dangerous Visions* (1967), writing an introduction that promised to address "a need for new horizons, new forms, new styles, new challenges in the literature of our times."[14]

Still, despite these ongoing efforts to nurture diversity in science fiction throughout the 1950s and 1960s, there also emerged new efforts to produce standardized science fiction, though mostly for juvenile audiences. The

Stratemeyer Syndicate revived its inventor-hero Tom Swift in a series of "Tom Swift, Jr." books featuring his equally brilliant son, beginning in 1954, that were mostly space adventures; around the same time, its publisher Grosset & Dunlap also published eight books featuring the protagonist of television's *Tom Corbett, Space Cadet* (1950–1955); in 1952, Doubleday recruited Asimov to write six juveniles, as "Paul French," starring intrepid scientist Lucky Starr in a series of adventures throughout the solar system; in Britain, Reginald Eric Martin, writing as E. C. Elliott, published fifteen novels about a youth living in a space station named Kemlo, beginning with *Kemlo and the Crazy Planet* (1954); and in 1961, Doubleday hired Wollheim to write eight novels about astronaut Mike Mars. And while DC's science fiction comic books continued to offer original adventures, they increasingly focused on the space adventures of recurring characters like Captain Comet, Adam Strange, Space Ranger, Star Hawkins, the Star Rovers, and Tommy Tomorrow.

Another new market for science fiction writers—film and television—offered lucrative, if not stimulating, opportunities for writers who were willing to produce formulaic work for younger viewers: Clarke briefly advised the television series *Captain Video* (1949–1955); Jerome Bixby, previously noted for the story "It's a *Good* Life" (1953), authored screenplays for the films *It! The Terror from Beyond Space* (1958) and *The Lost Missile* (1958); and I chronicle elsewhere the other science fiction authors of the era who wrote for film and television, some of whom later came to specialize in such work.

As for adult science fiction, pulp writers had regularly produced numerous sequels to popular magazine stories, and recurring heroes like Tarzan and John Carter of Mars were commonplace in the works of Edgar Rice Burroughs and other writers. The practice continued in the 1950s and 1960s, though writers could now repackage and republish related stories as books or produce new novels continuing their series. Examples that originated in the 1950s include Zenna Henderson's People stories involving telepathic aliens who migrate to Earth; Jack Vance's stories about the lovable scoundrel Magnus Ridolph; Poul Anderson's numerous stories about space adventurers Nicholas van Rijn and Dominic Flandry; Murray Leinster's Med Service stories, about spacefaring doctors in the future; and James White's Sector General stories (1957–1999), chronicling medical mysteries in an enormous space hospital. However, such series never developed the generic rigidity of the juvenile series, allowed characters to mature and change over time, and they generally remained the exception, not the norm, in science fiction publishing.

In the 1970s, though, a notoriously disastrous experiment in selling formulaic science fiction to adult readers lasted only two years. As Mike Resnick relates in one of his "Dialogues" with Barry N. Malzberg,

> the short-lived ill-fated Laser Books was published by wealthy and wildly-successful (to this point) Harlequin, its first attempt to infiltrate the science fiction field. But

because all Harlequin books at that time were essentially interchangeable, written to a rigid formula, they assumed that *all* category fiction must work that way. So they hired [Frank] Kelly Freas, who was probably the best science fiction artist going at that time, to do the cover of every Laser book, and then tied his hands by giving him a formula which had the books look as interchangeable as the romances.... No one could sell 50 near-identical-in-appearance science fiction novels in those pre–Trekbook days, and the line went down the tubes.

Yet Resnick acknowledges that Harlequin's project was not really "dumb," only premature, as he then says, "You had to wait for television audiences, reared on the same plots and characters week in and week out, to *want* to read the same books over and over before that concept would work."[15] Indeed, soon after Laser Books collapsed, a very successful series of formulaic science fiction books, inspired by a television series, would be launched.

Arguably, after Gernsback's and Campbell's editorial careers, the third most important event in the history of science fiction literature came in 1979, when Pocket Books began to regularly publish novels based on the television series *Star Trek* (1966–1969). True, *Star Trek* novels dated back to 1968, when Mack Reynolds's juvenile *Mission to Horatius* appeared, and Bantam Books published a second *Star Trek* novel in 1971 by James Blish (*Spock Must Die!*), followed by several others between 1976 and 1981. But it was Pocket Books that turned the production of *Star Trek* novels into a steady and profitable business by packaging them in standardized covers, numbering each book in the series, and imposing increasingly inflexible guidelines upon their authors. Soon, Pocket Books stopped publishing other science fiction books to focus exclusively on the *Star Trek* franchise, and it has now offered readers over six hundred *Star Trek* novels, including adaptations of all feature films; series of books starring the casts of the other five *Star Trek* series as well as original characters; and other series of books, including young-adult novels featuring various characters in the *Star Trek* universe.

The popularity of *Star Trek* novels inspired publishers to launch similar series based on other science fiction franchises. There were earlier precedents—series in the 1960s based on the television series *The Man from U.N.C.L.E.* (1964–1968) and *The Prisoner* (1967–1968)—but such books proliferated in the 1980s and thereafter. *Star Wars* novels enjoyed the greatest success, but there were also innumerable books based on the British series *Doctor Who* (1963–1989, 2005-), as well as books based on the *Terminator*, *Alien*, and *Godzilla* films and the television series *The X-Files* (1993–2002), *Babylon 5* (1994–1998), and *Stargate SG-1* (1997–2007), among many others. Later, as video games and other games emerged as a popular activity, there would also be series of novels based on popular games such as Dungeons and Dragons, Halo, and Warhammer.

To explain why such books became so common in the 1980s, there is merit in Resnick's suggestion that they reflected the growing popularity of science fiction television, but other factors were in play. By this time, Campbell had long been dead, the writers he had published in the 1940s were dying or fading from view, and his readers represented an aging minority within a field now dominated by new readers who did not know about or care about Campbell's crusade for constant originality in science fiction. Instead, they had learned to enjoy science fiction by watching *Star Trek* and *Star Wars*, and they were perfectly content to embrace their written equivalents: packaged, predictable books, guaranteed to provide the sorts of adventures they craved. Unaffected by Campbell or his concerns, they were simply typical readers of popular fiction, and publishers regularly attract such readers with repetitive books that minimized the risks of publishing. Setting up rigid guidelines eliminated the need for especially talented authors—any professional who could follow instructions would suffice—and new books could be printed with precise expectations as to how many copies would be sold. These are all standard practices in popular fiction; in the case of science fiction, the surprise is not that such policies emerged, but that they took so long to dominate the industry.

To further explain these developments, ongoing changes in the publishing industry increasingly marginalized what David G. Hartwell termed the "heroic" editors who had long fought to prevent science fiction from descending into formulaic patterns.[16] As their sales plummeted, all but a handful of science fiction magazines ceased publishing, and the few major magazines that survived had to adjust to shrinking circulation figures and their diminishing influence on writers who were understandably more attentive to the greater financial rewards that came from publishing books. One can praise creative editors like Gardner Dozois of *Asimov's Science Fiction* (1986–2004) and Gordon Van Gelder of *The Magazine of Fantasy and Science Fiction* (1997–2015), whose magazines published many award-winning stories, but they were no longer important figures in the field.

As for book publishers, the increasing consolidation of companies into large, bureaucratic conglomerates meant that individual editors had less control over what they published, as decisions were dictated by sales figures, the calculations of marketing experts, and the demands of chain bookstores. Today, only a few editors have retained a degree of power over what they want to publish: Betsy Wollheim, the daughter of Donald A. Wollheim, inherited his company, DAW Books, and has remained an independent force though her company was acquired by Penguin; Hartwell earned three Hugo Awards as an adventurous editor for Tor Books, and his work has been carried on by successors like Patrick Nielsen Hayden; Jim Baen launched another company devoted to certain preferred forms of science fiction, Baen Books, which has maintained Baen's policies after his death; and Lou Anders long oversaw Prometheus's Pyr Books, dedicated to publishing meritorious original works. One is hard pressed, though, to think of other examples.

Furthermore, no surveys of science fiction's history can ignore the growing prominence, and eventual dominance, of fantasy. After the 1960s, when the works of J. R. R. Tolkien became enormously popular, fantasy novels were regularly found in the science fiction sections of bookstores, soon renamed the science fiction and fantasy sections; and fantasies, unencumbered by any traditions requiring novelty or originality—indeed, governed by principles that almost demanded fidelity to time-honored patterns—faced no barriers to quickly adopting the format of interminable series. Some were produced by single authors like Terry Brooks, or teams of authors like David and Leigh Eddings, who annually produced new novels set in their elaborately developed fantasy worlds; others were franchises involving multiple authors, like the Forgotten Realms novels based on the Dungeons and Dragons role-playing game. And when such products began crowding science fiction out of bookstore shelves, the genre inevitably began to borrow moves from its competitor's playbook by offering similar series.

To be sure, there were still writers and readers in the 1980s who remained committed to Campbell's philosophy, believing that science fiction should be variegated and daringly imaginative, and they resented the growing number and prominence of these sequels and series. Several jeremiads condemning these works, and predicting the death of science fiction, inevitably emerged; prominent examples include Cristina Sedgewick's "The Fork in the Road: Can Science Fiction Survive in Postmodern, Megacorporate America?" (1991) and three essays in a 1996 critical anthology: Norman Spinrad's "Science Fiction in the Real World—Revisited," Hartwell's "The Distortion of the Product: Stresses on Science Fiction Literature," and Kathryn Cramer's "Our Pious Hope: Science Fiction Marketing, Counter-Marketing, and Transcendence."[17] Still, while gloomy about the present situation, all of these figures expressed the hope that the combined efforts of concerned writers, readers, and critics might somehow spark a counterrevolution that would restore the freedom and diversity that once characterized science fiction.

Surveying what has happened in the decades since they wrote these essays, one can safely say that their hopes were naïve. Indeed, the only discernible result of their outcries was that bookstores resolved to mollify readers who disliked formulaic products with a policy of segregation: *Star Trek* novels and other series, instead of being incorporated into the regular section for science fiction and fantasy, were isolated in a separate section for novels in franchises, which was convenient for readers looking for latest installments of their favorite series, but it also meant that the eyes of traditional connoisseurs would not be sullied by rows of science fiction books they despised.

Nevertheless, the mentality of series fiction gradually and inexorably invaded the sections of bookstores that theoretically excluded such works, as editors and agents encouraged writers to create recurring characters and worlds that could attract regular followings, instead of writing singletons that were less capable of ensuring steady audiences. The examples of Lois McMaster Bujold and David Weber, whose numerous novels respectively featuring diplomat Miles Vorkosigan and warrior Honor Harrington were highly profitable, inspired many writers to launch similar series about space travelers in the tradition of *Star Trek*-inspired space opera, usually with an emphasis on military matters, but other repetitive approaches also proved successful. As a result, science fiction today has finally became what Gernsback, Campbell, and others had vigorously resisted, a genuine form of popular fiction, as an overwhelming majority of its works now rigidly follow some standard conventions.

To document this claim, I visited a Barnes & Noble bookstore in Montclair, California, on January 3, 2012, for a snapshot of the science fiction then being offered to customers. Ignoring 19 shelves devoted to "Teen Fantasy/ Adventure," 19 shelves for "Teen Paranormal Romance," 9 shelves for comic books and graphic novels, and 24 shelves for manga, I only examined the section devoted to science fiction and fantasy books for adults, which had 48 shelves for general science fiction and fantasy, 23 shelves for series, and 24 shelves for new books of all varieties. Though not obsessive enough at the time to examine every single book to first distinguish science fiction from fantasy, and then distinguish original books from series books, I surveyed the 75 "New" books in this fashion. Some might quarrel with some of my classifications (novels about vampires, werewolves, and zombies were considered fantasy, though such stories may include scientific rationales, while a Terry Pratchett Discworld novel was counted as science fiction despite its kinship with fantasy), but different decisions in borderline cases would not have significantly changed my results. Books were classified into three groups: "classic" works first published decades ago; original works which to my knowledge had no related predecessors or successors; and works in series, ranging from a single sequel to one book that proudly proclaimed itself to be the one-hundredth novel in its series.

Overall, the "New" section featured 6 "classic" books (8 percent), 12 original books (16 percent), and 57 series books (76 percent). If those books are representative, they suggest that three out of every four science fiction books now being published are parts of series and are undoubtedly formulaic, at least to some extent. Further, while a few series books came from authors who have garnered some critical attention, like Bujold, Larry Niven, Pratchett, Vernor Vinge, and Connie Willis, the vast majority have authors who are unknown to scholars. To use myself as an example, I have never read anything by Taylor Anderson, Jack Campbell, William C. Dietz, Karen Traviss, and the team of Sharon Lee and Steve Miller, the only authors who had two books in the "New" section. And while series books featured a few detectives with special powers and post-apocalyptic warriors, most were examples of "military science fiction" set in outer space, precisely the sorts of stories that Gernsback had dismissed as "a lot of rays and bloodshed" and Siringer had condemned as "the formula type action story."[18]

To be sure, determined optimists would note that the section not reserved for new books did feature many examples of the variegated science fiction championed by Campbell, represented by at least one or two books from respected authors of the past and present like Poul Anderson, Asimov, Paolo Bacigalupi, Iain M. Banks, Greg Bear, Octavia E. Butler, Orson Scott Card, Clarke, Dick, Neil Gaiman, William Gibson, Joe Haldeman, Heinlein, Frank Herbert, Le Guin, Ian MacDonald, Jack McDevitt, China Miéville, Robert J. Sawyer, Dan Simmons, Neal Stephenson, Charles Stross, H. G. Wells, and Gene Wolfe. There were even classics that no one would expect to find in a 2012 bookstore, like John Brunner's *Stand on Zanzibar* (1968), Pat Frank's *Alas, Babylon* (1959), Walter M. Miller, Jr.'s *A Canticle for Leibowitz* (1960), and Yevgeny Zamyatin's *We* (1921). Still, these books only filled the gaps between lengthy arrays of contemporary works in series.

However, optimists might continue, one cannot dismiss all series fiction as derivative junk until one has read it, for talented writers may find ways to stimulatingly stretch generic boundaries even within such confines. For example, in the section devoted to series, I noticed a Doctor Who novel by Michael Moorcock and novels based on the Halo and Borderlands video games by, respectively, Greg Bear and John Shirley. Surely, if anyone could produce memorable texts in franchised universes, it would be writers like these, and some of their other authors, though unheralded, might be equally skilled. It does seem more probable, though, that all of these novels are no better or worse than others of their kind, despite the best efforts of their writers. (As evidence, I note that I once began reading a *Star Trek: Deep Space Nine* novel, *Warchild* [1994], written by the iconoclastic fantasy writer Esther M. Friesner, hoping to find a fresh and original approach to the franchise; however, I abandoned the book when I found that the book utterly lacked Friesner's trademark humor and was just as dull as all of the other *Star Trek* novels I had read.)

Optimists might further argue that science fiction has always been a literature with a few worthwhile works surrounded by mediocrities, as stipulated by "Sturgeon's Law"; though nostalgia edits from memory the many second-rate stories that appeared in *Astounding* and cluttered the paperback racks of the 1950s, discerning readers, they would say, have always had to seek scattered gems amidst the dross. But today's situation is significantly different. Writers in earlier generations shared certain ideas about science fiction, largely derived from Campbell, that they endeavored to apply when writing; some did this well, others did this poorly, accounting for the gap between memorable stories and forgettable ones. But most contemporary writers grew up without any exposure to the genre's traditions, having learned their trade almost exclusively from watching *Star Trek* and *Star Wars*, and they never even attempt to write anything exceeding those expectations; if asked why they were not drawing upon cutting-edge science to produce innovative, groundbreaking stories, they would be baffled to discover that anyone might expect them to do so. Also, in the past, the authors who best matched Campbell's ideals were the genre's stars, featured on magazine covers and bookstore shelves, while lesser writers lurked in the background; today, the successful writers of popular series garner more attention and shelf space in bookstores, while the writers admired and studied by scholars are marginalized. The authors who are still striving to produce provocative, original science fiction, then, are becoming a disregarded minority, with little impact on the genre.

Finally, optimists might wish to suggest that the results of a single bookstore survey are not necessarily definitive, especially since I limited my scrutiny to one small section of the science fiction and fantasy books; perhaps, if I had visited the bookstore at a different time, and studied its offerings more comprehensively, I would have found fewer series books and more original books. As it happens, as part of my research for a conference paper, I did complete a second survey of the science fiction and fantasy section of the same Barnes and Noble bookstore on April 18, 2018, and this time I attempted to count and classify every single one of the books on the shelves devoted to science fiction and fantasy books. My new results were eerily similar to the results of my earlier survey: about 77 percent of all science fiction and fantasy books available for purchase, I found, were installments of series, either linked to media franchises or created by individual authors, while about 23 percent were standalone novels or anthologies.[19] This only provides some mildly heartening news for traditional science fiction readers: the situation remains very bad, but it does not seem to be getting worse. Indeed, I may have stumbled upon the ratio that will define the state of science fiction for some time to come: about three-fourth series books, and one-fourth standalone books.

It is only natural for those who remain committed to Campbell's ideals to be displeased by contemporary developments; however, one might respond, devotees of a literature founded upon the principle that the world is destined to change should not be so resistant to changes in their own genre. For it is easy to argue that what has happened to science fiction is both natural and beneficial: the marketplace discovered what sorts of stories most people want to read, and it devised mechanisms to provide them with the products they desire. The notion that publishers, to fulfill a dead man's agenda, should instead endeavor to provide readers with stories they do not want to read runs counter to bedrock principles of democracy and free choice. To reverse Hartwell's argument, it is not the marketplace which "distorts the product" of science fiction; rather, it is people like Hartwell who long struggled to distort science fiction into the forms they prefer, instead of the forms most readers prefer that it should have assumed long ago.

One might also question whether there is any reason for traditional science fiction to remain in existence; yes, decades ago, when few people understood how technology would radically transform the world and the literary establishment seemed resistant to change, there might have been a need for fiction that would foreground the coming impact of science and break time-honored rules. But now, when examining the future is a cottage industry and calls for innovative literature are clichés, Campbell's variety of science fiction no longer seems essential. If science fiction is instead focusing on the standard purpose of popular fiction, to entertain undemanding readers, that hardly seems a catastrophe.

As for the readers and scholars who still esteem the sort of science fiction that Campbell espoused, they can keep it alive by means of small presses, webzines, and other forums for creative people on society's margins. Their works may garner increasingly little attention and income, but dedicated writers will find ways to carry on, and the resulting literature might become something like poetry, ignored by the masses but still a vibrant tradition to the minority of readers who value its works. Perhaps, however, we should stop describing such texts as "science fiction," for my survey indicates that science fiction, as it is now defined by a vast majority of readers, has become something entirely different from the literature that Campbell championed and many still cherish. Instead, one might revive a term long promoted as a more dignified alternative to "science fiction," "speculative fiction," to identify the innovative stories preferred by discerning readers and critics.

Indeed, however one feels about science fiction and the marketplace, the literary tradition inspired by the foes of the marketplace definitely seems worth maintaining, even though its champions do not always acknowledge its originator, John W. Campbell, Jr. Thus, the editors of the sometimes-valuable, sometimes-infuriating reference *Fifty Key Figures in Science Fiction* (2009)[20] found space for several persons of no real significance to the genre (Jean Baudrillard? Donna Haraway?), yet they excluded Campbell, despite the fact that the sort of superior science fiction written by most writers in that volume came into existence solely because Campbell insisted that it must. No figure in that book, not even Gernsback, had such a pervasive and significant impact on the genre; and even if his and others' herculean efforts to resist the inexorable forces of the marketplace ultimately proved unsuccessful, he and his cohorts still deserve the attention and respect of everyone today who remains committed to battling—however ineffectually—against the forces of the marketplace.

Conclusion

As I read through the manuscript for this book, making the usual sorts of last-minute revisions and minor improvements before sending it to the publisher, I was struck by the unusually personal tone of the later chapters, as I repeatedly discuss what I read and thought about science fiction as a youth in the 1950s and 1960s, almost transforming the book into my own version of Arthur C. Clarke's "science fictional autobiography," *Astounding Days* (1989). Those who are familiar with my work know that I am not generally inclined to talk a lot about myself; but it seemed important in this case, since I represent a source of information about a group of readers that have generally not been represented in histories of science fiction: avid readers in the 1950s and thereafter who never sent letters to the magazines, never contributed to fanzines, never attended science fiction conventions, and never had any real connections to the science fiction community. Only in my thirties did I finally communicate with other science fiction enthusiasts and begin to express my views in written form. But before then, I was a member of what could be termed the silent majority of science fiction readers, who have always far outnumbered the genre's more vocal writers, editors, and fans.

Nevertheless, people like myself have long been a powerful influence on the genre, for two reasons: first, they were purchasing certain science fiction magazines and certain science fiction books and avoiding others, and in that way they collectively shaped what sorts of works were most likely to be published. Thus, as noted, I was never attracted to the magazines, and many others like me were undoubtedly one of the reasons why they precipitously declined in their numbers; I might add that I quickly grew tired of series of original anthologies, which did not impress me as significantly better than the magazines, and many others like me were undoubtedly one of the reasons why, after briefly becoming commonplace in the late 1960s and early 1970s, they all soon faded away. My innumerable counterparts and I, then, may not have been saying anything, but somebody was paying attention to what we were purchasing, and was responding accordingly.

Second, publishers have grown more and more thorough and exacting in researching precisely what sorts of stories the silent majority of science fiction readers prefer, and they have more and more precisely sought to publish the sorts of books that they are most likely to purchase. Thus, it was utterly futile for prominent writers, editors, fans, and scholars to bemoan the growing tendency in the 1980s and thereafter to publish formulaic books in endless series often based upon media franchises—because the more numerous but voiceless readers of science fiction kept buying them and thus endorsed them. In the 1980s, I spoke with one of those readers, a student in one of my classes at the University of California, Riverside, who was obviously not proud of the fact but nonetheless confessed that, after a hard day of work, she enjoyed relaxing by reading *Star Trek* novels. And that, I suspect, remains the reason why most people read science fiction, and as I have said elsewhere, there is nothing wrong with that, and nothing wrong with publishers producing books to please those readers instead of catering to the peculiar preferences of a vocal and erudite minority of readers who would rather read more challenging material. Today, I suppose, I must be considered a defector from the ranks of the masses, as I grew out of a youthful willingness to be entertained by science fiction adventures and increasingly sought out stories that were unusual, stimulating, and thought-provoking. Thus, while growing up, I was never particularly fond of the works of Philip K. Dick, which I found odd, ill-shaped, and off-putting; but now, I regard Dick novels like *Clans of the Alphane Moon* (1964) and *Galactic Pot-Healer* (1969) as cherished favorites.

The twentieth-century history of science fiction, overall, is best regarded as a long series of heroic efforts to forge a genre that would defy the conventionality of other forms of popular fiction, with many wonderful results that are chronicled only imperfectly in this book, though I have addressed some of them at greater length elsewhere. And, as the American genre in the twenty-first century seems to be settling in to mass-market mediocrity and occasional small-press excellence, it may well be that the true future of science fiction will emerge outside of America—which after all is only to be expected, since no nation in history has indefinitely remained dominant in any area. While I have continued to focus my reading and research on achieving a better understanding of twentieth-century American science fiction, I did happen to read, and was greatly impressed, by Cixin Liu's *The Three-Body Problem* (2006) and its two sequels, one piece of evidence that readers in the future may have to look outside the United States and Great Britain to find superior works of science fiction.

Yet the increasing number of scholars who focus their attention on "global science fiction" will never be able to fully escape the obligation to study the twentieth-century tradition of American and British science fiction as one key to understanding the texts they examine, for any analysis of Cixin Liu must acknowledge the ways that he is avowedly, and manifestly, deeply indebted to the works of Arthur C. Clarke and other American writers; and surely, other science fiction writers from around the world are similarly indebted to other Anglophone writers. Perhaps, then, the ultimate value of the genre of science fiction created by Hugo Gernsback will be the manner in which it will continue to productively inspire so many other writers, both in America and throughout the world.

Chapter Notes

Chapter 1

1. Consider, for example, the tone of Brian Stableford's response to my first article on Gernsback (Brian Aldiss, Stableford, and Edward James, "On 'On the True History of Science Fiction,'" *Foundation: The Review of Science Fiction*, No. 47 [Winter 1989/1990], 28–33.

2. At greatest length in *The Mechanics of Wonder: A History of the Idea of Science Fiction* (Liverpool: Liverpool University Press, 1998) and *Hugo Gernsback and the Century of Science Fiction* (Jefferson, North Carolina: McFarland Publishers, 2007).

3. It is true that the term had been previously introduced by William Wilson in 1851, but no one noticed or remembered his work, as is discussed in *The Mechanics of Wonder* (21). Also, in an early issue of *Amazing Stories*, a response to a letter, probably written by Associate Editor T. O'Conor Sloane, called Jules Verne "a sort of Shakespeare in science fiction" ("Discussions," *Amazing Stories*, 1 [January, 1927], 974), a comment that officially qualifies as the first modern use of the term, though the reference went unnoticed at the time.

4. The history of efforts to name science fiction is surveyed in Sam Moskowitz's "How Science Fiction Got Its Name," *Explorers of the Infinite: Shapers of Science Fiction* (Cleveland: World Publishing Company, 1963), 313–333.

5. George Allan England, "The Fantastic in Fiction," excerpt published in "The Best Things from Printland," *The Writer's Monthly*, 22:3 (September, 1923), 244. It should perhaps be mentioned that England's adjective "Ananiacal" refers to Ananias, mentioned in the Bible as a notorious liar, and affirming England's assertion that science fiction stories amounted to little more than elaborate lies.

6. Hugo Gernsback, "A New Sort of Magazine," *Amazing Stories*, 1 (April, 1926), 3.

7. Gernsback, "The Lure of Scientifiction," *Amazing Stories*, 1 (June, 1926), 195.

8. I examine how the idea and subgenre of hard science fiction emerged in *Cosmic Engineers: A Study of Hard Science Fiction* (Westport, Connecticut: Greenwood Press, 1996) and in a chapter below.

9. Gernsback, "A New Sort of Magazine," 3.

10. Gernsback, "Science Wonder Stories," *Science Wonder Stories*, 1 (June, 1929), 5. At the top of the same page he listed their names, including F. (Frank) E. Austin of Dartmouth College, Margaret Clay Ferguson of Wellesley College, Donald H. Menzel of the University of California's Lick Observatory, and Samuel G. Barton of the University of Pennsylvania, all referenced below. I have confirmed by internet research that all of these people actually worked at those universities. The one woman on Gernsback's board, Ferguson, was distinguished enough (like Menzel) to earn an entry in Wikipedia.

11. Paul A. Carter, *The Creation of Tomorrow: Fifty Years of Magazine Science Fiction* (New York: Columbia University Press, 1977), 11.

12. Gernsback, "The Science Fiction League," *Wonder Stories*, 5 (May, 1934), 1062.

13. D. Mason, "The Proposed Science Club—a Constructive Letter with a Good Outline of Work" (letter), "Discussions," *Amazing Stories*, 3 (May, 1928), 188.

14. A. B. Maloire, "Tells of Science Correspondence Club" (letter), "The Reader Speaks," *Science Wonder Stories*, 1 (August, 1929), 283; Robert B. Konikow, "Another Club" (letter), "The Reader Speaks," *Science Wonder Stories*, 1 (April, 1930), 1052.

15. Allen Glasser, "The Scienceers" (letter), "The Reader Speaks," *Science Wonder Stories*, 1 (May, 1930), 1139; C. P. Mason, "Interplanetary Society Now Formed" (letter), "The Reader Speaks," *Wonder Stories*, 2 (June, 1930), 78.

16. Editorial response to Maloire's letter (probably written by managing editor David Lasser), "The Reader Speaks," *Science Wonder Stories*, 1 (August, 1929), 283; Paul J. McDermott, "To Promote the Advancement of Science" (letter), "The Reader Speaks," *Wonder Stories*, 2 (January, 1931), 908.

17. Gernsback, "The Science Fiction League: An Announcement," *Wonder Stories*, 5 (April, 1934), 933.

18. Gernsback, "The Science Fiction League," *Wonder Stories*, 5 (May, 1934), 1061.

19. Gernsback, "The Science Fiction League: An Announcement," 933.

20. Gernsback, "The Science Fiction League," 1062, 1064.

21. Dady A. Chandy, "A Voice from Far-Off India" (letter from India), "Discussions," *Amazing Stories*, 2 (June, 1927), 307; A. B. Chandler, "An English Criticism" (letter from England), "Discussions," *Amazing Stories*, 2 (July, 1927), 413; H. H. Currie, "An Indefatigable Reader's Favorable Criticism" (letter from Canada), "Discussions," *Amazing Stories*, 2 (July, 1927), 414–415; P. H. Ecclestone, "'Our Magazine' in the Antipodes: An Appreciation from an Australian Reader" (letter from Australia), *Amazing Stories*, 4 (April, 1929), 81; J. S. Bain, "On Lifting the Leviathan" (letter from Belgium), "The Reader Speaks," *Science Wonder Stories*, 1 (September, 1929), 376; Herbert Scheffler, "Another Classification" (letter from Mexico), "The Reader Speaks," *Science Wonder Stories*, 1 (November, 1929), 569. ("A. B. Chandler" later became a prominent science fiction writer who published as A. Bertram Chandler.) Letters from Canada and Great Britain were actually commonplace in Gernsback's magazines, though letters from other countries remained rare.

22. The history and evolution of space opera are discussed in two later chapters.

23. Cited in Gernsback, "Amazing Youth," *Amazing Stories*, 2 (October, 1927), 625.

24. Bernard Simon, "Some Very Pleasant Criticisms from a High School Student" (letter), *Amazing Stories*, 3 (August, 1928), 474.

25. Gernsback, "Reasonableness in Science Fiction," *Wonder Stories*, 4 (December, 1932), 585.

26. Gernsback, introduction to "A Martian Odyssey," *Wonder Stories*, 6 (July, 1934), 175 Unsigned, but attributed to Gernsback by outside sources.

27. "Wanted: Still More Plots," *Wonder Stories Quarterly*, 3 (Summer, 1932), 437. Unsigned, but probably by Lasser.

28. Everett C. Smith, plot, and R. F. Starzl, story, "The Metal Moon," *Wonder Stories Quarterly*, 3 (Winter, 1932), 246–259.

29. Wilson Tucker [writing as Bob Tucker], "Depts of the Interior" [sic], *Le Zombie*, 4 (January, 1941), 8.

30. Clyde F. Beck, *Hammer and Tongs* (Lakeport, California: Futile Press, 1937), 17–18.

31. John W. Campbell, Jr., "The Science of Science Fiction Writing," *Of Worlds Beyond*, edited by Lloyd Arthur Eshbach, 1947 (Chicago: Advent Publishers, 1964), 92.

32. Campbell, "Introduction," *Analog 1*, edited by Campbell (Garden City: Doubleday and Company, 1963), xvi.

33. Campbell, "Introduction," *Venus Equilateral*, by George O. Smith (New York: Prime Press, 1947), 9, 10.

34. Campbell, "Introduction," *Prologue to Analog*, edited by Campbell (Garden City: Doubleday and Company, 1962), 13.

35. Campbell, "History to Come," *Astounding Science-Fiction*, 27 (May, 1941), 5–6.

36. For an excellent study of the Anticipation series, see Bradford Lyau's *The Anticipation Novelists of 1950s French Science Fiction: Stepchildren of Voltaire* (Jefferson, North Carolina: McFarland Publishers, 2010).

37. Earl Kemp, *Who Killed Science Fiction?: An Affectionate Autopsy* (Chicago: Earl and Nancy Kemp, 1960).

Chapter 2

1. The entire issue is available online at archive.org: https://archive.org/details/Amazing_Stories_v03n05_1928-08_ATLPM-Urf.
2. Hugo Gernsback, "The Amazing Unknown," *Amazing Stories*, 3 (August, 1928), 389. All subsequent notes to "*Amazing*" refer to this issue.
3. Brian W. Aldiss with David Wingrove, *Trillion Year Spree: The History of Science Fiction* (New York: Atheneum, 1986), 202. Page references are to this edition.
4. William P. Keasbey, "Some Points in the Invisible Man Story from an Admirer of Mr. Wells and Good Words for Two Other Authors and the Editors" (letter), *Amazing*, 474.
5. Miles J. Breuer, "Physiological Effects of Nullification of Gravity" (letter), "Discussions," *Amazing*, 468. All Breuer quotations below are from this page; all subsequent letters appeared in the issue's "Discussions" section.
6. Editorial reply to Breuer's letter, *Amazing*, 468. Unsigned, written either by Gernsback or Sloane.
7. Charles E. Roe, "Something about Saurians and Their Successors. Paul's Cover Page Designs" (letter), *Amazing*, 477.
8. Frederick Bitting, "An Amusing Contribution to the Discussions Columns" (letter), *Amazing*, 466.
9. Marcley W. Fenten, "The Name 'Amazing Stories' and the Questionnaire Criticized. Some Brickbats. (Good natured ones)" (letter), *Amazing*, 469. A later Fenten quotation is from this page.
10. Bernard Simon, "Some Very Pleasant Criticisms from a High School Student" (letter), *Amazing*, 476.
11. Gary Westfahl, "'The Jules Verne, H. G. Wells, and Edgar Allan Poe Type of Story': Hugo Gernsback's History of Science Fiction," *The Mechanics of Wonder: The Creation of the Idea of Science Fiction* (Liverpool: Liverpool University Press, 1998), 67–91.
12. Introduction to "The Moth," *Amazing*, 461. Unsigned, but almost certainly written by T. O'Conor Sloane.
13. Clement Fezandié (as Henry Hugh Simmons), "Hicks' Inventions with a Kick: The Perambulating Home," *Amazing*, 456. Page references are to this edition.
14. Introduction to "Hicks' Inventions with a Kick: The Perambulating Home," *Amazing*, 450. Unsigned, but almost certainly written by Sloane. A later quotation is from this page.
15. Joe Kleier, "The Head," *Amazing*, 421. Later parenthetical page references are to this edition.
16. Introduction to "The Head," *Amazing*, 418. Unsigned, but almost certainly written by Sloane.
17. Philip Francis Nowlan, "Armageddon—2419 AD," *Amazing*, 426, 429. Page references are to this edition.
18. E. F. Bleiler with Richard Bleiler, *Science-Fiction: The Gernsback Years: A Complete Coverage of the Genre Magazines Amazing, Astounding, Wonder, and Others from 1926 to 1936* (Kent, Ohio: Kent State University Press, 1998), 310. Page references are to this edition.
19. Introduction to "Armageddon—2419 AD," *Amazing*, 422. Unsigned, probably written by Sloane, but possibly written by Gernsback.
20. As *Armageddon 2419 A.D.* (New York: Ace Books, 1962). As is true of other works published by Ace, Nowlan's text was unfortunately edited by publisher Donald A. Wollheim to achieve his desired length, usually in minor ways, but with some interesting exceptions. For example, perhaps worried that younger readers wouldn't want to read a story narrated by an eighty-eight-year-old man, Wollheim removed Nowlan's introductory reference to Rogers's age. Unedited texts of the two stories are available in *Armageddon 2419 A.D. and The Airlords of Han* (Mineola, New York: Dover Publications, 2015).
21. E. E. Smith with Lee Hawkins Garby, *The Skylark of Space, Amazing*, 390, 399. Page references are to this edition.
22. Sam Moskowitz, "Edward E. Smith, Ph.D.," *Seekers of Tomorrow: Masters of Modern Science Fiction* (Cleveland and New York: World Publishing, 1966), 14.
23. Introduction to *The Skylark of Space, Amazing*, 390. Unsigned, written by either Gernsback or Sloane.
24. F. J. Simmons, "One Brick, and a Bouquet. Description in Stories. Leading Up to the Ending of a Story" (letter), *Amazing Stories*, 3 (January, 1929), 959.
25. Captions to Frank R. Paul drawings, *Amazing*, 427, 430. Author unidentified, probably Sloane or Paul.

Chapter 3

1. If one considers book on science fiction art, one of the best available is undoubtedly Vincent Di Fate's *Infinite Worlds: The Fantastic Visions of Science Fiction Art* (New York: Penguin Studio: Wonderland Press, 1997). Other worthwhile studies include Anthony Frewin's *One Hundred Years of Science Fiction Illustration* (New York: Pyramid Books, 1975; first published 1974), though its coverage is limited to science fiction art from 1840 to 1940; Jacques Sadoul's *2000 A.D.: Illustrations from the Golden Age of Science Fiction Pulps* (Chicago: Henry Regnery, 1975; first published 1973); Brian W. Aldiss's *Science Fiction Art* (New York: Bounty Books, 1975)—both of the preceding books have good selections of illustrations, though they largely rely on thematic organization (Aldiss adds a "Gallery" of noteworthy artists); Lester del Rey's *Fantastic Science Fiction Art 1926–1954* (New York: Ballantine Books, 1975), which presents excellent reproductions of many magazine covers in chronological order; and Janet Sacks's *Visions of the Future* (1976), which offers an eclectic selection of art from the British magazine *Science Fiction Monthly*. For textual analyses of science fiction art, one relevant volume is *Unearthly Visions: Approaches to Science Fiction and Fantasy Art*, edited by Gary Westfahl, George Slusser, and Kathleen Church Plummer (Westport, Connecticut: Greenwood Press, 2002).

2. Aldiss, "1. Illustration (From the Beginning to 1978)," segment of "Illustration," by Westfahl, Aldiss, and Peter Nicholls, *The Encyclopedia of Science Fiction*, Third Edition, edited by John Clute, David Langford, Peter Nicholls and Graham Sleight, Gollancz, last updated November 3, 2018, at http://www.sf-encyclopedia.com/entry/illustration.

3. Aldiss, "Introduction," *Science Fiction Art*, 3.

4. Aldiss, "Illustration," 611.

5. For more information on Gernsback's theories, see my *The Mechanics of Wonder: The Creation of the Idea of Science Fiction* (Liverpool: Liverpool University Press, 1998).

6. Frewin points out this detail, 55.

7. "Our Cover," *Amazing Stories*, 1 (July, 1926), 289. This caption was unsigned, but probably written by either Gernsback or his associate T. O'Conor Sloane. It should be noted that, as was not the case when this survey was first published, virtually all of the magazine covers discussed in this chapter are now displayed at the online Internet Speculative Fiction Database (http://isfdb.org/); any search for the title of the relevant "Magazine" will eventually lead to a cover image (the one just cited, for example, can be seen at http://www.isfdb.org/cgi-bin/pl.cgi?56397). Many of the book covers discussed below can also be found by searching for the name of the book in question as a "Fiction Title," and the covers of numerous science fiction books are also available in the Picture Gallery of the online *Encyclopedia of Science Fiction* (http://www.sf-encyclopedia.com/).

8. "On the Cover," *Science Wonder Stories*, 1 (July, 1929), 99. This caption, and those cited in notes 9–14, were unsigned, but probably written by either Gernsback or his associate David Lasser.

9. "On the Cover," *Air Wonder Stories*, 1 (July, 1929), 1.

10. "On the Cover," *Science Wonder Stories*, 1 (August, 1929), 195.

11. "On the Cover," *Air Wonder Stories*, 1 (August, 1929), 99.

12. "On the Cover," *Science Wonder Stories*, 1 (October, 1929), 387.

13. "On the Cover This Month," *Air Wonder Stories*, 1 (October, 1929), 291.

14. "On the Cover This Month," *Air Wonder Stories*, 1 (January, 1930), 579.

15. Peter Nicholls and John Grant, "Earle K. Bergey," *The Encyclopedia of Science Fiction*, Second Edition (New York: St. Martin's Press, 1993), 111. This statement does not appear in the revised entry on Bergey in the online Third Edition.

16. Cited in Bryan Baugh, *Zap!: How to Draw Fantastic Sci-Fi Comics* (New York: Watson-Gupnill Publications, 2006), 18.

17. Aldiss (*Science Fiction Art*, 68) attributes the cover to Brown; Frewin (111) says it "may well be" by Brown; but del Rey (58) attributes the cover to Bergey. Here, I trust the judgments of Aldiss and Frewin more than del Rey's.

18. John W. Campbell, Jr., "Science-Fiction," *Astounding Science-Fiction*, 21 (March, 1938), 37.

19. For more information on Campbell's theories, see *The Mechanics of Wonder*.

20. Campbell, "In Times to Come," *Astounding Science-Fiction*, 22 (October, 1938), 11.

21. Campbell, "Mercury," *Astounding Stories*, 20 (February, 1938), 97.

22. For science fiction scholars, it is indeed fascinating that Campbell explained and achieved a new style of science fiction art well before he explained and achieved a new style of science fiction literature. This apparent reversal of priorities suggests that illustration in fact has been very important in the history of science fiction, which makes its relative neglect a major problem in our understanding of the genre.

23. Campbell, "In Times to Come," *Astounding Science-Fiction*, 22 (October, 1938), 6. Interestingly, just as Gernsback once made a story with a scientific error, Geoffrey Hewelke's "Ten Million Miles Sunward" (1928), "educational" by announcing a contest for readers to spot the error, Campbell similarly capitalized on an error in Brown's cover: "Jupiter" announced that "There is an error in the picturization.... I decided to let it go through as is for the interest of the reader.... The nature of the error—and why it is such—will be shown next month, in the Analytical Laboratory. I'll try to publish the names of those who spot the error correctly in the Brass Tacks column in the January issue. So go to it!" (*Astounding Science-Fiction*, 22 [November, 1938)], 6). He later explained that the shadow cast on Jupiter was incorrectly shaped ("The Analytical Laboratory," *Astounding Science-Fiction*, 22 [December, 1938], 154). Like his science fiction stories, then, Campbell's space art could provide useful practice in scientific thinking.

24. H. L. Gold, "For Adults Only," *Galaxy*, 1 (October, 1950), 2.

25. The choice was dictated entirely by circumstance: my first public discussion of the subject was at a conference that also featured a presentation by Frank Kelly Freas, so that another extended discussion of Freas's art seemed superfluous.

26. Aldiss, *Science Fiction Art*, 43.

27. Although, as pointed out by R. D. Mullen ("From Standard Magazines to Big Slicks: A Note on the History of U.S. General and Fiction Magazines," *Science-Fiction Studies*, 22 [March, 1995], 144–156), this common terminology is not accurate.

28. Grant and Nicholls, "Frank Kelly Freas," *The Encyclopedia of Science Fiction*, Second Edition, 452.

29. Another 1950s artist who produced "semi-abstract covers," Brian Lewis, is discussed in Aldiss, *Science Fiction Art*, 45.

30. I use the term "abstract" in its broadest sense to refer to all art which moves beyond the representational; the term also applies to non-objective art, where the art has no referent in the real or an imagined world, but I note in passing that true non-objective art seems rare in the science fiction field.

31. In the 1960s, Harlan Ellison hired the Dillons to work on virtually all of his books; his fondness for their work is best shown by the fact that his landmark anthology *Dangerous Visions* (1967) was dedicated "with love, respect, and admiration" to them (*Dangerous Visions #1* [New York: Berkley Books, 1969], [4].

32. Unusually for the time, the series was promoted using the Dillons's names: for example, the back-page advertisement for future Ace Science Fiction Specials in the first book of the series, Clifford D. Simak's *Why Call Them Back from Heaven?* (New York: Ace Books, 1967) said that these "major new novels" would be "presented with distinctive covers by Leo & Diane Dillon" ([192]). I have read that the original cover design of two squares on the cover was deemed problematic because it made books in the series appear too similar to each other, prompting the change to a different format.

33. Though some abstract art, as already implied, was commercially successful; Grant and Nicholls argue that "Powers was one of the first to show that semi-abstract images of some sophistication could sell sf; the Dillons went on to prove the point incontrovertibly" ("Leo and Diane Dillon," *The Encyclopedia of Science Fiction*, Second Edition, 334).

34. What is surprising about this apparent uniformity of style is that, as was pointed out from the audience in the question-and-answer session following the original presentation of this paper, *Omni* never commissioned cover art, but employed only "found art"; the magazine thus managed to promote a distinctive style of art entirely by careful selection, not by directly instructing or influencing artists.

35. Howard V. Hendrix, "Making the Pulpmonster Safe for Demography: *Omni* Magazine and the Gentrification of Science Fiction," 1996, *Bridges to Science Fiction and Fantasy: Outstanding Essays from the J. Lloyd Eaton Conferences*, edited by Gregory

Benford, Gary Westfahl, Hendrix, and Joseph D. Miller (Jefferson, North Carolina: McFarland Publishers, 2018), 109–118.

36. Bruce Sterling, Interview with Takayuki Tatsumi, *Science Fiction Eye*, No. 1 (Winter, 1987), 27.

37. *Longman Dictionary of Contemporary English* (London: Longmans, 1987), 1065.

38. Untitled and unattributed caption, Table of Contents page, *Omni*, 5 (August, 1983), 4. The next two notes similarly refer to untitled and unattributed captions.

39. Table of Contents page, *Omni*, 7 (November, 1984), 4.

40. Table of Contents page, *Omni*, 11 (December, 1988), 2.

41. The problem is that the term "surreal," commonly used in a variety of ways, may also apply to styles of art I am grouping together as "abstract"; thus, Nicholls and Grant refer to Powers's "Surrealist style" ("Richard M. Powers," *The Encyclopedia of Science Fiction*, Second Edition, 952). In my terminology, supported by several glossaries of art that I examined, "abstract" can properly refer to any art where objects are distorted beyond the representational; but I am using "surreal" more narrowly to refer to art which may depict objects representationally but combines or juxtaposes them in an unrealistic manner.

42. And we should expect this to be true even if the particular Clarke work in question is not hard science fiction. As one spectacular example, Ballantine Books in 1969 reprinted *Tales from the White Hart* (1957) with a cover depicting a detailed space station—although, of course, no space travel of any kind occurred in the atypically playful stories about ill-fated inventors on Earth that dominate the collection.

43. I argue at length that hard science fiction emerged during the 1950s in my *Cosmic Engineers: A Study of Hard Science Fiction* (Westport, Connecticut: Greenwood Press, 1996) and in a chapter below.

44. In addition to the issues of oversimplification and omitted artists, there are two other large areas neglected by my model. First, there is fantasy art, which arguably began as a modern, self-conscious genre in the pages of Farnworth Wright's *Weird Tales* magazine, not *Amazing Stories*, and which in its early stages clearly reflected the influence of Gothic art far more than did science fiction art, as seen, for example, in Hannes Bok's work. Later, fantasy art often combined Gothic imagery with a kind of prettified pastoral realism, Frank Frazetta being one obvious representative. At times, fantasy art has been closely intertwined with science fiction art; at other times—particularly today—it seems an entirely separate field. Another neglected area is comic book art, which initially, in the late 1930s and 1940s, employed a cartoonish style derived from comic strips that was never featured in the science fiction magazines. As the genre emerged, however, its art grew more sophisticated, roughly paralleling the evolution of science fiction art (though generally behind by about a decade); thus, it could be argued, one can find pulp art in 1950s comic books, slick art in 1960s comic books, and abstract and surreal art in 1970s and 1980s comic books. Overall, though it is possible to see fantasy art and comic book art as offshoots or relatives of science fiction art, I suspect that experts in these areas would prefer, with some justice, to develop their own explanatory models to characterize these fields.

45. Paul Carter, *The Creation of Tomorrow: Fifty Years of Magazine Science Fiction* (New York: Columbia University Press, 1977).

46. See Westfahl, "3. From 1992 to 2012," segment of "Illustration," *The Encyclopedia of Science Fiction*, Third Edition.

Chapter 4

1. Ursula K. Le Guin, "Introduction," *The Norton Book of Science Fiction*, edited by Le Guin and Brian Attebery (New York and London: W. W. Norton, 1993), 18.

2. "Ego & the Dying Planet," *Garygoyle*, 2:2 (April, 1941), 38–39. Officially uncredited, but almost certainly by Arthur C. Clarke.

3. Whenever two publication dates for a book are in parentheses, the first is the date of the book's original magazine appearance; the second is the date of its first publication in book form (usually revised).

4. E. E. "Doc" Smith, *Galactic Patrol* (1950; New York: Pyramid, 1964), 38.

5. Smith, *Galactic Patrol*, 67.

6. Robert A. Heinlein, "'If This Goes On —,'" *Revolt in 2100* (New York: Signet, 1953), 118–119.

7. Sam Moskowitz, "Robert A. Heinlein," *Seekers of Tomorrow: Masters of Modern Science Fiction* (Cleveland: World Publishing Company, 1966), 194.
8. Gary Westfahl, "Rules for Robots: Version 1.0," 2003, *An Alien Abroad: Science Fiction Columns from Interzone* ([Rockville, Maryland]: Wildside Press, 2016), 207–213.
9. Westfahl, "A.I.: Artificial Incompetence, or Robots Just Don't Understand: A Review of *I, Robot*," Locus Online website, posted on July 17, 2004, at http://www.locusmag.com/2004/Reviews/07_Westfahl_IRobot.html.
10. Leigh Brackett, "The Jewel of Bas," *Lorelei of the Red Mist* (Royal Oak, Michigan: Haffner Press, 2007), 90–91.
11. E. F. Bleiler and Richard Bleiler, *Science-Fiction: The Gernsback Years: A Complete Coverage of the Genre Magazines Amazing, Astounding, Wonder, and Others from 1926 to 1936* (Kent, Ohio: Kent State University Press, 1998), 330.
12. Moskowitz, "Edward E. Smith, Ph.D.," *Seekers of Tomorrow: Masters of Modern Science Fiction* (Cleveland: World Publishing Company, 1963), 20.

Chapter 5

1. Patricia Monk, "'Not Just Cosmic Skullduggery': A Partial Reconsideration of Space Opera," *Extrapolation*, 33 (Winter, 1992), 295–316. Page references are to this edition.
2. Gernsback's theories are discussed more thoroughly in my *The Mechanics of Wonder: The Creation of the Idea of Science Fiction* (Liverpool: Liverpool University Press, 1998).
3. Brian W. Aldiss, "Introduction," *Space Opera: An Anthology of Way-Back-When Futures*, edited by Aldiss (Garden City: Doubleday & Company, 1974), xi; my italics.
4. "The Readers' Corner" (readers' letters and responses), *Astounding Stories*, 2 (May, 1930), 279. Unsigned response presumably written by editor Harry Bates.
5. Cited in Malcolm J. Edwards, "Harry Bates," *The Encyclopedia of Science Fiction*, edited by John Clute and Peter Nicholls (New York: St. Martin's Press, 1993), 96.
6. Harry Bates, "Editorial Number One: To Begin," *A Requiem for Astounding*, by Alva Rogers (Chicago: Advent Publishers, 1964), x, xiii.
7. "The Reader Speaks" (readers' letters and responses), *Wonder Stories Quarterly*, 3 (Summer, 1932), 576. Unsigned response presumably written by managing editor David Lasser.
8. Hugo Gernsback, "Reasonableness in Science Fiction," *Wonder Stories*, 4 (December, 1932), 585.
9. "Wanted: Still More Plots," *Wonder Stories Quarterly*, 3 (Summer, 1932), 279. Unsigned; probably written by managing editor David Lasser.
10. Ultimately, though, there would be two ironic developments. After Gernsback's former magazine, *Amazing Stories*, was controlled for several years by the like-minded T. O'Conor Sloane, the publication passed to a new company and a new editor, Ray Palmer; and Gernsback's later magazine *Wonder Stories* would also be sold to another company, retitled *Thrilling Wonder Stories*, and assigned to editor, Mort Weisinger. And both Palmer and Weisinger quickly refashioned their magazines to emphasize space opera. In contrast, the magazine that originally championed the form of space opera—*Astounding Stories*—would later, under the editorship of John W. Campbell, Jr., become *Astounding Science-Fiction*, the magazine most responsible for introducing and promoting a form of science fiction that was both more thoughtful in its science and more mature in its literary values.
11. Wilson Tucker [writing as Bob Tucker], "Depts of the Interior" [sic], *Le Zombie*, 4 (January, 1941), 8.
12. Martin Alger, "The SFTPOBEMOTCOSFP" (letter), *Thrilling Wonder Stories*, 14:1 (August, 1939), 121.
13. Cited in Paul A. Carter, "'You Can Write Science Fiction If You Want To,'" *Hard Science Fiction*, edited by George Slusser and Eric S. Rabkin (Carbondale: Southern Illinois University Press, 1986), 150.
14. P. Schuyler Miller, "The Reference Library," *Astounding Science-Fiction*, 52 (May, 1953), 146; "The Reference Library," *Astounding Science-Fiction*, 52 (June, 1953), 78.
15. Particularly important, I would argue, is the influence of nineteenth-century melodrama and its written counterparts—acknowledged by Aldiss when he says that "What space opera does is take a few light years and a pinch of reality and inflate thor-

oughly with melodrama, dreams, and a seasoning of screwy ideas" ("Introduction," xi). I discuss the relationship between science fiction and melodrama in the sixth chapter of *Hugo Gernsback and the Century of Science Fiction* (Jefferson, North Carolina: McFarland, 2007).

16. As a parallel development, in response to the accumulation of more and more critical standards, the number of texts relegated to the category of space opera has tended to increase. That is, in the 1930s, E. E. "Doc" Smith was not considered a disreputable writer of space opera because of his obvious attention to scientific matters; by the 1940s, though, his pattern of juvenile-oriented action and adventure, now condemned as outdated, made his works seem like perfect exemplars of the form. In the 1950s and 1960s, an increased concern for style and sophisticated started to make writers like Isaac Asimov and Robert A. Heinlein, previously admired for their maturity and logic, now seem like space opera writers. And in the 1980s, even acknowledged stylists like Roger Zelazny were starting to be placed into the category of space opera fold because they lacked the hard-edged cynicism of cyberpunk writers.

17. John W. Campbell, Jr., "These Stories May Upset You," *The Permanent Implosion* (originally published in 1966 as *Analog 4*), edited by Campbell (New York: Curtis Books, 1970, 11.

18. Edmond Hamilton, "Space Mirror," *Thrilling Wonder Stories*, 10 (August, 1937), 43–51.

19. David Brin, "The Crystal Spheres," *Analog Science Fiction/Science Fact*, 104 (January, 1984), 128–143.

20. Aldiss, *The Eighty-Minute Hour: A Space Opera* (1974; New York: Leisure Books, 1975).

Chapter 6

1. Relevant commentaries, in addition to those cited below, include Norman Beswick, "The Machineries of Hokum, in Space Opera and Elsewhere," *Vector*, No. 171 (February/March, 1993), 16–18; Leigh Brackett, "Introduction: Beyond Our Narrow Skies," The *Best of Planet Stories No. 1*, edited by Brackett (New York: Ballantine, 1975), 1–8; Patricia Monk, "'Not Just Cosmic Skullduggery': A Partial Reconsideration of Space Opera," *Extrapolation*, 33 (Winter, 1992), 295–316; Joe L. Sanders, "Space Opera Reconsidered," *The New York Review of Science Fiction*, No. 82 (June, 1995), 1, 3–6; Jack Williamson, "On the Final Frontier," *Space and Beyond: The Frontier Theme in Science Fiction*, edited by Gary Westfahl (Westport, Connecticut: Greenwood Press, 2000), 49–52; David Langford, "Space Opera," *The Greenwood Encyclopedia of Science Fiction and Fantasy*, edited by Westfahl (Westport, Connecticut: Greenwood Press, 2005), 738–740; Richard L McKinney, "Space Opera," *Women in Science Fiction and Fantasy*, Volume 2, edited by Robin A. Reid (Westport, Connecticut: Greenwood Press, 2009), 284–287; David G. Hartwell and Kathryn Cramer, "Introduction: How Shit Became Shinola: Definition and Redefinition of Space Opera," *The Space Opera Renaissance*, edited by Hartwell and Cramer (New York: Tor Books, 2006), 9–18; Andy Sawyer, "Space Opera," *The Routledge Companion to Science Fiction*, edited by Mark Bould, Andrew M. Butler, Adam Roberts, and Sherryl Vint (New York: Routledge, 2009), 505–509; M. Keith Booker and Anne-Marie Thomas, "The Space Opera," *The Science Fiction Handbook* (Malden, Massachusetts: Wiley-Blackwell, 2009), 40–52; Alastair Reynolds, "Space Opera: This Galaxy Ain't Big Enough for the Both of Us," *Strange Divisions and Alien Territories: the Sub-Genres of Science Fiction*, edited by Keith Brooke (New York: Palgrave Macmillan, 2012), 12–25; and Cathy Cupitt, "Vacationing in the Neverending Empire: The Function of Space Opera," *Science Fiction: A Review of Speculative Literature*, 18:2 (2016), 27–38.

2. Wilson Tucker [writing as Bob Tucker], "Depts of the Interior" [sic], *Le Zombie*, 4 (January, 1941), 8.

3. See John Clute and David Langford, "Planetary Romance," *The Encyclopedia of Science Fiction*, Third Edition, edited by Clute, Langford, Peter Nicholls, and Graham Sleight, last updated December 4, 2013, at http://sf-encyclopedia.com/entry/planetary_romance.

4. Stilson Wray, letter, "Brass Tacks," *Astounding Science-Fiction*, 27 ((May, 1941), 129.

5. Brian W. Aldiss, "Introduction," *Space Opera: An Anthology of Way-Back-When Futures*, edited by Aldiss (Garden City:

Doubleday & Company, 1974), xi; Terry Carr, "Introduction," *Planets of Wonder: A Treasury of Space Opera*, edited by Carr (Nashville and New York: Thomas Nelson Inc., Publishers, 1976), 10.

6. "Wanted: Still More Plots," *Wonder Stories Quarterly*, 3 (Summer, 1932), 279. Unsigned instructions presumably written by managing editor David Lasser.

7. E. E. "Doc" Smith, *The Skylark of Space* (1928; New York: Pyramid Books, 1962), 70.

8. Hugo Gernsback, "Good News for Our Readers," *Wonder Stories Quarterly*, 4 (Fall, 1932), 5.

9. *Skylark Three* (1930; Reading, Pennsylvania: Fantasy Press, 1948) and *Skylark of Valeron* (1934–1935; Reading, Pennsylvania: Fantasy Press, 1949); much later came *Skylark DuQuesne* (New York: Pyramid Books, 1965).

10. The stories referenced—"At the Center of Gravity" (1936) and "The Men and the Mirror" (1938)—were republished in Rocklynne's *The Men and the Mirror* (New York: Ace Books, 1973).

11. The Arcot, Wade, and Morey stories were published in book form as *The Black Star Passes* (Reading, Pennsylvania: Fantasy Press, 1953), *Islands of Space* (Reading, Pennsylvania: Fantasy Press, 1957), and *Invaders from the Infinite* (Hicksville, New York: Gnome Press 1961).

12. E. E. "Doc" Smith, *Triplanetary* (1948; New York: Pyramid Books, 1965), 11; an early version of the novel (without this opening passage) first published in *Amazing Stories* in 1934. The other Lensman novels were *First Lensman* (Reading, Pennsylvania: Fantasy Press, 1950), *Galactic Patrol* (1937–1938; Reading, Pennsylvania: Fantasy Press, 1950), *Gray Lensman* (1939–1940; Reading, Pennsylvania: Fantasy Press, 1951), *Second Stage Lensman* (1941–1942; Reading, Pennsylvania: Fantasy Press, 1953), and *Children of the Lens* (1947–1948; Reading, Pennsylvania: Fantasy Press, 1954).

13. The stories that inspired the Buck Rogers comic strip, Philip Francis Nowlan's "Armageddon 2419 A.D." (1928) and "The Airlords of Han" (1929), were later published in book form as *Armageddon 2419 A.D.* (New York: Ace Books, 1962).

14. Cited in David Pringle, "What Is This Thing Called Space Opera?," *Space and Beyond: The Frontier Theme in Science Fiction*, edited by Gary Westfahl (Westport, Connecticut: Greenwood Press, 2000), 40.

15. Jack Vance, "The King of Thieves," *The Many Worlds of Magnus Ridolph* (New York: Ace Books, 1966), 82–83, 100; story first published in 1949. Other Magnus Ridolph stories include "Hard-Luck Diggings" (1948), "The Sub-Standard Sardines" (1949), and "Cosmic Hotfoot" (1950).

16. Books featuring or related to Nicholas van Rijn are Poul Anderson's *War of the Wing Men* (1958), *Trader to the Stars* (1965), *The Troubletwisters* (1966), *Satan's World* (1969), *The People of the Wind* (1973), *Mirkheim* (1977), and *The Earth Book of Stormgate* (1978). Books featuring or related to Dominic Flandry are Anderson's *We Claim These Stars* (1959), *Earthman, Go Home!* (1960), *Mayday Orbit* (1961), *Let the Spaceman Beware* (1963), *Agent of the Terran Empire* (1965), *Flandry of Terra* (1965), *Ensign Flandry* (1966), *The Rebel Worlds* (1969), *A Circus of Hells* (1970), *The Day of Their Return* (1973), *A Knight of Ghosts and Shadows* (1974), *A Stone in Heaven* (1979), *The Long Night* (1983), and *The Game of Empire* (1985).

17. The Retief books are Keith Laumer's *Envoy to New Worlds* (1963), *Galactic Diplomat* (1965) (which includes "The Prince and the Pirate"), *Retief's War* (1966), *Retief and the Warlords* (1968), *Retief: Ambassador to Space* (1969), *Retief of the CDT* (1971), *Retief's Ransom* (1971), *Retief: Emissary to the Stars* (1975), *Retief at Large* (1978), *Retief: Diplomat at Arms* (1982), *Retief to the Rescue* (1983), *The Return of Retief* (1984), *Retief and the Pangalactic Pageant of Pulchritude* (1986), *Retief in the Ruins* (1986), *Reward for Retief* (1989), and *Retief and the Rascals* (1993).

18. All but two John Carstairs stories are collected in Frank Belknap Long's *John Carstairs, Space Detective* (1949); Robert Sheckley's AAA Ace stories are "Ghost V" (1954), "The Laxian Key" (1955), "Milk Run" (1956), "Squirrel Cage" (1955), "The Lifeboat Mutiny" (1955), "The Necessary Things" (1955), and "The Skag Castle" (1956); Finch's Guild of Xenolinguists stories are collected in *The Guild of Xenolinguists* (Urbana, Illinois: Golden Gryphon Press, 2007), though another contribution to the series, "The Evening and the Morning," appeared in 2011.

19. James White's Sector General books are *Hospital Station* (1962), *Star Surgeon*

(1963), *Major Operation* (1971), *Ambulance Ship* (1979), *Sector General* (1983), *Star Healer* (1984), *Code Blue: Emergency* (1987), *The Genocidal Healer* (1991), *The Galactic Gourmet* (1994), *Final Diagnosis* (1997), *Mind Changer* (1998), and *Double Contact* (1999). Murray Leinster's Med Service books are *Med Service* (1959), *This World Is Taboo* (1961), *Doctor to the Stars* (1964), and *S.O.S. from Three Worlds* (1966). Most of Alan E. Nourse's Hoffman Medical Center and Hospital Earth stories are available in his collection *Rx for Tomorrow: Tales of Science Fiction, Fantasy, and Medicine* (1971), though each series also included a novel, respectively *A Man Obsessed* (1955), also known as *The Mercy Men*, and *Star Surgeon* (1960).

20. Brian W. Aldiss with David Wingrove, *Trillion Year Spree: The History of Science Fiction* (New York: Atheneum, 1986), 319–320.

21. The first two Harrison novels cited generated series: after *The Stainless Steel Rat* came *The Stainless Steel Rat's Revenge* (1970), *The Stainless Steel Rat Saves the World* (1972), *The Stainless Steel Rat Wants You!* (1978), *The Stainless Steel Rat for President* (1982), *A Stainless Steel Rat Is Born* (1985), *The Stainless Steel Rat Gets Drafted* (1987); *The Stainless Steel Rat Sings the Blues* (1994); *The Stainless Steel Rat Goes to Hell* (1996); *The Stainless Steel Rat Joins the Circus* (1999); and *The Stainless Steel Rat Returns* (2010). After *Bill, the Galactic Hero* came *Bill, the Galactic Hero on the Planet of Robot Slaves* (1989), *Bill, the Galactic Hero on the Planet of Bottled Brains* (with Robert Sheckley) (1990), *Bill, the Galactic Hero on the Planet of Tasteless Pleasure* (with David Bischoff) (1991), *Bill, the Galactic Hero on the Planet of the Zombie Vampires* (with Jack C. Haldeman II) (1991), *Bill, the Galactic Hero on the Planet of Ten Thousand Bars* (with Bischoff) (1991), and *Bill, the Galactic Hero: The Final Incoherent Adventure* (with David M. Harris) (1992).

22. Available in English in Stanislaw Lem's *The Star Diaries* (1976), *Memoirs of a Space Traveler: Further Reminiscences of Ijon Tichy* (1979), *Tales of Pirx the Pilot* (1979), and *More Tales of Pirx the Pilot* (1982).

23. Robert Sheckley, "Zirn Left Unguarded, the Jenghik Palace in Flames, Jon Westerley Dead," 1972, *Space Opera*, edited by Aldiss, 7.

24. As discussed in my "Where No Market Has Gone Before: 'The Science-Fiction Industry' and the Star Trek Industry," 1996, *A Sense-of-Wonderful Century: Explorations of Science Fiction and Fantasy Films* ([Rockville, Maryland]: Wildside Press/Borgo Press, 2012), 144–161.

25. Dana Stabenow, *Second Star* (New York: Ace Books, 1991), 1. There were two sequels, *A Handful of Stars* (1991) and *Red Planet Run* (1995).

26. Skyrider Melacha Rendell appeared in Melisa C. Michaels's *Skirmish* (1984), *First Battle* (1985), *Last War* (1986), *Pirate Prince* (1988), and *Floater Factor* (1988). Nicole Shea appeared in Chris Claremont's *FirstFlight* (1987), *Grounded!* (1991), and *Sundowner* (1994). Cherijo Grey Veil has appeared in S. L. Viehl's *StarDoc* (2000), *Beyond Varallan* (2000), *Endurance* (2001), *Shockball* (2001), *Eternity Row* (2002), *Rebel Ice* (2006), *Plague of Memory* (2007), *Omega Games* (2008), *Crystal Healer* (2009), and *Dream Called Time* (2010). Honor Harrington has appeared in David Weber's *On Basilisk Station* (1992), *The Honor of the Queen* (1993), *The Short Victorious War* (1994), *Field of Dishonor* (1994), *Flag in Exile* (1995), *Honor among Enemies* (1996), *In Enemy Hands* (1997), *Echoes of Honor* (1998), *Ashes of Victory* (2000), *War of Honor* (2002), *At All Costs* (2005), *Mission of Honor* (2010), *A Rising Thunder* (2012), and *Uncompromising Honor* (2018).

27. A list of all of C. J. Cherryh's novels connected in some way to the Alliance series would occupy a great deal of space; one may consult John Clute's "C. J. Cherryh" in the online *Encyclopedia of Science Fiction*, Third Edition (edited by Clute, David Langford, Peter Nicholls, and Graham Sleight) for a complete list: http://sf-encyclopedia.com/entry/cherryh_c_j. Her most esteemed novels in the series are *Downbelow Station* (1981) and *Cyteen* (1988), which both earned Hugo Awards as the best science fiction novel of the year. For a list of Bujold's numerous Miles Vorkosigan novels, see Peter Nicholls and Neil Tringham's "Lois McMaster Bujold" in the same reference: http://sf-encyclopedia.com/entry/bujold_lois_mcmaster. The most celebrated novels in the series are *The Vor Game* (1990), *Barrayar* (1991), and *Mirror Dance* (1994), which all also earned Hugo Awards.

28. The Culture novels are Iain M. Banks's *Consider Phlebas* (1987), *The Player*

of Games (1988), *The State of the Art* (1989), *Use of Weapons* (1990), *Excession* (1996), *Inversions* (1998), *Look to Windward* (2000), *Matter* (2008), *Surface Detail* (2010), *The Spheres and the Secret Courtyard* (2010), and *The Hydrogen Sonata* (2012).

29. Iain M. Banks, *Consider Phlebas* (New York: St. Martin's Press, 1987), 446.

Chapter 7

1. Milton A. Rothman, "Literature" (letter), *Amazing Stories*, 12:4 (August, 1938), 137.

2. Konrad Wm. Maxwell, "Brickbats" (letter), *Amazing Stories*, 14:8 (August, 1940), 142.

3. Clyde F. Beck, *Hammer and Tongs* (Lakeport, California: Futile Press, 1937), xiv, 16.

4. Phil Stong, "Foreword," *The Other Worlds*, edited by Stong (New York: Wilfred Funk, Inc., 1941), 14.

5. Dan Berad, letter, *Astounding Science-Fiction*, 23:6 (August, 1939), 99.

6. A. E. van Vogt, "Black Destroyer," 1939, *First Flight*, edited by Damon Knight (New York: Lancer Books, 1966), 36. Page references are to this edition.

7. Van Vogt, "On 'Black Destroyer,'" *Astounding Science-Fiction, July 1939*, facsimile of magazine issue edited by John W. Campbell, Jr., edited by Martin Harry Greenberg (Carbondale: Southern Illinois University Press, 1981), 169. Page references are to this edition.

8. These are the opening sentences of van Vogt's "Vault of the Beast," 1940, *Monsters*, by van Vogt, edited by Forrest J Ackerman (New York: Paperback Library, 1965), 134:

> The creature crept. It whimpered from fear and pain. Shapeless, formless thing yet changing shape and form with each jerky movement, it crept along the corridor of the space freighter, fighting the terrible urge of its elements to take the shape of its surroundings.

In "On 'Black Destroyer,'" van Vogt speculates that Campbell delayed this story's publication because it was about a shape-shifting alien, the subject of another story recently published in *Astounding*, Campbell's own "Who Goes There?" (1938).

9. Lew Cunningham, letter, *Astounding Science-Fiction*, 24:1 (September, 1939), 97. A later page reference is to this edition.

10. Campbell, "In Times to Come," *Astounding Science-Fiction*, 23:4 (June, 1939), 44.

11. Blurb, table of contents page, *Astounding Science-Fiction*, 23:5 (July, 1939), 4. Author unidentified but probably Campbell himself.

12. Robert Jackson, letter, *Astounding Science-Fiction*, 24:1 (September, 1939), 95.

13. Ted Crane, letter, *Astounding Science-Fiction*, 24:1 (September, 1939), 97.

14. Thomas A. Gardner, letter, *Astounding Science-Fiction*, 24:1 (September, 1939), 98.

15. Stanley Wells, letter, *Astounding Science-Fiction*, 24:2 (October, 1939), 153.

16. D. P. Bellaire, letter, *Astounding Science-Fiction*, 24:2 (October, 1939), 153.

17. Wilson Tucker (writing as Bob Tucker), letter, *Astounding Science-Fiction*, 24:3 (November, 1939), 155.

18. Forrest J Ackerman, "Introduction: The Monster Man, Sire of Slan," *Monsters*, 6–7.

19. Wilbur J. Widmer, letter, *Astounding Science-Fiction*, 24:4 (December, 1939), 104.

20. Damon Knight, "Cosmic Jerrybuilder: A. E. van Vogt," *In Search of Wonder: Essays on Modern Science Fiction*, 1956, Second Edition (Chicago: Advent Publishers, 1967), 58. Originally published in 1945 without added material as "The World of van Vogt." Page references are to this edition.

21. Robert A. Heinlein, "Life-Line," 1939, *First Flight*, 72. Page references are to this edition.

22. See, for example, Bradford Lyau, "Robert A. Heinlein Revisited: A Response to George Slusser's Calvinist Interpretation of His Works," *Science Fiction and the Dismal Science: Essays on Economics in and of the Genre*, edited by Gary Westfahl, Gregory Benford, Howard V. Hendrix, and Jonathan Alexander (Jefferson, North Carolina: McFarland Publishers, forthcoming).

23. Campbell, "In Times to Come," *Astounding Science-Fiction*, 24:2 (October, 1939), 159.

24. Blurbs, table of contents page and first page of story "Life-Line," *Astounding Science-Fiction*, 23:6 (August, 1939), 5, 84.

Author unidentified but probably Campbell himself.

25. R. A. Langevin, letter, *Astounding Science-Fiction*, 24:5 (January, 1940), 155.

26. Gardner, letter, *Astounding Science-Fiction*, 24:2 (October, 1939), 155. A later Gardner quotation is from this issue and this page.

27. D. L. Dobbs, letter, *Astounding Science-Fiction*, 24:2 (October, 1939), 156.

28. Samuel D. Russell, letter, *Astounding Science-Fiction*, 24:3 (November, 1939), 156.

29. Campbell, "In Times to Come," *Astounding Science-Fiction*, 24:5 (January, 1940), 29.

30. Brian W. Aldiss with David Wingrove, *Trillion Year Spree: The History of Science Fiction* (New York: Atheneum, 1986), 395.

Chapter 8

1. There was a six-month transition period—from September, 1937 to February 1938—when Campbell gradually took over the duties of the previous editor, F. Orlon Tremaine, and scholars debate precisely when he truly became the magazine's editor. However, the March, 1938 issue was the first one officially credited to Campbell, and first bearing the new title he had chosen, *Astounding Science-Fiction*.

2. Clifford D. Simak, cited in Sam Moskowitz, "Clifford D. Simak," *Seekers of Tomorrow: Masters of Modern Science Fiction* (Cleveland: World Publishing, 1966), 273.

3. H. Bruce Franklin, *Robert A. Heinlein: America as Science Fiction* (Oxford: Oxford University Press, 1980), 55–57.

4. Wilson Tucker [writing as Bob Tucker], "Depts of the Interior" [sic], *Le Zombie*, 4 (January, 1941), 8.

5. Robert A. Heinlein, *Have Space Suit—Will Travel* (1958; New York: Ace Books, [1969]), 237.

6. Darko Suvin, *Metamorphoses of Science Fiction: On the Poetics and History of a Literary Genre* (New Haven and London: Yale University Press, 1979), 4.

Chapter 9

1. Bud Webster, *Anthropology 101: Reflections, Inspections and Dissections of SF Anthologies* (West Warwick, Rhode Island: Merry Blacksmith Press, 2010), 4. Page references are to this edition.

2. Description on dust jacket flap, *Adventures to Come*, edited by J. Berg Esenwein (Springfield, Massachusetts: McLoughlin Bros. Inc., 1937); no author given.

3. Webster, *Past Masters, and Other Bookish Natterings* (West Warwick: Merry Blacksmith Press, 2013), 297.

4. Phil Stong, "Foreword," *The Other Worlds*, edited by Stong (New York: Wilfred Funk, Inc., 1941), 14. Page references are to this edition.

5. Wilson Tucker [writing as Bob Tucker], "Depts of the Interior" [sic], *Le Zombie*, 4 (January, 1941), 8.

6. "A. S." [possibly Albert Sidney], "Book Review," *Thrilling Wonder Stories*, 21:1 (October, 1941), 13.

7. Donald A. Wollheim (as "DAW"), "The Fantasy World," *Stirring Science Stories*, 2:1 (March, 1942), 66.

8. Wollheim, "Introduction," *The Pocket Book of Science-Fiction*, edited by Wollheim (New York: Pocket Books, 1943), viii. Page references are to this edition.

9. Ray Bradbury, "Introduction," *Timeless Stories for Today and Tomorrow*, edited by Bradbury (New York: Bantam Books, 1952), vii.

10. David G. Hartwell, "The Distortion of the Product: Stresses on Science Fiction Literature," *Science Fiction and Market Realities*, edited by Gary Westfahl, George Slusser, and Eric S. Rabkin (Athens: University of Georgia Press, 1996), 42–43. A page reference is to this edition.

11. Wollheim, "Introduction," *The Portable Novels of Science*, edited by Wollheim (New York: Viking Press, 1945), ix. Page references are to this edition.

12. James Gunn, *Alternate Worlds: The Illustrated History of Science Fiction* (New York: A & W Visual Library, 1975), 13.

13. John W. Campbell, Jr., "Introduction," *Prologue to Analog*, edited by Campbell (Garden City: Doubleday and Company, 1962), 13.

14. Wollheim, "Editor's Preface" to "The Shadow Out of Time," *The Portable Novels of Science*, 392.

15. Groff Conklin, "Introduction," *The Best of Science Fiction*, edited by Conklin (New York: Crown Publishers, 1946), xxvi. Page references are to this edition.

16. Campbell, "Concerning Science Fiction," *The Best of Science Fiction*, x–xi. Page references are to this edition.

17. Raymond J. Healy and J. Francis McComas, "Introduction," *Adventures in Time and Space: An Anthology of Modern Science-Fiction Stories*, edited by Healy and McComas (New York: Random House, 1946), xi. Page references are to this edition.

18. In an analysis written after I had completed a draft of this chapter, I discuss at length various science fiction anthologies prepared for the classroom, from the 1970s to today, in "Profiting from Prophecies: Science Fiction Scholars and Their Textbooks," *Science Fiction and the Dismal Science: Essays on Economics in and of the Genre*, edited by Gary Westfahl, Gregory Benford, Howard V. Hendrix, and Jonathan Alexander (Jefferson, North Carolina: McFarland Publishers, forthcoming).

19. Gary Westfahl, "What Is a Science Fiction Magazine? (And Why on Earth Are They Still Around?)," 2000, *An Alien Abroad: Science Fiction Columns from Interzone*. [Rockville, Maryland]: Wildside Press, 2016), 109.

20. Kathryn Cramer, "Our Pious Hope: Science Fiction Marketing, Counter-Marketing, and Transcendence," *Science Fiction and Market Realities*, edited by Westfahl, George Slusser, and Eric S. Rabkin (Athens, Georgia: University of Georgia Press, 1996), 56–70.

Chapter 10

1. John W. Campbell, Jr., "Concerning Science Fiction," *The Best of Science Fiction*, edited by Groff Conklin (New York: Crown Publishers, 1946), v.

2. Sam Moskowitz, "The Return of Hugo Gernsback," Part IV, *Fantasy Commentator*, 10:3/4 (Spring, 2003), 210.

3. Writing credits for *Captain Video and the Video Rangers* usually cannot be authoritatively verified because so few episodes of the series are still available, as the kinescopes of most series episodes were destroyed and the network that aired the series, DuMont, went out of business in the 1950s. The list provided is based on information from the Internet Movie Database, but it must be noted that the site perpetuates the false report that Arthur C. Clarke wrote for the series, though Clarke himself strongly denied that he did so.

4. The comic book is discussed at length in my *Hugo Gernsback and the Century of Science Fiction* (Jefferson, North Carolina: McFarland, 2007), 73–79.

5. Superman also began to make brief appearances as a member of the Justice League of America, beginning with their 1960 debut in *The Brave and the Bold* and continuing with their own comic in the same year, though these comics were under Schwartz's control, not Weisinger's.

6. This statement should be qualified by noting that Weisinger and its writers were *usually* coming up with new ideas for their stories; however, as noted below, they sometimes simply retold old stories for a new generation of readers.

7. The following reports are based on vivid memories of comic book stories that I repeatedly read as a child, though I now still possess only a few of them; references to specific stories to verify each example of a science fiction trope do not seem necessary, though internet research can easily verify that all of these elements were in fact introduced during Weisinger's tenure as the editor of Superman comic books. A useful compendium of information about Superman stories from the 1930s to the 1960s in print is Michael L. Fleisher's *The Great Superman Book* (New York: Warner Books, 1978).

8. Otto Binder, writer, Wayne Boring, artist, "The Lady and the Lion," *Action Comics*, No. 243 (August, 1958), 1–13. It should be noted that this particular story depicts Circe as an exiled Kryptonian scientist, but no science-fictional veneer is applied to the character when she is described as the sorceress who transformed Biron in Leo Dorfman, writer, Jim Mooney, artist, "The Secret Origin of Supergirl's Super-Horse," *Action Comics*, No. 293 (October, 1962), 21–31.

9. Jerry Coleman, writer, Wayne Boring, artist, "Superman's New Power," *Superman*, No. 125 (November, 1958), 23–30.

10. Robert Bernstein, writer, Al Plastino, artist, "The Menace of Metallo," *Action Comics*, No. 252 (May, 1959), 1–13. However, there have been previous and later versions of the villainous Metallo which do not accord with the events of this story.

11. Craig Shutt, "Twice-Told Superman

Tales," *Baby Boomer Comics: The Wild, Wacky, Wonderful Comic Books of the 1960s!* (Iola, Wisconsin: Krause Publications, 2003), 186–189.

12. John Broome, writer, Bob Oskner, artist, "It's a Woman's World," *Mystery in Space*, No. 8 (July, 1952). Republished in *Mysteries in Space: The Best of DC Science Fiction Comics*, edited by Michael Uslan (New York: Simon & Schuster, 1980), 91. This book, by the way, provides a valuable if imperfect portrait of DC's ventures in science fiction during the 1950s, almost all of them overseen by Julius Schwartz.

13. Otto Binder, writer, Gil Kane, artist. "Follow the Space-Leader." *Mystery in Space*, No. 42 (March, 1958). Republished in *Mysteries in Space*, 142–147.

14. Morris B. Holbrook and Barbara Stern, "The Use of Space-Travel and Rocket-Ship Imagery to Market Commercial Music: How Some Jazz Albums from the 1950s, 1960s, and 1970s Burned Brightly but Fizzled Fast," *Extrapolation*, 41:1 (Spring, 2000), 57, 58. Page references are to this edition.

15. Album Cover Artists: The Master List, compiled by monocle, Rate Your Music, updated June 17, 2018, at https://rateyourmusic.com/list/monocle/album_cover_artists__the_master_list/1/.

16. Joachim Boaz, "Update: Hilarious 1960s/1950s Sci-Fi Themed Ads," Science Fiction and Other Suspect Ruminations, posted October 3, 2010, at https://sciencefictionruminations.com/2010/10/03/update-hilarious-1960s-sci-fi-themed-ads/.

17. Hugo Gernsback, "The Science-Fiction Industry," *Science-Fiction Plus*, 1 (May, 1953), 2.

Chapter 11

1. Allen M. Steele, "Hard Again," *The New York Review of Science Fiction*, No. 46 (June, 1992), 4.

2. David G. Hartwell, "Hard Science Fiction," *The Ascent of Wonder: The Evolution of Hard Science Fiction*, edited by Hartwell and Kathryn Cramer (New York: Tor Books, 1994), 31.

3. See Gary Westfahl, *Cosmic Engineers: A Study of Hard Science Fiction* (Westport, Connecticut: Greenwood Press, 1996).

4. C. S. Lewis, "On Science Fiction," *Of Other Worlds: Essays and Stories*, edited by Walter Hooper (New York: Harcourt Brace Jovanovich, 1966), 66. From the text of a lecture presented in 1955.

5. John W. Campbell, Jr. "Science Fiction and the Opinion of the Universe," *Saturday Review*, 39 (May 12, 1956), 9–10, 42–43.

6. Cited in Gordon Jones, "Jules Verne at Home, *Temple Bar*, 129 (June, 1904), 664–671. Available online at http://jv.gilead.org.il/evans/Gordon_Jones_interview_of_JV.html.

7. H. G. Wells, "Preface" to *The Sleeper Awakes*, 1921, *H. G. Wells's Literary Criticism*, edited by Patrick Parrinder and Robert M. Philmus (Sussex: The Harvester Press, 1980), 238.

8. Wells, "Preface" to *Seven Famous Novels*, by Wells (1933; New York: Alfred A. Knopf, 1934), viii.

9. As discussed at length in my *The Mechanics of Wonder: The Creation of the Idea of Science Fiction* (Liverpool: Liverpool University Press, 1998).

10. Hugo Gernsback, "Reasonableness in Science Fiction," *Wonder Stories*, 4 (December, 1932), 585.

11. Gernsback, "Science Fiction vs. Science Faction," *Wonder Stories Quarterly*, 2 (Fall, 1930), 5.

12. Robert A. Heinlein, "Shooting *Destination Moon*," *Astounding Science-Fiction*, 45 (July, 1950), 7, 16.

13. Hal Clement, "Whirligig World," *Astounding Science-Fiction*, 51 (June, 1953), 102. Page references are to this edition.

14. Cited in Donald M. Hassler, *Hal Clement*, Starmont Reader's Guide 11 (Mercer Island, Washington: Starmont House, 1982), 21.

15. Poul Anderson, "The Creation of Imaginary Worlds: The World Builder's Handbook and Pocket Companion," *Science Fiction: Today and Tomorrow*, edited by Reginald Bretnor (Baltimore: Penguin Books, 1974), 235–257.

16. As discussed in *Cosmic Engineers*, 8–9.

17. P. Schuyler Miller, "The Reference Library," *Astounding Science Fiction*, 60 (November, 1957), 143.

18. Larry Niven, untitled introduction to an excerpt from *Ringworld*, *N-Space* (New York: Tor Books 1990), 123–124.

19. For another perspective on recent developments in hard science fiction, see Don-

ald M. Hassler, "The Renewal of 'Hard' Science Fiction," *A Companion to Science Fiction*, edited by David Seed (Oxford: Blackwell Publishers, 2005), 248–258.

20. See David Brin, "Running Out of Speculative Niches: A Crisis for Hard Science Fiction?," 1986, *Bridges to Science Fiction and Fantasy: Outstanding Essays from the J. Lloyd Eaton Conferences*, edited by Gregory Benford, Gary Westfahl, Howard V. Hendrix, and Joseph D. Miller (Jefferson, North Carolina: McFarland Publishers, 2018), 53–57.

Chapter 12

1. Isaac Asimov writing as Paul French, *David Starr, Space Ranger* (1952; New York: Signet Books, 1971), 9–10. Page references are to this edition.
2. Asimov writing as Paul French, *Lucky Starr and the Pirates of the Asteroids* (1953; New York: Signet Books, 1971), 122.
3. Arthur C. Clarke, *Islands in the Sky* (1952; New York: Signet Books, 1960), 12. Page references are to this edition.
4. Clarke, *Dolphin Island: A Story of the People of the Sea* (1963; New York: Berkley, 1968), 5. Page references are to this edition.
5. Robert A. Heinlein, *Rocket Ship Galileo* (1947; New York: Ace Books, [1970]), 38. Page references are to this edition.
6. Robert A. Heinlein, *Space Cadet* (1948: New York: Ace Books, [1969]), 7. Page references are to this edition.
7. Gregory Benford, "Terraforming Ganymede with Robert A. Heinlein," Baen Books website, posted in 2011, at https://www.baen.com/terraformingganymede1.
8. C. S. Lewis, "On Science Fiction," *Of Other Worlds: Essays and Stories*, edited by Walter Hooper (New York and London: Harcourt Brace Jovanovich, 1966), 67.

Chapter 13

1. Gary Westfahl, "Guest Editor's Pad: Combativeness and Science Fiction, or, Look Forward in Anger," *Extrapolation*, 41 (Spring 2000), 3–6.
2. See Sam Moskowitz, *The Immortal Storm: A History of Science Fiction Fandom* (Westport, Connecticut: Hyperion Press, 1974); Harry Warner, Jr., *All Our Yesterdays: An Informal History of Science Fiction Fandom in the Forties* (Chicago: Advent Publishers, 1969); and Warner, *A Wealth of Fable: An Informal History of Science Fiction Fandom in the 1950s*, edited by Dick Lynch (Van Nuys, California: SCIFI Press, 1992).

3. Earl Kemp, editor, *The Complete and Unexpurgated Who Killed Science Fiction?*, *Efanzines*, 5:6 (December, 2006), at https://efanzines.com/EK/eI29/. Along with some material identified as having been written after 1960, this includes the entire text of the original 1960 publication, with the Heinlein and Farmer contributions now attributed to their authors. All quotations are from this edition.

4. Westfahl, "What Is a Science Fiction Magazine? (And Why on Earth Are They Still Around?)," 2000, *An Alien Abroad: Science Fiction Columns from Interzone* (Holicong, Pennsylvania: Wildside Press, 2016), 109.

5. Paul A. Carter, "From 'Nat' to 'Nathan': The Liberal Arts Odyssey of a Pulpster," *Styles of Creation: Aesthetic Technique and the Creation of Fictional Worlds*, edited by George Slusser and Eric S. Rabkin (Athens: University of Georgia Press, 1992), 58–78.

6. Gregory Benford, *Deep Time: How Humanity Communicates across Millennia* (New York: Avon Books, 1999), 39. The phrase appears elsewhere in Benford's writings.

7. P. Schuyler Miller, "The Reference Library," *Analog Science Fact/Science Fiction*, 68:3 (November, 1961), 167.

8. Harlan Ellison, "Introduction: Thirty-Two Soothsayers," *Dangerous Visions #1*, edited by Ellison (1967; New York: Berkley Books, 1969), 23–24.

9. Ellison, "A Time for Daring," *The Book of Ellison*, edited by Andrew Porter (New York: ALGOL Press, 1978), 112. Speech originally published in *ALGOL* (March, 1967).

10. Mark R. Kelly, The Science Fiction Awards+ Database, Locus Online, updated monthly, at http://www.sfadb.com/.

11. Advertisements, *Galaxy*, 26:5 (June, 1968), 4–5.

Chapter 14

1. Hugo Gernsback, "A New Sort of Magazine," *Amazing Stories*, 1 (April, 1926), 3.

2. Gernsback, "Fiction Versus Facts," *Amazing Stories*, 1 (July, 1926), 291.
3. Gernsback, "Thank You!," *Amazing Stories*, 1 (May, 1926), 99.
4. Walter Nash, *Language in Popular Fiction* (London: Routledge, 1990), 3–4.
5. "Wanted: Still More Plots" (no author given), *Wonder Stories Quarterly*, 3 (Summer, 1932), 437.
6. Norman Spinrad, "Science Fiction in the Real World—Revisited," *Science Fiction and Market Realities*, edited by Gary Westfahl, George Slusser, and Eric S. Rabkin (Athens: University of Georgia Press, 1996), 26.
7. John W. Campbell, Jr., "Introduction," *Who Goes There?* (Chicago: Shasta, 1948), 5.
8. Campbell, "The Science of Science Fiction Writing," *Of Worlds Beyond: The Science of Science Fiction Writing*, edited by Lloyd Arthur Eshbach (1947; Chicago: Advent, 1964), 100.
9. Campbell, "Introduction," 5.
10. Campbell, "In Times to Come," *Astounding Science-Fiction*, 22 (October, 1938), 11.
11. Damon Knight, *In Search of Wonder: Essays on Modern Science Fiction*, Second Edition (Chicago: Advent, 1967), 6, 8)
12. Norman Siringer, "Literature and Science Fiction," *The Rhodomagnetic Digest*, 2 (August, 1950), 22, 21.
13. Spinrad, 28.
14. Harlan Ellison, "Introduction: Thirty-Two Soothsayers," *Dangerous Visions #1*, edited by Ellison (1967; New York: Berkley, 1969, 19.
15. Mike Resnick and Barry N. Malzberg, "Really Dumb Ideas," 2006, *The Business of Science Fiction: Two Insiders Discuss Writing and Publishing*, by Resnick and Malzberg (Jefferson, North Carolina: McFarland, 2010), 175.
16. David G. Hartwell, "The Distortion of the Product," *Science Fiction and Market Realities*, 38.
17. Cristina Sedgewick, "The Fork in the Road: Can Science Fiction Survive in Postmodern, Megacorporate America?" *Science-Fiction Studies*, 18 (March, 1991), 11–52; Kathryn Cramer, "Our Pious Hope: Science Fiction Marketing, Counter-Marketing, and Transcendence," *Science Fiction and Market Realities*, 56–70; David G. Hartwell, "The Distortion of the Product: Stresses on Science Fiction Literature," *Science Fiction and Market Realities*, 36–55; and Spinrad, cited above.
18. For anyone wishing to check my results, I am listing the 75 books I observed below (for the standard umbrella titles of series, I generally relied upon the Internet Speculative Fiction Database). Reading through the entire list—omitted when the results of the survey were first published—is also enlightening, as it vividly illustrates the huge disconnect between the works that science fiction scholars are now examining and the works that are now being purchased and read by large numbers of readers.

I. "Classic" Works (6 = 8%)
  Christopher Anvil, *The Power of Illusion* (collection)
  Ray Bradbury, *The Golden Apples of the Sun* (collection)
  H. P. Lovecraft, *The Call of Cthulhu and Other Weird Stories* (collection)
  Lovecraft, *Horror Out of Arkham* (collection)
  Lovecraft, *The Other Gods and More Unearthly Tales* (collection)
  Anne McCaffrey, *The Rowan*

II. Original Works (12 = 16%)
  Michael Dempsey, *Necropolis*
  Eric Flint, *Worlds* (collection)
  Marty Halpern, editor, *Alien Contact* (anthology)
  Ian McDonald, *The Dervish House*
  Ryu Mitsuse, *10 Billion Days and 100 Billion Nights*
  Lev A. C. Rosen, *All Men of Genius*
  Jason Stoddard, *Winning Mars*
  Harry Turtledove, *Atlantis and Other Places* (collection)
  Turtledove, *Supervolcano: Eruption*
  Sayuri Ueda, *The Cage of Zeus*
  David Weber, *Out of the Dark*
  Rob Ziegler, *Seed*

III. Works in Series (57 = 76%) (Series title in parentheses)
  Anne Aguirre, *Aftermath* (Sirantha Jax)
  Taylor Anderson, *Firestorm* (Destroyermen)
  Anderson, *Rising Tides* (Destroyermen)
  Neil Asher, *Brass Man* (Polity Universe)
  James Axler, *Infestation Cubed* (Outlanders)

Axler, *Prodigal's Return* (Deathlands)
John Barnes, *Daybreak Zero* (Directive 51)
Lois McMaster Bujold, *Cryoburn* (Miles Vorkosigan)
Jack Campbell, *Stark's Command* (Ethan Stark)
Campbell, *Stark's War* (Stark)
Greg Cox, *Final Crisis* (DC Comics Universe)
Peter Crowther, *Darkness Falling* (Forever Twilight)
Hank Davis, editor, *The Best of the Bolos* (anthology) (Bolo)
Guillermo del Toro and Chuck Hogan, *The Night Eternal* (Strain)
del Toro and Hogan, *The Strain* (Strain)
William C. Dietz, *Bones of Empire* (Zak Cato)
Dietz, *A Fighting Chance* (Legion of the Damned)
David Drake, *Voyage Across the Stars* (Hammer's Slammers)
Alan Dean Foster, *The Human Blend* (Tipping Point)
Eric Flint, editor, *Grantville Gazette IV* (anthology) (Assiti Shards)
Christie Golden, *Ascension* (Star Wars)
James Goss, *First Born* (Torchwood)
Paula Guran, editor, *New Cthulhu: The Recent Weird* (anthology) (Cthulhu Mythos)
Peter F. Hamilton, *The Evolutionary Void* (Void Trilogy)
Steven Harper, *The Doomsday Vault* (Clockwork Empire)
Brian Herbert and Kevin J. Anderson, *Hellhole* (Hellhole Trilogy)
Tanya Huff, *The Truth of Valor* (Confederation Novels)
Kameron Hurley, *Infidel* (God's War)
Alex Irvine, *Exiles* (Transformers)
William H. Keith, Jr., *Free Fall* (Android)
Paul S. Kemp, *Riptide* (Star Wars)
Steven L. Kent, *The Clone Redemption* (Clone Republic)
Nate Kenyon, *Spectres* (Starcraft Universe)
E. E. Knight, *March in Country* (The Vampire Earth)
Sharon Lee and Steve Miller, *The Crystal Variation* (Liaden Universe)
Lee and Miller, *Mouse and Dragon* (Liaden)
Andrew P. Mayer, *Hearts of Smoke and Steam* (Society of Steam)
Kelly Meding, *Trance* (Trance West)
Jonathan Morris, *Touched by an Angel* (Doctor Who)
Larry Niven and Steven Barnes, *The Moon Maze Game* (Dream Park)
Stefan Petrucha, *Dead Mann Walking* (Hessius Mann)
Terry Pratchett, *Snuff* (Discworld)
Cherie Priest, *Ganymede* (Clockwork Century Universe)
Andy Remic, *Theme Planet* (The Anarchy)
John Ringo, *Citadel* (Troy Rising)
Michael Schuster and Steve Mollmann, *A Choice of Catastrophes* (Star Trek)
Stirling, S. M. *The High King of Montival* (The Change)
Karen Traviss, *Coalition's End* (Gears of War)
Traviss, *Glasslands* (Halo)
Harry Turtledove, *Liberating Atlantis* (Lost Continent of Atlantis)
Patrick A. Vanner, *Ragnarok* (Xan-Sskarn War)
Vernor Vinge, *The Children of the Sky* (Zones of Thought)
David Weber, *How Firm a Foundation* (Safehold)
Steve White, *Wolf Among the Stars* (Lokaran)
Michael Z. Williamson, *Rogue* (Freehold Universe)
Connie Willis, *All Clear* (Time Travel)
Timothy Zahn, *Cobra Guardian* (Cobra Universe)

19. Gary Westfahl, "The Homeostatic Culture Machine Revisited, or, The Contemporary Wordmills of Science Fiction," *Science Fiction and the Dismal Science: Essays on Economics in and of the Genre*, edited by Westfahl, Gregory Benford, Howard V. Hendrix, and Jonathan Alexander (Jefferson, North Carolina: McFarland Publishers, forthcoming).

20. Mark Bould, Andrew M. Butler, Adam Roberts, and Sherryl Vint, editors, *Fifty Key Figures in Science Fiction* (London: Routledge, 2009).

Bibliography

This bibliography lists secondary resources on science fiction that are likely to be useful to scholars studying twentieth-century American science fiction, including all of the relevant sources cited in individual chapters. Some texts are included because they offer provocative perspectives on the genre as a whole while saying relatively little about the modern tradition. I have generally excluded studies of individual authors, except for biographies and autobiographies that regularly mention other writers, editors, and publishers.

Aldiss, Brian W. *Science Fiction Art.* New York: Crown, 1975.
_____. *The Shape of Further Things: Speculation on Change.* 1970. London: Corgi Books, 1974.
_____, with David Wingrove. *Trillion Year Spree: The History of Science Fiction.* New York: Atheneum, 1986.
Amis, Kingsley. *New Maps of Hell.* New York: Ballantine Books, 1960.
Ash, Brian, editor. *The Visual Encyclopedia of Science Fiction.* New York: Harmony Books, 1977.
Ashley, Mike. *Gateways to Forever: The Story of the Science-Fiction Pulp Magazines from 1970 to 1980.* Liverpool: Liverpool University Press, 2007.
_____. *Science Fiction Rebels: The Story of the Science-Fiction Pulp Magazines from 1981 to 1990.* Liverpool: Liverpool University Press, 2016.
_____. *The Time Machines: The Story of the Science-Fiction Pulp Magazines from the Beginning to 1950.* Liverpool: Liverpool University Press, 2000.
_____. *Transformations: The Story of the Science-Fiction Pulp Magazines from 1950 to 1970.* Liverpool: Liverpool University Press, 2005.
_____, and Robert A. W. Lowndes. *The Gernsback Days: A Study of the Evolution of Modern Science Fiction from 1911 to 1936.* Holicong, Pennsylvania: Wildside Press, 2004.
Asimov, Isaac. *Asimov on Science Fiction.* Garden City: New York: Doubleday, 1981.
_____. *I, Asimov: A Memoir.* New York: Doubleday, 1994.
_____. *I, Robot.* 1950. New York: Bantam, 2008.
_____. *In Joy Still Felt: The Autobiography of Isaac Asimov, 1954–1978.* Garden City, New York: Doubleday, 1980.
_____. *In Memory Yet Green: The Autobiography of Isaac Asimov, 1920–1954.* Garden City, New York: Doubleday, 1979.
_____, editor. *Before the Golden Age: A Science Fiction Anthology of the 1930s.* Garden City: Doubleday, 1974.
Bacon-Smith, Camille. *Science Fiction Culture.* Philadelphia: University of Pennsylvania Press, 1999.

Bibliography

Bailey, J. O. *Pilgrims through Time and Space: Trends and Patterns in Scientific and Utopian Fiction.* New York: Argus Books, 1947.
Bainbridge, William Sims. *Dimensions of Science Fiction.* Cambridge, Massachusetts: Harvard University Press, 1986.
Barr, Marleen S. *Lost in Space: Probing Feminist Science Fiction and Beyond.* Chapel Hill: North Carolina University Press, 1993.
_____, editor. *Future Females: A Critical Anthology.* Bowling Green, Ohio: Bowling Green Popular Press, 1981.
Barron, Neil, editor. *Anatomy of Wonder: A Critical Guide to Science Fiction.* Fifth Edition. Westport, Connecticut: Libraries Unlimited, 2004.
Beck, Clyde F. *Hammer and Tongs.* Lakeport, California: Futile Press, 1937.
Berger, Albert I. *The Magic That Works: John W. Campbell and the American Response to Technology.* San Bernardino, California: Borgo Press, 1993.
Bleiler, Everett F., with Richard Bleiler. *Science-Fiction: The Early Years: A Full Description of More Than 3, 000 Science-Fiction Stories from Earliest Times to the Appearance of Genre Magazines in 1930.* Kent, Ohio: Kent State University Press, 1990.
_____, with Richard Bleiler. *Science-Fiction: The Gernsback Years: A Complete Coverage of the Genre Magazines* Amazing, Astounding, Wonder, *and Others from 1926 to 1936.* Kent, Ohio: Kent State University Press, 1998.
Bleiler, Richard, editor. *Science Fiction Writers: Critical Studies of the Major Authors from the Early Nineteenth Century to the Present Day.* Second Edition. New York: Scribner's, 1999.
Blish, James. *The Issues at Hand: Critical Studies in Contemporary Science Fiction.* Chicago: Advent Publishers, 1964.
_____. *More Issues at Hand: Critical Studies in Contemporary Science Fiction.* Chicago: Advent Publishers, 1970.
Booker, M. Keith, and Anne-Marie Thomas. *The Science Fiction Handbook.* Malden, Massachusetts: Wiley-Blackwell, 2009.
Bould, Mark, Andrew M. Butler, Adam Roberts, and Sherryl Vint, editors. *Fifty Key Figures in Science Fiction.* London: Routledge, 2009.
_____, Andrew M. Butler, Adam Roberts, and Sherryl Vint, editors. *The Routledge Companion to Science Fiction.* New York: Routledge, 2009.
_____, and Sherryl Vint. *The Routledge Concise History of Science Fiction.* New York: Routledge, 2011.
Bretnor, Reginald, editor. *The Craft of Science Fiction.* New York: Harper & Row, 1976.
_____, editor. *Modern Science Fiction: Its Meaning and Its Future.* 1953. Chicago: Advent, 1979.
_____, editor. *Science Fiction: Today and Tomorrow.* Baltimore: Penguin Books, 1974.
Bridgstock, Martin, "A Psychological Approach to 'Hard' Science Fiction." *Science-Fiction Studies,* 10 (March, 1983), 50–57.
Campbell, John W., Jr. *Collected Editorials from Analog.* Edited by Harry Harrison. Garden City: Doubleday and Company, 1966.
_____. "Concerning Science Fiction." *The Best of Science Fiction.* Edited by Groff Conklin. New York: Crown Publishers, 1946, v-xi.
_____. "History to Come," *Astounding Science-Fiction,* 27 (May, 1941), 5–6.
_____. "Introduction," *Analog 1.* Edited by Campbell. Garden City: Doubleday and Company, 1963, xv-xviii.
_____. "Introduction." *Prologue to Analog.* Edited by Campbell. Garden City: Doubleday and Company, 1962, 9–16.
_____. "Introduction." *Venus Equilateral.* By George O. Smith. New York: Prime Press, 1947, 8–12.
_____. *The John W. Campbell Letters with Isaac Asimov and A. E. van Vogt.* [Volume 2] Edited by Perry A. Chapdelaine, Tony Chapdelaine, and George Hay. Franklin, Tennessee: AC Projects, 1987.

_____. *The John W. Campbell Letters, Volume I.* Edited by Perry A. Chapdelaine, Tony Chapdelaine, and George Hay. Franklin, Tennessee: AC Projects, 1985.

_____, editor. *The Astounding Science Fiction Anthology.* New York: Simon and Schuster, 1952.

Carter, Paul A. *The Creation of Tomorrow: Fifty Years of Magazine Science Fiction.* New York: Columbia University Press, 1977.

Cheng, John. *Astounding Wonder: Imagining Science and Science Fiction in Interwar America.* Philadelphia: University of Pennsylvania Press, 2012.

Clareson, Thomas D. *Some Kind of Paradise: The Emergence of American Science Fiction.* Westport, Connecticut: Greenwood Press, 1985.

_____, and Joe Sanders. *The Heritage of Heinlein: A Critical Reading of the Fiction.* Jefferson, North Carolina: McFarland, 2014.

Clarke, Arthur C. *Astounding Days: A Science Fictional Autobiography.* London: Victor Gollancz, 1989.

_____. *Greetings, Carbon-Based Bipeds!: Collected Essays, 1934–1998.* Edited by Ian T. Macauley. New York: St. Martin's Press, 1999.

_____. *Profiles of the Future: An Inquiry into the Limits of the Possible.* Millennial Edition. London: Victor Gollancz, 1999.

Clute, John. *SF: The Illustrated Encyclopedia.* London, New York, and Stuttgart: Dorling Kindersley, 1995.

_____, David Langford, Peter Nicholls, and Graham Sleight, editors. *The Encyclopedia of Science Fiction.* Third Edition. London: Gollancz, 2012, at http://www.sf-encyclopedia.com/.

Conklin, Groff. "Introduction." *The Best of Science Fiction.* Edited by Conklin. New York: Crown Publishers, 1946, xv-xxviii.

Cowart, David, and Thomas L. Wymer, editors. *Twentieth Century American Science-Fiction Writers.* Dictionary of Literary Biography, Volume. 8. Detroit: Gale, 1981.

Csicsery-Ronay, Istvan, Jr. *The Seven Beauties of Science Fiction.* Middletown, Connecticut: Wesleyan University Press, 2008.

Davenport, Basil. *Inquiry into Science Fiction.* New York: Longman, Green, and Co., 1955.

_____, editor. *The Science Fiction Novel: Imagination and Social Criticism.* Chicago: Advent Publishers, 1959.

Davin, Eric Leif. *Partners in Wonder: Women and the Birth of Science Fiction, 1926–1965.* Lanham, Maryland: Lexington, 2006.

_____. *Pioneers of Wonder: Conversations with the Founders of Science Fiction.* Amherst, New York: Prometheus Books, 1999.

de Camp, L. Sprague and Catherine Crook de Camp. *Science Fiction Handbook, Revised: how to Write and Sell Imaginative Stories.* New York: McGraw-Hill, 1975.

del Rey, Lester. *Fantastic Science Fiction Art 1926–1954.* New York: Ballantine Books, 1975.

_____. *The World of Science Fiction, 1926–1976: The History of a Subculture.* New York: Garland Publishing, 1979.

Delany, Samuel R. *Silent Interviews: On Language, Race, Sex, Science Fiction, and Some Comics.* Hanover, NH: Wesleyan University Press, 1994.

_____ *Starboard Wine: More Notes on the Language of Science Fiction.* Pleasantville, New York: Dragon, 1984.

Di Fate, Vincent. *Infinite Worlds: The Fantastic Visions of Science Fiction Art.* New York: Penguin Studio: Wonderland Press, 1997.

Disch, Thomas M. *The Dreams Our Stuff Is Made Of: How Science Fiction Conquered the World.* New York: Free Press, 1998.

_____. *On SF.* Ann Arbor: University of Michigan Press, 2005.

Eller, Jonathan R. *Becoming Ray Bradbury.* Urbana: University of Illinois Press, 2013.

_____. *Ray Bradbury Unbound.* Urbana: University of Illinois Press, 2014.

Ellison, Harlan. *The Book of Ellison.* Edited by Andrew Porter. New York: ALGOL Press, 1978.

_____. *Sleepless Nights in the Procrustean Bed: Essays by Harlan Ellison.* Edited by Marty Clark. San Bernardino, California: Borgo Press, 1984.
Elrick, George S. *Science Fiction Handbook for Readers and Writers.* Chicago: Chicago Review Press, 1978.
Eshbach, Lloyd Arthur, editor. *Of Worlds Beyond: The Science of Science Fiction Writing.* 1947. Chicago: Advent Publishers, 1964.
Frank, Jane. *Science Fiction and Fantasy Artists of the Twentieth Century: A Biographical Dictionary.* Jefferson, North Carolina: McFarland Publishers, 2009.
Franklin, H. Bruce. *Robert A. Heinlein: America as Science Fiction.* Oxford: Oxford University Press, 1980.
_____. *War Stars: The Superweapon and the American Imagination.* Oxford: Oxford University Press, 1988.
Freedman, Carl. *Critical Theory and Science Fiction.* Middletown, Connecticut: Wesleyan University Press, 2000.
Frewin, Anthony. *One Hundred Years of Science Fiction Illustration.* 1974. New York: Pyramid Books, 1975.
Gernsback, Hugo. "Amazing Youth." *Amazing Stories,* 2 (October, 1927), 625.
_____. "The Lure of Scientifiction." *Amazing Stories,* 1 (June, 1926), 195.
_____. "A New Sort of Magazine." *Amazing Stories,* 1 (April, 1926), 3.
_____. *The Perversity of Things: Hugo Gernsback on Media, Tinkering, and Scientifiction.* Edited by Grant Wythoff. Minneapolis: University of Minnesota Press, 2016.
_____. "Reasonableness in Science Fiction." *Wonder Stories,* 4 (December, 1932), 585.
_____. "The Science Fiction League," *Wonder Stories,* 5 (May, 1934), 1061–1065.
_____. "The Science Fiction League: An Announcement," *Wonder Stories,* 5 (April, 1934), 933.
_____. "Science Wonder Stories." *Science Wonder Stories,* 1 (June, 1929), 5.
Golder, Dave, Jess Nevins, Russ Thorne, and Sarah Dobbs. *The Astounding Illustrated History of Science Fiction: Movies, Art, Comics, Pulp Magazines, Fiction.* Consultant editor David Langford. London Flame Tree Publishing, 2017.
Greenberg, Martin Harry, editor. *Astounding Science-Fiction, July 1939.* Facsimile of magazine issue edited by John W. Campbell, Jr., with added material. Carbondale: Southern Illinois University Press, 1981.
Gunn, James. *Alternate Worlds: The Illustrated History of Science Fiction.* New York: A & W Visual Library, 1975.
_____. *Inside Science Fiction.* San Bernardino, CA: Borgo Press, 1992.
_____. *Star Begotten: A Life Lived in Science Fiction.* Jefferson, North Carolina: McFarland Publishers, 2017.
_____, Marleen S. Barr, and Matthew Candelaria, editors. *Reading Science Fiction.* Basingstoke, Hampshire, and New York: Palgrave Macmillan 2009.
Hamilton, Edmond. *The Star of Life.* Greenwich, Connecticut: Fawcett, 1959.
Hartwell, David G. *Age of Wonders: Exploring the World of Science Fiction.* Second Edition. New York: Tor Books, 1996.
Hassler, Donald M. *Hal Clement.* Starmont Reader's Guide 11. Mercer Island, Washington: Starmont House, 1982.
Heinlein, Robert A. *Grumbles from the Grave.* Edited by Virginia Heinlein. New York: Ballantine, 1989.
_____. *The Heinlein Letters: Volume I: Correspondence of John W. Campbell, Jr., and Robert A. Heinlein.* Houston, Texas: The Virginia Edition, Inc., 2011.
_____. *The Heinlein Letters: Volume II: General Correspondence of Robert Heinlein, Volume 1.* Houston, Texas: The Virginia Edition, Inc., 2011.
_____. *The Heinlein Letters: Volume III: General Correspondence of Robert Heinlein, Volume 2.* Houston, Texas: The Virginia Edition, Inc., 2011.
_____. *The Nonfiction of Robert A. Heinlein: Volume I.* Houston, Texas: The Virginia Edition, Inc., 2011.

_____. *The Nonfiction of Robert A. Heinlein: Volume II.* Houston, Texas: The Virginia Edition, Inc., 2011.
Holdstock, Robert, editor. *Encyclopedia of Science Fiction.* London: Octopus Books, 1978.
Hubble, Nick, and Aris Mousoutzanis, editors. *The Science Fiction Handbook.* New York: Bloomsbury, 2013.
Huntington, John. *Rationalizing Genius: Ideological Strategies in the Classic American Science Fiction Short Story.* New Brunswick, New Jersey: Rutgers University Press, 1989.
James, Edward. *Science Fiction in the 20th Century.* Oxford and New York: Oxford University Press, 1994.
_____, and Farah Mendlesohn, editors. *The Cambridge Companion to Science Fiction.* Cambridge: Cambridge University Press, 2003.
Jones, Gwyneth. *Deconstructing the Starships: Science, Fiction, and Reality.* Liverpool: Liverpool University Press, 1999.
_____. *Imagination/Space: Essays and Talks on Fiction, Feminism, Technology, and Politics.* Seattle, Washington: Aqueduct Press, 2009.
Kemp, Earl, editor. *The Complete and Unexpurgated Who Killed Science Fiction?, Efanzines,* 5:6 (December, 2006). At https://efanzines.com/EK/eI29/. Originally published in 1960.
Kilgore, De Witt D. *Astrofuturism: Science, Race, and Visions of Utopia in Space.* Philadelphia: University of Pennsylvania Press, 2003.
Knight, Damon. *The Futurians: The Story of the Great Science Fiction "Family" of the 30s That Produced Today's Top SF Writers and Editors.* New York: Day, 1977.
_____. *In Search of Wonder: Essays on Modern Science Fiction.* 1956. Revised and Enlarged. Chicago: Advent Publishers, 1967.
Kyle, David. *A Pictorial History of Science Fiction.* London: Hamlyn Publishing, 1976.
Landon, Brooks. *Science Fiction after 1900: From the Steam Man to the Stars.* Boston: Twayne Publishers, 1997.
Latham, Rob, editor. *Science Fiction Criticism: An Anthology of Essential Writings.* London: Bloomsbury, 2017.
_____. *The Oxford Handbook of Science Fiction.* London and New York: Oxford University Press, 2014.
Le Guin, Ursula K. *The Language of the Night: Essays on Fantasy and Science Fiction.* Edited by Susan Wood. New York: Perigee, 1980.
_____. *Words Are My Matter: Writings About Life and Books, 2000–2016.* Easthampton, Massachusetts: Small Beer Press, 2016.
Lewis, C. S. *Of Other Worlds: Essays and Stories.* Edited by Walter Hooper. New York: Harcourt Brace Jovanovich, 1966.
Link, Eric Carl, and Gerry Canavan, editors. *The Cambridge Companion to American Science Fiction.* Cambridge and New York: Cambridge University Press, 2015.
Lundwall, Sam J. *Science Fiction: An Illustrated History.* 1977. New York: Grosset, 1978.
_____. *Science Fiction: What It's All About.* New York: Ace Books, 1971. Revision, expansion, and translation of book published in Sweden in 1969.
Magill, Frank N., editor. *Survey of Science Fiction Literature.* 5 volumes. Englewood Cliffs, NJ: Salem Press, 1979.
Malzberg, Barry N. *The Bend at the End of the Road.* New York: Fantastic Books, 2018.
_____. *Breakfast in the Ruins: Science Fiction in the Last Millennium.* New York: Baen Books, 2007.
_____. *The Engines of the Night: Science Fiction in the Eighties.* 1982. New York: Bluejay Books, 1984.
McConnell, Frank. *The Science of Fiction and the Fiction of Science: Collected Essays on SF Storytelling and the Gnostic Imagination.* Edited by Gary Westfahl. Foreword by Neil Gaiman. North Carolina: McFarland Publishers, 2009.
McGiveron, Rafeeq, editor. *Critical Insights: Robert A. Heinlein.* Ipswich, Massachusetts: Salem Press, 2015.

Mendlesohn, Farah. *The Inter-Galactic Playground: A Critical Study of Children's and Teens' Science Fiction*. Jefferson, North Carolina: McFarland, 2009.

Merril, Judith. *The Merril Theory of Lit'ry Criticism: Judith Merril's Nonfiction*. Edited by Ritch Calvin. Seattle, Washington: Aqueduct Press, 2016.

Morrison, Grant. *Supergods: What Masked Vigilantes, Miraculous Mutants, and a Sun God from Smallville Can Teach Us about Being Human*. New York: Spiegel & Grau, 2011.

Moskowitz, Sam. *Explorers of the Infinite: Shapers of Science Fiction*. Cleveland: World Publishing Company, 1963.

_____. *The Immortal Storm: A History of Science Fiction Fandom*. Westport, Connecticut: Hyperion Press, 1974.

_____. *Seekers of Tomorrow: Masters of Modern Science Fiction*. Cleveland: World Publishing Company, 1966.

_____. *Strange Horizons: The Spectrum of Science Fiction*. New York: Scribner's, 1976.

Nadis, Fred. *The Man from Mars: Ray Palmer's Amazing Pulp Journey*. New York: Jeremy P. Tarcher/Penguin, 2014.

Nevala-Lee, Alec. *Astounding: John W. Campbell, Isaac Asimov, Robert A. Heinlein, L. Ron Hubbard, and the Golden Age of Science Fiction*. New York: William Morrow Dey Street, 2018.

Nicholls, Peter, General Editor. David Langford and Brian Stableford, Contributors. *The Science in Science Fiction*. 1982. New York: Alfred A. Knopf, 1983.

Nicolson, Marjorie Hope. *Voyages to the Moon*. New York: Macmillan, 1948.

Panshin, Alexei, and Cory Panshin. *The World Beyond the Hill: Science Fiction and the Quest for Transcendence*. Los Angeles: Jeremy P. Tarcher, 1989.

Park, Paul. "The Shadow of Hard Science Fiction." *The New York Review of Science Fiction*, No. 38 (October, 1991), 1, 3–4.

Patterson, William H., Jr. *Robert A. Heinlein in Dialogue with His Century, Volume 1, 1907–1948: Learning Curve*. New York: Tor, 2010.

_____. *Robert A. Heinlein in Dialogue with His Century, Volume 2, 1948–1988: The Man Who Learned Better*. New York: Tor, 2014.

Peterson, Jay P., editor. *St. James Guide to Science Fiction Writers*. Detroit: Gale Research, 1996.

Pierce, John J. "The Literary Experience of Hard Science Fiction." *Science-Fiction Studies*, 20 (July, 1993), 176–183.

Platt, Charles. *Dreammakers: Science Fiction and Fantasy Writers at Work: Profiles*. New York: Ungar, 1987.

Pohl, Frederik. *The Way the Future Was: A Memoir*. New York: Ballantine, 1978.

Pringle, David. *Science Fiction: The 100 Best Novels*. London: Xanadu, 1985.

_____, general editor. *The Ultimate Encyclopedia of Science Fiction: The Definitive Illustrated Guide*. North Dighton, Massachusetts: JG Press, 1996.

Reid, Robin A., editor. *Women in Science Fiction and Fantasy*. Two volumes. Westport, Connecticut: Greenwood Press, 2009.

Resnick, Mike, and Barry N. Malzberg. *The Business of Science Fiction: Two Insiders Discuss Writing and Publishing*. Jefferson, North Carolina: McFarland, 2010.

Rieder, John. *Science Fiction and the Mass Cultural Genre System*. Middletown, Connecticut: Wesleyan University Press, 2017.

Roberts, Adam. *The History of Science Fiction*. Second Edition. New York: Palgrave/Macmillan, 2016.

_____. *Science Fiction*. Second Edition. London and New York: Routledge, 2010.

Robinson, Frank M. *Science Fiction of the 20th Century*. Portland, Oregon: Collectors Press, 1999.

Rogers, Alva. *A Requiem for Astounding*. Chicago: Advent Publishers, 1964.

Rollyson, Carl, editor. *Critical Survey of Long Fiction: Science Fiction Novelists*. Ipswich, Massachusetts, and Hackensack, New Jersey: Salem Press, 2012.

Rose, Mark. *Alien Encounters: Anatomy of Science Fiction*. Cambridge, Massachusetts: Harvard University Press, 1981.

Russ, Joanna. *The Country You Have Never Seen: Essays and Reviews*. Liverpool: Liverpool University Press, 2007.
_____. *To Write Like a Woman: Essays in Feminism and Science Fiction*. Bloomington: Indiana University Press 1995.
Sadoul, Jacques. *2000 A.D.: Illustrations from the Golden Age of Science Fiction Pulps*. 1973. Chicago: Henry Regnery, 1975.
Samuelson, David N. "Modes of Extrapolation: The Formulas of Hard Science Fiction." *Science-Fiction Studies*, 20 (July, 1993), 176–183.
Sands, Karen, and Marietta Frank. *Back in the Spaceship Again: Juvenile Science Fiction Series Since 1945*. Westport, Connecticut: Greenwood Press, 1999.
Sawyer, Andy, and Peter Wright, editors. *Teaching Science Fiction*. London: Palgrave/McMillan, 2011.
Scholes, Robert, and Eric S. Rabkin. *Science Fiction: History, Science, Vision*. Oxford and New York: Oxford University Press, 1977.
Searles, Baird, Martin Last, Beth Meacham, and Michael Franklin. *A Reader's Guide to Science Fiction*. New York: Avon Books, 1979.
Seed, David. *Science Fiction: A Very Short Introduction*. New York: Oxford University Press, 2011.
_____, editor. *A Companion to Science Fiction*. Oxford: Blackwell Publishers, 2005.
Shippey, Tom. *Hard Reading: Learning From Science Fiction*. Liverpool Science Fiction Texts and Studies 53. Liverpool: Liverpool University Press, 2016.
_____, consulting editor. A. J. Sobchak, project editor. *Magill's Guide to Science Fiction and Fantasy Literature*. 4 volumes. Pasadena, CA: Salem Press, 1996.
Shutt, Craig. *Baby Boomer Comics: The Wild, Wacky, Wonderful Comic Books of the 1960s*. Iola, Wisconsin: Krause Publications, 2003.
Silverberg, Robert. *Reflections and Refractions: Thoughts on Science Fiction, Science, and Other Matters*. Revised and Expanded Edition. New York: Nonstop Press, 2016.
Slusser, George and Eric S. Rabkin, editors. *Aliens: The Anthropology of Science Fiction*. Carbondale: Southern Illinois University Press, 1987.
_____, and Eric S. Rabkin, editors. *Hard Science Fiction*. Carbondale: Southern Illinois University Press, 1986.
Spinrad, Norman. "On Books: The Hard Stuff." *Isaac Asimov's Science Fiction Magazine*, 12 (March, 1988), 177–191.
_____. *Science Fiction in the Real World*. Carbondale: Southern Illinois University Press, 1990.
Stableford, Brian. *The Dictionary of Science Fiction Places*. New York: Fireside/Wonderland Press, 1999.
_____. "The Last Chocolate Bar and the Majesty of Truth: Reflections on the Concept of 'Hardness' in Science Fiction." *The New York Review of Science Fiction*, No. 71 (July, 1994), 1, 8–12, and No. 72 (August), 10–16.
Stong, Phil. "Foreword." *The Other Worlds*. Edited by Stong. New York: Wilfred Funk, Inc., 1941), 1–16.
Suvin, Darko. *Metamorphoses of Science Fiction: On the Poetics and History of a Literary Genre*. New Haven: Yale University Press, 1979.
_____. *Positions and Presuppositions in Science Fiction*. Kent, Ohio, and London: Kent State University Press, 1989.
Toronto, Richard. *War over Lemuria: Richard Shaver, Ray Palmer and the Strangest Chapter of 1940s Science Fiction*. Jefferson, North Carolina: McFarland Publishers, 2013.
Tucker, Wilson. [As Bob Tucker]. "Depts of the Interior" [sic]. *Le Zombie*, 4 (January, 1941), 8.
Tymn, Marshall B., and Mike Ashley, editors. *Science Fiction, Fantasy, and Weird Fiction Magazines*. Westport, Connecticut: Greenwood Press, 1986.
van Vogt, A. E. *Reflections of A .E. van Vogt: The Autobiography of a Science Fiction Giant*. Lakemont, Georgia: Fictioneer, 1975.

Vint, Sherryl. *Science Fiction: A Guide for the Perplexed*. London and New York: Bloomsbury Academic, 2014.
Warner, Harry, Jr., *All Our Yesterdays: An Informal History of Science Fiction Fandom in the Forties*. Chicago: Advent Publishers, 1969.
_____. *A Wealth of Fable: An Informal History of Science Fiction Fandom in the 1950s*. Edited by Dick Lynch. Van Nuys, California: SCIFI Press, 1992.
Webster, Bud. *Anthropology 101: Reflections, Inspections and Dissections of SF Anthologies*. West Warwick, Rhode Island: Merry Blacksmith Press, 2010.
_____. *Past Masters, and Other Bookish Natterings*. West Warwick: Merry Blacksmith Press, 2013.
Westfahl, Gary. *An Alien Abroad: Science Fiction Columns from Interzone*. [Rockville, Maryland]: Wildside Press, 2016.
_____. *Cosmic Engineers: A Study of Hard Science Fiction*. Westport, CT: Greenwood Press, 1996.
_____. "Guest Editor's Pad: Combativeness and Science Fiction, or, Look Forward in Anger." *Extrapolation*, 41 (Spring, 2000), 3-6.
_____. *Hugo Gernsback and the Century of Science Fiction*. Jefferson, North Carolina: McFarland Publishers, 2007.
_____. *The Mechanics of Wonder: The Creation of the Idea of Science Fiction*. Liverpool: Liverpool University Press, 1998.
_____, editor. *The Greenwood Encyclopedia of Science Fiction and Fantasy: Themes, Works, and Wonders*. Advisory Board Richard Bleiler, John Clute, Fiona Kelleghan, David Langford, Andy Sawyer, and Darrell Schweitzer. Foreword by Neil Gaiman. Three volumes. Westport, Connecticut: Greenwood Press, 2005.
_____, editor. *Space and Beyond: The Frontier Theme in Science Fiction*. Westport, Connecticut: Greenwood Press, 2000.
_____, and George Slusser, editors. *Nursery Realms: Children in the Worlds of Science Fiction, Fantasy, and Horror*. Athens, Georgia: University of Georgia Press, 1999.
_____, George Slusser, and Eric S. Rabkin, editors. *Science Fiction and Market Realities*. Athens: University of Georgia Press, 1996.
_____, Gregory Benford, Howard V. Hendrix, and Jonathan Alexander, editors. *Science Fiction and the Dismal Science: Essays on Economics in and of the Genre*. Jefferson, North Carolina: McFarland Publishers, forthcoming.
_____, and George Slusser, editors. *Science Fiction, Canonization, Marginalization, and the Academy*. Westport, Connecticut: Greenwood Press, 2002.
_____, George Slusser, and Kathleen Church Plummer, editors. *Unearthly Visions: Approaches to Science Fiction and Fantasy Art*. Westport, Connecticut: Greenwood Press, 2002.
Williamson, Jack. *Wonder's Child: My Life in Science Fiction*. New York: Bluejay, 1984.
Winter, Jerome. *Science Fiction, Space Opera and Neoliberal Globalism*. Cardiff: University of Wales Press, 2016.
Wolfe, Gary K. *Critical Terms for Science Fiction and Fantasy: A Glossary and Guide to Scholarship*. Westport, CT: Greenwood Press, 1986.
_____. *Evaporating Genres: Essays on Fantastic Literature*. Middletown, Connecticut: Wesleyan University Press, 2011.
_____. *The Known and the Unknown: The Iconography of Science Fiction*. Kent, Ohio: Kent State University Press, 1979.
Wollheim, Donald A. "Introduction." *The Pocket Book of Science-Fiction*. Edited by Wollheim. New York: Pocket Books, 1943, viii-x.
_____. "Introduction." *The Portable Novels of Science*. Edited by Wollheim. New York: Viking Press, 1945, vii-xiii.
_____. *The Universe Makers: Science Fiction Today*. New York: Harper, 1971.

Index

AAA Ace Interplanetary Decontamination series (Sheckley) 91
Abe, Kōbō 20, 192; *Inter Ice Age 4* 192
Ace-High Magazine 27
The Ace Science Fiction Reader (Wollheim) 140
Ackerman, Forrest J 12, 104, 161, 166, 216, 230; "Introduction" 104
Action Comics 166–167
Adam Strange comics 89, 173–174, 239
Adams, Douglas 92–93; *The Hitchhiker's Guide to the Galaxy* 92; The Hitchhiker's Guide to the Galaxy series 92–93; *Life, the Universe, and Everything* 92; *Mostly Harmless* 92; *The Restaurant at the End of the Universe* 92; *So Long, and Thanks for All the Fish* 92
Adams, Neal 177
Adamski, George 119–120, 157; *Flying Saucers Have Landed* (with Leslie) 119–120, 123, 157
"The Adaptive Ultimate" (Weinbaum) 133, 162–163
Adventure Comics 167
Adventures in Time and Space (Healy and McComas) 124, 125, 127, 140, 145–147
Adventures of the Batman (Greenberg) 219–220
Adventures to Come (Esenwein) 125, 127–131, 136
After Things Fell Apart (Goulart) 211
After Worlds End (Williamson) 63
Again, Dangerous Visions (Ellison) 229
Against the Fall of Night (Clarke) 63–64, 67, 73, 190
Air Wonder Stories 43–44, 234
"The Airlords of Han" (Nowlan) 31–32, 36, 67
Alas, Babylon (Frank) 244

Alderson, Dan 193
Aldiss, Brian W. 20, 23, 30, 32, 39–41, 48, 51, 75, 78, 84, 92, 110, 195, 221–222, 223–224, 229, 254n, 257–258n; *Barefoot in the Head* 229; *Billion Year Spree* 40; *The Eighty-Minute Hour* 84, 92; Helliconia series 195; *Helliconia Spring* 195; *Helliconia Summer* 195; *Helliconia Winter* 195; *The Malecia Tapestry* 84; *A Report on Probability* 229; *Science Fiction Art* 40–41, 75, 221–222; *Space Opera* 92; *Trillion Year Spree* (with Wingrove) 40
Alger, Martin 80
Alien 94, 113
Alien films 94, 240
"All" (Campbell) 32, 67–68
All-Story 238
"All the Time in the World" 162
"All the Time in the World" (Clarke) 162
"'All You Zombies—'" (Heinlein) 112
Allen, Irwin 218, 220
Alliance series (Cherryh) 94–95
Alphaville 20
Alter Ego 219
Alternate Kennedys (Resnick) 150
Alternate Tyrants (Resnick) 150
Alternate Worlds (Gunn) 137
"Amazing Life" (Gernsback) 22
"An Amazing Phenomenon" (Gernsback) 22
"The Amazing Space-Flight of North America" (Binder) 172
Amazing Stories 8, 9, 10, 11, 12, 14, 21–38, 40, 42–43, 51–52, 57, 59, 72–73, 79, 87, 99–100, 116–117, 118–119, 129–130, 131, 134, 144, 146–147, 154, 159, 184, 224, 233–234, 251n, 256n, 257n
Amazing Stories Quarterly 21, 24–25
"Amazing Thinking" (Gernsback) 22

Index

"The Amazing Unknown" (Gernsback) 21, 22–23
American Legion Magazine 155–156
American Science Fiction: Four Classic Novels, 1953–1956 (Wolfe) 140
American Science Fiction: Five Classic Novels, 1956–1958 (Wolfe) 140
Amis, Kingsley 49–50, 159–160; *New Maps of Hell* 49–50, 159–160
Analog: Science Fact/Science Fiction 191–192, 237–238
Analog: Science Fiction/Science Fact 52, 181, 191–192, 194, 237–238
"The Analytical Laboratory" (Campbell) 108
Ancient Aliens 227–228
"And a Star to Steer Her By" (Correy) 188
"'—And He Built a Crooked House—'" (Heinlein) 236–237
Anders, Lou 241–242
Anderson, Gerry 218
Anderson, Kevin J. 72, 145, 151; *Assemblers of Infinity* (with Beason) 151; *Slan Hunter* (with van Vogt) 72; *The War of the Worlds: Global Dispatches* 145
Anderson, Poul 91, 158, 183, 189, 190, 196, 212, 230, 239, 244; *Brain Wave* 190; "The Creation of Imaginary Worlds" 190; Dominic Flandry series 91, 239; *The High Crusade* 91; *Is There Life on Other Worlds?* 158; Nicholas van Rijn series 91, 238; *Tau Zero* 190; *A World Named Cleopatra* (with Elwood) 190
Anderson, Sylvia 218
Anderson, Taylor 243–244
The Angry Red Planet 117
Another Science Fiction (Prelinger) 177–178
Anthony, Piers 126–127; *Uncollected Stars* (with Malzberg, Greenberg, and Waugh) 126–127
Anthropology 101 (Webster) 101
"Anthropology 101" articles (Webster) 101
The Anticipation Novelists of 1950s French Science Fiction (Lyau) 252n
Apollo at Go (Sutton) 227
Appleseed (Clute) 95–96
Appleton, Victor (pseudonym) 128
Appleton, Victor, II (pseudonym) 188; *Tom Swift, Jr. and His Outpost in Space* 188
Aquaman comics 166
Arcot, Morey, and Wade series (Campbell) 36
Argosy 155–156
"Armageddon 2419 A.D." (Nowlan) 21, 29–33, 36, 37, 67

Armageddon 2419 A.D. (Nowlan) 16, 67, 75, 253n
Arnold, Jack 128, 129; "A Life by Television" 129
Arnold, Kenneth 159; *The Coming of the Saucers* (with Palmer) 159
Artsutanov, Yuri 193
The Ascent of Wonder (Hartwell and Cramer) 54–56
Ash, Brian 80
Asimov, Isaac 13, 17–18, 19, 62, 69–70, 71, 72, 73, 75, 81, 90, 101, 109, 113, 116, 126, 127, 137, 156–158, 159, 161–162, 186, 189, 196, 197–201, 202, 204–205, 206, 212, 215, 218, 223–224, 226, 230, 236, 238–239, 244, 258n; *Asimov's Guide to Shakespeare* 226; *Before the Golden Age* 62, 75, 127; *Biochemistry and Human Metabolism* (with Walker and Boyd) 159; *Building Blocks of the Universe* 159; *The Caves of Steel* 70, 114; *The Chemicals of Life* 159; *Chemistry and Human Health* (with Walker and Nicholas) 159; *David Starr, Space Ranger* 196, 197–201; *Fantastic Voyage* 218; *Foundation* 113; *Foundation and Empire* 113; Foundation series 70, 81, 113, 156–157; *I, Robot* 69–70, 113; *Inside the Atom* 159; *Lucky Starr and the Big Sun of Mercury* 198; *Lucky Starr and the Moons of Jupiter* 198; *Lucky Starr and the Oceans of Venus* 198; *Lucky Starr and the Pirates of the Asteroids* 196, 197–201; *Lucky Starr and the Rings of Saturn* 198; Lucky Starr series 174, 196, 197–201, 202, 206, 238–239; *The Naked Sun* 70; "Nightfall" 113; *Only a Trillion* 159; *Pebble in the Sky* 157; *Races and People* (with Boyd) 159; *Robots and Empire* 70; *The Robots of Dawn* 70; Robots series 81, 113; *Second Foundation* 113
Asimov's Guide to Shakespeare (Asimov) 226
Asimov's Science Fiction 241
Assemblers of Infinity (Anderson and Beason) 151
Asteroids (video game) 221
Astonishing Stories 116–117
Astounding Days (Clarke) 18, 62, 247
Astounding Science-Fiction 16, 18, 41, 45, 47–48, 52, 56, 63, 66, 72, 80, 81–82, 86, 99, 100, 101, 104, 105, 107, 111–115, 118, 121, 144, 146, 176, 177, 186, 189, 190, 191–192, 235–236, 237, 241, 244, 257n, 262n
The Astounding Science Fiction Anthology (Campbell) 75
Astounding Stories 16, 46–47, 56, 65, 78–

79, 99, 100, 111, 131, 146–147, 185–186, 235, 257n, 262n
Astounding Stories of Super-Science 78–79
"At the Center of Gravity" (Rocklynne) 186
Atom comics 166, 174
Atomic Knights comics 173
The Atomic Story (Campbell) 158
The Atomic Submarine 176
Attack of the 50-Foot Woman 176
Attebery, Brian 61; *The Norton Book of Science Fiction* (with Le Guin) 61
Austin, Frank E. 251n
Aviation Week 177–178

Babel-17 (Delany) 231
Baby Boomer Comics (Shutt) 171
Babylon 5 240
Bacigulapi, Paolo 244
Baen, Jim 241–242
Bailey, J.O. 1, 159; *Pilgrims Through Space and Time* 1, 159
Bails, Jerry 219
"Balance of Terror" 93
Ballantine, Betty 157, 238
Ballantine, Ian 157, 238
Ballard, J.G. 20, 54–56, 156, 180
Balmer, Edwin 144, 162–163; *When Worlds Collide* (with Wylie) 162–163
Banks, Iain M. 96, 244; *Consider Phlebas* 96; Culture series 96
Bantha Tracks 217
Barefoot in the Head (Aldiss) 229
Barrett, C.L. 213
Barrow, Marjorie 130; *Science Fiction and Reader's Guide* 130
Barton, Samuel G. 251n
Bass, Saul 175
Bates, Harry 19, 80, 162–163, 179; "Farewell to the Master" 162–163; *Space Hawk* (with Hall) 80
Batman (TV series) 220
Batman comics 117, 166, 219–220
Battle Beyond the Stars 94
Battlestar Galactica 94
Baudrillard, Jean 246
Baxter, Stephen 195
Bear, Greg 94, 183, 194–195, 244; *Blood Music* 194–195; *Hegira* 194–195
Beason, Doug 151; *Assemblers of Infinity* (with Anderson) 151
The Beast from 20,000 Fathoms 162–163
Beaumont, Charles 162
"Becalmed in Hell" (Niven) 192
Beck, Clyde F. 15, 100; *Hammer and Tongs* 15, 100

"Beep" (Blish) 130
Before the Dawn (Taine) 136, 138, 139
Before the Golden Age (Asimov) 62, 75, 127
Bellaire, D.P. 103
Bellamy, Edward 138; *Looking Backward* 138
Belloc, Hilaire 138; *The Man Who Made Gold* 138
Benét, Stephen Vincent 134, 155; "By the Waters of Babylon" 155
Benford, Gregory 13, 64, 94, 150, 182, 183, 189, 194, 207–208; *Beyond Infinity* 64; *Beyond the Fall of Night* 64; *Jupiter Project* 194, 207–208; *Timescape* 194; *What Might Have Been, Volume 1* (with Greenberg) 150
Beresford, J.D. 138; *The Hampdenshire Wonder* 138
Bergey, Earle K. 45, 55, 254n
The Best Alternate History Stories of the 20th Century (Turtledove and Greenberg) 149
The Best Military Science Fiction Stories of the 20th Century (Turtledove and Greenberg) 149
The Best of Science Fiction (Conklin) 124, 125, 127, 140–144, 147, 154–155
The Best Time Travel Stories of the 20th Century (Turtledove and Greenberg) 149
Bester, Alfred 90, 114, 165, 212, 215, 224
Between Planets (Heinlein) 206–207
Beyond Infinity (Benford) 64
Beyond Jupiter (Clarke) 222
Beyond the Fall of Night (Benford) 64
Beyond the Solar System (Ley) 222
Beyond This Horizon (Heinlein) 69, 236–237
Bierce, Ambrose 134, 144; "The Damned Thing" 134; "Moxon's Master" 134
The Big Book of Science Fiction (VanderMeer and VanderMeer) 147, 149
The Big Sleep 74
The Big Trick and Puzzle Book (Keasbey) 23–24
The Big X (Searls) 227
Bill, the Galactic Hero (Harrison) 92
Billion Year Spree (Aldiss) 40
Binder, Eando 12, 158
Binder, Earl 12
Binder, Otto 12, 158, 172, 175; "The Amazing Space-Flight of North America" 175; "The Lady and the Lion" 170; *The Moon* 158; *Planets* 158
Biochemistry and Human Metabolism (Asimov, Boyd, and Walker) 159

280　　　　　　　　　　　Index

Bird, Cordwainer *see* Ellison, Harlan
Bitting, Frederick 23, 25
Bixby, Jerome 126–127, 162, 217, 218, 239; "It's a *Good* Life" 126, 139; "Little Boy" 126–127
Bizarro comics 168
Black Cats and Broken Mirrors (Greenberg and Helfers) 150
The Black Cloud (Hoyle) 190
"Black Destroyer" (van Vogt) 101–105, 107, 108, 113
The Black Hole 94
Blade Runner 176
Bleiler, E.F. 31, 75, 139–140; *Science-Fiction: The Gernsback Years* (with Bleiler) 31; *The Year's Best Science Fiction Novels* anthologies (with Dikty) 139–140
Bleiler, Richard 31, 75; *Science-Fiction: The Gernsback Years* (with Bleiler) 31
Blish, James 78, 130, 161–162, 191, 212, 218, 224, 240; "Beep" 130; *Spock Must Die!* 240; *Star Trek* 218, 224, 240; *Star Trek* series 218, 224
Bloch, Robert 156, 212, 214, 218
Blood Music (Bear) 194–195
"Blowups Happen" (Heinlein) 236–237
"The Blue Behemoth" (Brackett) 73–74
Blue Book 155–156, 238
"The Blue Men of Yrano" (Van Lorne) 101
The Body Snatchers (Finney) 162–163
Bodyguard and Four Other Short Science Fiction Novels from Galaxy (Gold) 126, 160
Bok, Hannes 57, 175, 256n
Bond, Nelson 155, 162; *Exiles of Time* 155
Bonestell, Chesley 47–48, 55, 176–177, 187, 232
Borderlands (video game) 244
"Born of the Sun" (Williamson) 88
Bosch, Hieronymus 51
Boucher, Anthony 48, 114, 124, 165–166, 214, 237
Boulle, Pierre 20, 192, 217–218; *Planet of the Apes* 192, 217–218
Bourbon Street Beat 162
Bova, Ben 183, 192, 193, 195; *Colony* 193; *The Weathermakers* 192
Boyd, William C. 159; *Biochemistry and Human Metabolism* (with Asimov and Walker) 159; *Races and People* (with Asimov) 159
Boys' Life 155–156
Bracken, Alexandra 208–209; *The Darkest Minds* 208; Darkest Minds series 208
Brackett, Leigh 73–74, 90, 109, 115; "The Blue Behemoth" 73–74; *The Coming of the Terrans* 74; "The Dancing Girl of Ganymede" 74; "The Jewel of Bas" 73, 115; *Lorelei of the Red Mist* 73–74; "Lorelei of the Red Mist" (with Bradbury) 73–74; "Quest of the Starhope" 73–74; "Thrall of the Endless Night" 74, 115; "The Veil of Astrellar" 74
Bradbury, Ray 13, 61, 73–74, 109, 114, 115, 136, 155, 156, 157–158, 162–163, 166, 212, 218, 223–224; *Fahrenheit 451*, 61, 157; "The Fog Horn" 162–163; "Frost and Fire" 74, 115; "Lorelei of the Red Mist" (with Brackett) 73–74; "Mars Is Heaven" 115; *The Martian Chronicles* 61, 74, 115, 157; *Timeless Stories for Today and Tomorrow* 136
Bradley, Marion Zimmer 212
"Brain" (Wright) 146
The Brain Eaters 163
Brain Wave (Anderson) 190
The Brave and the Bold 263n
Brave New World (Huxley) 138
Brennan, John F. 90
Bretnor, Reginald 159; *Modern Science Fiction* 159
Breuer, Miles J. 24, 25
Brick Bradford (comic strip) 16, 89, 154, 235
Brick Bradford (serial) 16, 89, 235
Bright, Laura 217
Brin, David 83–84, 94, 183, 194–195; "The Crystal Spheres" 83–84; "Running Out of Speculative Niches" 195; *Startide Rising* 194–195; *Sundiver* 194–195
Briney, Robert P. 224–225
British Future Fiction, 1700–1914 (Clarke) 140
Brooks, Terry 242
Brown, Fredric 45, 162; *What Mad Universe* 45
Brown, Howard V. 46–48, 55, 254n, 255n
Brown, Reynold 176
Brunner, John 90, 157, 207, 229, 231, 238, 244; *Stand on Zanzibar* 207, 231, 244
Buck Rogers (comic strip) 16, 21, 31, 32, 36, 75, 89, 128, 129–130, 154–155, 164, 178, 235, 238
Buck Rogers (serial) 16, 21, 89, 164, 178, 238
Buck Rogers in the Twenty-Fifth Century (TV series) 94
Buckskin 162
Budrys, Algis 191
Bugs Bunny cartoons 164
Building Blocks of the Universe (Asimov) 159

Bujold, Lois McMaster 94–95, 243; *Miles Vorkosigan* series 94, 243
Bullwinkle comics 174–175
Bulmer, Kenneth 229
Burke's Law 162
Burks, Arthur J. 101; "The First Shall Be Last" 101
Burroughs, Edgar Rice 7, 29, 72–73, 74, 138, 166, 173, 223–224, 239; *Llana of Gathol* 72–73; Mars series 72–73, 158, 166, 173, 239; *A Princess of Mars* 72–73; Tarzan series 239
Burroughs, William S. 227; *Nova Express* 227
"But Without Honor" (Page) 138
Butler, Octavia E. 182, 183, 195, 244; *Wild Seed* 195
"By His Bootstraps" (Heinlein) 112, 121, 236–237
"By the Waters of Babylon" (Benét) 155

Caidin, Martin 227; *Four Came Back* 227; *The Long Night* 227; *Marooned* 227
Calkins, Gregg 213
Calvin, John 106
Campbell, Jack 243–244
Campbell, John W., Jr. 1–2, 8, 14–15, 16–18, 19, 20, 32, 36, 41, 42, 46–49, 52, 63, 66, 72, 75, 79, 81–82, 88, 89, 90, 99–101, 102, 10, 3, 104, 107, 108–109, 111–115, 116, 118, 121, 123, 131, 133, 134, 137, 138, 140–142, 144, 145, 146, 154–155, 158, 162, 181, 184–186, 188, 190–192, 206, 212, 214, 230, 234, 235–238, 239, 241, 242, 244, 255*n*, 257*n*, 261*n*, 262*n*; "All" 32, 67–68; "The Analytical Laboratory" 108; Arcot, Morey, and Wade series 36, 88; *The Astounding Science Fiction Anthology* 75; *The Atomic Story* 158; "Concerning Science Fiction" 140–142, 154–155; "History to Come" 17; "In Times to Come" (July 1939) 107; "In Times to Come" (June 1939) 103; "The Irrelevant" 184; *Islands of Space* 191; *The Mightiest Machine* 16–17; "Piracy Preferred" 36; *The Space Beyond* 67; "Space Rays" 16–17, 79, 185; "Twilight" 16–17, 111, 133, 235; "Who Goes There?" 16–17, 111, 162–163, 235, 261*n*
"Can We Get to Mars?" (von Braun and Ryan) 176
A Canticle for Leibowitz (Miller) 61, 244
Captain Comet comics 89, 239
Captain Future 89, 116–117, 235, 237
Captain Future series (Hamilton) 81, 89
Captain Video and His Video Rangers 89, 161–162, 239, 263*n*

Card, Orson Scott 192, 208, 209; *Ender's Game* 208, 209
Carnell, John 13, 148, 214; *New Writings in SF* anthologies 148
Carr, John F. 148; *Endless Frontier* anthologies (with Pournelle) 148
Carr, Terry 50, 131, 148, 224; *Science Fiction for People Who Hate Science Fiction* 131; *Universe* anthologies 148
Carter, Paul A. 11, 57, 224; *The Creation of Tomorrow* 57
Cartier, Edd 175
cartoons 164, 175
Cat-Women of the Moon 176
"The Cavern of Deadly Spheres" (Fox) 219
The Caves of Steel (Asimov) 70, 114
The Centrifugal Rickshaw Dancer (Watkins) 193
The Challenge of the Spaceship (Clarke) 158
Challengers of the Unknown 174
Chandler, A. Bertram 19, 252*n*
Chariot of the Gods? (von Däniken) 227–228
The Chemicals of Life (Asimov) 159
Chemistry and Human Health (Asimov, Nicholas, and Walker) 159
Cherijo Grey Veil series (Viehl) 94
Cherryh, C.J. 94–95, 96, 195; Alliance series 94–95, 195; *Downbelow Station* 195
Cheyenne 162
Chiang, Ted 124
Childhood's End (Clarke) 61, 121, 157, 190–191, 247
Chiller 165
Christopher, John 19, 155
Cimarron Strip 162
Cioffi, Frank 80
"Cities in the Air" (Hamilton) 43
Citizen Kane 176
Citizen of the Galaxy (Heinlein) 206–207
City (Simak) 75, 112
The City and the Stars (Clarke) 64, 190
City of Illusions (Le Guin) 32
"The City of the Living Flame" (Hasse) 115–116
City on the Moon (Leinster) 188
Clans of the Alphane Moon (Dick) 248
Claremont, Chris 94, 219; Nicole Shea series 94
Clareson, Thomas D. 228
Clarke, Arthur C. 10, 13, 19, 48, 54, 61, 62, 63–64, 73, 90, 97, 109, 114, 121, 126, 155–158, 162, 183, 186, 188, 190–191, 193, 194, 195, 196, 197, 199, 201–203, 217, 222, 223–224, 238, 244, 247, 248–249, 256*n*,

263n; *Against the Fall of Night* 63–64, 67, 73, 190; "All the Time in the World" 162; *Astounding Days* 19, 62, 247; *Beyond Jupiter* 222; *The Challenge of the Spaceship* 158; *Childhood's End* 61, 114, 121, 157, 190–191, 238; *The City and the Stars* 64, 190; *The Coast of Coral* 158; *Dolphin Island* 196, 201–202; *Earthlight* 188; "Ego and the Dying Planet" 63; *The Exploration of Space* 158; *The Exploration of the Moon* 158; *A Fall of Moondust* 188; *The Fountains of Paradise* 193, 194; "Hide and Seek" 186; *Interplanetary Flight* 158; *Islands in the Sky* 188, 196, 201–202; *The Making of a Moon* 158; "A Meeting with Medusa" 156; "The Other Side of the Sky" 188; *Prelude to Space* 54, 90, 188, 189; Rama series (with Lee) 193; *Rendezvous with Rama* 193; *Sands of Mars* 188; "The Secret" 155–156; "The Sentinel" 121; *Tales from the White Hart* 256n; *2001: A Space Odyssey* 64, 121; "Venture to the Moon" 188; "We Can Rocket to the Moon—Now!" 63; *The Young Traveller in Space* 158
Clarke, I.F. 140; *British Future Fiction, 1700–1914*, 140
Clement, Hal 10, 48, 55, 56, 109, 182, 183, 186, 189–190, 194, 196–197, 233–234, 236; "Fireproof" 182; *Mission of Gravity* 185, 189–190, 193; *Needle* 190; *The Nitrogen Fix* 194; "Proof" 186; "Whirligig World" 189–190
Cleopatra 168
Clues 27
Clute, John 95–96; *Appleseed* 95–96
The Coast of Coral (Clarke) 158
Cogswell, Theodore R. 130; "The Specter General" 130
"The Cold Equations" (Godwin) 126, 181
"The Coldest Place" (Niven) 192
Cole, Dandridge M. 194
Cole, Robert W. 86; *The Struggle for Empire* 86
Collier, John 134
Collier's magazine 176–177
Collins, Suzanne 208, 209; *The Hunger Games* 208; The Hunger Games series 208, 209
Colony (Bova) 193
Combat! 162
Comet (Sagan) 222
The Comet 11
comic books 16, 89, 116–117, 165–175, 200–201, 215, 216, 219–220, 221, 222, 239, 256n, 263n

"The Coming of the Ice" (Wertenbaker) 28
The Coming of the Saucers (Arnold and Palmer) 159
The Coming of the Terrans (Brackett) 74
"Common Sense" (Heinlein) 236
Conan series (Howard) 156–157
Conan Doyle, Arthur 144, 150; Sherlock Holmes series 150
"Concerning Science Fiction" (Campbell) 140–142, 154–155
Conklin, Groff 124, 125, 127, 140–146, 147, 154–155; *The Best of Science Fiction* 124, 125, 127, 140–144, 154–155; *Enemies in Space* 144–145; *Great Science Fiction about Doctors* (with Fabricant) 145; *Great Stories of Space Travel* 144–145; "Introduction" 140, 147; *Invaders of Earth* 145; *Science Fiction Adventures in Dimension* 144–145; *Science Fiction Adventures in Mutation* 145; *Science-Fiction Thinking Machines* 145
A Connecticut Yankee in King Arthur's Court (Twain) 144
Conquest of Space 176, 188
The Conquest of Space (Ley) 177, 222
Consider Phlebas (Banks) 95
Corben, Richard 177
Correy, Lee 188, 194; "And a Star to Steer Her By" 188; "The Plains of St. Augustine" 188; *Shuttle Down* 194
Cosmic Engineers (Westfahl) 3, 189
The "Cosmic Frame" (Fairman) 162–163
Cosmos (magazine) 214
Cosmos (TV series) 222
Coulson, Robert 214, 218
Countdown 227
"Coventry" (Heinlein) 69, 236–237
Cover, Arthur Byron 93; *Planetfall* 93; *Stationfall* 93
"The Crab Lice" (Feeley) 150
Cramer, Kathryn 54–56, 148–149, 242; *The Ascent of Wonder* (with Hartwell) 56–55; "Our Pious Hope" 242
Crane, Ted 103
The Creation of Tomorrow (Carter) 57
The Creature from the Black Lagoon 176
"The Creatures of Man" (Myers) 126–127
"The Creatures That Time Forgot" *see* "Frost and Fire"
"Crossing the Space Frontier" (von Braun) 176
"The Crystal Spheres" (Brin) 83–84
Ctein 193
Cthulhu Mythos series (Lovecraft) 118
Culture series (Banks) 96

Cummings, Ray 89
Cunningham, Lew 102, 103
"Curiosities" (Webster) 125
"Curiosities" articles 125
cyberpunk 41–42, 52, 53, 55, 57, 58, 182, 258n

Daffy Duck cartoons 164
"The Damned Thing" (Bierce) 134
"The Dancing Girl of Ganymede" (Brackett) 74
Dangerous Visions (Ellison) 127, 229, 238, 255n
Dangerous Visions anthologies (Ellison) 124–125, 255n
The Dark Destroyers (Wellman) 100–101
The Dark Forest (Liu) 96–97, 195
The Darkest Minds (Bracken) 208
Darkest Minds series (Bracken) 208
Darrow, Jack 12
The D.A.'s Man 162
Dashner, James 208, 209; *The Maze Runner* 208; The Maze Runner series 208
Davenport, Basil 159; *The Science Fiction Novel* 159
David Starr, Space Ranger (Asimov) 196, 197–201
Davin, Eric Leif 62; *Partners in Wonder* 62
Davis, Don 222
The Day the Earth Stood Still 162–163
"Dead Planet" (Hamilton) 89
"Deadly City" (Fairman) 162–163
Dean, Roger 177
Death's End (Liu) 96–97, 195
de Camp, L. Sprague 100, 158–159, 212, 224–225, 244, 248; *Energy and Power* 158–159; *Engines* 158–159; "The Incorrigible" 100; *Lands Beyond* 158–159; *Lost Continents* 158–159; *Lovecraft: A Biography* 158–159; *Man and Power* 158–159; *The Science Fiction Handbook* 159
Decline of the West (Spengler) 103
Delany, Samuel R. 148, 231, 238; *Babel-17*, 231; *The Einstein Intersection* 231; *Quark* anthologies (with Hacker) 148
de la Ree, Gerry 104, 213
del Rey, Judy-Lynn 148; *Stellar* anthologies 148
del Rey, Lester 81, 133, 158, 188, 196, 221–222, 254n; *Fantastic Science Fiction Art 1926-1954*, 221–222; "Helen O'Loy" 81, 133; *It's Your Atomic Story* 158; *Mission to the Moon* 188; *Moon of Mutiny* 188; *The Mysterious Earth* 158; *The Mysterious Sea* 158; "The Pipes of Pan" 133; *Rockets Through Space* 158; *Rocks and What They Tell Us* 158; *Space Flight* 158; *Step to the Stars* 188
Demon (Varley) 194
"Design for Great-Day" (Russell) 49
Destination Moon 90, 161, 176, 187–188, 190, 204
DeWeese, Gene 218
"Dialogues" (Resnick and Malzberg) 239–241
DiChario, Nicholas A. 150; "The Winterberry" 150
Dick, Philip K. 18, 40, 71, 72, 74, 76, 110, 113, 114, 123, 126, 157, 207, 225–226, 231, 236–237, 238, 248; *Clans of the Alphane Moon* 248; *Do Androids Dream of Electric Sheep?* 74, 207, 231; *Galactic Pot-Healer* 248; "Null-O" 126
Dickson, Gordon R. 188
Dietz, William C. 243–244
Di Fate, Vincent 57
Dikty, T.E. 139–140; *The Year's Best Science Fiction Novels* anthologies (with Bleiler) 139–140
Dille, John F. 31
Dillon, Diane 50–51 55, 224, 255n
Dillon, Leo 50–51, 55, 224, 255n
Disch, Thomas M. 218, 224; *The Prisoner* 218, 224
"Discord in Scarlet" (van Vogt) 103
Discworld series (Pratchett) 243
Disneyland 163–164
"The Distortion of the Product" (Hartwell) 242
Ditko, Steve 174
Do Androids Dream of Electric Sheep? (Dick) 74, 207, 231
Dobbs, D.L. 108
Doc Savage series 167
"Dr. Hackensaw's Secrets" series (Fezandié) 26
Doctor Who 217, 218, 240, 244
Doctor Who novels 240, 244
Dolphin Island (Clarke) 196, 201–202
Dominic Flandry series (Anderson) 91, 239
Donald Duck cartoons 175
"Donovan's Brain" 163
Donovan's Brain 162–163
Donovan's Brain (Siodmak) 162–163
"The Doomsday Machine" 93
Dos Passos, John 50
Downbelow Station (Cherryh) 195
Dozois, Gardner 150, 241; *The Year's Best Science Fiction* anthologies 150
Dragon's Egg (Forward) 194
The Dragons of Eden (Sagan) 222

Drake, David A. 149; *The Fleet* anthologies (with Fawcett) 149
Druillet, Philippe 177
"Duck Dodgers in the 24 1/2 Century" 164
Duncan, David 162, 217
Dune (Herbert) 78, 190
Dune series (Herbert) 190
Dungeons and Dragons (novels) 240, 242
Dungeons and Dragons (role-playing game) 94, 240, 242
Dunsany, Lord 25
Dynamic Science Fiction 99
Dyson, Freeman 193

Earthlight (Clarke) 188
Eclipse Three (Strahan) 59
Eddings, David 242
Eddings, Leigh 242
Edison, Thomas Alva 8
Edison's Conquest of Mars (Serviss) 86
Edwards, Frank 227; *Flying Saucers—Serious Business* 227
Egan, Greg 183, 195
"Ego and the Dying Planet" (Clarke) 63
Ehrlich, Max 162
The Eighty-Minute Hour (Aldiss) 84, 92
Einstein, Albert 8, 105
The Einstein Intersection (Delany) 231
Elam, Richard M., Jr. 130; *Teen-Age Science Fiction Stories* 130; *Teen-Age Super Science Stories* 130
Elastic Lad comics 167–168
"Elayn of Troyius" 83
The Electronic Monster 162–163
Eliot, T.S. 96; *The Waste Land* 96
Eliott, E.C. 238–239; *Kemlo and the Crazy Planet* 238–239; Kemlo series 238–239
Ellis, Dean 48
Ellison, Harlan 13, 41, 50–51, 78, 124–125, 132–133, 162, 165, 190, 191, 218, 219, 229, 230, 238, 255n; *Again, Dangerous Visions* 229; *Dangerous Visions* 127, 229, 238, 255n; *Dangerous Visions* anthologies 124–125, 129; *From the Land of Fear* 50–51; *I, Robot: The Illustrated Screenplay* 70; "Introduction: Thirty-Two Soothsayers" 229; *Medea: Harlan's World* 190
"Elsewhen" (Heinlein) 236–237
Elwood, Roger 124–125, 148–149, 190; *A World Named Cleopatra* (with Anderson) 190
Empire of the Ants 176
The Empire Strikes Back 74
Emshwiller, Edward 48–49, 55, 175
Ender's Game (Card) 208, 209

Endless Frontier anthologies (Pournelle and Carr) 148
Endymion (Simmons) 95
Enemies in Space (Conklin) 144–145
Energy and Power (de Camp) 158–159
Engines (de Camp) 158–159
England, George Allan 8–9, 144, 251n
England Swings SF (Merril) 229
Entoverse (Hogan) 194
Escapement (Maine) 162–163
Esenwein, J. Berg 125, 127–131; *Adventures to Come* 125, 127–131, 136; *Field and Campus Stories for Girls* 129; *Sport and Adventure Stories for Boys* 129
Eshbach, Lloyd Arthur 159; *Of Worlds Beyond* 159
E.T.: The Extra-Terrestrial 176, 221
"Evans of the Space Guard" (Hamilton) 87–88
Exiles of Time (Bond) 155
The Exploration of Space (Clarke) 158
The Exploration of the Moon (Clarke) 158
Extrapolation 211, 228

Fabricant, Noah D. 146; *Great Science Fiction about Doctors* (with Conklin) 146
The Fabulous World of Jules Verne 162–163
Facing the Flag (Verne) 162–163
The Facts Behind Superman 219
Fahrenheit 451 (Bradbury) 61, 157
Fahrer, Howard 23
Fairman, Paul W. 162–163; "The Cosmic Frame" 162–162; "Deadly City" 162–163
The Fall of Hyperion (Simmons) 95
"The Fall of Mercury" (Stone) 88
A Fall of Moondust (Clarke) 188
Famous Fantastic Mysteries 99
Famous Monsters of Filmland 216
Fantastic Adventures 99, 116–117
Fantastic Four comics 220
Fantastic Science Fiction Art 1926–1954 (del Rey) 221–222
Fantastic Voyage 217, 218
Fantastic Voyage (Asimov) 218
"Farewell to the Master" (Bates) 162–163
Farmer, Philip Jose 56, 212–213, 225; *The Lovers* 56
Farmer in the Sky (Heinlein) 206
Fate 119
Fate of Worlds (Niven and Lerner) 193
Fawcett, Bill 149; *The Fleet* anthologies (with Drake) 149
Fearn, John Russell 115–116; "Vampire Queen" 115–116
Feeley, Gregory 150; "The Crab Lice" 150
Felten, Marcley W. 23, 25, 36

Index 285

Ferguson, Margaret Clay 251*n*
Fezandié, Clement 21–22, 26–27, 28, 29, 31, 35; "Dr. Hackensaw's Secrets" series 26; "Hicks' Inventions with a Kick: The Perambulating Home" 21–22, 26–27
Field and Campus Stories for Girls (Esenwein) 129
The 5th Wave (Yancey) 208
The 5th Wave series (Yancey) 208
Fifty Key Figures in Science Fiction (Bould, Butler, Roberts, and Vint) 246
Final Blackout (Hubbard) 75
Final Report of the Scientific Study of Unidentified Flying Objects 227
Finch, Sheila 91; Guild of Xenolinguists series 91
Finger, Bill 172; "The Last Television Broadcast on Earth" 172
Finlay, Virgil 57
Finney, Jack 162–163; *The Body Snatchers* 162–163
"Fireproof" (Clement) 182
First Lensman (Smith) 65
First Man into Space 165
First Men in the Moon 217–218
The First Men in the Moon (Wells) 136, 139, 184, 217–218
The First Science Fiction Novel Megapack 190
"The First Shall Be Last" (Burks) 101
First Through Time (Gordon) 224
Flash comics 166, 174
Flash Gordon (comic strip) 16, 89, 128, 154, 235
Flash Gordon (serial) 16, 89, 128, 235
Flash Gordon (TV series) 89
Flash Gordon Conquers the Universe 16, 89, 235
Flash Gordon Strange Adventure Magazine 235
Flash Gordon's Trip to Mars 16, 89, 235
The Fleet anthologies (Drake and Fawcett) 149
Flint, Homer Eon 146, 161; "The Nth Man" 161
The Fly 162–163
"The Fly" (Langelaan) 162–163
Flying Saucers Have Landed (Leslie and Adamski) 119–120, 123, 157
Flying Saucers—Serious Business (Edwards) 227
"The Fog Horn" (Bradbury) 162–163
"Follow the Space-Leader" 172
Food of the Gods 176
"For Adults Only" (Gold) 48, 237
For Us the Living (Heinlein) 69

Forbidden Planet 16, 89, 117
The Forever War (Haldeman) 230
"Foreword" (Stong) 131–132
Forgotten Realms series 242
"The Fork in the Road" (Sedgewick) 242
Fort, Charles 146–147; *Lo!* 146–147
Forward, Robert F. 182, 183, 194; *Dragon's Egg* 194
Foster, Alan Dean 218
Foundation (Asimov) 113
Foundation and Empire (Asimov) 113
Foundation series (Asimov) 70, 81, 113, 156–157
The Fountains of Paradise (Clarke) 193
Four Came Back (Caidin) 227
Four-Sided Triangle 162–163
Four-Sided Triangle (Temple) 162–163
"The Fourth-Dimensional Demonstrator" (Leinster) 133
The Fourth Galaxy Reader (Gold) 126, 160
Fox, Gardner 165–166, 172–173, 219; "The Cavern of Deadly Spheres" 219; Justice League of America comics 174, 219, 263*n*; "The Maze of Time" 172; "Yes, Virginia, There Is a Martian" 172–173
Frank, Howard 221
Frank, Jane 221; *Science Fiction Artists of the Twentieth Century* 221
Frank, Pat 244; *Alas, Babylon* 244
Frankenstein (Shelley) 40, 138, 146
Franklin, Benjamin 168
Franklin, H. Bruce 112
Frau im Mond 65, 176
Frazetta, Frank 177, 256*n*
Freas, Frank Kelly 48, 54, 55, 175, 177, 240, 255*n*
French, Paul *see* Asimov, Isaac
Frewin, Anthony 221–222, 254*n*; *One Hundred Years of Science Fiction Illustration* 221–222, 254*n*
Friesner, Esther M. 244; *Warchild* 244
From the Earth to the Moon 162–163
From the Earth to the Moon (Verne) 138, 162–163, 184
From the Land of Fear (Ellison) 50–51
"Frost and Fire" (Bradbury) 74, 115
Futura comics 116
Futurama 29
"Future History" chart (Heinlein) 112
"Future History" series (Heinlein) 66–69
Future Science Fiction 99
Futures to Infinity (Moskowitz) 100, 126–127
The Futurians (Knight) 134

Gaiman, Neil 150, 219, 244; "A Study in Emerald" 150

Galactic Patrol (Smith) 65–66
Galactic Pot-Healer (Dick) 248
Galaga (video game) 94, 220
Galaxy 4, 48–49, 61, 81–82, 114, 124, 160, 188–189, 230, 237
Gallun, Raymond Z. 115–116, 133, 163; "Old Faithful" 133; "Space Oasis" 115–116
Garby, Lee Hawkins 33–37, 86–87, 93; *The Skylark of Space* (with Smith) 14, 21, 33–37, 86–87, 129–130, 234
Gardner, Martin 181
Gardner, Thomas S. 103, 108, 110
The Gentle Giants of Ganymede (Hogan) 194
Gernsback, Hugo 1, 2–3, 8–16, 17–18, 20, 21–38, 40, 41, 42, 43, 44, 45, 48, 51, 58, 78, 79, 80, 81–82, 86, 87, 105, 107–108, 109, 118, 127, 128, 132, 134, 135, 144, 161, 165, 178, 181, 184, 185, 191, 212, 246, 249, 251n, 255n, 257n; "Amazing Life" 22; "An Amazing Phenomenon" 22; "Amazing Thinking" 22; "The Amazing Unknown" 21–23; *Baron Munchausen's New Scientific Adventures* 24–25; "New Amazing Facts" 22; "Our Amazing Minds" 22; "Our Amazing Senses" 22; "Our Amazing Universe" 22; *Ralph 124C 41+*, 24–25, 30, 161, 184, 233; "Reasonableness in Science Fiction" 79; "The Science-Fiction Industry" 178; "Science Fiction vs. Science Faction" 185
"The Gernsback Continuum" (Gibson) 44
Get Out of My Sky (Marguiles) 49–50
Giants' Star (Hogan) 194
Giesy, J.U. 144
Gibson, William 40, 41, 44, 57, 78, 219, 230, 244; "The Gernsback Continuum" 44; *Neuromancer* 41, 78
Gilmore, Anthony *see* Bates, Harry; Hall, Desmond W.
Gladiator (Wylie) 138
Godard, Jean-Luc 20
Godwin, Tom 126, 181; "The Cold Equations" 126, 181
Godzilla films 240
Gog 161
Gold, H.L. 41, 42, 48, 114, 126, 160, 164, 237; *Bodyguard and Four Other Short Science Fiction Novels from Galaxy* 126, 160; "For Adults Only" 48, 237; *The Fourth Galaxy Reader* 126, 160; *The Third Galaxy Reader* 160; *Mind Partner and 8 Other Novelets from Galaxy* 160; *The World That Couldn't Be and 8 Other Novelets from Galaxy* 160
Golden Argosy 238

"Goldfish Bowl" (Heinlein) 236–237
Gordon, Rex 224; *First Through Time* 224
Goulart, Ron 211; *After Things Fell Apart* 211
Grant, John 45, 49
Gravity's Rainbow (Pynchon) 227
Great Science Fiction About Doctors (with Fabricant) 145
Great Stories of Space Travel (Conklin) 144–145
The Great War Syndicate (Stockton) 144
Green Lantern comics 166, 173
The Green Man of Graypec (Pragnell) 75
"The Green Splotches" (Stribling) 134
Greenberg, Martin 114, 156–157
Greenberg, Martin H. 126–127, 149, 150, 219–220; *Adventures of the Batman* 219–220; *The Best Alternate History Stories of the 20th Century* (with Turtledove) 149; *The Best Military Science Fiction of the 20th Century* (with Turtledove) 149; *The Best Time Travel Stories of the 20th Century* (with Turtledove) 149; *Black Cats and Broken Mirrors* (with Helfers) 150; *Uncollected Stars* (with Anthony, Malzberg, and Waugh) 126–127; *What Might Have Been, Volume 1* (with Benford) 150
Greenland, Colin 95–96; *Mother of Plenty* 95–96; *Plenty* series 95–96; *Season of Plenty* 96–96; *Take Back Plenty* 95–96
Gregor, Lee *see* Rothman, Milton A.
Griffith, George 86; *A Honeymoon in Space* 86
"The Gryb" (van Vogt) 103
Guild of Xenolinguists series (Finch) 91
Gulliver's Travels (Swift) 137, 143–144
Gundam Mobile Suit series 94
Gunn, James 137, 212; *Alternate Worlds* 137
Gygax, Gary 220
Gyro Gearloose comics 174

Haas, Cliveden Chew 217
Hacker, Marilyn 148; *Quark* anthologies (with Delany) 148
Haenchen, F.C. 23
Haggard, H. Rider 144
Haldeman, Joe 230, 244; *The Forever War* 230
Hall, Austin 144
Hall, Desmond W. 80; *Space Hawk* (with Bates) 80
Halo (video game) 240, 244
Hamilton, Alexander 224
Hamilton, Edmond 1, 12, 14, 41, 43, 75, 81,

82–83, 87–88, 89, 133, 165, 171, 184–185, 234; Captain Future series 81, 89; "Cities in the Air" 43; "The Dead Planet" 89; "Evans of the Space Guard" 87–88; "The Man Who Evolved" 106, 133; "Space Mirror" 82–83; *The Star of Life* 75; "The Story Behind the Story" 83; "Under the Red Sun" 171

Hammer and Tongs (Beck) 15, 100

The Hampdenshire Wonder (Beresford) 138

Haraway, Donna 246

hard science fiction 3, 10, 41–42, 48, 51, 52, 55, 57–58, 180–195, 237–238, 256*n*

Hard Science Fiction (Slusser and Rabkin) 192

The Hard SF Renaissance (Hartwell and Cramer) 195

"Haredevil Hare" 164

"Hareway to the Stars" 164

Harness, Charles L. 110, 165–166

Harris, Clare Winger 25; "The Miracle of the Lily" 25

Harrison, Harry 92, 148; *Bill, the Galactic Hero* 92; *Nova* anthologies 148; *The Stainless Steel Rat* 92; Stainless Steel Rat series 92; *Star Smashers of the Galaxy Rangers* 92

Harry Potter series (Rowling) 208

Hartwell, David G. 54–56, 136, 180, 195, 241–242, 246; *Ascent of Wonder* (with Cramer) 54–56; "The Distortion of the Product" 242; *The Hard SF Renaissance* (with Cramer) 195; *The World Treasury of Science Fiction* 136

Hasse, Henry 115–116, 165–166; "City of the Living Flame" 115–116

"The Hasty Hare" 164

Have Space Suit—Will Travel (Heinlein) 114, 122, 206–207

Hawkman comics 166, 173–174

Hawthorne, Julian 144

Hayden, Patrick Nielsen 211–212

"The Head" (Kleier) 21–22, 27–30, 37

Healy, Raymond J. 124, 125, 127, 140, 145–147; *Adventures in Time and Space* (with McComas) 124, 125, 127, 140, 145–147

"Heavy Planet" (Rothman) 108

Hefner, Hugh 156

Hegira (Bear) 194–195

Heinlein, Robert A. 1–2, 3–4, 13, 17, 19, 32, 47, 65, 61, 66–69, 70, 72, 73, 90, 101, 105–110, 112–113, 116, 121, 122, 123, 126, 130, 133, 134, 138, 141, 155–158, 160, 161, 163, 176, 186, 187–188, 189, 196–197, 199, 202–209, 212, 220, 231, 233–234, 236–238, 244, 258*n*; "'All You Zombies—'" 112; "'—And He Built a Crooked House—'" 236–237; *Between Planets* 206–207; *Beyond This Horizon* 69, 236–237; "The Black Pits of Luna" 130; "Blowups Happen" 236; "By His Bootstraps" 112, 121, 236–237; *Citizen of the Galaxy* 206–207; "Common Sense" 236; "Coventry" 69, 236–237; "Elsewhen" 236–237; *Farmer in the Sky* 206; *For Us the Living* 69; "Goldfish Bowl" 236–237; "The Green Hills of Earth" 155; "Future History" chart 112; "Future History" series 66–69; *Have Space Suit—Will Travel* 114, 122, 206–207; "'If This Goes On—'" 32, 66–68, 108–109, 236–237; "It's Great to Be Back" 107 ; "'Let There Be Light'" 107; "Life-Line" 105–108, 133, 236–237; "Logic of Empire" 236; *Methuselah's Children* 69, 72, 236; "Misfit" 69, 107–108; *The Moon Is a Harsh Mistress* 231; *The Number of the Beast* 69; *Podkayne of Mars* 196, 207; *The Puppet Masters* 163; *Red Planet* 197, 206; "Requiem" 107, 108, 236; *Revolt in 2100* 66; "The Roads Must Roll" 112, 236–237; *Rocket Ship Galileo* 161, 187, 196, 202–204, 205; *The Rolling Stones* (Heinlein) 207; "Shooting Destination Moon" 187–188; *Sixth Column* 32, 67–68; "Solution Unsatisfactory" 141, 236–237; *Space Cadet* 196–197, 204–206; "Space Jockey" 107; *The Star Beast* 206–207; *Starman Jones* 206–207; *Starship Troopers* 61, 196, 197, 207, 208, 220; "They" 112–113, 236–237; *Time Enough for Love* 68, 69; *Time for the Stars* 207; *Tunnel in the Sky* 206–207; "Universe" 112–113, 236; "The Unpleasant Profession of Jonathan Hoag" 112–113, 236–237; "Waldo" 236–237; "'We Also Walk Dogs'" 236

Heinlein in Dimension (Panshin) 197

The Heiress 155–156

"Helen O'Loy" (del Rey) 81, 133

Helfers, John 150; *Black Cats and Broken Mirrors* (with Greenberg) 150

Helliconia series (Aldiss) 195

Helliconia Spring (Aldiss) 195

Helliconia Summer (Aldiss) 195

Helliconia Winter (Aldiss) 185

Henderson, Zenna 239; People series 239

Hendrix, Howard V. 52

Herbert, Frank 78, 190, 244; *Dune* 78, 190; Dune series 190

Hewelke, Geoffrey 255*n*; "Ten Million Miles Sunward" 255*n*

"Hicks' Inventions with a Kick: The Perambulating Home" (Fezandié) 21–22, 26–27
"Hide and Seek" (Clarke) 186
The High Crusade (Anderson) 91
High Justice (Pournelle) 194
Hildebrandt, the Brothers 177
The History of Science Fiction (Roberts) 149
"History to Come" (Campbell) 17
Hitchcock, Alfred 176
The Hitchhiker's Guide to the Galaxy (Adams) 92
The Hitchhiker's Guide to the Galaxy (film) 92
The Hitchhiker's Guide to the Galaxy (radio series) 92
The Hitchhiker's Guide to the Galaxy (TV series) 92
The Hitchhiker's Guide to the Galaxy series (Adams) 92–93
The Hobbit (Tolkien) 158
Hoffman Medical Center series (Nourse) 92
Hoffman's Adventure 238
Hogan, James P. 194, 208; *Entoverse* 194; *The Gentle Giants of Ganymede* 194; *Giants' Star* 194; *Inherit the Stars* 194; *Outward Bound* 208, 209
Holbrook, Morris B. 177
Holiday 224
Holly, J. Hunter 218
A Honeymoon in Space (Griffith) 86
Honor Harrington series (Weber) 59
Hornig, Charles 165
Hoskins, Robert 148; *Infinity* anthologies 148
Hospital Earth series (Nourse) 92
Howard, Robert E. 156–157; Conan series 156–157
Hoyle, Fred 190; *The Black Cloud* 190
Hubbard, L. Ron 75; *Final Blackout* 75
"Huddling Place" (Simak) 112
Hugo Gernsback and the Century of Science Fiction (Westfahl) 3, 36–37, 59
Hull, E. Mayne 109
The Hunger Games (Collins) 208
The Hunger Games series (Collins) 208, 209
Hunter, Evan *see* Lombino, S.A.
Huntington, John 127; *Rationalizing Genius* 127
Huxley, Aldous 138, 144; *Brave New World* 138
Hyperion (Simmons) 95
Hyperion series (Simmons) 95, 96

"I Remember Lemuria" (Shaver) 118
I, Robot 70
I, Robot (Asimov) 69–70, 112
I, Robot: The Illustrated Screenplay (Ellison) 70
If 126
"'If This Goes On—'" (Heinlein) 32, 66–68, 108–109, 236–237
Ijon Tichy series (Lem) 92
"The Immortality Seekers" 172
In Search of Wonder (Knight) 159, 238
"In the Abyss" (Wells) 134
"In Times to Come" (July 1939) (Campbell) 107
"In Times to Come" (June 1939) (Campbell) 103
"The Incorrigible" (de Camp) 160
Incredible Hulk comics 220
The Incredible Shrinking Man 162–163
Infinity anthologies (Hoskins) 148
Ing, Dean 194
Inherit the Stars (Hogan) 194
Inside the Atom (Asimov) 159
Inter Ice Age 4 (Abe) 192
Interplanetary Flight (Clarke) 158
Interzone 148
"Introduction" (Ackerman) 104
"Introduction" (Conklin) 140, 147
"Introduction" (Wollheim) 136–138
"Introduction: Thirty-Two Soothsayers" (Ellison) 229
Invaders of Earth (Conklin) 145
Invasion of the Body Snatchers 162–163
Invasion of the Saucer Men 162–163
Iron Man comics 220
"The Irrelevant" (Campbell) 185
Is There Life on Other Worlds? (Anderson) 148
Isaacs, John 193
The Island of Dr. Moreau (Wells) 139
Islands in the Sky (Clarke) 188, 196, 201–202
Islands in the Sky (Westfahl) 188
Islands of Space (Campbell) 191
It! The Terror from Beyond Space 89, 163, 239
"It's a *Good* Life" (Bixby) 126, 239
"It's a Woman's World" 171–172
"It's Great to Be Back" (Heinlein) 107
It's Your Atomic Story (del Rey) 158

Jackson, Robert 103
Jaime Retief series (Laumer) 91
Jameson, Malcolm 100–101, 115–116; "Mill of the Gods" 100–101; "Stellar Showboat" 115–116

Jefferson, Thomas 224
Jenkins, Will F. *see* Leinster, Murray
La Jetée 20
The Jetsons 164
"The Jewel of Bas" (Brackett) 73
Jimmy Olsen comics 167–169
John Carstairs series (Long) 91
John Colbie series (Rocklynne) 186
Jones, Neil R. 100
Jones, Raymond F. 162–163; *This Island Earth* 162–163
"Journey to Babel" 93
Journey to the Center of the Earth 162–163
Journey to the Center of the Earth (Verne) 138, 162–163
Journey to the Seventh Planet 117
Joyce, James 50
"Judgment Day" 166
Jupiter novels 208
Jupiter Project (Benford) 194, 207–208
Justice League of America comics (Fox) 174, 219, 263n
juvenile science fiction 2, 4, 41–42, 67, 114, 117, 130, 153, 155, 194, 196–204, 238–239, 240

Kasdan, Lawrence 74
Kaveney, Roz 193
Keasbey, William P. 23–24; *The Big Trick and Puzzle Book* 23–24; *Wonder Stories from Nature* 23
Keep Watching the Skies! (Warren) 216
Keller, David H. 12, 25, 29; "The Yeast Men" 25
Kelly, Frank K. 14, 234
Kelly, Mark R. 231
Kemlo and the Crazy Planet (Eliott) 238–239
Kemlo series (Eliott) 238–239
Kemp, Earl 19, 160, 211–215, 224–226; *Who Killed Science Fiction?* 19, 160, 211–215, 224–226
Kepler, Johannes 145–146; *Somnium* 145–146
Kersh, Gerald 155
"The King of Thieves" (Vance) 90–91
"King Superman vs. Clark Kent, Metallo" 171
King's College Review 155, 156
Kingsbury, Donald 194
Kirby, Jack 174
Kleier, George 27
Kleier, Joe 21–22, 27–30, 31, 35; "The Head" 21–22, 27–30, 37
Kleier, Josephine Walter 27
Klushantsev, Pavel 163–164

Knight, Damon 78, 104, 113, 124–125, 134, 148, 159, 161, 212, 230, 238; *The Futurians* 134; *In Search of Wonder* 159, 238; *Orbit* anthologies 124–125, 148; "The World of van Vogt" 104
Knight, Norman L. 101; "Saurian Valedictory" 101
Knights of the Galaxy comics 171–172
Kornbluth, C.M. 162
Kosmicheskiy Reys 65
Krypto the Super-Dog comics 169
Kubrick, Stanley 46, 176
Kuttner, Henry 75, 115–116, 162–163, 165, 186; "The Twonky" (with Moore) 162–163; "War-Gods of the Deep" 115–116
Kyle, David A. 114, 156–157

"The Lady and the Lion" 170
Lafferty, R.A. 223–224, 230
Lagrange Five (Reynolds) 193
Lana Lang, Insect Queen comics 167–168
The Land Unknown 176
Lands Beyond (de Camp) 139
Lang, Fritz 48, 65, 176
Langelaan, George 162–163; "The Fly" 162–163
Last and First Men (Stapledon) 139
"The Last Television Broadcast on Earth" (Finger) 172
Latham, Philip *see* Richardson, Robert S.
Latham, Rob 229
Laumer, Keith 91; Jaime Retief series 91; "The Prince and the Pirate" 91
Lawlor, R.E. 37
Lawman 162
Le Guin, Ursula K. 32, 40, 61, 156, 182, 230, 231, 238, 244; *City of Illusions* 32; *The Left Hand of Darkness* 231; "Nine Lives" 156; *The Norton Book of Science Fiction* (with Attebery) 61; "The Word for World Is Forest" 230
Lee, Gentry 193; Rama series (with Clarke) 183
Lee, Sharon 243–244
Lee, Stan 174
The Left Hand of Darkness (Le Guin) 231
Legion of Super Heroes comics 168
The Legion of Time (Williamson) 64–65
Leiber, Fritz 191, 212, 215
Leinster, Murray 15, 81, 92, 133, 155, 162, 188, 217–218, 239; *City on the Moon* 188; "The Fourth-Dimensional Demonstrator" 133; Med Service series 92, 239; *Men into Space* 218; "The Power Planet" 81; *Space Platform* 188; *Space Tug* 188; *The Wailing Asteroid* 217–218

Lem, Stanislaw 4, 20, 40, 92, 192; Ijon Tichy series 92; Pirx the Pilot series 92; *Solaris* 92
Lensman 66
Lensman: Galactic Patrol 66
Lensman series (Smith) 65–66,
Leslie, Desmond 119–120, 157; *Flying Saucers Have Landed* (with Adamski) 119–120, 123, 157
Leslie, Norman 128
"'Let There Be Light'" (Heinlein) 107
Lewis, Brian 255n
Lewis, C.S. 4, 51, 138, 144, 158, 181, 209; *Out of the Silent Planet* 138; *Perelandra* 138; Space trilogy 158
Ley, Willy 163, 177, 187, 222; *Beyond the Solar System* 222; *The Conquest of Space* 177, 222; *Rockets and Space Travel* 187
"A Life by Television" (Arnold) 129
"Life-Line" (Heinlein) 105–108, 133, 236–237
Life, the Universe, and Everything (Adams) 92
Lilliput 155–156
Limbo (Wolfe) 224
Lincoln, Abraham 168
Lindsay, David 144
"Little Boy" (Bixby) 126–127
Liu, Cixin 96–97, 195, 248, 249; *The Dark Forest* 96–97, 195; *Death's End* 96–97, 195; *The Three-Body Problem* 96–97, 195, 248; The Three-Body Problem series 96–97, 195, 248
Llana of Gathol (Burroughs) 72–73
Lo! (Fort) 146–147
Locke, Richard Adams 144; *The Moon Hoax* 144
"Logic of Empire" (Heinlein) 236
Lois Lane comics 167, 170–171
Lombino, S.A. 162
London, Jack 144
Long, Frank Belknap 91; John Carstairs series 91
The Long Night (Caidin) 227
Looking Backward (Bellamy) 138
Lord of Light (Zelazny) 231
The Lord of the Rings (Tolkien) 158
Lorelei of the Red Mist (Brackett) 73–74
"Lorelei of the Red Mist" (Brackett and Bradbury) 73–74
Lost Cities and Vanished Civilizations (Silverberg) 158, 160, 226
Lost Continents (de Camp) 158–159
Lost in Space 220
The Lost Missile 230
The Lost World comics 116

Lovecraft, H.P. 29, 118, 136, 138, 139, 150, 156, 158–159; Cthulhu Mythos series 118; "The Shadow Out of Time" 136, 139
Lovecraft: A Biography (de Camp) 158–159
Lowell, Percival 74
Lowndes, Robert W. 196
Lucas, George 66, 74, 81, 88–89
Lucifer's Hammer (Niven and Pournelle) 194
Lucky Starr and the Big Sun of Mercury (Asimov) 198
Lucky Starr and the Moons of Jupiter (Asimov) 198
Lucky Starr and the Oceans of Venus (Asimov) 198
Lucky Starr and the Pirates of the Asteroids (Asimov) 196, 197–201
Lucky Starr and the Rings of Saturn (Asimov) 198
Lucky Starr series (Asimov) 174, 196, 197–201, 238–239
Ludwig von Drake comics 175
Lupoff, Pat 219
Lupoff, Richard A. 219
Luna 163–164
Lyau, Bradford 252n; *The Anticipation Novelists of 1950s French Science Fiction* 252n

MacDonald, Anson *see* Heinlein, Robert A.
MacDonald, Ian 244
MacLean, Katherine 165–166
Macrolife (Zebrowski) 194
Mad magazine 175
"Mad as a Mars Hare" 164
Mad in Orbit 175
The Magazine of Fantasy and Science Fiction 48, 49, 61, 81–82, 114, 124, 125, 181, 188–189, 214, 237, 241
Maggin, Elliot S. 219–220; *Superman: Last Son of Krypton* 219–220; *Superman: Miracle Monday* 219–220
The Magnetic Monster 161
Magnus Ridolph series (Vance) 90–91, 239) 101
Maine, Charles Eric 162–163; *Escapement* 162–163
The Making of a Moon (Clarke) 158
The Malecia Tapestry (Aldiss) 84
Maloire, A.B. 11, 12
Malzberg, Barry N. 126–127, 239–241; "Dialogues" (with Resnick) 239–241; *Uncollected Stars* (with Anthony, Greenberg, and Waugh) 126–127
Man and Power (de Camp) 158–159

"Man and the Moon" 163–164
"The Man from Ariel" (Wollheim) 138
The Man from U.N.C.L.E. 218, 240
The Man from U.N.C.L.E. novels 218, 240
"Man in Space" 163
"The Man Who Evolved" (Hamilton) 106, 133
The Man Who Made Gold (Belloc) 138
Mantley, John 162–163; *The 27th Day* 162–163
Marguiles, Leo 49–50; *Get Out of My Sky* 49–50
Marker, Chris 20
Markham 162
Marooned 227
Marooned (Caidin) 227
Mars (Richardson) 222
"Mars and Beyond" 163–164
"Mars Is Heaven" (Bradbury) 115
Mars series (Burroughs) 72–73, 158, 166, 173, 239
Marsten, Richard *see* Lombino, S.A.
The Martian Chronicles (Bradbury) 61, 74, 115, 157
"A Martian Odyssey" (Weinbaum) 15, 23, 133
Martin, Reginald Eric *see* Elliot, E.C.
Marvel Science Fiction 99
Marvin the Martian cartoons 164
Matheson, Richard 162–163, 218; *The Shrinking Man* 162–163
Mattingly, David 59
Maxwell, Konrad 99–100, 105
"The Maze of Time" (Fox) 172–173
The Maze Runner (Dashner) 208
The Maze Runner series (Dashner) 208
McBain, Ed *see* Lombino, S.A.
McComas, J. Francis 48, 114, 124, 125, 127, 140, 145–147, 237; *Adventures in Time and Space* (with Healy) 124, 125, 127, 140, 145–147
McDevitt, Jack 244
McKean, Dave 177
McLaughlin, Dean 188, 213, 215, 225
McMichael, Stanley 23
The Mechanics of Wonder (Westfahl) 3
Med Service series (Leinster) 92, 239
Medea: Harlan's World (Ellison) 190
"A Meeting with Medusa" (Clarke) 156
Men into Space 164, 188, 218
Men into Space (Leinster) 218
"The Menace of Metallo" 170–171
Menzel, Donald H. 11, 251*n*
Merril, Judith 78, 229, 230; *England Swings SF* 229
Merritt, A. 144

Meskys, Edmund S. 213–213
"The Metal Moon" (Smith and Starzl) 15
Methuselah's Children (Heinlein) 69, 72, 236
Metropolis 44, 48, 176
Michaels, Melisa C. 94; Skyrider series 94
"Microcosmic God" (Sturgeon) 113, 121
Miéville, China 244
The Mightiest Machine (Campbell) 16–17
Mighty Mouse comics 174–175
Mighty Mouse in Outer Space 174–175
Mike Mars series (Wollheim) 238–239
Miles Vorkosigan series (Bujold) 94–95, 243
"Mill of the Gods" (Jameson) 100–101
Miller, P. Schuyler 12, 80, 191, 229; "The Reference Library" 191
Miller, Steve 243–244
Miller, Walter M., Jr. 18, 61, 244; *A Canticle for Leibowitz* 61, 244
Mind Partner and 8 Other Novelets from Galaxy (Gold) 160
"The Miracle of the Lily" (Harris) 25
"Misfit" (Heinlein) 69, 107–108
Mission of Gravity (Clement) 185, 189–190, 193
Mission to Horatius (Reynolds) 240
Mission to the Moon (del Rey) 188
Modern Science Fiction (Bretnor) 159
Moebius 177
Monk, Patricia 77–78, 80, 82; "Not Just Cosmic Skulduggery" 77–78
Monsters (van Vogt) 103–104
The Moon (Binder) 158
The Moon Hoax (Locke) 144
The Moon Is a Harsh Mistress (Heinlein) 231
Moon of Mutiny (del Rey) 188
Moorcock, Michael 20, 41, 42, 50, 78, 124, 229, 230, 238, 244
Moore, C.L. 75, 133, 162–163; "Shambleau" 133; "The Twonky" (with Kuttner) 162–163
Moore, Ward 155
More, Thomas 138; *Utopia* 138
More Adventures on Other Planets (Wollheim) 49–50, 224
More Fun Comics 167
More Stories from the Twilight Zone (Serling) 223–224
More Than Human (Sturgeon) 61, 114
Moskowitz, Sam 33, 75, 100, 126–127, 161, 211; *Futures to Infinity* 100, 126–127; "The Return of Hugo Gernsback" 161
Mostly Harmless (Adams) 92
The Mote in God's Eye (Niven and Pournelle) 194

"The Moth" (Wells) 21–22, 26, 37
Mother of Plenty (Greenland) 95–96
"Moxon's Master" (Bierce) 134
Mullen, R.D. 23
Myers, Howard L. 126–127; "The Creatures of Man" 126–127
Mysta of the Moon comics 116
The Mysterious Earth (del Rey) 158
Mysterious Island (serial) 162–163
Mysterious Island (Verne) 162–163
The Mysterious Sea (del Rey) 158
Mystery in Space 16, 166, 171–173, 174
Mystery Magazine 27
Mystic Magazine 119

N-Space (Niven) 192–193
The Naked Sun (Asimov) 70
Nash, Walter 234
Needle (Clement) 190
Neuromancer (Gibson) 41, 78
"Neutron Star" (Niven) 190, 192
The New Adam (Weinbaum) 75, 138
"New Amazing Facts" (Gernsback) 22
New Dimensions anthologies (Silverberg) 148
New Maps of Hell (Amis) 49–50, 159–160
"New Wave" 228–230, 237–238
New Worlds 124, 229, 238
New Writings in SF anthologies (Carnell) 148
News of the World 177
Nicholas, M. Kolaya 159; *Chemistry and Human Health* (with Asimov and Walker) 159
Nicholas van Rijn series (Anderson) 91, 239
Nicholls, Peter 45, 49
Nicole Shea series (Claremont) 94
Nicolson, Marjorie Hope 159; *Voyages to the Moon* 159
Night Gallery 218
"Nightfall" (Asimov) 113
Nimoy, Leonard 217
"Nine Lives" (Le Guin) 156
1984 162–163
Nineteen Eighty-Four (Orwell) 162–163
The Nitrogen Fix (Clement) 194
Niven, Larry 48, 55, 56, 94, 150, 183, 185, 190, 192–193, 231, 243; "Becalmed in Hell" 192; "The Coldest Place" 192; *Fate of Worlds* (with Lerner) 193; *N-Space* 192–193; "Neutron Star" 190, 192; "The Return of William Proxmire" 150; *Ringworld* 48, 185, 192–193, 231; *The Ringworld Engineers* 193; Ringworld series 192–193; *Ringworld's Children* 193

Norton, Andre 130, 212, 214; *Space Pioneers* 130; *Space Police* 130; *Space Service* 130
The Norton Book of Science Fiction (Le Guin and Attebery) 61
"Not Just Cosmic Skulduggery" (Monk) 77–78
Nourse, Alan E. 92, 188; Hoffman Medical Center series 92; Hospital Earth series 92
Nova anthologies (Harrison) 148
Nova Express (Burroughs) 227
Nowlan, Philip Francis 16, 21, 23, 29–33, 36, 37–38, 67, 75, 154, 235, 253n; "The Airlords of Han" 31–32, 36, 67, 154, 235; "Armageddon 2419 A.D." 21, 29–33, 36, 37, 67, 154, 235; *Armageddon 2419 A.D.* 16, 67, 253n
"The Nth Man" (Flint) 161
"Nuisance Value" (Wellman) 100–101
Null-A Three (van Vogt) 110
"Null-O" (Dick) 126
The Number of the Beast (Heinlein) 69

Oberth, Hermann 93
O'Brien, Fitz-James 144
Odd John (Stapledon) 136, 139
Of Worlds Beyond (Eshbach) 159
"Old Faithful" (Gallun) 133
Oliver, Chad 182, 196
Omni 51–55, 255n
"On 'Black Destroyer'" (van Vogt) 261n
On the Beach 162–163
On the Beach (Shute) 162–163
One Hundred Years of Science Fiction Illustration (Frewin) 221–222, 254n
O'Neill, Gerard 193
Only a Trillion (Asimov) 159
Orbit anthologies (Knight) 124–125, 148
Orbitsville (Shaw) 193
Orbitsville Departure (Shaw) 193
Orbitsville Judgment (Shaw) 193
Orbitsville series (Shaw) 193
Orwell, George 162–163; *Nineteen Eighty-Four* 162–163
The Oscar 162
"The Other Side of the Sky" (Clarke) 188
The Other Worlds (Stong) 100, 127, 131–133, 142
"Our Amazing Minds" (Gernsback) 22
"Our Amazing Senses" (Gernsback) 22
"Our Amazing Universe" (Gernsback) 22
"Our Pious Hope" (Cramer) 242
"Out of the Sub-Universe" (Starzl) 174
Out There 162, 163
Outward Bound (Hogan) 208, 209

Page, Norvell 138; "But Without Honor" 138
Pal, George 187, 204
The Palace of Eternity (Shaw) 51
Pale Blue Dot (Sagan) 222
Palmer, Ray 11, 43, 49, 118–119, 120, 146–147, 159, 174, 257n; *The Coming of the Saucers* (with Arnold) 159; "The Shaver Mystery No. 2" (with Shaver) 119
Palunian, Dickman 52–53
Panshin, Alexei 197, 231; *Heinlein in Dimension* 197; *Rite of Passage* 197, 231
The Paranoid Fifties 140
paranormal literature 3, 117–121, 122, 123, 157, 159, 216, 227–228
Partners in Wonder (Davin) 62
Paul, Frank R. 21–22, 36–37, 42–45, 47, 48, 51, 52, 55, 56, 59, 109, 129–130, 165
Pebble in the Sky (Asimov) 157
Peck, Bob 176
Pelan, John 150; *Shadows Over Baker Street* (with Reaves) 150
People series (Henderson) 239
Perelandra (Lewis) 138
The Persistence of Vision (Varley) 194
Phillifent, John T. 218
Phillips, A.M. 146; "Time Travel Happens!" 146
Phillips, Rog 126; "Rat in the Skull" 126
Phillips, Vic 101; "Maiden Voyage" 101
The Pilgrim Project (Searls) 227
Pilgrims Through Time and Space (Bailey) 1, 159
"The Pipes of Pan" (Leinster) 133
"Piracy Preferred" (Campbell) 36
Pirx the Pilot series (Lem) 92
"The Plains of St. Augustine" (Correy) 188
Planet Comics 16, 116–117, 165, 235
Planet of the Apes 217–218, 220
Planet of the Apes (Boulle) 192, 217–218
Planet Stories 16, 49, 57, 72, 80, 90, 99, 115–117, 123, 165, 235, 237
Planetfall (Cover) 93
Planets (Binder) 158
Plastic Man comics 167–168
Plauger, P.J. 194
Playboy 156
The Playboy Book of Science Fiction and Fantasy (Russell) 156
The Players of Null-A (van Vogt) 110
Plenty series (Greenland) 95–96
The Pocket Book of Science Fiction (Wollheim) 124, 127, 133–136, 142, 145
Podevin, Jean François 53, 54
Podkayne of Mars (Heinlein) 196, 207
Poe, Edgar Allan 1, 4, 78, 139, 194

Pohl, Frederik 62, 124–125, 156, 157, 160, 162, 238; *Star Science Fiction anthologies* 124–125, 157, 238; *The Way the Future Was* 62
Porky Pig cartoons 164
The Portable Novels of Science (Wollheim) 127, 136–140, 143
Pournelle, Jerry 148, 183, 194, 208; *Endless Frontier* anthologies (with Carr) 148; *High Justice* 194; *Lucifer's Hammer* (with Niven) 194; *The Mote in God's Eye* (with Niven) 194
The Power 217–218
The Power (Robinson) 217–218
"The Power Planet" (Leinster) 81
Powers, Richard M. 49–50, 55–57, 59, 119, 222, 255n, 256n
Pragnell, Festus 75; *The Green Man of Graypec* 75
Pratchett, Terry 243; Discworld series 243
Pratt, Fletcher 139–140; "Twayne Triplets" anthologies 139–140
Prelinger, Megan 177–178; *Another Science Fiction* 177–178
Prelude to Space (Clarke) 54, 90, 188, 189
"The Price of Doom" 218
"The Prince and the Pirate" (Laumer) 91
A Princess of Mars (Burroughs) 72–73
"Prison Planet" (Tucker) 115–116
The Prisoner 218, 240
The Prisoner (Disch) 218, 224
The Problems of Space Flying (von Noordung) 81
"Proof" (Clement) 186
Purdom, Tom 194
The Purple Cloud (Shiel) 138, 162–163
Pynchon, Thomas 227; *Gravity's Rainbow* 227

Quachri, Trevor 192
Quark anthologies (Delany and Hacker) 148
Queen 177
"Quest of the Starhope" (Brackett) 73–74
"Quest of Thig" (Wells) 115–116
Quinn, Gerald 47–48
Quick, W.T. 194

Rabkin, Eric S. 192; *Hard Science Fiction* (with Slusser) 192
Races and People (Asimov and Boyd) 159
Ralph 124C 41+ (Gernsback) 24–25, 30, 161, 233
Rama series (Clarke and Lee) 193
The Ranger Boys in Space (Clement) 196–197

"Rat in the Skull" (Phillips) 126
Rationalizing Genius (Huntington) 127
"Reasonableness in Science Fiction" (Gernsback) 79
Reaves, Michael 150; *Shadows Over Baker Street* (with Pelan) 150
Red Dwarf 93
Red Planet 197
Red Planet (Heinlein) 197, 206
Reed, Donald A. 217
"The Reference Library" (Miller) 191
Rendezvous with Rama (Clarke) 193
Report on Probability A (Aldiss) 229
"Requiem" (Heinlein) 107, 108, 236
Resnick, Mike 150, 239–240; *Alternate Kennedys* 150; *Alternate Tyrants* 150; "Dialogues" (with Malzberg) 239–240
The Restaurant at the End of the Universe (Adams) 92
"The Return of Hugo Gernsback" (Moskowitz) 161
"The Return of William Proxmire" (Niven) 250
Revolt in 2100 (Heinlein) 66
Reynolds, Mack 193, 202, 240; *Lagrange Five* 193; *Mission to Horatius* 240
Richardson, Robert S. 161–162, 222; *Mars* 222
Riders to the Stars 161, 188
The Right Stuff (Wolfe) 227
Ring Around the Sun (Simak) 114
Ringworld (Niven) 48, 185, 192–193, 231
The Ringworld Engineers (Niven) 193
Ringworld series (Niven) 192–193
Ringworld's Children (Niven) 193
Rio Bravo 74
Rip Hunter, Time Master 174
Ripcord 162
The Rise of Endymion (Simmons) 95
Rite of Passage (Panshin) 197, 231
Road Runner cartoons 164
Road to the Stars 163–164
"The Roads Must Roll" (Heinlein) 112, 236–237
Roadside Picnic (Strugatsky and Strugatsky) 192
Roberts, Adam 149; *The History of Science Fiction* 149
Robida, Albert 63–64
Robinson, Frank M. 217–218; *The Power* 217–218
Robots and Empire (Asimov) 70
The Robots of Dawn (Asimov) 70
Robots series (Asimov) 81
Rocket Ship Galileo (Heinlein) 161, 196, 202–204, 205

Rockets and Space Travel (Ley) 187
Rockets Through Space (del Rey) 158
Rocklynne, Ross 87, 186; "At the Center of Gravity" 186; John Colbie series 186
Rocks and What They Tell Us (del Rey) 158
Rockwood, Roy (pseudonym) 128
Rocky and His Friends 174–175
Rocky Jones, Space Ranger 16, 117
Rocky the Flying Squirrel comics 174–175
Rod Brown of the Rocket Rangers 162
Roddenberry, Gene 217, 218
Roddenberry, Majel Barrett 217
Roe, Charles E. 24–25
Rogers, Bruce Holland 150; "Thirteen Ways to Water" 150
Rogers, Hubert 45, 46
Rollerball 176
The Rolling Stones (Heinlein) 207
Rosny aîné, J.-H. 7
Rothman, Milton A. 99, 108; "Heavy Planet" 108
Route 66 162
Rowling, J.K. 108; Harry Potter series 108
"Running Out of Speculative Niches" (Brin) 195
Russell, Eric Frank 19, 32, 49, 212; "Design for Great Day" 49; *Sinister Barrier* 32
Russell, Ray 156; *The Playboy Book of Science Fiction and Fantasy* 156
Russell, Samuel D. 108
Ryan, Cornelius 176; "Can We Get to Mars?" (with von Braun) 176

Sacks, Janet 221–222; *Visions of the Future* 221–222
Sadoul, Jacques 221–222; *2000 A.D.*, 221–222
SaFari Annual 211
Sagan, Carl 222; *Comet* 222; *The Dragons of Eden* 222; *Pale Blue Dot* 222
Sands of Mars (Clarke) 188
The Saturday Evening Post 49, 155, 176–177
"Saurian Valedictory" (Knight) 101
Sawyer, Robert J. 244
Schachner, Nat 224
Schiff, Jack 174
Schismatrix (Sterling) 95
Schismatrix Plus (Sterling) 95
Schmidt, Stanley 192
Schomburg, Alex 175
Schulz-Neudamm, Heinz 176
Schwartz, Julius 117, 166, 171–175, 264n
Science Fiction 99
Science Fiction Adventures in Dimension (Conklin) 144–145

Science Fiction Adventures in Mutation (Conklin) 145
Science Fiction and Market Realities (Westfahl, Slusser, and Rabkin) 3
Science Fiction and Reader's Guide (Barrow) 130
science fiction anthologies 4, 49–50, 54–56, 59, 61, 62, 75, 92, 113–114, 124–151, 154–155, 156, 157, 160, 190, 195, 219–220, 229, 238, 255n
science fiction art 3, 36–37, 39–59, 75, 153, 155, 175–178, 179, 221–222, 240, 254n, 255n
Science Fiction Art (Aldiss) 40–41, 75
Science Fiction Artists of the Twentieth Century (Frank) 221
Science Fiction for People Who Hate Science Fiction (Carr) 131
The Science Fiction Hall of Fame, Volume 1 (Silverberg) 113–114, 127
The Science Fiction Handbook (de Camp) 159
"Science Fiction in the Real World—Revisited" (Spinrad) 242
"The Science-Fiction Industry" (Gernsback) 178
science fiction marketplace 3, 8–9, 19, 59, 233–246
science fiction merchandise 153, 155, 178–179
The Science Fiction Novel (Davenport) 159
Science-Fiction Plus 24–25, 178
Science-Fiction: The Gernsback Years (Bleiler and Bleiler) 31
Science Fiction Theatre 164
Science-Fiction Thinking Machines (Conklin) 145
"Science Fiction vs. Science Faction" (Gernsback) 185
Science Wonder Quarterly 15
Science Wonder Stories 10, 11, 12, 43–44
Scientific Detective Monthly 23, 234
The Scientific Romances (Wells) 184
"The Sea Thing" (van Vogt) 103
Searls, Hank 227; *The Big X* 227; *The Pilgrim Project* 227
Season of Plenty (Greenland) 95–96
Second Foundation (Asimov) 113
Second Star (Stabenow) 93–94
"The Secret" (Clarke) 155–156
The Secret of Saturn's Rings (Wollheim) 16
"The Secret of the Men in the Moon" *see* "The Secret"
Secrets of Our Spaceship Moon (Wilson) 120
Sector Twelve General Hospital series (White) 91–92, 239

Sedgewick, Christina 242; "The Fork in the Road" 242
Seetee series (Williamson) 115, 186
Seetee Ship (Williamson) 115
Seetee Shock (Williamson) 115
Senior Prom 155–156
"The Sentinel" (Clarke) 121
Serling, Rod 164–165, 218, 220, 223–224; *More Stories from the Twilight Zone* 223–224
Serviss, Garrett P. 7, 86, 144; *Edison's Conquest of Mars* 86
Seven Famous Novels see The Scientific Romances
"The Shadow Out of Time" (Lovecraft) 136, 139
Shadows Over Baker Street (Reaves and Pelan) 150
Shakespeare, William 251n
"Shambleau" (Moore) 133
Shaver, Richard 118–119, 120, 125, 146–147, 159; "I Remember Lemuria!" 118; "The Shaver Mystery No. 2" (with Palmer) 119
"The Shaver Mystery No. 2" (Palmer and Shaver) 119
Shaw, Bob 51, 193; *Orbitsville* 193; *Orbitsville Departure* 193; *Orbitsville Judgment* 193; Orbitsville series 193; *The Palace of Eternity* 51
Shaw, Larry T. 225
She Devil 162–163
Sheckley, Robert 91, 92, 156, 161–162, 163; AAA Ace Interplanetary Decontamination Service series 91; "Zirn Left Unguarded, the Jenghik Palace in Flames, Jon Westerly Dead" 92
Sheffield, Charles 183, 193, 194, 208; *The Web Between the Worlds* 193, 194
Shelley, Mary 4, 40, 138, 144, 146; *Frankenstein* 40, 138, 146
Sherlock Holmes series (Conan Doyle) 150
Shiel, M.P. 138, 162–163; *The Purple Cloud* 138, 162–163
The Shining 176
Shirley, John 244
"Shooting *Destination Moon*" (Heinlein) 187–188
Short Stories Magazine 155–156
The Shrinking Man (Matheson) 162–163
Shuster, Joe 165, 166–167
Shute, Nevil 162–163; *On the Beach* 162–163
Shutt, Craig 171; *Baby Boomer Comics* 171
Shuttle Down (Correy) 194
Siegel, Jerry 165, 166–167

Silverberg, Robert 13, 27, 148, 158, 160, 212, 225–226; *Lost Cities and Vanished Civilizations* 158, 160, 226; *New Dimensions* anthologies 148; *The Science Fiction Hall of Fame, Volume 1* 113–114, 127
Simak, Clifford D. 13, 15–16, 49–50, 51, 75, 89, 113, 114, 157–158, 233–234, 235, 236; *City* 75, 113; "Huddling Place" 113; *Ring Around the Sun* 114; *Time Is the Simplest Thing* 49–50; *Why Call Them Back from Heaven?* 51
Simmons, Dan 57, 95, 96, 244; *Endymion* 95; *The Fall of Hyperion* 95; *Hyperion* 95; Hyperion series 95; *The Rise of Endymion* 95
Simmons, Henry Hugh *see* Fezandié, Clement
Simon, Bernard 25
Sinister Barrier (Russell) 32
Siodmak, Curt 157, 162–163; *Donovan's Brain* 162–163
Siringer, Norman 238, 244
Sixth Column (Heinlein) 32, 67–68
Sketch 155–156
Skidmore, Joseph W. 100
Skylark Duquesne (Smith) 35
The Skylark of Space (Smith and Garby) 14, 21, 33–37, 129–130, 234
Skylark series (Smith) 14, 21, 33–37, 79, 86–87, 129–130, 132
Skyrider series (Michaels) 94
Slan (van Vogt) 71–72, 103–104, 113, 138, 161
Slan Hunter (van Vogt and Anderson) 72
Sloane, T. O'Conor 21, 23, 24, 25, 26, 27, 28, 31, 37, 128, 251n, 257n
Slonczewski, Joan 183, 195; *Still Forms on Foxfield* 195
Slusser, George 3, 106, 192; *Hard Science Fiction* (with Rabkin) 192; *Science Fiction and Market Realities* (with Westfahl and Rabkin) 3
Smith, Clark Ashton 12
Smith, Cordwainer 42, 49, 90, 114
Smith, E.E. "Doc" 1, 3–4, 14, 21, 22, 23, 33–38, 41, 42, 65–66, 71, 75, 79, 86–87, 88–89, 93, 104, 109, 115, 129–130, 138, 184–185, 212, 234, 258n; *First Lensman* 65; *Galactic Patrol* 65–66; Lensman series 65–66, 75, 88–89, 104, 115; *Skylark Duquesne* 35; *The Skylark of Space* (with Garby) 14, 21, 33–37, 79, 86–87, 129–130, 234; Skylark series 14, 21, 33–38, 79, 86–87, 129–130, 132, 158, 234; *Triplanetary* 65, 75
Smith, Everett C. 15; "The Metal Moon" (with Starzl) 15

Smith, George O. 115, 182, 186; *Venus Equilateral* 115, 186
So Long, and Thanks for All the Fish (Adams) 92
Sohl, Jerry 162
Solaris (1971) 20, 192
Solaris (2003) 192
Solaris (Lem) 192
"Solution Unsatisfactory" (Heinlein) 141, 236–237
Somnium (Kepler) 145–146
The Space Beyond (Campbell) 67
Space Cabby comics 89, 172
Space Cadet (Heinlein) 196–197, 204–206
The Space Dreamers see Prelude to Space
Space Flight (del Rey) 158
Space Hawk (Bates and Hall) 80
Space Invaders (video game) 94
"Space Jockey" (Heinlein) 107
"Space Mirror" (Hamilton) 82–83
Space Museum comics 173
"Space Oasis" (Gallun) 115–116
space opera 3, 13–16, 33–37, 41–42, 55, 57, 58, 65–66, 70–71, 72, 77–97, 115–117, 121–122, 131, 182, 234–235, 243, 252n, 257–258n
Space Opera (Aldiss) 92
Space Opera (role-playing game) 94
Space Opera (Vance) 91
Space Patrol 16, 89, 117, 178
Space Pioneers (Norton) 130
Space Platform (Leinster) 188
Space Police (Norton) 130
Space Ranger comics 89, 174, 200–201, 239
Space Rangers comics 116
"Space Rays" (Campbell) 14–15, 79
Space Service (Norton) 130
"Space Station No. 1" (Wellman) 81
Space trilogy (Lewis) 158
Space Tug (Leinster) 188
Spaceway 214
"The Specter General" (Cogswell) 130
Spengler, Oswald 103; *Decline of the West* 103
Spider-Man comics 220
Spielberg, Steven 221
Spinrad, Norman 218, 235, 238, 242
Spock Must Die! (Blish) 240
Sport and Adventure Stories for Boys (Esenwein) 129
Stabenow, Dana 93–94; *Second Star* 93–94; Star Svensdotter series 93–94
Stableford, Brian 251n
The Stainless Steel Rat (Harrison) 92
Stainless Steel Rat series (Harrison) 92

Stalker 192
Stand on Zanzibar (Brunner) 207, 231, 244
Stapledon, Olaf 4, 40, 136, 138, 139, 144; *Last and First Men* 139; *Odd John* 136, 139; *Star Maker* 139
The Star Beast (Heinlein) 206–207
Star Hawkins comics 173
Star Maker (Stapledon) 139
The Star of Life (Hamilton) 75
Star Pirate comics 116
Star Rovers comics 239, 272–273
Star Science Fiction anthologies (Pohl) 124–125, 157, 238
Star Smashers of the Galaxy Rangers (Harrison) 92
Star Svensdotter series (Stabenow) 93–94
Star Trek 41, 65–66, 85, 89, 93–94, 117, 149, 179, 216–217, 218, 220, 221, 240, 241, 243, 245
Star Trek (Blish) 218, 224
The Star Trek Concordance (Trimble) 217
Star Trek: Deep Space Nine 244
Star Trek films 176, 240
Star Trek novels 149, 218, 240–241, 242, 248
Star Trek: The Motion Picture 176
Star Wars 41, 65–66, 74, 81, 85, 88–89, 94, 117, 179, 217, 221, 240, 241, 245
Star Wars novels 240
Starcrash 94
Stargate SG-1 240
Starman Jones (Heinlein) 206–207
Starship Troopers 197, 208
Starship Troopers (Heinlein) 61, 196, 197, 207, 208, 220
Startide Rising (Brin) 194–195
Startling Stories 45, 46, 57, 99, 190
Starzl, R.F. 12, 15, 174; "The Metal Moon" (with Smith) 15; "Out of the Sub-Universe" 174
Stationfall (Cover) 93
Steele, Allen 180, 245
Stellar anthologies (del Rey) 148
"Stellar Showboat" (Jameson) 115–116
Step to the Stars (del Rey) 188
Stephenson, Neal 244
Sterling, Bruce 41, 42, 52, 57, 95, 227, 230; *Schismatrix* 95; *Schismatrix Plus* 95
Stern, Barbara 177
Stern, Philip Van Doren 134
Stewart, Potter 78
Stewart, Will *see* Williamson, Jack
Still Forms on Foxfield (Slonczewski) 195
Stilson, Charles B. 144
Stine, G. Harry *see* Correy, Lee

Stirring Science Stories 131
Stockton, Frank 144; *The Great War Syndicate* 144
Stone, Leslie F. 14, 88, 234; "The Fall of Mercury" 88
Stong, Phil 100, 127, 131–133, 140–141, 142; "Foreword" 131–132; *The Other Worlds* 100, 127, 131–133, 142
"The Story Behind the Story" (Hamilton) 93
Stover, Leon 106
Strahan, Jonathan 59; *Eclipse Three* 59
Strange Adventures 16, 166, 171–173, 174, 175
Stribling, T.S. 134; "The Green Splotches" 134
Stross, Charles 195, 244
Strugatsky, Arkady 4, 20, 192; *Roadside Picnic* (with Strugatsky) 192
Strugatsky, Boris 4, 20, 192; *Roadside Picnic* (with Strugatsky) 192
The Struggle for Empire (Cole) 86
Struzan, Drew 176
Stuart, Don A. *see* Campbell, John W., Jr.
Studio One 163
"A Study in Emerald" (Gaiman) 150
Sturgeon, Theodore 61, 109, 113, 121, 134, 156, 162, 165–166, 186, 218, 236, 244n; "Microcosmic God" 113, 121; *More Than Human* 61, 114; "Thunder and Roses" 113; *Voyage to the Bottom of the Sea* 218
Sundiver (Brin) 194–195
"The Super-Prisoner of Amazon Island" 167
Super Science Stories 116–117
Superboy 167
Supergirl comics 169, 170
Superman 166–167, 175
Superman (film) 176
Superman comics 117, 132, 165, 166–171, 178, 220, 263n
Superman: Last Son of Krypton (Maggin) 219–220
"Superman Meets the Goliath-Hercules" 171
Superman: Miracle Monday (Maggin) 219–220
Superman's Girl Friend Lois Lane 167
"Superman's New Power" 170
Superman's Pal Jimmy Olsen 167
Superworld Comics 117, 165
Sutton, Jeff 227; *Apollo at Go* 227
Swann, Thomas Burnett 230
Swanwick, Michael 57, 95; *Vacuum Flowers* 95
Swift, Jonathan 143–144; *Gulliver's Travels* 137, 143–144

Taine, John 75, 136, 138, 139; *Before the Dawn* 136, 138, 139; *The Time Stream* 75
Takacs, Stephen 215
Take Back Plenty (Greenland) 95–96
Tales from the White Hart (Clarke) 256n
Tales of Frankenstein 162
Tales of the Unexpected 174
Tales of Tomorrow 162, 163, 164
Tarantula 176
Target Comics 117
Target Earth 162–163
Tarkowsky, Andrei 20
Tarzan series (Burroughs) 239
Tau Zero (Anderson) 190
Tcherevkoff, Michel 52, 54
Teen-Age Science Fiction Stories (Elam) 130
Teen-Age Super Science Stories (Elam) 130
Temple, William F. 162–163; *Four-Sided Triangle* 162–163
"Ten Million Miles Sunward" (Hewelke) 255n
Tenn, William 163
Terada, Takashi 53, 54
Terminator films 240
The Terrornauts 217–218
"They" (Heinlein) 112–113, 236–237
The Thing (1982) 16–17, 111, 176
The Thing (2011) 16–17, 111
The Thing (from Another World) 16–17, 111, 162–163
Things to Come 44
The Third Galaxy Reader (Gold) 160
"Thirteen Ways to Water" (Rogers) 150
This Island Earth 16, 89, 117, 162–163, 176
This Island Earth (Jones) 162–163
This Week 155–156
Thomas, Roy 219
"The Thought-Men of Mercury" (Winterbotham) 115–116
"Thrall of the Endless Night" (Brackett) 74
The Three-Body Problem (Liu) 96–97, 195, 248
The Three-Body Problem series (Liu) 96–97, 248
Thrilling Wonder Stories 45, 57, 80, 82, 99, 116–117, 131, 137, 257n
"Thunder and Roses" (Sturgeon) 113
Time Enough for Love (Heinlein) 68, 69
Time for the Stars (Heinlein) 207
Time Is the Simplest Thing (Simak) 49–50
The Time Machine (Wells) 28, 139
The Time Stream (Taine) 75
"Time Travel Happens!" (Phillips) 146

The Time Traveller 166
Timeless Stories for Today and Tomorrow (Bradbury) 136
Timescape (Benford) 194
Titan (Varley) 194
Titan A.E. 94
Titan series (Varley) 194
Tolkien, J.R.R. 158, 209, 242; *The Hobbit* 158; *The Lord of the Rings* 158
Tom Corbett, Space Cadet 16, 89, 117, 163, 178, 197, 238–239
Tom Corbett, Space Cadet novels 238–239
Tom Swift, Jr. series (Appleton) 188, 238–239
Tom Swift, Jr. and His Outpost in Space (Appleton) 188
Tom Swift series (Appleton) 238–239
Tommy Tomorrow comics 89, 239
Tors, Ivan 161
Traviss, Karen 243–244
Tremaine, F. Orlon 19, 56, 100, 146–147, 185–186, 236, 262n
Tremaine, Nelson *see* Van Lorne, Warner
Trillion Year Spree (Aldiss and Wingrove) 40
Trimble, Bjo 217; *The Star Trek Concordance* 217
Triplanetary (Smith) 65
Tsiolkovsky, Konstantin 163–164
Tubb, E.C. 229
Tucker, Bob *see* Tucker, Wilson
Tucker, Wilson 15, 78, 80, 85–86, 100, 103, 115–116, 131, 234; "Prison Planet" 115–116
Tunnel in the Sky (Heinlein) 206–207
Turtledove, Harry 149; *The Best Alternate History Stories of the 20th Century* (with Greenberg) 149; *The Best Military Science Fiction of the 20th Century* (with Greenberg) 149; *The Best Time Travel Stories of the 20th Century* (with Greenberg) 149
Twain, Mark 68, 144; *A Connecticut Yankee in King Arthur's Court* 144
"Twayne Triplets" anthologies (Pratt) 139–140
The 27th Day 162–163
The 27th Day (Mantley) 162–163
20,000 Leagues Under the Sea 162–163
20,000 Leagues Under the Sea (Verne) 162–163
"Twilight" (Campbell) 16–17, 111, 133, 235
The Twilight Zone 164, 218, 220, 224
2000 A.D. (Sadoul) 221–222
2001: A Space Odyssey 54, 64, 121, 217
2001: A Space Odyssey (Clarke) 64, 121
The Twonky 162–163

"The Twonky" (Kuttner and Moore) 162–163

Uffelman, Francis 23
Uncollected Stars (Anthony, Malzberg, Greenberg, and Waugh) 126–127
Uncompromising Honor (Weber) 59
"Under the Red Sun" (Hamilton) 171
"Universe" (Heinlein) 112–113, 236
Universe anthologies (Carr) 148
Unknown 101, 111, 131, 236
Unknown Worlds 111, 236
"The Unpleasant Profession of Jonathan Hoag" (Heinlein) 236–237
Utopia (More) 138

Vacuum Flowers (Swanwick) 95
"Vampire Queen" (Fearn) 115–116
The Vampire's Ghost 74
Van Campen, Karl *see* Campbell, John W., Jr.
Vance, Jack 16, 80, 90–91, 196, 239; "The King of Thieves" 90–91; Magnus Ridolph series 90–91, 239; *Space Opera* 91; *Vandals of the Void* 16
Vandals of the Void (Vance) 16
Vandals of the Void (Walsh) 81
VanderMeer, Ann 147, 149; *The Big Book of Science Fiction* (with VanderMeer) 147, 149
VanderMeer, Jeff 147, 149; *The Big Book of Science Fiction* (with VanderMeer) 147, 149
Van Gelder, Gordon 241
Van Lorne, Warner 100, 101; "The Blue Men of Yrano" 101
van Vogt, A.E. 1–2, 3–4, 57, 70–72, 90, 101–105, 108–110, 113, 126, 161, 163; *The Beast* 110; "Black Destroyer" 101–105, 107, 108, 113, 163; "Discord in Scarlet" 103; "The Gryb" 103; *Monsters* 103–104; *Null-A Three* 110; "On 'Black Destroyer'" 261*n*; *The Players of Null-A* 110; "The Sea Thing" 103; *Slan* 71–72, 103–104, 113, 138, 161; *Slan Hunter* (with Anderson) 72; "Vault of the Beast" 102, 261*n*; *The War Against the Rull* 110; "The Weapon Shop" 113; *The World of Null-A* 72, 103–104, 110, 113, 126
Varley, John 194; *Demon* 194; *The Persistence of Vision* 194; *Titan* 194; Titan series 194; *Wizard* 194
"Vault of the Beast" (van Vogt) 102, 261*n*
"Veil of Astrellar" (Brackett) 74
"Venture to the Moon" (Clarke) 188
Venus Equilateral (Smith) 115, 186

Verne, Jules 1, 4, 25, 40, 78, 138, 144, 146, 162–163, 183–184, 251*n*; *Facing the Flag* 162–163; *From the Earth to the Moon* 138, 162–163, 184; *Journey to the Center of the Earth* 138, 162–163; *Mysterious Island* 162–163; *20,000 Leagues Under the Sea* 162–163
Verrill, A. Hyatt 29
Vertigo 176
video games 94, 220, 221, 240, 244
Viehl, S.L. 94; Cherijo Grey Veil series 94
Vincent, Harl 234
Vinge, Vernor 194, 243
Visions of the Future (Sacks) 221–222
von Braun, Wernher 176, 187; "Can We Get to Mars?" (with Ryan) 176; "Crossing the Space Frontier" 176
von Däniken, Erich 120, 227–228; *Chariots of the Gods?* 227–228
Vonnegut, Kurt, Jr. 212, 225–226
von Noordung, Hermann 43–44, 81; *The Problems of Space Flying* 81
Voyage to the Bottom of the Sea (film) 218
Voyage to the Bottom of the Sea (Sturgeon) 218
Voyage to the Bottom of the Sea (TV series) 218, 220
Voyages to the Moon (Nicolson) 159

The Wailing Asteroid (Leinster) 217–218
"Waldo" (Heinlein) 236–237
Walker, Burnham J. 159; *Biochemistry and Human Metabolism* (with Asimov and Boyd) 159; *Chemistry and Human Health* (with Asimov and Nicholas) 159
Walsh, J.M. 81; *Vandals of the Void* 81
Walt Disney's Wonderful World of Color 175
Wandrei, Donald 165–166
Wanted: Dead or Alive 162
The War Against the Rull (van Vogt) 110
"The War-Gods of the Void" (Kuttner) 115–116
War of the Satellites 165
The War of the Worlds (film) 162–163, 176
The War of the Worlds (radio play) 139
The War of the Worlds (Wells) 42–43, 139, 145, 162–163
The War of the Worlds: Global Dispatches (Anderson) 145
Warchild (Friesner) 244
Warhammer (game) 240
Warner, Harry, Jr. 211
Warren, Bill 215; *Keep Watching the Skies!* 215
Washington, George 168

The Waste Land (Eliot) 96
Watkins, William John 193; *The Centrifugal Rickshaw Dancer* 193
Waugh, Charles G. 126–127; *Uncollected Stars* (with Anthony, Malzberg, and Greenberg) 126–127
The Way the Future Was (Pohl) 62
We (Zamiatin) 244
"'We Also Walk Dogs'" (Heinlein) 236
"We Can Rocket to the Moon—Now!" (Clarke) 63
"The Weapon Shop" (van Vogt) 113
The Weathermakers (Bova) 192
The Web Between the Worlds (Sheffield) 193, 194
Weber, David 59, 94, 243; Honor Harrington series 59, 94, 243; *Uncompromising Honor* 59
Webster, Bud 125, 128, 130, 131, 134, 147; *Anthropology 101*, 125, 147; "Anthropology 101" articles 125; "Curiosities" 125
Weinbaum, Stanley G. 1, 15, 23, 133, 134, 162–163; "The Adaptive Ultimate" 133, 162–163; "A Martian Odyssey" 15, 23, 133; *The New Adam* 75, 138
Weird Fantasy 166
Weird Science 16, 165–166
Weird Tales 131, 134, 256n
Weisinger, Mort 99, 117, 166–167, 170–171, 175, 257n, 263n
Welles, Orson 139
Wellman, Manly Wade 81, 100–101; "Nuisance Value" 100–101; "Space Station No. 1" 81
Wells, Basil 115–116; "Quest of Thig" 115–116
Wells, H.G. 1, 4, 7, 21–22, 25–26, 28, 40, 42–43, 75, 78, 134, 138, 139, 144, 146, 183–184, 217–218, 244; *The First Men in the Moon* 136, 139, 184, 217–218; "In the Abyss" 134; *The Island of Dr. Moreau* 139; "The Moth" 21–22, 26, 37, 42–43, 44–45; "Preface" 184; *The Time Machine* 28, 139; *The War of the Worlds* 42–43, 139, 145, 162–163
Wells, Stanley 103
Wertenbaker, G. Peyton 28, 29, 224; "The Coming of the Ice" 28
The Wesleyan Anthology of Science Fiction (Evans, Csicsery-Ronay, Jr., Gordon, Hollinger, Latham, and McGuirk) 147
West, Wallace 134
Western Adventures Magazine 27
Westfahl, Gary 2–3, 36–37, 59, 148, 149, 213; *Cosmic Engineers* 190; *Hugo Gernsback and the Century of Science Fiction* 36–37, 59; *Islands in the Sky* 188; "What Is a Science Fiction Magazine?" 148
"What Is a Science Fiction Magazine?" (Westfahl) 148
What Mad Universe (Brown) 45
What Might Have Been, Volume 1 (Benford and Greenberg) 150
Whelan, Michael 66, 177
When Worlds Collide 162–163, 176
When Worlds Collide (Wylie and Balmer) 162–163
"Whirligig World" (Clement) 189–190
White, James 91–92, 239; Sector Twelve General Hospital series 91–92, 239
White, Ted 219
"Who Goes There?" (Campbell) 16–17, 111, 162–163, 235, 261n
Who Killed Science Fiction? (Kemp) 19, 160, 211–215, 224–225
Why Call Them Back from Heaven? (Simak) 51
Widner, Wilbur J. 104
Wild Seed (Butler) 195
Wile E. Coyote cartoons 164
"Will the Star Rovers Abandon Earth?" 172–173
Willey, Robert *see* Ley, Willy
Williamson, Jack 1, 13, 14, 17–18, 62, 63, 64–65, 79, 89, 115, 184–185, 186, 212, 215, 230, 234; *After Worlds End* 63; "Born of the Sun" 88; *The Legion of Time* 64–65; Seetee series 115, 186; *Seetee Ship* 115; *Seetee Shock* 115; *Wonder's Child* 62
Willis, Connie 243
Wilson, Don 120; *Secrets of Our Spaceship Moon* 120
Wilson, William 251n
Wingrove, David 40, 110; *Trillion Year Spree* (with Aldiss) 40
"The Winterberry" (DiChario) 150
Winterbotham, R.R. 115–116; "The Thought Men of Mercury" 115–116
Wizard (Varley) 194
Wolfe, Bernard 224; *Limbo* 224
Wolfe, Gary K. 140; *American Science Fiction: Four Classic Novels, 1953–1956* 140; *American Science Fiction: Five Classic Novels, 1956–1958* 140
Wolfe, Gene 244
Wolfe, Tom 227; *The Right Stuff* 227
Wollheim, Betsy 241–242
Wollheim, Donald A. 16, 49–50, 114, 117, 124, 127, 133–140, 142, 145, 147, 175, 196, 212, 213, 214, 224, 230, 238–239, 241–242, 253n; *Ace Science Fiction Reader* 140; "Introduction" 136–138; "The Man

from Ariel" 138; Mike Mars series 238–239; *More Adventures on Other Planets* 49–50, 224; *The Pocket Book of Science Fiction* 124, 127, 133–136, 142, 145; *The Portable Novels of Science* 127, 136–140, 143; *The Secret of Saturn's Rings* 16
Wonder Stories 10, 11, 12, 75, 79, 99, 165, 234, 257n
Wonder Stories from Nature (Keasbey) 23
Wonder Stories Quarterly 15
Wonder's Child (Williamson) 62
Woodroffe, Patrick 177
"The Word for World Is Forest" (Le Guin) 230
A World Named Cleopatra (Anderson and Elwood) 190
The World of Null-A (van Vogt) 72, 103–104, 110, 113, 126
"The World of van Vogt" (Knight) 104
The World That Couldn't Be and 8 Other Novelets from Galaxy (Gold) 160
The World, the Flesh, and the Devil 162–163
The World Treasury of Science Fiction (Hartwell) 136
World's Finest Comics 166–167
Wright, Farnsworth 256n
Wright, S. Fowler 144, 146; "Brain" 146

Wylie, Philip 138, 144, 155, 162–163; *Gladiator* 138; *When Worlds Collide* (with Balmer) 162–163

The X-Files 121, 240
X-Men comics 220
Xero 219

Yancey, Rick 208, 209; *The 5th Wave* 208; The 5th Wave series 208
The Year's Best Science Fiction anthologies (Dozois) 150
The Year's Best Science Fiction Novels anthologies (Bleiler and Dikty) 139–140
"The Yeast Men" (Keller) 25
"Yes, Virginia, There Is a Martian" (Fox) 172–173
Youd, Sam *see* Christopher, John
The Young Traveller in Space (Clarke) 158

Zebrowski, George 194; *Macrolife* 194
Zelazny, Roger 231, 258n; *Lord of Light* 231
Zhuravlev, Vasili 65
Zingaro, Charles 130
"Zirn Left Unguarded, the Jenghik Palace in Flames, Jon Westerley Dead" (Sheckley) 92

www.ingramcontent.com/pod-product-compliance
Lightning Source LLC
Chambersburg PA
CBHW021347300426
44114CB00012B/1107